The Painter 5 Wow! Book

Cher Threinen-Pendarvis

Peachpit Press

The Painter 5 Wow! Book

Cher Threinen-Pendarvis

Peachpit Press
1249 Eighth Street
Berkeley, CA 94710
(510) 524-2178
(800) 283-9444
(510) 524-2221 (fax)

Find us on the World Wide Web at: http://www.peachpit.com/peachpit/titles/categories/
titles.wow.html

Peachpit Press is a division of Addison Wesley Longman

Series Editor: Linnea Dayton
Cover design: TMA Ted Mader + Associates
Cover illustration: Cher Threinen-Pendarvis
Book design: Jill Davis
Art direction and layout: Cher Threinen-Pendarvis
Editing: Linnea Dayton
Copyediting and proofreading: Susan Bugbee
Index: Jackie Estrada
Production and prepress: Jonathan Parker

This book was set using the Stone Serif and Stone Sans families. It was written and composed in Adobe Pagemaker 6.0. Final output was computer to plate.

ISBN 0-201-69651-7

0 9 8 7 6 5 4 3 2
Printed and bound in the United States of America.

To my husband Steven,
for his friendship,
encouragement and understanding;
and to our Creator
from whom all inspiration comes. . . .

— Cher Threinen-Pendarvis

Mount Brushmore, *by Mark Zimmer*

ACKNOWLEDGMENTS

The Painter 5 Wow! Book would not have been possible without a great deal of help from some extraordinary people and sources.

My heartfelt thanks go to Linnea Dayton, the *Wow!* Series Editor and a treasured friend and colleague. At times when it was needed most during the first, second and *third* editions, her inspiration, advice and cheerleading proved invaluable. Thank you, Linnea, for the creative edit of *The Painter 5 Wow! Book*.

Warmest thanks go to my friends at Peachpit Press, especially Ted Nace for his inspiration, Nancy Ruenzel for her guidance during this edition, Jeanne Woodward for her sincere encouragement and help when it was needed most, and the rest of the publishing team for their support. Thank you Peachpit, for giving me the opportunity to do this book.

A big "thank you" goes to the folks at MetaCreations Corporation: Mark Zimmer, Tom Hedges, John Derry, Jon Bass and John Wilczak, for creating such a *Wow!* program and for their inspiration, enthusiasm and openness; to Kim Kern for her support with communications; to Shawn Grunberger, for answering Web-related questions, and to MetaCreations' outstanding technical support team for fielding many questions about the program.

I am grateful to the talented Painter artists who contributed their work and techniques; their names are listed in Appendix D in the back of the book. I would especially like to thank Sharon Steuer, author of *The Illustrator Wow! Book*, who helped me locate artists who use Painter and became an encouraging friend as our two books developed.

Statue of Creative Liberties, *illustrated by John Derry*

Painthenge, *illustrated by Chet Phillips*

The Leaning Tower of Painter, *illustrated by Steve Guttman*

I'd also like to thank the companies who supplied the *Wow!* book team with supporting software during the development of the book—Adobe Systems for supplying me with Photoshop, Illustrator, Premiere and PageMill, so I could demonstrate how nicely these programs work with Painter; Macromedia, for contributing Director for the Multimedia chapter; Netscape Communications for providing Netscape for the Web graphics chapter; MetaCreations and Xaos Tools for their filters, and Baseline Publishing for Screenshot.

Thanks to Digital Stock and PhotoDisc for their support during all three editions of the book; these two "stock on CD-ROM" companies allowed us to use their photos for demonstration purposes in the book. I am also grateful to the other companies who provided images or video clips for The Painter 5 Wow! CD-ROM; their names are listed in Appendix A in the back of the book.

Additionally, the following companies donated, loaned or gave us a good deal on hardware that helped to create the book: Wacom, for their great pressure-sensitive tablets, Mitsubishi Electronics America for their monitors; Number Nine for their graphics accelerators and Hewlett-Packard for color printers (for the testing of printing techniques).

I'm grateful to Linnea Dayton, Jack Davis, Victor Gavenda and Donal Jolley for their helpful technical reads. My warmest thanks go to Michele Lill for sharing her knowledge about reflection maps, and Steven Gordon for his experience with terrain maps. Special thanks also go to Jon Lee and Geoff Hull of Fox Television for sharing their experience of designing for broadcast television; Cindy and Dewey Reid of Reid Creative for sharing their expertise in animation and film; and Lynda Weinman for sharing her knowledge about designing graphics for the Web.

I'd like to thank my co-workers "behind the scenes" on the Wow! book team. Warmest thanks go to Jill Davis for her brilliant book design; Susan Bugbee for her friendship and excellent copyediting and proofreading; Jackie Estrada for her careful indexing; and Pagemaker whiz Jonathan Parker for his production and prepress expertise. His calm assurance during the deadlines of all three editions of this book was much appreciated!

My very special thanks go to Victor Gavenda at Peachpit Press for his fine work on the Painter Wow! CD-ROM.

Finally, I would like to thank my family, friends and colleagues for their patience and understanding during the development of three editions of this book.

Cher Threinen-Pendarvis

Mark Zimmer, Chief Technology Officer of MetaCreations Corporation, and a developer of Painter

FOREWORD

"Mark, this *Painter 5 Wow! Book* is full of great new stuff, huh?"

"Sure is, John . . . Cher has definitely explored some of the more remote regions of Painter."

"Yeah . . . like the Great Liquid Metal Sea and the Valley of Plug-in Brushes."

My, how time flies. Here we are at the third edition of *The Painter Wow! Book* . . . And like Painter itself, this book has grown in both size and popularity. As you look over the table of contents, you will notice quite a few new subject areas. In just a few short pages, you will begin a creative journey into the fascinating world of Painter 5.

In its initial 1.0 release, Painter was a simple painting application that created a new metaphor for software . . . "natural media." Painter 1.0's spartan interface employed tools and techniques from the world of traditional art and design media. Pencils, chalk, charcoal, erasers, brushes. This, coupled with a pressure-sensitive pen and tablet, offered remarkable ease-of-use, even for the computer illiterate.

As Painter has evolved, we have listened to what our users had to say. We've talked with you at trade shows and conferences. We've read your e-mail. Your wish lists started to grow like weeds! These suggestions (along with a few of our own) have been incorporated into each new Painter release. Reflecting this, Painter 5 now con-

John Derry, Vice President of Creative Design at MetaCreations Corporation and a developer of Painter

tains a remarkable array of tools that encompass much more than natural media. Photo-editing, the Web, and multimedia have all become creative territories in Painter's brave new world.

Along with this evolving growth comes the challenge to provide users with easy access to the tools. This is no easy task. In fact, there is no single solution to the problem. For that reason, we've built several user-customizable features into the interface, like tear-off tools and custom palettes and layouts. This allows you to organize the tools according to your liking. Even so, Painter's varied landscape encourages the creative traveler to take advantage of any navigational aids available.

With so many realms to explore in Painter, wouldn't it be great to have a travel guide that could help keep you on the path instead of wandering into that quicksand just over there? Well, you do have one, and her name is Cher Pendarvis. And the item you are holding in your hands right now is your indispensable guidebook.

Cher has done all the trail-blazing in advance so you can navigate your way through Painter without getting lost. Better yet, she has discovered many interesting techniques that she generously shares with one and all. Finally, she has recruited many of the best Painter users and chronicled their real-world experiences for your benefit. Whether you're a well-traveled veteran or curious tenderfoot, this *Painter Wow! Book* will get you to your creative destination safely and in record time.

"Say, Mark . . . did you gas up the Range Rover?"

"Sure did, John. Gas stations are gonna be few and far between where we're goin'."

"Look here on the map. This is where we're headed. It says terra incognita . . . What's that mean?"

"I think it's Latin for more work, John."

"Let's Go!"

As we head off into yet more uncharted territory, we hope that both Cher and you will continue your own vast, creative world with Painter.

Mark Zimmer
John Derry

November 1997

CONTENTS

WELCOME TO *PAINTER 5 WOW!*

SOME PEOPLE EMPHASIZE THE DIFFERENCES between traditional and digital art tools—almost as if "real" art and the computer are not compatible. But during the early development of this book, we discovered many working artists who had bought computers specifically because they were thrilled by the promise of MetaCreations Painter. It seemed logical that *The Painter Wow! Book* should become a bridge connecting conventional tools and techniques with their electronic counterparts. Early chapters of the book, in particular, touch on color theory, art history and conventional media, and explain how to translate foundational art theory using Painter's tools.

This book addresses the needs of a wide variety of creative professionals: artists making the transition from traditional to digital media; photographers looking to expand their visual vocabulary; screen or print graphic designers hunting for special effects to apply to type; even creative explorers out for some thrills. For those of you with a long history in a traditional art form and a short history with computers, we've done our best to guide you through Painter's interface, making it as simple as possible for you to achieve the desired effect. And if you've spent more time with a keyboard and mouse than you have with an artist's palette and paintbrush, you may learn a lot about conventional art terms and techniques as you read the book.

The folks at MetaCreations are famous for their creativity, innovation and dedication to improving and expanding their software tools. Along with new Painter 5 features such as custom palettes, the dynamic capabilities of plug-in floaters, and tools that make it easy to prepare graphics for use on the World Wide Web, MetaCreations has also made changes to Painter's interface that make it easier to use.

Painter 5's Impasto brushes and floaters let you paint with exciting, realistic three-dimensional strokes that leave bristle marks and thick paint on the surface of the image as you paint.

ORIGINAL PHOTO: DIGITAL STOCK

Painter 5 offers several new plug-in brush variants designed specifically for photographers, such as the Add Texture brush used here.

CHER THREINEN-PENDARVIS

With the Bevel World dynamic plug-in floater you can create beveled type and buttons easily, varying their size and shape on the fly!

WHAT'S NEW IN PAINTER 5?

To make *The Painter 5 Wow! Book* complete and up-to-date for Painter 5, we've revised every page. And we've expanded the book—adding pages of brand-new real-world tips and techniques that specifically profile features added in version 5. Here's a quick overview of some of Painter 5's exciting new features and a description of where in this book you can find information about them.

The area of the program that's most likely to change the way you work is Painter 5's new industry-standard **selection and masking** model, which will be familiar to users of Adobe Photoshop. With Painter 5, you can make selections and save them as user masks into the Mask List, much like saving selections as masks into the Channels palette in Photoshop. Painter's powerful and easier-to-use masking tools also include a versatile new **Magic Wand**. To find out about these useful new functions, turn to Chapter 4, "Selections, Shape Paths and Masks."

Among the changes that make Painter easier to use are these: The Painter **toolbox** has been expanded and the list of single key shortcuts has been extended to include the new tools. A **Crop tool** has been added. The **Paint Bucket tool** has been enhanced to include a tolerance slider that lets you adjust the range of colors affected by the fill. New **custom palettes** allow you to design your workspace by setting up special palettes to store tools and menu commands. And you can make your own set of **function keys** for favorite commands, making it easier to access the commands nested two or three layers deep in Painter's menus and palettes. Read about these time-saving enhancements in Chapter 1, "Getting to Know Painter." Turn to the beginning of Chapter 4 for information about selection tools such as the Magic Wand.

Painter 5's new **plug-in brushes** bring great versatility: They can lay down paint, or smear it; the Fire Brush paints with special effects; and the Add Grain brush puts 3D texture on the end of your brush! Read more about plug-in brushes (and **Impasto plug-in floaters**) in "Painting with Super-Media Plug-in Brushes," on pages 40–41, and "More Super-Media Painting Tools," on pages 42–43. And see "Advanced Painting with Impasto" for a step-by step tutorial using Impasto plug-in floaters. Painter 5's new **layer brushes** and **transparent layers** offer great flexibility to digital illustrators. (Read about layer brushes in the beginning of Chapter 3, and turn to "Using Transparent Layers" in Chapter 5 to read more about painting and compositing techniques with transparent layers.

In addition to new painting tools, Painter 5 includes many tools designed specifically for photographers. Plug-in brushes (such as **Add Grain**) and new plug-in floaters such as **Brightness and Contrast** allow you to make adjustments to an image without actually changing the original image. See Chapter 6, "Enhancing Photos, Collage and Montage," to read about these new tools.

Painter 5's new features help you get images ready for use on the World Wide Web. For instance, Painter can create some of the coding for interactive buttons and can convert colors to Web-friendly palettes.

HUGO HIDALGO / BOXTOP INTERACTIVE

Several of the dynamic plug-ins can be used to apply special effects. The **Bevel World** plug-in floater lets you apply complex beveled edges to objects easily. To read about Bevel World and other special effects plug-ins such as **Glass Distortion** and **Liquid Metal**, turn to Chapter 7, "Exploring Special Effects." You'll find basic information about how different kinds of **dynamic plug-in floaters** work in the beginning of Chapter 5, "Using Floaters and Shapes."

Designers preparing graphics for display on the Web love Painter's ability to make **image maps**. And now you can add motion to your web pages by exporting **GIF animations** directly from Painter 5. See the beginning of Chapter 9, "Multimedia and Film with Painter," and Chapter 10, "Using Painter for Web Graphics," for more about animation, video and web graphics using Painter.

If you need to prepare images for print, Painter 5 offers a useful new **Kodak Color Management System**. Turn to Chapter 11, "Printing and Archival Concerns," to read about this useful system.

DO YOU USE MAC OR WINDOWS?

Because Painter works so similarly on Macintosh and PC/Windows platforms, we've taken the path of least resistance by using only one platform's keyboard commands—Macintosh, our native language. (Just to make sure of our techniques, though, we also tested them under Windows 95.) If you're a Windows user, use the **Control key** wherever the **Command key** is mentioned, and substitute the **Alt key** for the **Option key**. Also, because versions of Windows prior to Windows 95 require shorter file names, PC users looking for texture libraries will need to find them under somewhat different names from their Mac counterparts. For instance, "More Wild Textures" Paper library on the Mac is "morewild.pap" on the PC. The few differences are covered in Chapter 1.

FOR BEGINNERS

If you're new to Painter, welcome! We assume that you're familiar with the basic Mac and Windows mouse functions, that you know how to open and save files, copy items to the clipboard and navigate through the Mac's hierarchical file system or through Windows directories. We suggest reading Chapter 1, "Getting to Know Painter," Chapter 4, "Selections, Shape Paths and Masks," and Chapter 5, Using Floaters and Shapes," before jumping into the more advanced techniques. It's also a good idea, though it isn't essential, to have worked with the *Painter 5 User Guide* and to have completed the tutorial that comes with the program.

Just a few words on some of the "shorthand" naming conventions that we've used to pack more information into the book. Because Painter uses nested palettes that have long names—for instance, the "Art Materials:Paper palette"—we frequently direct you only to the "child" palette. In this case we'd refer to the "Paper palette." Another space-saving measure: In the Brushes palette, we refer to the "Method Subcategory" as the "submethod."

3

SAMPLING PAINT

You can temporarily switch to the Dropper tool and sample colors by holding down the Command key while you're using many of Painter's other tools.

4

5

HOW TO USE THIS BOOK

In chapters 2 through 11, the information we're presenting generally progresses from simple to complex. We've organized these chapters into four types of information: "Basics" sections, techniques, practical tips and galleries. In addition, hardware, software and other resources are listed at the back of the book.

1 The **Basics** sections teach how Painter's tools and functions work, and give real-world applications for the tools. *The Painter 5 Wow! Book* wasn't designed to be a replacement for the *Painter 5 User Guide* that comes with the program. We've focused on the tools and functions that we think are most useful. In some cases we've explained items covered in the manual, and, where important, we've dug deeper to help you understand how the tools and functions work. In other cases, we've covered undocumented functions and practical applications, either shared by contributing artists or uncovered in our own research.

2 Within each **Technique** section, you'll find step-by-step, real-world methods that give you enough information to re-create the process yourself. In the *Wow!* format, pictures illustrating the stages of the process are positioned alongside the appropriate step in the project. Browse the pictures in the art column within a technique for a quick overview of the development of an image. We've done our best to give you enough information so that you won't have to refer to the manual to follow the steps.

3 The **Tips** are easily identified by their gray title bar. We've placed them in the Basics and Technique sections where we thought they'd be the most helpful, but each tip is a self-contained tidbit of useful information, so you can learn a lot very quickly by taking a brisk walk through the book, reading only the tips.

4 The **Galleries** are there for inspiration, and one appears at the end of every chapter. With each gallery image, you'll find a short description of how the artwork was produced.

5 No book is an island, so in the **Appendixes** in the back of this one, we've included lists of other resources for your use. If you want to contact a vendor, an artist, or a fine art print studio or locate an art-related book or other publication, you'll find the information you need there.

The Painter 5 Wow! Book was created to share useful techniques and tips and to provide creative suggestions for using the program. We hope that you'll use it as inspiration and a point of departure for your own creative exploration. Above all, don't be overwhelmed by Painter's richness. . . Just dig in and enjoy it!

Cher Threinen-Pendarvis

www.peachpit.com/peachpit/meetus/authors/
cher.threinen.pendarvis.html

GETTING
TO KNOW
PAINTER

Chelsea Sammel's illustration, Le Can de Triomphe

SIT RIGHT DOWN AND POWER UP! This chapter explores Painter's basic needs and functions, as well as its unique strengths and idiosyncrasies. If you're new to Painter, you'll benefit the most from this chapter if you've already spent some time with the *Painter 5 User Guide* that ships with the program.

PAINTER'S REQUIREMENTS FOR MAC AND PC

Here are Painter's *minimum* requirements: If you use a Macintosh you'll need a Power Macintosh with a minimum of 12 MB application RAM (at least 24 MB is recommended). To run Painter on Windows 95, you'll need at least 16 MB of application RAM (32 MB is recommended). For both platforms you'll need a hard disk with approximately 30 MB of free space to perform a minimum installation.

When you open an image in Painter—for example, a 5 MB image—and begin working with it, Painter needs three to five times that file size in RAM in order to work at optimal speed—in our example, that would be 15–25 MB of RAM. Opening more than one image, adding floaters or shapes, or increasing the number of Undos (under Edit, Preferences, Undos) adds further demands on RAM. When Painter runs out of RAM, it uses the hard disk chosen in Edit, Preferences, General as a RAM substitute. This "scratch disk" holds the Temp file you may have seen.

ABOUT FLOATERS AND SHAPES

Floaters and *shapes* are image elements that reside in layers above the Painter image canvas. Both floaters and shapes can be manipulated independently of the image canvas—allowing for exciting compositing effects.

PAINTER TEMP FILE OVERHEAD

If you open a large image in Painter, the Painter Temp file increases to reflect the working size of the image, and it stays on your scratch disk until you quit the program. The Painter Temp file size may be several times the size of the file. It includes the image background, the wet layer, enough steps to handle the specified number of Undos, and any clones that you may have open. Simply closing a file will not clear the scratch disk—you must quit Painter to unload the Temp file.

Here are two ways to make quick copies without going through the clipboard and using valuable RAM. To make a copy of your entire document, use File, Clone. (This is also a quick way to make a "flat" copy with the floaters in the document dropped.) To quickly duplicate a floater, choose the Floater Adjuster tool and Option-drag a floater copy.

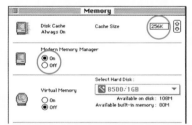

On the Mac, Painter runs faster with these settings in the Memory Control Panel: Virtual Memory off (it interferes with Painter's own virtual memory scheme, the Painter Temp file) and Disc Cache Size on a low setting.

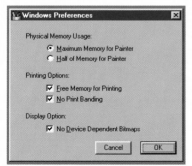

Setting the Maximum Memory for Painter in Windows 95

Since hard disks operate much slower than RAM, performance suffers accordingly—even if you have a fast hard disk.

Ideally, to work with Painter, you would use a computer with a speedy processor; a large, fast hard disk; and lots of RAM. In addition, you'll want a large, 24-bit-color monitor—probably no less than 16 inches—and perhaps a second monitor on which to store palettes. Also highly recommended—some might say *essential*—is a drawing tablet with a pressure-sensitive stylus. Not only is it a more natural drawing and painting tool than a mouse, but many of Painter's brushes lose their personality without a pressure-sensitive input device.

Mac memory allocation. To allot maximum RAM to Painter on a Mac, first quit all open applications. In the Finder, under the Apple menu, choose About This Macintosh. Write down the number next to Largest Unused Block. This is the total amount of RAM in which you can run applications. Subtract 500 or 1000 K (as a buffer) from this number. Now, in the Painter folder, click once (not twice!) on the Painter application icon and choose File, Get Info. Enter the result of your math in the Preferred Size box. This method won't let you open any other applications of significant size while Painter is running, but it assures you of the use of nearly all available RAM while you're in Painter.

Windows memory allocation. To make maximum RAM available for your Windows 95–based PC, choose Edit, Preferences, Windows to access the Windows Preferences dialog box. Under Physical Memory Usage click the "Maximum Memory for Painter" button. Quit all applications and relaunch Painter. Painter will run faster if you let Windows 95 manage the virtual memory scheme.

FILE SIZE AND RESOLUTION

If you're new to the computer, here's important background information regarding file sizes: Painter is primarily a *pixel-based* program, also known as a *bitmap*, *painting* or *raster* program (see "Painter's Vector Capabilities" on page 8), not a *drawing* program, also known as an *object-oriented* or *vector* program. Drawing programs use mathematical expressions to describe the outline and fill attributes of

You can speed up your scratch disk by using hard disk driver software to make a separate partition just for the Painter Temp file. Additionally, use a hard disk utility program like Norton Utilities, Mac Tools or PC Tools (all from Symantec) to regularly defragment the partition. Over time, hard drives become fragmented (space is broken into smaller and smaller blocks)—and thus, slower—as file data is split up in order to be written to them.

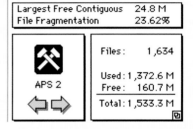

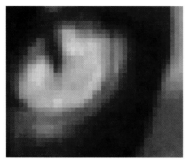

This scan of a photograph is a pixel-based image. Enlarging it to 1200% reveals the grid of pixels.

USING PAPER COLOR

Besides offering a multitude of mark-making tools and unlimited textured surfaces to paint on, Painter also lets you specify Paper Color. You can set Paper Color in the New Picture dialog box (File, New) by clicking the Paper Color icon and choosing a color in the Select Paper Color dialog box, or you can change it midway through the painting process by selecting a color in the Color palette and choosing Canvas, Set Paper Color to apply the current color. The color of the existing background doesn't change, but if you make a selection and delete an area of the image or choose an Eraser variant (Bleaches don't work) and erase an area of the image, the new color appears.

Cher Threinen-Pendarvis's Tienda Verde *in progress. Using the Rectangular Selection tool, we selected an area of the image sky and deleted the area to reveal the new purple Paper Color.*

objects in the drawing, while pixel-based programs describe things dot-by-dot. Because its components are mathematically described, art created with drawing programs can be resized or transformed with no loss of quality. Not so with Painter, Photoshop and other pixel-based programs. Increasing the size of an existing image in these programs means that additional pixels must be created to accommodate the larger size by filling in spaces as the existing pixels spread apart. As a result of the interpolated (manufactured) pixels, resized images can lose their crispness.

There are ways of working around this "soft image" dilemma. One solution is to do studies using a small file size (for instance, an 8 x 10-inch image at 75 pixels per inch), then start over with a large image to do final art at full size (for instance an 8 x 10-inch file at 300 pixels per inch). You can also block in the basic form and color in a small file, then scale the image up to final size (using Canvas, Resize) to add texture and details (textures seem particularly vulnerable to softening). You'll notice that many of the artists whose work is featured in this book use another efficient method: They create the components of a final piece of art in separate documents, then copy and paste the components into a final "master" image. Painter 5 offers yet another solution for working with large file sizes—composing with reference floaters (small versions of actual larger images that are kept outside the document). Because data for the large image is not kept in the working file, performance improves. The introduction to Chapter 5 contains more information about using reference floaters.

Painter's vector capabilities. Although it's primarily a pixel-based program, Painter does have some object-oriented features—shapes, shape paths and outline-based selections. Painter's shapes and shape paths exist as floating elements above the image canvas and have mathematically described outlines with stroke and fill attributes. And Painter's selections (areas of the image designated for work) are versatile; they can be used as pixel-based selections (similar to Photoshop's selections), or they can be transformed into outline-based selections or converted into shapes. Other elements in Painter—the image background and the image floaters—are pixel-based. Chapters 4 and 5 tell more about selections and shapes.

Pixel size and resolution. There are two commonly used ways of describing file sizes: in terms of their pixel measurements, or in a unit of measure (such as inches) plus a resolution. An image is a fixed number of pixels wide and tall—like 1200 x 1500—or a measurement combined with a resolution—4 x 5 inches at 300 ppi. (Either way, the full-color file is 7 MB.) If you use pixels as a measurement for Width and Height in the New File dialog box, notice that the file size doesn't change, regardless of the numbers you type into the Resolution box. The pixel number does not change

Expressing width and height in pixels in the New Picture dialog box keeps the file size the same, regardless of how you change the Resolution.

Whether the Constrain File Size checkbox in the Canvas, Resize dialog box is checked or unchecked, if you're using "pixels" as the units, the file size stays the same, regardless of how you change the Resolution.

FASTER STARTUP

Painter reads all open fonts and loaded plug-in filters when it starts up. For faster startup, consider organizing your fonts with a utility that enables you to turn them on and off (Suitcase or MasterJuggler). And, if you have a large number of third-party filters, create several plug-ins folders. To change to an alternate plug-ins folder choose Edit, Preferences, Other Raster Plug-ins, and navigate to the folder. Restart Painter, and the alternate filter set will appear under the Effects, Plug-in Filters menu.

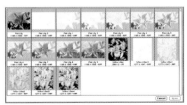

Click the Browse button in the Open dialog box to preview all of the images in a folder. The watercolor studies in Mary Envall's "Lilies" folder are shown here. (Some files may not have a preview—for example, some PICT or JPEG files created by other programs).

unless you resize the image using Canvas, Resize. Increasing or decreasing the number of pixels in the Width and Height fields in the Canvas, Resize dialog box to add (or reduce) pixel information in the picture automatically unchecks the Constrain File Size box.

INCREASING FILE RESOLUTION WITH SCRIPTS

You can use Painter's Scripts function to record your work at low resolution, then play it back at a higher resolution. This technique gives you a much crisper result than simply resizing the original image to a new resolution. Here's how to do it: Start by opening the Objects:Scripts palette. From the Script menu, select Script Options. In the Script Options dialog box check the Record Initial State box, then click OK. Open a new file (File, New) and choose Select, All (Command-A). Choose Script, Record Script and begin painting. When you're finished, choose Script, Stop Recording Script. Open a new document two to four times as large as the original (this technique loses its effectiveness if your new file is much bigger than this), press Command-A, then Scripts, Playback Script. Painter will replay the script in the larger image, automatically scaling brushes and papers to perfectly fit the new size. A word of caution—scripts can be quirky: Your higher-resolution image may not match the lower-resolution one if you use imported photos, complex selections, shapes or the Image Hose, for instance.

Choosing Script Options from the pull-down menu on the Objects:Scripts palette

OPENING FILES

Images in Painter are 24-bit color, made up of RGB (red, green and blue) components consisting of 8 bits each. Painter will recognize and open grayscale images, not in grayscale mode (since it doesn't have one), but in Painter's own RGB mode. CMYK, CIE LAB, Kodak Photo CD format and other color formats used by other applications will need to be converted to RGB in one of these programs (such as Adobe Photoshop or Equilibrium's Debabelizer), before Painter can read them.

SAVING FILES

Painter offers numerous ways to save your image under Edit, Save or Save As. If you've created an image with a mask (Chapter 4 tells how to create masks), some of the formats will allow you to preserve the mask (by checking the Save Mask Layer box in the Save or Save As dialog box), while others won't. Here's a list of the current formats that includes their "mask-friendliness" and other advantages and disadvantages:

RIFF. Thrifty (files are saved quite small) and robust (allows for multiple layers), RIFF (Raster Image File Format) is Painter's native format. Few other programs recognize RIFF, so if you want to

You can preserve floaters in files by saving in either RIFF or Photoshop 3.0 format, but RIFF (even uncompressed) is usually significantly smaller. Rick Kirkman's 663 x 663-pixel image with 150 floaters weighs in at 1.7 MB as a compressed RIFF, 6.1 MB as an uncompressed RIFF, and 7.1 MB when saved in Photoshop 3.0 format.

KEYBOARD SHORTCUTS

Use these shortcuts to switch tools from the keyboard:

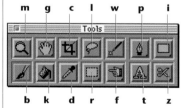

In the Tools palette, several tools are nested with other tools. Use these keys to select these tools: Rotate Page, **e**; Oval Selection, **o**; Quick Curve, **q**; Oval Shape, **j**; Add Point, **a**; Delete Point, **x**; Convert Point, **y**; Oval Selection, **o**; Selection Adjuster, **s**; Shape Selection, **h**. In addition to choosing tools in the Tools palette, you can change settings in the Controls palette for the Brush tool using your keyboard. Press **b** to navigate to the brush, then press **v** to paint straight lines, press **b** to toggle back to freehand.

work with a Painter image in another program, save a copy in a different format. If you're using elements unique to Painter, such as the Wet Layer, image floaters, transparent layers, reference floaters, plug-in floaters, shapes, selections or mosaics, saving in RIFF format will preserve them. (Selections, floaters and shapes are described in depth in Chapters 4 and 5). If you have *lots* of free hard disk space, check the Uncompressed box in the Save dialog box when you're saving in RIFF: Files will become many times larger, but will save and open much more quickly.

Photoshop 2.0 and 3.0. Saving files in Photoshop 3.0 format gives you nearly all the flexibility of RIFF, and is ideal if you frequently move data between Painter and Photoshop. When you use Photoshop to open a file saved in this format, Painter's floaters become Photoshop layers (Chapter 8, "Using Painter with Photoshop," contains more information about working with Painter and Photoshop); Painter's masks (explained in depth in Chapter 4) become Photoshop channels; and Painter's Bézier paths translate perfectly to Photoshop's paths and subpaths, appearing in Photoshop's Paths palette. Photoshop 2.0 format saves the image with information from one Painter mask (this becomes Channel 4), but without the file's floater or path information.

TIFF. Probably the most popular and widely recognized of the bitmap file formats, TIFF allows you to save a mask with your image (check the Save Alpha checkbox). Unfortunately, unlike Photoshop, Painter's Save As dialog box gives you no option to compress the TIFF file—the Uncompressed check box is checked and grayed-out.

PICT. PICT is the format of choice for many multimedia programs and other on-screen display. Painter's PICT format lets you save a single mask (but not floaters), and save a Painter movie as a sequence of numbered PICT files to export and animate in another program (described in Chapter 9). Painter also opens PICT files very quickly.

JPEG. When you save a file in JPEG format, a dialog box will appear with four choices:

WORKING WITH CMYK

Here are some hints for working with Painter in a CMYK production environment. If you're starting with scanned images, scan them in RGB instead of CMYK—RGB has a significantly broader color gamut. If possible, avoid importing your image into another program (like Photoshop) to convert it to CMYK until you're ready to print, since you lose colors when you convert from RGB to CMYK. And, it's a good idea to save a copy of the RGB image in case you want to convert it again with different RGB-to-CMYK conversion settings.

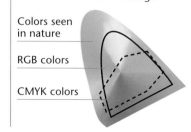

Colors seen in nature

RGB colors

CMYK colors

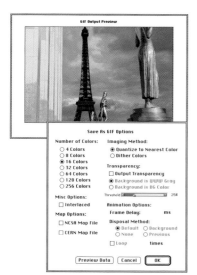

The GIF file format dialog box has been expanded in Painter 5 to include GIF Animation Options.

A SAVING GRACE

Saving multiple versions of your art at various steps along the way makes good sense: It helps you remember how you created your art, and it could be your saving grace if a file gets corrupted.

QUICK CLOSING KEYS

To quickly close a file without having to click the on-screen buttons in the warning box that appears during the closing process, use these keyboard shortcuts: press **D** for Don't Save, **C** for Cancel, and **S** (or Return) for Save.

Excellent, High, Good and Fair. You'll get the best results by choosing Excellent. The advantage of saving a file in JPEG format is that you get superb space savings: a JPEG file is usually only one tenth as large as a TIFF file of the same image if you choose Excellent, and only one-hundredth the size if you choose Fair. The drawbacks: No mask, floaters or paths are saved; and the compression is a lossy compression—which means that some data (color detail in the image) is lost in the compression process. While JPEG is a good way to archive images once they're finished (especially images that have no sharp edges), many artists prefer not to use JPEG because it alters pixels. Don't save in JPEG format if you're continually opening and closing an image—you'll lose more data every time you do so.

JPEG is also useful for preparing 24-bit images with the tiny file sizes that are needed for use with World Wide Web site graphics. (See Chapter 10 for more information on JPEG use in projects created for the Web.)

GIF. GIF is the graphics format of choice for the World Wide Web on the Internet. Like TIFF, PICT or JPEG, saving in GIF format combines floaters with the background. It also reduces the number of colors to a maximum of 256, so remember to Save As in a different file format if you want to be able to access the original image structure again. When you save in GIF, a dialog box appears that gives you a number of options for saving your file. Click the Preview Data button to see how your choices will affect your image. For more information about using Painter's GIF format turn to Chapter 10, "Using Painter for Web Graphics."

EPS. Saving in this format drops floating elements into the background and ignores the mask layer, so it's best to choose Save As in another format if you'll want to make changes to your document at a later time. Saving in EPS format also converts the file into a five-part DCS file: four separate files for the four process printing colors, and a fifth file as a preview of the composite image. Check Painter's *User Guide* for a complete explanation of the EPS Options dialog box.

PC formats. BMP, PCX and Targa are formats commonly used on DOS and Windows platforms. BMP (short for "bitmap") is a Windows-based graphics file format, and PCX is the PC Paintbrush native format. Neither of these two formats supports floaters or masks. Targa is a popular format used for creating sophisticated 24-bit graphics; it was originally developed by the Truevision company as a proprietary format for use with its video capture boards. The Targa format is often used (in place of PICT) when preparing numbered files for import into Windows animation applications.

Movie formats. Movies in Painter (described in Chapter 9) are saved as Frame Stacks, but you can choose Save As to export the

You can set your own set of function keys for favorite commands, making it easier to access the commands nested in Painter's menus and palettes. Choose Edit, Preferences, Function keys, then select a key from the Function key list. Now, choose a command, we chose Select, Hide Marquee (to hide a selection marquee while keeping the area selected). Then choose the Set button and click OK.

Making a new function key using the Customize Keys dialog box

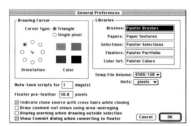

The General Preferences dialog box lets you specify libraries, cursor type and orientation, Temp File Volume (location of scratch disk) and units, among other defaults.

current frame of your movie, the entire Frame Stack as a Quicktime or AVI/VFW (on the PC) movie, or the entire Frame Stack as numbered PICT files. See Chapter 8's introduction for more information about multimedia formats.

Pyramid files. The Pyramid file structure is useful for composing high-resolution documents. A file with Pyramid data structure is capable of containing multi-resolution information. When an image is placed into a document (File, Place), it comes in as a reference floater (a low-resolution *reference* to the original placed image). The introduction to Chapter 5 contains more information about working with reference floaters and Pyramid files.

SETTING PREFERENCES

Painter's Preferences (under the Edit menu) go a long way in helping you create an efficient workspace. Here are a few pointers:

Brush tracking. Before every work session, it's a good idea to first choose Edit, Preferences, Brush Tracking. Make a brushstroke with your stylus using a typical amount of pressure. Painter accepts this as the average stroke and adjusts to give you the maximum amount of range and pressure-sensitivity based on your sample stroke. Unfortunately, Painter doesn't remember your custom setting after you quit the program; hence the need to re-establish your typical brushstroke every time you launch.

Multiple undos. Painter lets you set the number of Undos you want under Edit, Preferences, Undo. It's important to note that this option applies cumulatively across all open documents within Painter. For example, if the number of Undos is set to 5 (the default) and you have two documents open, if you use two Undos on the first document, you'll be able to perform only three Undos on the second document. And, since a high setting for the number of Undos will burden your RAM and scratch disk, unless you have a good reason (such as working on a small sketch where you'll need to make many changes), it's best to leave the Undo setting at 5.

PAINTER BASICS

Here's a guide to some of Painter's basic operating procedures.

Opening drawers. Many of Painter's palettes display a push bar with an arrowhead that you can click on to open (the arrow turns green) or close a drawer. An open drawer gives you access to a wide choice of brushes, gradients, papers and so on from whatever library is active at the time. A closed drawer (you see only the "front" of the drawer) shows your five most recent choices and may give you additional controls. Clicking the "grow" or the "zoom-out" box in the upper-right portion of the palette will show more controls—brush methods and submethods, for instance.

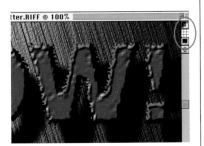

The Tracing Paper, Grid Overlay and Output Preview icons reside at the top of Painter's vertical scroll bar.

The Drawing Mode icons are located in the lower left of the image window. They are from left to right: Draw Anywhere, Draw Outside and Draw Inside. To read more about them turn to Chapter 4.

VIEW FROM POINT LOMA / CHER THREINEN-PENDARVIS

Screen management shortcuts. Like other programs, Painter offers lots of shortcuts designed to cut down on your trips to the menus, palettes or scroll bars. To *scroll* around the page, press the spacebar (a grabber hand appears), then click and drag on your image. To *zoom in* on an area of your image at the next level of magnification, hold down Command-spacebar (a magnifier tool appears) and click in your image. Add the Option key to *zoom out*. (You can also use Command-plus to *zoom in* one magnification level and Command-minus to *zoom out*.) These are the same zooming shortcuts used in Photoshop and Adobe Illustrator.

To *rotate the page* to better suit your drawing style, press Option-spacebar (the Rotate Page icon appears) and click and drag in your image until the dotted outline preview shows you the angle you want. (The Rotate Page command rotates the view of the image only, not the actual pixels.) Restore your rotated image to its original position by holding down Option-spacebar and clicking once on your image.

Two other frequently used screen management shortcuts are Command-M (Window, Screen Mode Toggle), which replaces a window's scroll and title bars with a frame of gray (or toggles back to normal view), and Command-H (Window, Hide Palettes), which hides (or restores) all palettes.

Helpful icon buttons. Just outside the Painter image window are two sets of very helpful icon buttons. At the top right on the Painter Window scroll bar are three icon buttons: the Tracing Paper icon (allowing you to toggle Tracing Paper on and off), the Grid overlay icon (which turns the Grid View on and off) and the Output Preview icon (to toggle between the full-color, RGB view and the Output Preview view). Turn to Chapter 11, "Printing and Archival Concerns," for information about Painter's Output Preview. To the left of Painter's bottom scroll bar are the Drawing Mode icons, which allow

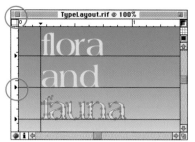

Positioning the baseline of active letterform shapes with the help of the Ruler and horizontal Guides pulled from the ruler. The circled items show the Ruler Origin field (top) and a triangular marker (bottom).

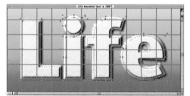

Using the Grid overlay to help when positioning text selections

you to control where you paint—anywhere in the image, outside of a selection, or inside of a selection. See the beginning of Chapter 4 to read more about the Drawing Modes.

Measuring and positioning elements. The Ruler, Guides and Grid overlay can help you measure and position shapes and floaters. The commands for all three of these features reside in the Canvas menu. They are especially helpful for aligning type shapes and selections (see Chapter 5 for more about working with type in Painter).

To set up a guide using precise measurements or to change the default guide color, double-click on the Ruler to access the Guide Options. Double-click on a triangle marker on the Ruler to access options for an individual guide. Delete guides by dragging their triangles off the document window or by pressing the Delete All Guides button in Guide Options.

To easily measure the exact *width* of an item, try moving the Ruler Origin. Press and drag it from the upper-left corner of the Ruler, where the horizontal and vertical measurements meet, to the left end of the item you want to measure. Then see where the right end falls on the ruler.

The Grid overlay is useful for aligning items. Choose Canvas, Grid, Show Grid or click on the checkered Grid icon above the scroll bar. To change the grid's appearance (for example, to create a grid of only horizontal lines), choose Canvas, Grid, Grid Options and adjust the settings.

ALIGNING SHAPES AND FLOATERS AUTOMATICALLY

The Align dialog box (Effects, Objects, Align) is helpful for lining up several shapes or floaters (or a combination of the two). To align a series of items, start by selecting the Floater Adjuster tool, pressing the Shift key and clicking on each item. When all the items are selected, go to the Effects menu and choose Objects, Align, and choose your settings. The dialog box preview will update to show you how your horizontal and vertical choices will affect alignment of the objects, and you can click OK to accept, or Cancel. The shapes (below, center,) are aligned using Horizontal: Center, and Vertical: None. The floaters (below, right), were aligned using the tops of their bounding boxes. The settings were Horizontal: None, and Vertical: Top.

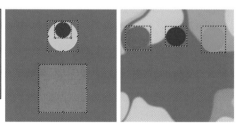

The Objects, Align dialog box with settings for the shapes

Interactive dialog boxes. In most programs, clicking to make choices outside of a dialog box will reward you with an error beep, but Painter's interactive dialog box design encourages you

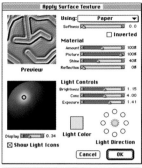

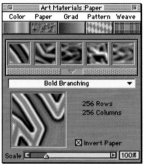

The Surface Texture dialog box preview window (here shown Using Paper Texture) updates when a new choice is made in the Paper palette.

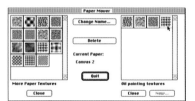

Dragging an item into the Oil Painting Textures library

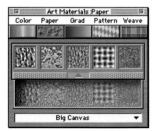

The open Papers drawer showing the newly created Oil Painting texture library

to continue to make the choices you need. As an example, you can open a piece of artwork or a photo, and then choose Effects, Surface Control, Apply Surface Texture and click and drag in the Preview window until you see a part of the image that you like. If you then choose Paper in the Using pop-up menu you can go outside the dialog box to choose a different paper (even a paper in another library) in the Paper palette. You can even move the Scale slider in the Paper palette and watch as the Preview image in the Apply Surface Texture dialog box updates to reflect your choice. When you've arrived at a result that you like, you can click OK in the Apply Surface Texture dialog box. The Effects, Surface Control, Color Overlay dialog box behaves in a similar way, allowing you to choose Uniform Color in the pop-up menu and test different colors from the Color palette before you click OK. The Edit, Fill dialog box (Command-F) is also interactive, giving you the ability to preview your image before it's filled with a Current Color, a Pattern, a Gradation or a Weaving.

LIBRARIES AND MOVERS

Painter uses *libraries* and *movers* to help you manage the huge volume of custom textures, brushes and other items that the program can generate. Libraries are the "storage bins" for those items, and movers let you customize those bins by transferring items into or out of them.

How libraries work. You'll find the Load Library command at the bottom of the resource list on every palette—for instance, the brush list on the Brushes palette, the paper list on the Art Materials:Paper palette and the Script list on the Objects:Scripts palette. Scroll down to the bottom of the list and choose Load Library to display the standard Mac or Windows Open dialog box so you can search through folders on any hard disk or CD-ROM (like the Painter 5 CD-ROM or the Wow! CD-ROM) until you find the library you want; then double-click to open it. Fortunately, Painter is smart enough to show only libraries that can be opened in the palette of origin. For instance, if you clicked on the Library button in the Paper palette, you'll see Paper libraries only, not the Grad or Brush libraries.

Using movers to customize your libraries. If you find that you're continually switching Paper texture libraries, it's probably time to use the Paper Mover to compile several textures into a single library for your work. You can create a Paper texture library containing five textures that work well

To save libraries of "effects scripts" separate from the Painter Script Data file (so the Script Data file does not become too large), you can make new script libraries to store automated effects. From the Objects palette's Script menu choose Script Mover. The Painter Script Data file will open on the left side of the mover. Click the New button on the right side of the mover to make a new library and name it when prompted. Select the scripts you want to copy to the new library and drag and drop them into the new library. When you've finished copying, delete the items from the Painter Script Data file to keep file size trim. (For more information about effects scripts, see Chapter 9.)

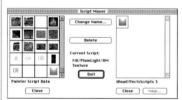

Using the Script Mover to import scripts saved in the Painter Script Data file (left side) into a custom library of special effects scripts (right side)

The Script library containing special effects "macros" that can be applied to images

with Painters's oil-painting brushes and the Wow! Permanent Media brush library on the Wow! CD-ROM—Big Canvas, Small Canvas, Canvas 2, Big Grain Rough (all from the More Paper Textures library in Free Stuff, Papers, on the Painter 5 CD-ROM) and Sandy texture from the Drawing Paper Textures (in the Extra Art Materials folder). Here's how to build it: From the Paper pull-down menu on the Art Materials palette, choose Paper Mover. Create a new, empty Paper library by clicking on the New button on the right side of the mover, then name your Paper Texture file and save it. To move a texture from the left side of the mover (your currently active library) into the new library, select a texture's icon on the left side of the mover: A preview of the texture will appear in the center of the mover window; drag the texture icon from the original library (left side) and drop it into the new library (right side).

Continue adding textures to the new library in this fashion. We selected each of the four textures from the More Paper Textures library and dropped each icon into the new Oil Painting library. Next, we added the Sandy texture from the Drawing Paper Textures library to our new library. To add a texture from another library to your new library, click on the left-hand Close button, then click again when it changes to an Open button and open the next library that you want to draw from. (Don't forget the libraries on the Wow! and Painter 5 CD-ROMs!) We selected the Sandy texture and dragged and dropped it to our new library. When you've finished, click Quit. Now open your new library by choosing Load Library from the Paper palette's paper list menu. If you want your new library to open every time you launch Painter, choose Edit, Preferences, General and type its exact name in the Paper Textures box.

All movers work in the same way, so you can follow the above procedure to, say, create a new Brushes library that contains the only five brushes that you ever use. (See "Expressive Custom Brushes" in Chapter 3 for an example of using the Brush mover.)

SCROLLING IN A DRAWER

When a library contains over 25 icons (although libraries this large are not recommended), a scroll bar will appear so you can scroll to items at the bottom of the drawer.

CUSTOMIZING YOUR WORKSPACE

Painter 5 makes it even easier to customize your work space. You can tear a subpalette off a main palette (such as tearing the Color palette away from the Art Materials palette). And the program now allows you to build your own custom palettes to store favorite menu commands, brushes and textures, for instance.

Dragging off palettes. Painter lets you tear off inactive "child" palettes from the "parent" palette to customize your workspace. For example, in the Art Materials palette, click on the Color icon to make the Color palette active, then click and drag the Paper icon

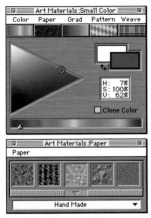

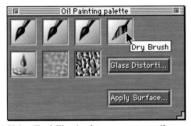

The Art Materials: Compact Colors palette, above, with the Paper palette dragged off, below

Using Tool Tips in the new custom oil painting palette to display the name of the brush. Tool Tips are turned on by default; if you've turned them off, choose Show Tool Tips from the Help menu.

to another location on your monitor. An outline of the palette appears as you drag, and when you release, the Paper palette appears. Although separating palettes in this manner can quickly fill your screen, if you frequently use palettes that are on the same parent palette (such as Color and Paper), creating child palettes will save you many mouse-clicks. To return a child palette to its parent, click the close box in the child palette's upper-left corner.

Building a custom palette. You can make your own palettes to store menu commands and art materials for your work. To make a custom palette for oil painting, begin by selecting the Brush icon in the Brushes palette and choose a brush variant that you prefer (we chose the Big Wet Oils variant). Click the Brush icon and drag it off the Brushes palette—this action will create a new custom palette. The palette will expand automatically when you add a new item. Select another brush variant and drag it to the palette. (We added the Oil Paint and Brushy variants of the Brush). We needed a blending brush to mix colors, so we added the Grainy Water variant of the Water brush. Then we chose Window, Custom Palettes, Shortcut to New Brushes to quickly access Painter 5's exciting New Paint Tools library. We dragged the New Paint Tools icon onto our new custom palette.

Now for the texture: We clicked on the Raw Silk texture from Painter 5's default Paper library and dragged it into our palette, then we loaded the More Paper Textures library (located in Free Stuff, in Papers folder on the Painter 5 CD-ROM). We clicked on the Big Canvas texture and dragged it into the new custom palette.

To add a menu command to a custom palette, choose Window, Custom Palette, Add Command, then select the menu item that you'd like to add to the palette. We added two commands that are useful for adding texture to paintings after the brushwork is complete: Effects, Focus, Glass Distortion and Surface Control, Apply Surface Texture. 🖌

THE POWER OF COLOR

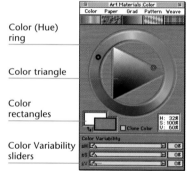

Color (Hue) ring

Color triangle

Color rectangles

Color Variability sliders

The Standard Colors palette (with the Hue ring), expanded to show the Color Variability (± H, ± S, ±V) sliders

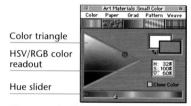

Color triangle

HSV/RGB color readout

Hue slider

Change to the Compact Colors palette by selecting Color Picker, Compact Colors from the Color pull-down menu list.

Change to the RGB Colors palette by choosing Color Picker, RGB Colors from the Color pull-down menu list.

"COLOR, THE FRUIT OF LIGHT, is the foundation of the painter's means of painting—and its language." Abstract painter Robert Delaunay's observation mirrors our own appreciation of color as an expressive and essential element of the visual arts. Getting the most out of Painter's powerful color tools is an important first step for those of us who work with "the fruit of light."

HUE, SATURATION AND VALUE

Painter's interface for choosing color is built around a model that uses *hue*, *saturation* and *value* (HSV) as the three basic properties of color. The program is designed so that you'll typically first choose a hue, then alter it by changing its saturation or value. Painter's Standard Colors palette and Compact Colors palette are designed to work with these properties, but the program also includes an RGB (red, green, blue) palette for those who prefer working in that color space. Click the Color button in the Art Materials palette to open the Color palette. Switch palette views by choosing from the Color, Color Picker menu on the Color palette.

Hue. The term *hue* refers to a predominant spectral color, such as red or blue-green. Hue indicates a color's position on the color wheel or spectrum, and also tells us the color's temperature. A red-orange hue is the warmest color; a blue-green hue is the coolest. (Keep in mind, though, that temperatures are relative. Blue-violet is a cool color, but it warms up when it's placed next to blue-green.)

In the traditional pigment-based color system, red, yellow and blue are *primary* hues—colors

QUICK SWITCH TO RGB

Click on the HSV color readout on the Standard Colors or Compact Colors palette to show color in RGB mode. Click again to switch back to HSV.

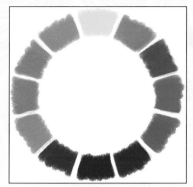

A pigment-based color wheel

A study created in a fiery, analogous palette dominated by orange

Saturating a color   Desaturating a color

Creating a shade of a color   Creating a tint of a color

An example of atmospheric perspective. The illusion of distance is enhanced in this piece because distant hills are painted with reduced saturation and less value contrast.

that cannot be obtained by mixing. *Secondary* hues—green, orange and violet—are those colors located midway between two primary colors on the color wheel. Yellow-green, blue-violet and red-orange are examples of *tertiary* hues, each found between a primary and a secondary color.

Analogous hues are adjacent to each other on the color wheel and have in common a shared component—for instance, blue-green, blue and blue-violet. *Complementary hues* sit opposite one another on the color wheel. Red and green are complements, as are blue and orange. (Painter's Hue ring is based on the RGB components of the computer screen, so it doesn't exactly match a traditional pigment-based color wheel.)

To change hues in Painter's Color palette, drag the slider on the Hue ring or click anywhere on the ring. Dragging and clicking also work with the Hue slider in the Compact Colors palette.

Saturation. Also known as *intensity* or *chroma*, *saturation* indicates the color's purity or strength. The most common way of changing a color's saturation is by adjusting the amount of its gray component. In the Color triangle, move the Color ring to the left to desaturate a color, or to the right to saturate it. Fully or very saturated colors—those at or near the tip of the Color triangle—won't print the way they look on the screen. To see their printed equivalent colors while you paint, choose Canvas, Output Preview, Kodak Color Correction. For more information about the Output Preview option, turn to Chapter 10, "Printing and Archival Concerns" and to Chapter 17 of the *Painter 5 User Guide*.

Value. A color's lightness or darkness is its *luminance* or *value*. To create a *tint* of a color (lightening it, or increasing its value), move the Color ring higher in the Color triangle. To create a *shade* of a color (darkening it, or decreasing its value), move the Color ring lower in the Color triangle.

PUTTING HSV TO WORK
Here are several practical suggestions and creative solutions for solving artistic problems using hue, saturation and value.

Reduce saturation and value to indicate distance. Artists have been creating *atmospheric* (or *aerial*) *perspective* in their work for thousands of years. The wall paintings of Pompeii in the first century B.C. show this technique. Hills we see in the distance have less intensity than nearer hills, and they also have less variation in value. This effect increases in hazy or foggy conditions. To depict this in your art, you can reduce the color saturation and value range as the landscape recedes from the foreground.

Use saturation to indicate time of day. At dawn or dusk, colors appear to be less saturated, and it becomes more difficult to distinguish colors. At noon, on a bright sunny day, colors seem saturated and distinct. (See Richard Noble's solutions on page 31.)

19

A study in value contrast, based on a drawing by Michelangelo

Detail from Dennis Orlando's Bend in the Epte, *showing shadows modulated with complementary color*

Red Mask *was painted by Janet Martini. She used color to express intense emotion.*

Simultaneous contrast at work. Notice how the gold looks brighter next to the dark blue than it does next to pink.

Use color temperature to indicate distance. The eye puts warm colors in front of cool colors. For example, orange flowers in the foreground of a hedge appear closer than blue ones.

Create drama with light-to-dark value contrast. Baroque and Romantic period artists as diverse as Caravaggio, Zurbarán, Géricault and Rembrandt are known for their use of extreme light-to-dark contrast. They accomplished this by limiting their palette to only a few hues, which they either tinted with white or shaded by adding black. A close look at the shadows and highlights that these artists created reveals complex, modulated tone. Digital artists can use Painter's Apply Lighting feature (from Effects, Surface Control) to add a dramatic splash of contrast to an image and also to unify a painting's color scheme, although achieving genuine tonal complexity requires additional painting.

Use complementary colors to create shadows. The Impressionists Monet, Renoir and Degas frequently avoided the use of black in the shadow areas of their paintings. They embraced a more subjective view of reality by layering complementary colors to create luminous shadows.

Neutralize with a complement or gray. One way to tone down a hue is to paint on top of it with a translucent value of its complement. El Greco painted his backgrounds in this manner to draw attention to more saturated foreground subjects. Try painting with a bright green hue, then glaze over it with a reduced opacity of red. The result will be an earthy olive. You can also neutralize a hue using shades of gray, as did the French artist Ingres. Although he often limited his palette to red, blue, gold and flesh tones, he created the illusion of a larger palette by adding varying proportions of gray and white.

Blending, pulling and thinning colors. Subtle changes in hue and saturation take place when colors are blended in a painting. Use the Just Add Water or Grainy Water variants of the Water brush to blend, for instance, two primary colors (red and blue) to get a secondary color (violet). For a more dramatic blending, you can pull one color into another by using the Total Oil Brush variant of the Liquid brush. Artists using traditional tools often thin paint by mixing it with an extender. In Painter, you get a similar effect by reducing a brush's opacity in the Controls palette.

Draw attention with simultaneous contrast. If two complementary colors are placed next to one another, they intensify each other: Blue looks more blue next to orange, and white looks more white next to black. In the 1950s, Op artists used the principle of simultaneous contrast to baffle the eye. Advertising art directors understand the power of simultaneous contrast and use it to gain attention for their ads.

The flowers were painted in reds and red-oranges to unify the composition

A landscape with figures, based on Mahana no atua (The Day of the God) by Paul Gauguin

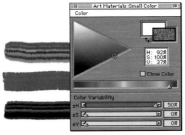

These brushstrokes were painted with the Loaded Oils variant of the Brush and varying amounts of Color Variability: top, Hue slider only set to 50%; middle, Saturation slider only set to 50%; bottom, Value slider only set to 50%.

MORE COLORFUL STROKES

To paint with two colors using criteria other than pressure, open the Controls:Sliders palette and move the Color slider to Velocity. Move slowly to paint using the color in the front color rectangle; speed up your strokes to paint with the back color. Now, drag the Color slider to Direction. Start drawing horizontal brushstrokes (front color) and then gradually turn the strokes vertical (back color).

Use a family of colors to evoke an emotional response. Create a calm, restful mood by using an analogous color theme of blues and blue-greens. Develop another family of hues using reds and red-oranges to express passion and intensity. You can also use a color family to unite a composition.

Create your own color world. Post-Impressionist Paul Gauguin (among others) created a powerful, personal color language by combining several of the above techniques. He used warm, bright colors to bring a subject forward in his composition, and used cool, dark colors to convey distance and mystery. He also made the bright foreground colors seem brighter by surrounding them with darker, more subdued colors.

PAINTING WITH MULTIPLE COLORS

Painter has several brushes that paint with several colors at once; for instance, nearly all of the Artists brushes do so. Here are some customizing tips:

Randomize colors with Color Variability. Choose a multiple-bristle brush such as the Big Loaded Oils variant of the Brush. (If you keep the Brush Controls:Spacing palette open as you choose various brushes, you'll see their Stroke Types appear. Both Multi and Rake are multiple-bristle brushes. You can open this palette by choosing Control, Spacing from the Brushes palette menu.) Now zoom-out the Color palette to display the Color Variability sliders. Choose a color and paint with the brush, then experiment by adjusting the Hue (± H), Saturation (± S) or Value (± V) slider and painting again. You can see the effects of the sliders more easily if you make a series of short strokes rather than one long one.

Change colors with stylus pressure. Use your pressure-sensitive stylus to paint in two colors. Start by choosing the Graduated Brush variant of the Brush. In the Standard Colors or Compact Colors palette, click on the front Color rectangle and choose a bright blue color. Choose the back Color rectangle and select a rose color. If you paint with a light touch, you'll be painting in rose. If you press heavily, the stroke turns blue. (If the balance between the two colors seems uneven, choose Edit, Preferences, Brush Tracking. Make a typical brushstroke in the Scratch Pad area, click OK, and try the Graduated Brush again.)

COLOR ADJUSTMENTS ON EXISTING IMAGES

Painter offers several ways to modify color in your art *after* you have created it. To see the results of your choices in many of these dialog boxes, you'll need to click and drag in the Preview window.

Correct Colors. Do you see an unnatural color cast in your image? The Correct Colors, Curves feature can help you correct this problem. This feature is especially useful when working with scanned photos, for instance.

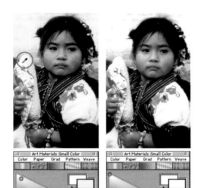

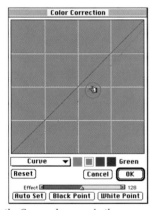

Before and after: Sampling in the image with the Dropper to determine the color cast on a bright highlight on the aluminum foil reveals these values: Red: 227, Green: 241, and Blue 213: (left); and the corrected image (right) with pure white highlights shows Red, Green and Blue values of 255.

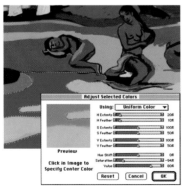

Pulling the Green color curve in the Correct Colors dialog box to lessen the green cast in the image above

To adjust an image, begin by determining the color cast. Use the Dropper tool to sample a bright highlight in your image. (The brightest highlights should be pure white.) In the Color palette, click on the HSV values box to toggle the palette to RGB view. Check the RGB values in the Color palette. In our example, the color and numbers show that the unwanted color cast is green. A bright white should have R, G and B values of 255 in the Color palette. Choose Effects, Tonal Control, Correct Colors and choose Curve from the pop-up menu. Curve will allow you to adjust the individual RGB values. Click on the color that you want to adjust. (We clicked on the Green icon—to constrain the adjustment to *only* the green values in the image.) Then, position the crosshair cursor over the diagonal line, and when you see the hand cursor appear, pull down and to the right. Pulling down (as shown) will decrease the selected color in the image. Click the Reset button to try out another adjustment without leaving the dialog box.

Adjust Colors. To change the hue, saturation or value of all of the colors in an image, choose Effects, Tonal Control, Adjust Colors. Experiment with the sliders and view the changes in the Preview window. Adjust Colors is also useful for quickly desaturating a full-color image—converting it to black and white. To desaturate an image, move the Saturation slider all the way to the left.

Adjust Selected Colors. You may want to make color adjustments in particular areas of your image. Painter's Adjust Selected Colors feature lets you make dramatic changes (turning a blue sky yellow) or more subtle ones (removing the red cast from a subject's face). Choose Effects, Tonal Control, Adjust Selected Colors. In the dialog box, click in your image (*not* in the Preview window) on the color you want to change. Adjust the Hue Shift, Saturation and Value sliders at the bottom of the dialog box. When the basic effect is in place, use the Extents sliders to fine-tune the color range. Use the Feather sliders to adjust transitions between colors: 100% gives a soft transition, 0% gives an abrupt one.

Color Overlay and Dye Concentration. Found under Effects, Surface Control, these two dialog boxes don't allow the radical color replacement options you get with the Adjust Colors feature, but they have their strengths. Color Overlay lets you tint an image with a color using either a dye concentration model (which makes the paper appear to absorb the color) or a hiding power model (which covers the image with the color). Dye Concentration adds or removes pigment. Both of these dialog boxes allow you to add texture by selecting Paper in the pop-up menu.

Negative. Creating a negative of all or part of an image can have dramatic, artistic purposes or more practical ones—such as converting a scanned negative to a positive. Select Effects, Tonal Control, Negative to convert your image.

Using Adjust Selected Colors to neutralize a bright blue

While you're using many of Painter's other tools, you can temporarily switch to the Dropper tool and sample colors by holding down the Command key.

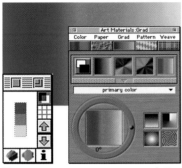

You can create your own custom gradation based on selected colored pixels using Art Materials, Grad, Capture Grad. Create a new document (ours was 144 x 144 pixels) and zoom-in to 1200%. Choose the Single Pixel variant of the Pens brush. Paint a single row of pixels (similar to the one above). Now marquee the pixels with the Rectangular Selection tool and choose Grad, Capture Grad from the pull-down menu on the palette. When the Save Color Ramp dialog box appears, give the grad a descriptive name. Click OK and the new gradation will appear in the Grad palette.

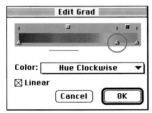

Moving a Color control point in the gradation editor; the Hue Clockwise Color option is chosen.

To name your colors so you can search for them by name, click on the Display Text button at the bottom of the Color Sets palette, double-click on the color in the Color Set, type a name and click OK. To search for a named color in a set, click the Find Color button.

Output Preview and Video Colors. Your monitor can display more colors than can be reproduced in the four-color printing process, and if you are creating images for video, some highly saturated colors will not make the transition to video tape. It's a good idea to convert your out-of-gamut colors while you're in Painter so there won't be any surprises. Choose Canvas, Output Preview, Kodak Color Correction or Effects, Tonal Control, Video Legal Colors, depending on whether your image is destined for paper or tape.

MORE COLOR TOOLS

Adding color with Gradations. Painter's powerful Grad palette lets you fill selected areas with preset gradations or ones that you've created. See "Adding Color and Gradations to Line Art" and "Filling with Gradations" later in this chapter. You can also colorize an image with a gradation using Grad, Express in Image.

The gradation editor is a powerful tool for creating custom color ramps. You can't use this tool to alter all of Painter's existing gradations, however—it's used primarily for creating new ones. On the Art Materials palette, click on the Grad icon, and choose Edit Grad from the pop-up menu to bring up the gradation editor. Select one of the triangular color control points and choose a color from the Color palette. The color ramp will update to reflect your choice. Add new color control points by clicking directly in the color bar; the sliders can be positioned anywhere along the ramp. To delete a control point, select it, and press the Delete key; Option-click on the color bar to add a new control point in the current color. Clicking on the squares above the ramp brings up the Color menu; experiment with the options available there to get quick rainbow effects. To store the new grad in the Grad palette, choose Save Grad from the Grad palette menu.

Filling images. You can fill images or masks using either Effects, Fill (Command-F) or the Paint Bucket tool. The Fill command lets you fill your image or a selected portion of it with a color, a gradient, a clone source (if one is available), a pattern (if no clone source is available) or a weave. The Paint Bucket gives you the same fill options, and gives you additional choices of what to fill: the image or a cartoon cel. (The Paint Bucket options appear on the Controls palette when you select the Paint Bucket tool.) Cartoonists and others who fill line art with color will want to explore the Lock Out Color feature (to preserve black line art, for example) by double-clicking on the Paint Bucket tool icon in the Tools palette.

Keep colors in Color Sets. Painter can store your most frequently used colors in the Color Sets palette, found under the Art Materials: Color, Adjust Color Set pull-down menu. Painter Colors is the default set. Switch Color Sets by clicking on the Library button in the Color Sets palette. You'll find more Color Sets (including a full Pantone set) in Free Stuff, Colors on the Painter 5 CD-ROM. For more about Color Sets turn to "Capturing a Color Set" on page 26.

Filling with Gradations

Overview _Fill the background image with a custom gradation; add paper texture using Dye Concentration; create shapes; convert the shapes to floaters; resize, reposition and fill them._

Flight Adventures

FLIGHT TRAINING
RENTALS
SKY TOURS
PHOTOGRAPHY

CHER THREINEN-PENDARVIS

Reducing the amount of purple in the gradation using the gradation editor

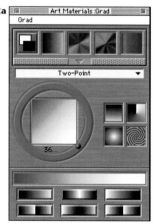

The zoomed-out Grad palette showing the custom gradation, ready to fill the background

PAINTER'S TWO-POINT GRADATION is a great way to create an equal blend of two colors, but if you want to see a larger percentage of one of the colors, you'll need to create a custom gradation. For this prototype design for a flying service's interactive CD-ROM, we initially tried a two-point, purple-to-white gradation on the background, but later chose to make a custom gradation to reduce the amount of purple.

1 Modifying a color ramp with the gradation editor. To create a custom two-color gradation that emphasizes one color more than another, you could select colored pixels in an image and choose Art Materials, Grad, Capture Gradation, but Painter's gradation editor gives you greater precision and flexibility. Begin by choosing the two colors you want to blend (we chose white and a blue-purple). Select the Two-Point gradation in the Art Materials:Grad palette, then close the drawer so you can see the drawer front showing the gradation with the surrounding direction ring. Choose the Linear Type (the top left of the four icons to the right of the ring). Open the gradation editor by choosing Grad, Edit Grad. Click on the triangular slider under the color that you want to de-emphasize (purple, in our example), and uncheck the Linear box so the Color Spread slider bar appears. Drag the Color Spread slider to the left (we set the slider to 33%). The color ramps in the gradation editor and in the Grad palette will update as you move the slider. Click OK. Back in the Grad palette, choose Grad, Save Grad if you want to keep your new gradation for later use.

2 Filling the background image. Choose File, New and create a 640 x 480-pixel document, a standard size for an interface screen. In the Grad palette, drag the red ball on the direction ring so that the darker color (in our example, the blue) starts at the upper left. To fill with the gradation, choose Effects, Fill (Command-F) with Gradation at 100% Opacity and click OK.

2b

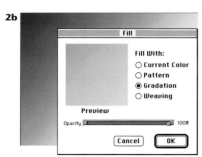

Filling the background with the gradation

3

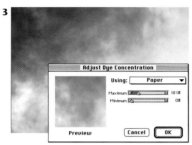

Using Dye Concentration to apply the Clouds paper texture to the background

4

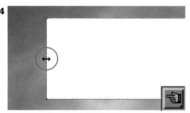

Resizing the rectangular shape with the Floater Adjuster tool

5

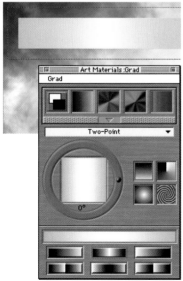

Applying the gradation to the title bar

3 Applying a paper grain to the gradation. To add "atmosphere" to the image, we added a paper texture using Dye Concentration, since that method adds grain based on an image's luminance (darker areas receive more texture). Start by choosing a texture in the Paper palette (we chose the Clouds paper texture from the Nature paper library), then choose Effects, Surface Control, Dye Concentration. Choose Paper from the pop-up menu and experiment with the Maximum and Minimum sliders until you're pleased with the result in the Preview window (we set Maximum to 181% and Minimum to 0%). Click OK.

4 Preparing the title bar. The easiest way to create a long, editable rectangle is to resize a shape made with the Rectangular Shape tool. The shape will appear in your document filled with the current color. (We chose white, it helped us see the shape against the purple background). Use the Rectangular Shape tool to draw a rectangle on your image. You can resize the rectangle by choosing the Floater Adjuster tool and clicking and dragging on one of the corner or side handles. You can reposition the shape by clicking inside of it and dragging it to a new location.

Satisfied with the size and position of our shape, we converted the shape to an image floater before applying the gradation effect. To do this, select the shape by clicking on it with the Floater Adjuster tool, and choose Shapes, Convert to Floater.

5 Creating and applying a gold gradation. We wanted a gold color on both ends of the title bar and an area of white in the center. Choose a gold color in the Color palette, it will appear in the Primary Color Rectangle (front rectangle). To designate a second color for your gradation, click on the Secondary Color Rectangle (back rectangle), then choose the color in the Color palette.

To apply the gradation, first make sure the title bar floater is selected. In the Grad palette, set the angle to 0 and click the top left button to choose the Linear Type. To create a gradation with gold at the ends, click the grow box in the upper right corner of the palette to zoom-out the palette and display the Orders options. Click the top center option (mirrored). Apply the gradation by choosing Effects, Fill (Command-F), select the Gradation button and click OK.

Adding other elements. We repeated the filling process to add gradations and solid colors to the remaining elements of the design. We created the drop shadows behind several of the buttons by selecting each floater and using Effects, Objects, Create Drop Shadow. Finally, we added purple text using the Text tool, kerning the type shapes with the arrow keys and filling them with purple. (To kern the type, choose the Floater Adjuster tool, click outside the newly set type to deselect it, then click individual letters with the Floater Adjuster tool and move them using either the left or right arrow key.) 🖐

Capturing a Color Set

Overview *Capture color from a reference using the Dropper; build and customize a Color Set; use the Color Set to paint a new image.*

1a

The reference photograph

1b

Using the Dropper to sample color from the image

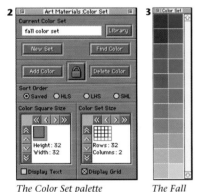

The Color Set palette

The Fall Colors Set

4

Applying colored brushstrokes with the Square Chalk brush using the Fall Colors Set

CHER THREINEN-PENDARVIS

TRADITIONAL ARTISTS USE PALETTES to hold paint; digital artists can turn to Painter's Color Sets. Use this technique of sampling color from a photo or painting to quickly build a full palette of colors as we did here to create the pastel painting *Tienda Verde*, using our custom color set and various Pastel brushes. If you're planning a series of illustrations based on the same color theme, you'll find Color Sets invaluable.

1 Sampling the color. Open an image that contains the color range you want. To sample the color, choose the Dropper tool and click it on a colored pixel in the image. The Color palette will display the color. If the displayed color isn't the one you want, you can click and drag the Dropper around your image. The Color palette will update to show the new color as you drag.

2 Creating a Color Set. In the Art Materials palette, choose Color, Adjust Color Set from the pull-down menu to open the Color Set palette, and click on the New Set button. A very small Color Set palette title bar will appear. Click on the Add Color button to add the selected color to the Color Set. Continue to sample and add more colors by clicking the Add Color button. To save your colors, click on the Library button in the Color Sets palette, then click Save, name the set and Save. We named ours "Fall Colors."

3 Arranging the Color Set display. You can arrange your colors in the Color Set to fit your drawing environment. To change the shape of the individual color squares, click on the Color Square Size arrow buttons, or click on Color Set Size arrow buttons to change the shape of the layout. We built our Color Set of 32-pixel-wide squares with 2 columns and 11 rows.

4 Using your new colors. To paint with the new Color Set, start a new file, click on a color in the set, choose a brush and begin painting. We drew a sketch using a dark blue-gray from our set with the 2B Pencil variant, and added brushstrokes in other colors using the variants of the Pastel brush.

Colorizing Scratchboard

Overview *Create black-and-white art; float it and apply the Gel Composite Method; paint on the background in color.*

CHET PHILLIPS

Phillips' black-and-white scratchboard art

Choosing the Gel Composite Method

Adding color to the image background using the Thin Stroke Airbrush variant

HERE'S A QUICK WAY TO ADD COLOR to black-and-white art, a favorite technique of artist Chet Phillips. To paint *Creation*, Phillips used a floater and the Gel Composite Method, which makes the white areas of the floater appear transparent.

1 Creating black-and-white art. Start a new document with a white background. Choose black, then Effects, Fill (Command-F) using Current Color. Click OK. Use white and the Scratchboard Tool variant of the Pens brush to "etch" into the black fill.

2 Floating the image. Select All (Command-A), choose the Floater Adjuster tool and click once on the image to float it. The black-and-white image is now floating over a white background. In the Controls palette, choose Gel from the Composite Method pop-up menu. This method makes the white areas of the floater transparent, which will allow any color you will add on the background in step 2 to completely show through without affecting the black in the floater.

3 Painting on the background. In the Objects, Floater List palette, click in the blank area below the floater's name to deselect it. This makes sure that you'll be painting on the background. Choose a brush and a color and begin painting. To view your artwork without the floater, toggle the eye icon to the left of the floater name shut. Phillips used the Thin Stroke and Fat Stroke Airbrush variants in varying sizes and colors. In addition to painting freehand with the brush, he also made selections and filled the selections with color (Effects, Fill). If you need to edit the black areas, click on the floater's name in the Floater List and then paint.

Adding Color and Gradations to Line Art

Overview *Use the Pens brush to create line art; fill areas with flat color and gradations; add highlights with the Airbrush.*

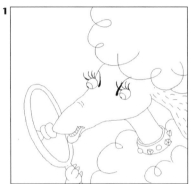

Line art created with the Single Pixel variant of the Pens brush

Filling the drawing with flat color

A TOLERANT PAINT BUCKET

To fill an area of modulated color with the Paint Bucket, use the Tolerance slider on the Controls:Paint Bucket palette to increase the amount of Tolerance. To sample a narrower color range, decrease the Tolerance setting.

FILLING LINE ART WITH COLOR AND GRADATIONS is slick and efficient in Painter, using what children's book illustrator Linda Davick calls "the coloring-book technique." Davick employed the Paint Bucket tool to create the vain, arrogant Zuba, the protagonist in Debbie Smith's *Beauty Blow-Up*.

1 Creating a black-and-white line drawing. Choose the Pens brush, Single Pixel variant, and choose the Flat Cover submethod. Flat Cover lets you draw a solid-color line, a necessity for this technique that fills all neighboring pixels of the same color. Choose black (in the Color palette) and draw your line art, making sure all your shapes are completely enclosed with black lines. If you need to correct your work, switch the color to pure white in the Color palette and erase.

2 Filling with flat color. To test color choices and tonal values, fill areas of your illustration with flat color. Choose the Paint Bucket tool, and in the Controls palette, choose Image under What To Fill and Current Color under Fill With. Choose a color, then click in the area of your drawing you want to fill. Since the Paint Bucket fills all neighboring pixels of the same color, you can refill by choosing another color and clicking again. If you're filling small areas, it's important to know that the Paint Bucket's "hot spot" (where it fills from) is the tip of the red paint in the icon. Davick filled all areas except Zuba's face using this method.

3 Adding color ramps. To fill the background with a gradation, open the drawer of the Art Materials:Grad palette and choose Two-Point from the pop-up menu. Close the drawer, choose the upper-left Types button, from the four buttons on the lower right) and set an angle for your fill by rotating the red ball

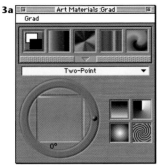

A Two-Point linear gradation

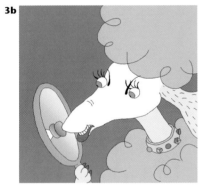

Filling the background with the gradation

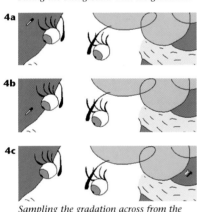

Sampling the gradation across from the top of the area to be filled (a); sampling across from the bottom of the area to be filled (b); filling the area with the gradation (c). Repeat this process for each flat color (negative) area to be filled.

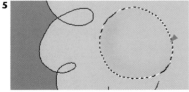

Adding dimension to Zuba's hair using the Fat Stroke Airbrush inside a selected area

around the direction ring. In the Color palette, choose colors for both the front and back Color rectangles. In the Controls palette, choose Fill with Grad. Finally, to apply the gradation, click in the area that you want to fill. Davick filled the largest background area and the mirror with linear gradations.

4 Duplicating color ramps. To duplicate the large background gradation in each of the smaller background shapes—under Zuba's chin and below and above her ear—Davick created a new gradation using color sampled from areas in the background gradation. She then filled the smaller background shapes with the new gradation. If you need to do this on the "negative" shapes in your image, first check the Color palette to make sure that the Color rectangle that contains the starting color of your original gradation is selected. Choose the Dropper tool and position it over the gradation in your image at approximately the same height as the top of the negative area that you want to fill. Click in the gradation to sample the color. To sample the bottom portion of the gradation, select the opposite Color rectangle, then position and click the Dropper at about the same height as the bottom of the area to be filled. Click in the negative area with the Paint Bucket to fill with the new sampled gradation.

5 Adding airbrush details. Davick finished the piece using the Fat Stroke variant of the Airbrush within circular selections to add dimension to Zuba's hair and fur. (You can make roughly circular selections using the Lasso tool.) She used the same Airbrush with unrestricted strokes on Zuba's face and ear.

Davick used her "coloring-book technique" for this editorial illustration for Aspire magazine. The related article offered suggestions on how to keep kids entertained during the summer.

■ Judicious use of saturated color, loose, illustrative strokes and an eclectic mix of brushes and paper textures let **Susan LeVan**, of LeVan/Barbee Studio, create a strong emotional quality in her work.

In *Schizophrenia,* cover illustration for *Pharmacy and Therapeutics (P & T),* a peer-reviewed journal (right), she combined bright, highly saturated colors with dark, somber ones to express the pain and disassociation of the disease. LeVan roughed in the image with the Large Chalk variant of the Chalk brush, then added and blended transparent color with the Simple Water variant of the Water Color brush. She used the Large Chalk, Default Crayons, Scratchboard (Pens) tools, and Simple Water brushes for the details, switching between a variety of subtle and coarse paper textures.

To create *The Garden Within* (below), an illustration for *Home and Garden Magazine* in *The Boston Globe,* LeVan used a palette composed primarily of highly saturated colors, including many reds, yellows and greens. She applied and mixed strokes using the Simple Water variant of the Water Color brush for the underpainting. Then she used the Artist Pastel Chalk and Square Chalk variants and a rough paper texture to apply strokes on the background and the vegetables. LeVan painted with a soft touch, allowing the color in the underpainted areas to show through.

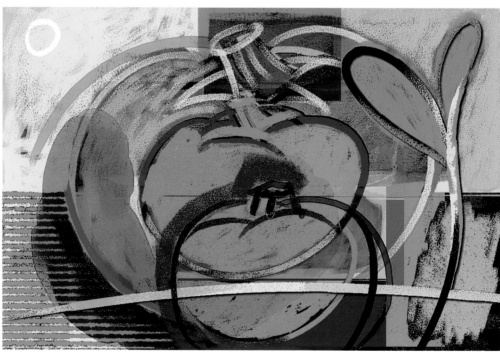

■ **Margaret Sweeney** is an accomplished traditional watercolorist. Today she paints most of her work in Painter directly on screen, without the use of photographic scanning. To begin *Setting Traps* (above), she referred to a sketch drawn on location. Painting with several Brush variants (the Small Loaded Oils, Brushy, and the Sable Chisel Tip Water) on custom made paper textures, she used a palette of pastel colors with subtle contrast to depict the tranquil light of early morning.

■ Artist **Richard Noble** has successfully recreated the look of traditional acrylic using Painter. In *Marina by Moonlight* (left), he used a limited palette and soft brush work to create an atmosphere of low light. Highlights and shadows are subdued and painted with reduced detail. After roughing in color with the Chalk brushes, he blended colors with the Just Add Water variant and used the Distorto (Liquid brush) to pull one color into another, then he added highlights with the Airbrush. Noble outputs his pieces onto canvas, then stretches and finishes them with a clear glaze and touches of acrylic paint.

■ **Cher Threinen-Pendarvis** often makes color studies for a painting on location, carefully observing how light and atmosphere affect color in highlights and shadows.

A passing storm and mysterious, late afternoon light reflecting onto surfaces of century-old buildings in San Jose Del Cabo, Mexico provided the inspiration for *Distribudoria* (top). Pendarvis began by making color studies on location. In Painter, she used the 2B Pencil variant and Basic Paper texture to sketch a rough composition. She blocked in loose areas of color with the Soft Oil brush, a custom brush she designed. Pendarvis's custom brush contains a small amount of Color Variability which helps to modulate the color. To build up layers of color interest, she dabbed small strokes of paint on top using a smaller Soft Oil brush.

■ **Dennis Orlando's** sensitive use of light combined with layered color in the shadowed areas in his paintings has earned him the name "The Modern Impressionist."

Orlando painted *The Bend in the Epte* (bottom)—inspired by Claude Monet's technique of painting highlight and shadow—with soft, warm light on the backlit trees and blue and purple hues in the shadows. He used the Grainy Water variant of the Water brush and the Total Oil Brush variant of the Liquid brush to pull and blend colors into each other.

■ **Richard Biever's** brushy, spontaneous style translates nicely to the digital realm. Value contrast plays a primary role in his compositions, often inspired by the light-to-dark value contrast used by the masters Rembrandt and John Singer Sargent. He typically begins with a gestural sketch on paper, which he then traces on his digital tablet.

Biever was commissioned to paint the cover illustration *Lightning Trap!* (top), by *Earthdawn*, a science fiction gaming magazine. Biever began by sketching with the Oil Pastel variant of the Chalk brush, making large strokes to block in the composition. He opened the Painter sketch in Fractal Design Poser, where he positioned and rendered the figures, and saved the image as a PICT file. He opened the image again in Painter, and using the Poser renderings as an underpainting, he painted over the figures using the Chalk and Oil Pastel, and to further develop the forms and detail in color. He used the Just Add Water and Water Rake variants of the Water brush to move color around in a painterly fashion, then added final details with the Chalk brushes.

In *Grounder* (bottom), Biever painted dark, low-saturation blue and gray strokes behind the ball player to make the background recede and bring the player forward. He added type with the Text tool, filling the letters with a bright red, and then desaturating them by softly stroking over them with a low-opacity white Chalk brush. He blended the colors in the type using his custom Water Rake.

3
PAINTING WITH BRUSHES

India. *Janet Martini added interest to her painting—maximizing the interaction between brush and virtual texture in Painter—by exaggerating the size of the texture. Before painting, she adjusted the Scale slider on the front of the Paper drawer.*

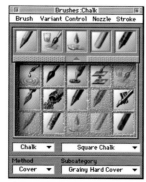

The expanded Brushes palette. From left to right and down: Brush, Variant, Method and Submethod (or Subcategory)

PAINTER'S BRUSHES ARE THE PROGRAM'S HEART: Without them, Painter would be a lot like other image editors. What sets Painter apart is the way it puts pen to paper and paint to canvas—the way its brushes interact with the surface below them. Here's a primer on getting the most from Painter's brushes.

Painting basics. If you're new to Painter, follow these steps to jump right in and begin painting. Create a new file (File, New). If the Brushes palette is not open, choose Window, Show Brushes to open it, and choose a brush. Select a color in the Color palette (Window, Show Art Materials, Color). On the Art Materials palette, you'll also find the Paper palette. Click its icon to open the Paper palette, and choose a texture. Make strokes on the image canvas. Experiment by changing brushes, colors, and paper textures. As you paint, you'll be working on the background canvas. It's also possible to paint on a user mask or on a floater. Painting on masks is covered in the introduction of Chapter 4; for information regarding painting on floaters, turn to the introduction of Chapter 5.

Brush variants. Variants are the options that appear in the pop-up menu on the bottom of the Brushes palette drawer. Every brush has its own variants, so every time you choose a different brush, the list of variants changes. While many artists will be content to use only a

Although it's fun to assign whimsical names (such as Monster Airbrush), informative names are more useful. Try listing brush size, color variability, percentage of opacity, and any change in method or submethod in your variants.

Switch methods to make dramatic changes in brush characteristics. Here we've applied the Crayons brush over a gradient using the default Buildup method (top), Cover method (center), and Eraser method (bottom).

The Gritty Charcoal variant of the Charcoal brush was applied using various submethods: the semi-anti-aliased default Grainy Hard Cover (top); the aliased Grainy Edge Flat Cover (middle); and the soft-edged Soft Cover (bottom).

few of the many brush variants that come standard with the program, others will create dozens of their own. Even if you're an intuitive artist, you'll probably find yourself wanting, for instance, "that scrubby-edged oil brush." Since you lose your custom settings when you switch brushes or brush variants, you'll want to save a variant of that special brush so you're not continually adjusting your settings. (For in-depth information on creating your own brushes, turn to "Building Brushes" on page 44.)

If you've made changes to an existing brush variant, and you'd like to store it in the Brushes palette, check that all your settings are the way you want them. Then choose Save Variant from the Variant pull-down menu on the Brushes palette, name it and click OK. Your new variant will appear in the variant list for that brush and will stay there, even after you leave the program, until you remove it by selecting (on the Brushes palette) Variant, Delete Variant.

Methods. Methods are the backbone of the brushes. To see the Methods pop-up menu, click the zoom-out box in the upper-left corner of the Brushes palette. A brush's method controls how the paint will interact with the background and with other paint. For instance, the Pencil brush uses the Buildup method, meaning that overlapping strokes will darken. The Chalk brush uses the Cover method, which means that strokes—even light-colored ones—will cover other strokes. You can, however, switch methods for the variant that you design. For example, you can save a Cover method variant of the Pencil brush.

Painter 5 introduces a new kind of method, the "plug-in" brush, bringing new special effects to the tips of your brushes. See "Painting with Super-Media Plug-in Brushes" later in the beginning of this chapter to learn more about plug-in brushes.

CHANGING EXISTING VARIANTS

To change the settings of a variant temporarily, first modify the settings of the current variant, then (on the Brushes palette) from Variant pull-down menu choose Save Built Variant. To recover the original variant, select the Variant pull-down menu, and choose Restore Default Variant. This works with Painter's standard brushes as well as with brushes that you have built and saved.

THE LOOKS YOU LIKE

If you like the look of a particular brush-and-paper combination (for instance, the Big Wet Oils brush on Big Canvas from the More Paper Textures library, located in the Free Stuff folder on the Painter 5 CD-ROM), save the combo as a Brush Look so you can quickly call it up when you want to use it again: Select the texture from the Paper palette and the brush variant from the Brushes palette. Choose Brush, Brush Looks Designer—draw a stroke in the dialog box to preview your combination—and click the Save button. Naming your Brush Look saves it to the current Brush Look library. To paint with your new Brush Looks, choose Brush, Brush Looks and select it.

Submethods. While each method gives a radically different effect to a brush, the subcategories, or submethods, make more subtle changes, affecting the edges of brush strokes. Submethods that include the word *flat* produce hard-edged, aliased strokes. Those that include the word *hard* give semi-anti-aliased strokes. Strokes made using *soft* submethods appear with feathered edges. And strokes with the word *grainy* in their submethods will be affected by the active paper texture.

Paper textures. "Grainy" brush methods will reveal the paper texture you've selected in the Art Materials:Paper palette. You can use Painter's standard papers or create your own (see "Applying Scanned Paper Textures," on page 48). Adjust the Grain slider on the Controls: Brush palette to vary the intensity of the grain on your brush strokes. For all brushes except Watercolor brushes, a lower grain setting means that less of the color will penetrate the grain, so your strokes will actually look grainier: They are hitting only the "peaks" of the paper surface. But to make grain more prominent when using a Watercolor brush, move the Grain slider to the right.

EASIER ACCESS TO CUSTOM CONTROLS

In Painter 5, you can add important brush modification commands to the Controls:Brush palette. From the Brushes palette's Control pull-down menu choose Custom Controls. The Custom Controls palette will appear showing available settings for the current brush. To make it easy to customize our Simple Water Watercolor brush as we worked, we added two controls from the Advanced Controls:Water palette, specific to Watercolor brushes. In the Customize Control palette dialog box we selected a palette from the Cat-

egory menu—we chose Water and checked the Wet Fringe and Diffuse checkboxes. To save the brush variant with the custom control added to the Controls:Brush palette, choose Variant, Save Variant. To delete the added controls choose Control, Custom Controls. Water, and uncheck the Wet Fringe and Diffuse checkboxes.

The Controls:Brush palette with added settings from the Water palette (Diffuse and Wet Fringe) that were used with the Simple Water variant to paint this watercolor sketch of Needle's Eye, Sunset Cliffs.

EMULATING TRADITIONAL TECHNIQUES

Here's a brief description of several traditional art techniques and how to re-create them in Painter. There are a number of ways to obtain similar results, so only one or two techniques for each medium are outlined as a starting point for your own experimentation.

Sketch created with the 2B Pencil variant

Still life study painted with Sharp Chalk, Artist Pastel Chalk and Square Chalk

Detail from Coastal Meadow. *The Artist Pastel Chalk and Large Chalk variants were used on Big Canvas texture to paint this pastel image.*

Inspired by a Michelangelo drawing, this charcoal study was drawn with Gritty Charcoal and blended with Grainy Water.

Pencil. Pencil sketches using traditional materials are typically created on location. Tools include soft-leaded graphite pencils (HB to 6B), various erasers and white paper with a smooth to medium grain. To create a pencil sketch in Painter, select a relatively smooth paper such as Plain Grain (in the Drawing Papers library from the Extra Art Materials folder) and choose the Pencils brush, 2B Pencil variant. Select a black or dark gray and begin sketching. To erase or add white highlights, choose a white color and switch the method from Buildup to Cover.

Colored pencil. Conventional colored pencils are highly sensitive to the surface used: Layering strokes with light pressure on a smooth board will create a shiny look, while switching to a rougher surface creates more of a "broken color" effect (color that doesn't completely cover the existing art). To closely match the grainy, opaque strokes of a soft Prismacolor pencil on cold-pressed illustration board with Painter, select a finer medium-grained paper such as Plain Grain (from the Drawing Papers library). Choose the Pencils brush, Colored Pencils variant. Switch the method from Buildup to Cover and change the submethod to Grainy Edge Flat Cover. See "Drawing with Colored Pencils," later in this chapter for a full description of this technique.

Pastel. Pastels encourage a bold, direct style: Edgar Degas preferred pastels for his striking compositions because they simultaneously yield tone, line and color. A great variety of hard and soft pastels are used on soft or rough-grain papers. Pastel artists often use a colored paper stock to unify a composition.

Use Painter's Chalk brush variants to mimic traditional hard or soft pastels, and if you want to use a colored paper, click on the Paper Color box as you open a new document and choose a color. The Chalk brushes are among Painter's most popular; turn to "Blending and Feathering with Pastels," or "Spontaneous Pastels," later in this chapter for two different techniques using them.

Conté crayon. Popular in Europe since the 1600's and used today for life drawing and landscapes, Conté crayons have a higher oil content than conventional chalk or pastel; as a result, they work successfully on a greater variety of surfaces.

To get a realistic Conté crayon look in Painter, start with the Chalk brush, Sharp Chalk variant. Reveal more paper grain in the brushwork by moving the Grain slider in the Controls:Brush palette to 14%. On the Brushes palette, choose Control, Spacing to open the Spacing palette. Set the Spacing/Size at 25%. Now open the Size palette (Control, Size) and choose the upper left brush tip. Set the ± Size slider at 1.45, increasing the brush's effective diameter by 45%. Click the Build button and begin drawing. To see another Conté variant, turn to "Spontaneous Pastels," later in this chapter.

A study created with the Scratchboard Tool variant of the Pens brush

Charcoal. One of the oldest drawing tools, charcoal is ideal for life drawing and portraiture in *chiaroscuro* (high value contrast) style. Renaissance masters frequently chose charcoal because images created with it could be transferred from paper (where corrections could be made easily) to canvas or walls in preparation for painting.

To create a charcoal drawing in Painter, select a rough paper and the Soft Charcoal variant of the Charcoal brush. Create a gestural drawing, then blend the strokes—as you would traditionally with a tortillion, a tissue or your fingers—with the Water brush, Grainy Water variant, changing the submethod to Grainy Soft Cover. Finish with more strokes using the Charcoal brush, this time using the Gritty Charcoal variant.

Scratchboard illustration. Scratching white illustrations out of a dark (usually black) background surface became popular in the late 1800's. Illustrations created in this manner often contained subtle, detailed tone effects, making them a useful alternative to photographic halftones in the publications of that era. Modern scratchboard artists use knives and gougers on a variety of surfaces, including white board painted with India ink. To duplicate this look in Painter, start with the Pens tool, Flat Color variant and increase its size in the Size palette. Choose black from the Color palette and rough out the basic shape for your illustration. To "scratch" the image out of the shape with hatch marks, switch to white and change to the Scratchboard Tool variant. Use the Scratchboard Rake to add texture. Turn to Chapter 5's gallery to see Chet Phillips's Painter-generated scratchboard work, or check out John Fretz's blending of traditional and digital scratchboard in Chapter 4's gallery.

A glazing technique was used for a watercolor portrait study of Sabina Gaross

Calligraphy. With the exception of "rolling the nib" and a few other maneuvers, you can imitate nearly all conventional calligraphic strokes in Painter. Choose the Calligraphy variant of the Pens brush and begin your brushwork. To make guides for your calligraphy, select Canvas, Rulers, Show Rulers and drag guides out from the ruler, or you can use Painter's Grid overlay (Canvas, Grid, Show Grid). If you want a rougher edge to your strokes, try switching submethods to Flat Cover or Grainy Edge Flat Cover. To fine-tune the "nib," choose Size from the Control pull-down menu in the Brush palette and zoom-out the palette. Create a flatter nib by setting a smaller value on the Squeeze slider; if you want to adjust the angle of the brush, drag the Angle slider until you like what you see in the preview.

A pen and watercolor wash study of the king of beasts. Washes were added with the Simple Water and Broad Water variants.

Watercolor. Landscape artists like Turner and Constable helped popularize watercolors in the nineteenth century, and the medium's portability lends itself nicely to painting on location. Traditional watercolor uses transparent pigment for color, and the paper is often moistened and stretched prior to painting.

Detail from John Dismukes's airbrushed Meteor Man logo

Detail of Nancy Stahl's Tennis Woman, *showing her gouache technique*

Richard Noble blends color with a variant of the Liquid brush to get the look of conventional acrylic

Painter lets you achieve many traditional watercolor effects—without paper-stretching! Choose the Simple Water variant of the Water Color brush, a rough paper (such as Cold Press 1 from Drawing Papers library) and a color, and begin painting. When you choose a Water Color brush, you automatically paint on Painter's Wet Layer, which stays "wet" until you choose Canvas, Dry to drop it to the background. For more details about repeatedly drying the Wet Layer for a *glazing* (translucent layering) effect, turn to "Glazing with Watercolor" later in this chapter. If you want your strokes to appear to *diffuse* into the paper, switch to the Diffuse Water variant. (If the color created with this variant is too intense, reduce the opacity in the Controls palette.) You can also diffuse all existing strokes in the Wet Layer using the Post-diffuse command: Shift-D. Repeat the keystroke to increase the effect.

Pen and wash. Tinted, translucent washes over pen work has been a medium of choice of Asian painting masters for many centuries. Painter's Wet Layer lets you add a wash to any drawn (or scanned) image without smearing or hiding it. Choose the Simple Water or Broad Water Brush variant of the Water Color brush, pick a color and a medium-textured paper and begin painting on top of line work.

Airbrush. The trademark of most traditional airbrush work is a slick, super-realistic look; photo retouching is a more subtle use of the tool. A traditional airbrush is a miniature spray gun with a hollow nozzle and a tapered needle. Pigments include finely ground gouache, acrylic, watercolor and colored dyes, and a typical support surface is a smooth illustration board. Airbrush artists protect areas of their work from overspraying with pieces of masking film, or flexible friskets cut from plastic.

In Painter, choose one of the Airbrush variants and begin sketching or retouching. To get the most from the tool, use Painter's selections just as you would traditional airbrush friskets. Turn to "Selections and Airbrush" in Chapter 4 and the gallery in Chapter 5 to see John Dismukes's masterful airbrush work using selections and floaters.

Gouache. Roualt, Vlaminck, Klee and Miro were a few of the modern artists who experimented with this opaque watercolor, used most frequently in paintings that called for large areas of flat color. Gouache contains a blend of the same type of pigment used in transparent watercolor, a chalk that makes the pigment opaque, and an extender that allows it to flow more easily.

Artist Nancy Stahl has created several complex brushes in Painter that emulate traditional gouache applied to cold-pressed illustration board. To learn her secrets, turn to "Gouache and Opaque Watermedia" later in this chapter.

Detail from Paths to Water 1. *The "3D" appearance of thick paint was built by adding highlights and shadows based on Image Luminance.*

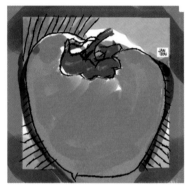

To complete Speedy Persimmon *Janet Martini used the Calligraphy variant of the Pens brush on top of Watercolor and Pastel strokes.*

Detail from Paths to Water 1. *We created texture in grass by scratching out with a modified Scratchboard Tool variant and white paint. To bring out soft highlights in the grasses on the path, the Medium Bleach variant of the Eraser was also used at low opacity.*

Oil paint and acrylic. These opaque media are "standards" for easel painting. Both can be applied in a thick impasto with a palette knife or stiff brush, or they can be *extended* (thinned) with a solvent or gel and applied as transparent glazes. They are typically applied to canvas that has been primed with paint or gesso.

To get the look of oil or acrylic in Painter, choose a very rough paper (Big Grain Rough, Big Canvas or Small Canvas, all from More Paper Textures in the Free Stuff folder on the Painter 5 CD-ROM) and one of the Brush variants (Small Loaded Oils, Big Wet Oils, Hairy Brush or Oil Paint) and begin painting. Blend colors using short strokes with a Liquid brush. For a variation on this technique, see Dennis Orlando's version of a traditional oil look in "Painting With Oils," later in this chapter.

To get textured brushstrokes (the "3D paint" look) when you're finished, choose Effects, Surface Control, Apply Surface Texture. Choose Image Luminance from the pop-up menu, and an Amount setting of 20–30%. If you want to mimic the look of acrylic paint extended with a glossy gel medium, drag the Shine slider to 100%. To get a semi-matte finish, move the Shine slider to between 20% and 30%. You may also want to experiment with the Impasto techniques (requiring setting up an Impasto plug-in floater) as described in "Painting with Realistic Impasto Paint" on page 42.

Mixed media. You can create media combinations in Painter that would be impossible (or at least very messy!) in traditional media. Try adding strokes with a Water Color or Pencils brush atop oils, or use a Pens brush on a base of chalk and gouache. See how artist Phil Howe combines media in "Mixing Media," later in this chapter.

Erasing techniques. Painter provides several ways to emulate traditional erasing techniques. Use the Pure Water Brush variant of the Water Color brush to pull up pigment from a "wet" watercolor (similar to *sponging up* a traditional watercolor). Use the Scratchboard Tool variant of the Pens brush and a white or light color to *scratch out* pigment from a pastel or oil painting; to create strokes with a hint of texture, switch to the Grainy Hard Cover submethod. *Pull paint out* of an image but leave some pigment in the "valleys" of the paper grain by using one of the Bleach variants of the Eraser brush, lowering the Opacity slider (in the Controls palette) to 10%.

PAINTING WITH SUPER-MEDIA PLUG-IN BRUSHES
Painter 5 offers several new brush variants, "plug-in brushes," that involve an open programming architecture. These brushes (that we call "super-media") use brand-new submethods, such as Add Grain and Diffuse Pull. They can make marks on the image background canvas, or on any active image floater. Transparent Layer brushes are also plug-in brushes, and they require a transparent layer. Read more

Detail from study for Paths to Water 4. *Using the Palette Knife variant of the New Art Tools brush to pull and spread color in the clouds and sky.*

about them (and Impasto plug-in floaters) in "More Super-Media Painting Tools," on pages 42–43.

Find these new brushes by selecting Load Library from the Brush library pop-up list on the Brushes palette, or by choosing Window, Custom Palette, Shortcut to New brushes. Click the appropriate icon on the custom palette to quickly access each brush library. "Painting with Super-Media Plug-in Brushes" touches on several techniques using the New Paint Tools, Gooey and Photo libraries. To read more about the Photo plug-in brushes, turn to the beginning of Chapter 6. Use the following techniques as inspiration for your own experimentation.

Mixed media paint with a liquid feel. The plug-in brushes in the New Paint Tools library offer Liquid submethod brushes to lay down color and smear, such as the Sargent brush and Big Wet Luscious. Liquid submethod tools for pulling paint include: Big Wet Turpentine and tools using the Diffuse Pull submethod for distorting and smearing paint on the canvas—the Palette Knife and Dry Brush.

In the *Paths to Water 4* study, color was laid down with the Square Chalk variant of the Chalk brush, and the Big Wet Luscious and Sargent brushes on top of Big Grain Rough (from More Paper Textures). Then color was blended with the Palette knife.

Painting with these new brushes is a very tactile experience—as you drag the stylus and the Palette Knife, you observe large areas of paint being moved on the canvas. Exciting!

To paint and blend using these brushes, choose the Big Wet Luscious brush and a color, and begin painting. When you are ready to pull and blend paint, switch to the Palette Knife or the Dry Brush variant. Try reducing its Opacity to 10% in the Controls:Brush palette for a more subdued effect. Experiment with the Opacity and Grain settings.

Painting with texture. The Add Grain plug-in brush puts 3D texture on the end of your brush. You can switch textures at any time during the painting process, and any brush can be used with the Add Grain submethod for a variety of effects. This submethod is useful for adding texture to colored areas or to a white canvas. Two brushes that work well are the Chalk and Airbrush variants.

To begin, open an existing illustration on which you would like to paint grainy strokes. Choose the Square Chalk variant, and switch its method to Plug-in. Change the Submethod to Add Grain. The submethod is very sensitive to pressure, so use very light pressure on the stylus. Make a few marks in the document to preview the effect. For a more subtle look, try lowering the Opacity and Grain Penetration in the Controls:Brush palette.

Dolphins and Wave, *a card illustration, was originally airbrushed in Photoshop. To enhance it in Painter, we made selections and painted with the Add Grain submethod, using various textures.*

Pulling and distorting paint. The Gooey plug-in variants were created as a tribute to MetaCreations Goo. These brushes are

Zinnias began with a photo. We painted on the photo with Chalk brushes, completely covering it with colored strokes. Then we used Gooey brushes to distort the illustration, add texture and emphasize the focal point.

Detail from Le Can de Triomphe *by Chelsea Sammel. To add textured brushstrokes to the image, she painted with a variety of brushes on top of an Impasto floater.*

To paint the study, Cutting Back at Rincon, *we used the Pen, Brush and Airbrush from the Layer brush library (in the New Brushes folder), to paint on transparent layers. After drawing the line sketch on its own transparent layer, we created a second layer for the color work. Using low-opacity color, we painted on the "color" layer to build up brushstrokes without altering the image canvas or the layer with the line sketch. We finished by dragging the line sketch layer to the top of the Floater List, placing it on top of the "color" layer.*

similar to the Liquid brushes that came with earlier versions of Painter, but much stronger—like liquid brushes on steroids. Brush strength is controlled by Opacity in the Controls:Brush palette.

To create *Zinnias*, we used the Bulge brush to enlarge the pink flowers, and the Diffuse Pull brush to pull pixels and add diffused texture to the edges of the pink flowers. Then the Marble Rake variant was used to add linear texture and to pull pixels up and around the image to create a sense of movement.

MORE NEW "SUPER-MEDIA" PAINTING TOOLS

The exciting new advanced painting techniques that follow use new brushes available with Painter 5 in conjunction with two new tools that are useful to painters—Impasto and Transparent Layers.

Painting with realistic Impasto paint. Impasto lets you go beyond showing the texture of paper as you paint. It gives you the power to show the texture of brushmark striations and the paint itself with realistic highlights and shadows—Impasto brings thick paint to the tip of your stylus!

Painter 5 ships with a useful library of Impasto brushes (you'll find it in the Extra Art Materials folder), and the Wow! Permanent Media brushes on the CD-ROM that accompanies this book also work well. Used in conjunction with an Impasto *dynamic plug-in floater*, these brushes can help you create the look of paint with luscious 3D relief. Impasto plug-in floaters (Objects palette: Plug-in Floaters) are the devices that contain the color and depth information making painting with textured brushstrokes possible.

To create a blank Impasto floater that you can paint on, begin with a new file. Choose Objects and click on P. Float, select Impasto from the pop-up menu, and click the Apply button. To load the Impasto brush library, open the Brush palette, from the brush list pull-down menu, choose Load library, open the Extra Brushes folder and select Impasto brushes. To read about modifying other brushes to include Impasto Options, turn to "Building Brushes" on page 44; to read about using selections and masks with Impasto see "Advanced Painting with Impasto," later in this chapter.

Painting with layer brushes. Painter 5 lets you paint not only on the program's canvas or floaters, but on transparent layers. A *transparent layer* is similar to a clear piece of acetate that hovers above the image canvas. When you paint on a transparent layer with a layer brush, you can see the canvas underneath, as well as color on other layers that you may have stacked up, and you can change the stacking order of the acetate sheets.

If you work with Adobe Photoshop, you'll find painting on Painter 5's transparent layers familiar—with one exception. To paint the transparent layer in Painter you must use brushes that employ the Transparent Layer submethod. You can transform *any* brush into a Transparent Layer brush by changing its method to

IMPASTO AND CLONING

Here are two speedy Impasto illustration methods. If there's not time to paint from scratch, choose a photo you'd like to use for reference. Make a clone (File, Clone). Now, turn the entire clone image into an Impasto Floater. Open the Objects palette, click P. Float, and choose Impasto from the pop-up menu. Choose Edit, Select all. (Tracing Paper is not available when using an Impasto floater, so you may not want to delete the clone canvas.) Click the Apply button to generate an Impasto floater. Apply color and depth to the floater based on the clone source by choosing the Clone Color option in the Colors palette. You may also want to try changing an Impasto brush into a cloner. From the Impasto Brush library (found in the Extra Art Materials folder), choose the Big Thick Wash brush. Change its method to Cloning, and begin painting.

ORIGINAL PHOTO: DIGITAL STOCK

Painting with Impasto using the custom Big Thick Wash "cloner"

Plug-in and submethod (subcategory) to Transparent Layer Brushes in the Brushes palette.

Before you start making your own, though, you may want to try out the set of ready-made Transparent Layer brushes that comes with Painter 5. You'll find more information about modifying brushes for use on transparent layers in "Using Transparent Layers" in Chapter 5.

To add a transparent layer to an existing file, open the Objects: Floater List palette. From the Floater pull-down menu choose Transparent Layer. To paint on the new layer, load the Layer Brush library (found in the New Brush Libraries folder), choose one of the Layer brush variants (such as the Airbrush), select the layer in the Objects:Floater List and begin painting.

Layer brushes and transparent layers offer great flexibility to digital illustrators. Some artists prefer to draw each item in an image on its own layer, which isolates the item so that it can be repositioned, painted on, or composited as an individual element. Transparent layers are also useful when creating *glazes*. A *glaze* is a thin, clear layer of color applied over existing color. Use glazes on transparent layers to build up colored brushstrokes without altering the image canvas. (Turn to "Using Transparent Layers" in Chapter 5 to read more about painting and compositing techniques.

GESSOING A DIGITAL CANVAS WITH IMPASTO

Inspired by traditional canvas preparation, artist John Derry recommends a useful way to add the color and texture of conventional gessoed canvas to a Painter canvas. Begin by creating a new file the size and resolution you need. In the New Picture dialog box, click on the Paper Color icon and select an off-white background color. (Our file was 883 pixels wide.) The color will improve the look of the highlights and shadows when you brush on the texture. Choose Raw Silk texture from the default Painter 5 default texture library. (For our file size, we left the texture scaled at 100%.) Select the entire canvas (Command-A) and from the Objects:Plug-In floater palette menu and choose Impasto. Click the Apply button. Painter will generate an Impasto floater, and the Impasto Options dialog box will appear. In the dialog box, turn off Draw with Color. From the How Depth is Drawn pop-up menu, choose Paper. Check the Grain Controls Depth checkbox. Click OK. Now, choose the Fat Stroke variant of the Airbrush from the default Painter Brushes library. Experiment with the brush size. The grain will appear through the depth layer of the Impasto floater, as you make soft strokes onto the Impasto floater. When you have brushed over the entire canvas and have a realistic texture reminiscent of conventional canvas, save the file in RIFF format, naming it "Blank Canvas." Leave the floater as a live Impasto plug-in floater ready for future Impasto paintings.

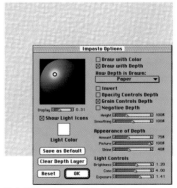

Painting a warm-white gesso onto a Painter canvas using Impasto

Building Brushes

Overview *Creating these custom brushes will give you insight into the workings of the palettes that control them.*

CHER THREINEN-PENDARVIS

Adding thick Impasto brushstrokes to Lighthouse Wall *using an Impasto version of the Soft Oil brush to give the masonry more relief. To read about adding Impasto Options to the Soft Oil brush turn to page 47.*

To read about adding Impasto Options to the Soft Oil brush turn to page 47.

PAINTER 5 SHIPS WITH MANY NEW BRUSHES, and makes customizing them even easier than before. If you like trying new brushes but don't want to build them, check out the Brush libraries on the Wow! CD-ROM in the back of this book—you'll find the brushes shown on these pages and more. But if you can't rest until you get exactly the brushstroke you want, read on. *Lighthouse Wall*, above (based on a photo by Melinda Holden), was created with several of the custom brushes described here.

DAB TYPES

It's important to distinguish between the terms *dab* and *stroke*. Think of a *dab* as the footprint of the brush—a cross-section of its shape. Open the Brush Controls:Size palette by choosing Control, Size in the Brushes palette. You can switch Dab Types at the bottom of the zoomed-out Size palette. Painter has four Dab Types:

Circular. Most of Painter's brushes use this Dab Type. Don't be fooled by the term "Circular"; you can change a brush's Squeeze setting so that its footprint looks elliptical, but it's still considered a Circular Dab Type.

1-Pixel. Just like it sounds, this is a 1-pixel-wide brush.

Bristle. Since Bristle brushes are made up of several "hairs," they have a richer potential than Circular brushes. You can make adjustments in Bristle Thickness, Clumpiness and other settings in the Spacing and Bristle palettes (in the Brushes palette's Control menu).

Captured. You can capture any area of a document to act as a footprint for a Captured brush. Use the Rectangular Selection tool and draw a marquee (press the Shift key if you want to constrain the selection to a perfect square) around a mark or group of markings. Go to the Brushes palette and choose Brushes, Capture Brush; the brush footprint will appear in the Brush Controls:Size palette.

TAKE A SHORTCUT

Painter 5's Shortcut to New Brushes organizer (available under Window, Custom Palette), offers a quick way to navigate to and from new brush libraries in the Painter 5 folder—from left to right: Default Painter Brushes, FX, Gooey, Mouse, New Paint Tools, Photo, Layer, and Super Cloners—experiment with them and use the Pencil icon to return to the default Painter Brushes library.

QUICKER CAPTURES

When you want to design and capture a brush, start by opening a variant that's close to the effect you want. That way you'll have fewer adjustments to make.

AN ANGLE WITH A SQUEEZE

If you want a Captured Dab Type brush to change angle as you draw, set Squeeze (choose Control:Size from the Brushes palette), to 99% or less. Choose Control:Sliders in the Brushes palette and set Angle to Direction. If Squeeze is set to 100%, Painter ignores the Angle/Direction setting. The captured leaf brush dab is circled below. To create the Wisteria brush, follow this recipe: *Method:* Cover *Submethod:* Soft Cover. *Brush Controls:* Opacity, 80; Grain, 20; *Control: Size:* Size, 41.5; ± Size, 2.03; Size Step, 5; Squeeze, 99; Angle Range, 180; Angle Step, 5. *Color Variabilty.* ± H, 5; ± V 5 (in the Color palette)*; Sliders:* Size/Pressure; Angle/Direction; all others/None.

VIEWING THE DAB

Click on the brush footprint in the Size palette's Preview window to switch between "hard" (showing the maximum and minimum sizes) and "soft" (showing bristles) views.

The Brush Controls: Size palette showing a "soft" view of the bristled dab used to create the Feathering Brush

STROKE TYPES

The *stroke* is a dab applied over a distance. You can switch Stroke Types by choosing Control:Spacing from the Brushes palette.

Single. Just as it sounds, Single Stroke Type brushes have only one stroke path. Because of this, they're fast. If you use a Bristle or Captured Dab Type, you can create a fast Single Stroke Type brush with a lot of complexity.

Multi. Painter's computation-intensive Multi Stroke brushes are the slowest (and therefore least spontaneous) of Painter's brushes. For example, try drawing a line with the Hairy Brush variant of the Brush. Instead of a stroke, you'll see a dotted "preview" line that shows its path; the stroke appears a moment later. Multi brushes are built from several randomly distributed dabs that may or may not overlap. Lovely, variable strokes can be made using a Multi Stroke brush, however you can create much faster, "real-time" brushes using a Rake Stroke, or a Single Stroke brush with a Bristle Dab Type.

Rake. The Rake Stroke Type is like a garden rake; each of the evenly-spaced tines is a bristle of the brush. Painter gives you a lot of control over the bristles; for instance, you can make them overlap, letting you create wonderfully complex, functional brushes. You can change the number of Rake Bristles in the Spacing palette (keeping in mind that fewer bristles make faster brushes), and adjust the way the bristles interact in the Bristle palette and also the Advanced Controls:Rake palette. To try out an existing Rake brush, paint with the Big Wet Oils variant of the Brush.

Hose. The Hose Stroke Type sprays a variety of images when you paint each stroke. To read about painting with the Image Hose turn to "Creating a Tidepool" in Chapter 7 of this book and to Chapter 7, "The Image Hose," in the *Painter 5 User Guide.*

BUILDING CUSTOM BRUSHES

For the custom brushes that follow, we start with an existing Painter brush and radically modify its appearance by making adjustments in the palettes that affect brush behavior. After you've created the brush (and perhaps after having made further modifications on your own), you may want to choose Variant, Save Variant from the Brushes palette menu to save it into your current palette.

Try these settings on images of 1000 pixels square or less. If you work with larger files, you'll want to proportionally increase the Size slider settings that we list here. Also, don't worry if your slider numbers don't exactly match ours—just get them as close as you can. And don't think your computer has crashed if you hit the Build button (or Command-B) and nothing happens for a while when you try to paint: Painter is working away, building a very complex brush.

To make room for more brushes, we've shortened our descriptions of how to make the brushes. For instance, "*Well:* Resaturation, 80" means, "From the Brushes palette choose Control, Well and set

Blocking in window panes with the Fast Flat Oil brush

Adding horizontal strokes to masonry with the Feathering brush

Using the Blender brush to add graduated tones to masonry

Footprint of the Random Leaves brush and strokes made in a lighter color. To cover an area with fallen leaves, try recording a stroke and playing it back automatically. Choose Brushes, Stroke, Record Stroke and paint a stroke with the Random Leaves brush, then choose Brushes, Stroke, Auto Playback, and watch the leaves fall!

Footprint of the Soft Captured Oil brush with strokes

Resaturation to 80 but leave all other sliders where they are." *"Color Variability"* stands for the Color Variability settings in the zoomed-out Color palette. Many of the palettes you will use (such as the Size, Bristle, Rake, Well and Spacing palettes) are found under the Control menu in the Brushes palette. For a full description of the functions of the controls in each of the palettes, you can refer to Painter's *User Guide*, although painting with the brush after you make each adjustment will teach you a lot, too.

Fast Flat Oil brush. A Circular Dab Type and a Single Stroke Type make this a fast-painting brush, great for painting short dabs of color with a hint of transparency at the end of the stroke.

Start with the Fine Brush variant of the Brush. *Submethod:* Grainy Hard Cover. *Controls:* Opacity, 100; Grain, 18. *Size:* Size, 25.3; ± Size, 1.00; Size Step, 5; Squeeze, 25; Angle, 0; Dab Type, Circular. *Sliders:* Opacity/Pressure; all others/None.

Feathering brush. Created for feathering over existing color to add interest and texture, this Single Stroke, Bristle brush paints tapered strokes quickly, thanks to optimized Spacing settings.

Start with the Loaded Oils variant of the Brush. *Submethod:* Soft Cover. *Controls:* Opacity, 9; Grain, 100. *Size:* Size, 21.0; ± Size, 1.41; Size Step, 5. *Spacing:* Spacing/Size, 8; Min Spacing, 0.1; Single Stroke Type. *Bristle:* Thickness, 40; Clumpiness, 0 (for smooth strokes), Hair Scale, 495; Scale/Size, 0. *Color Variability:* ±H, 1; ± V, 5. *Well:* Resaturation and Dryout, maximum; Bleed, 0.

Blender brush. The *Well* palette settings for this Single Stroke, Bristle brush let you pick up existing color and blend with it.

Start with the Fine Brush variant of the Brush. *Controls:* Opacity, 100; Grain, 20. *Size:* Size, 20; ± Size, 1.44; Size Step, 5; Bristle Dab Type. *Spacing:* Spacing/Size, 1; Min Spacing, 2.0. *Bristle:* Thickness, 71; Clumpiness, 100; Hair Scale, 221; Scale/Size, 0. *Well:* Resaturation, 74; Bleed, 51; Dryout, 4.9. *Sliders:* Size/Pressure; Grain/Velocity; all others/None.

Random Leaves brush. This Single Stroke, Captured Dab Type brush with variable color, random size and direction is useful for texturizing—adding a natural look of random fallen leaves to a painting. It looks richest when used over a rough paper texture.

To create the brush dab, use the Smooth Ink Pen variant of the Pens brush to make a few simple leaf shapes—similar to the footprint shown—and capture the dab (see Captured, on page 44). *Submethod:* Grainy Soft Cover. *Controls:* Opacity, 83; Grain, 9; *Size:* Size, 25.3; ± Size, 2.72; Size Step, 16; Squeeze, 98; Angle Range, 180; Angle Step, 5. *Color Variability:* ± H, 20; ± V, 7; *Sliders:* Size/Random; Angle/Random; all others/None.

Soft Captured Oil brush. The captured gray dots and a medium Dryout setting give this Single Stroke brush a soft feel.

Start with the Loaded Oils variant of the Brush. To create the dab, draw several tiny black and gray dots to make a circular footprint,

Footprint and lettering made with the Bamboo Pen brush

Soft horizontal strokes of color made with the Soft Oil brush

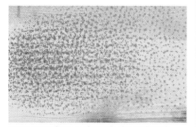

Grainy strokes made with the Colorful Texture brush

then capture the dab. *Submethod:* Soft Cover. *Controls:* Opacity and Grain, 100. *Size:* Size: 26.6; ± Size, 1.34; Size Step, 10. *Spacing:* Spacing/Size, 10; Min Spacing, 1.0; Single Stroke Type. *Well:* Resaturation, 100; Bleed, 75; Dryout, 90.4.

Bamboo Pen brush. This Captured, Single Stroke brush's irregular edges, color variability and changing stroke thickness make it an expressive calligraphy brush. The bleed and resaturation settings make brushstrokes appear to soak into the image surface and to pick up color when the brush is dragged over existing strokes.

Use the Sharp Chalk variant of the Chalk brush to draw a rough-edged oval footprint, with "splinters" on the leading and trailing edges. Switch to the Dirty Marker variant of the Felt Pens brush and capture the dab. *Controls:* Opacity, 16; Grain, 79. *Size:* Size, 25.3; ± Size, 1.91; Size Step, 10; Squeeze, 60, Angle Range, 180; Angle Step, 5. *Spacing:* Spacing/Size, 10; Min. Spacing 0.6; *Well:* Resaturation 42%, Bleed 43%; *Sliders:* Size/Direction; Angle/Direction; all others/None.

Soft Oil brush. This Rake Stroke Type, Bristle brush was created to feel like a traditional soft, flat brush with long bristles.

Start with the Big Wet Oils variant of the Brush. *Submethod:* Soft Cover. *Controls:* Opacity, 50; Grain, 100. *Size:* Size, 22.1. *Spacing:* Bristles, 7. *Bristle:* Thickness, 50; Clumpiness, 70; Hair Scale, 323; Scale/Size, 0. *Color Variability:* ± H, 1; ± V, 3. *Well:* Resaturation, 70; Bleed, 40; Dryout, maximum. *Sliders:* Opacity/Pressure; Grain/Pressure; all others/None. *Rake:* Contact Angle, 59°; Brush Scale, 0; Turn Amount, 200; check Soften Bristle Edge; check Spread Bristles.

Colorful Texture brush. This Bristle Dab Type, Rake Stroke Airbrush is great for painting grainy textures. Decrease the Hue (± H) Color Variability setting for more monochromatic strokes.

Start with the Spatter Airbrush variant of the Airbrush. *Submethod:* Grainy Hard Cover. *Controls:* Opacity, 68; Grain, 44. *Size:* Size, 63.9; ± Size, 2.72; Size Step, 5; Squeeze, 75; Dab Type, Bristle. *Spacing:* Rake Stroke Type. *Color Variability:* ± H, 40. *Rake:* Turn Amount, 136; *Random:* Placement 4.00, *Sliders:* Size/Pressure; Grain/Velocity; Opacity/Pressure; all others/None.

BRUSHES WITH IMPASTO OPTIONS

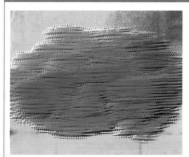

Strokes made using the Soft Oil brush on an Impasto floater

Saving Impasto Options within a brush variant will automatically set up the Impasto Options dialog box when you choose the brush. To set up a brush for Impasto, begin by making an Impasto floater: Open a file, open the Objects palette and click on the plug icon below P.Float. From the Plug-in Floater palette list choose Impasto and click the Apply button to display the Impasto Options dialog box. Now, select the Soft Oil brush (in the Permanent Media brush library in the Wow! Brushes folder, on the Painter 5 Wow! CD-ROM). We used these settings to create the Soft Oil Impasto brush: Draw With Color, Draw with Depth, Height 85%, Smoothness, 200% and Shine 0%. Click OK to close the dialog box. To save your variant, from the Brushes palette's Variant menu choose Save Variant. To read more about Impasto turn to the beginning of this chapter and to "Advanced Painting with Impasto," later in the chapter.

Applying Scanned Paper Textures

Overview *Scan a textured paper; open the file in Painter and capture the texture; use a grain- sensitive brush and Painter's special effects to apply the texture to your image.*

CORRINE OKADA

1a

The scanned paper textures: rice paper (left) and maple leaf (right)

1b

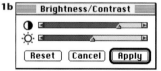

Increasing the contrast of the paper scan

2a

Capturing a selected area of the paper scan

2b

Saving and naming the new paper texture

WHILE PAINTER OFFERS A SEEMINGLY ENDLESS assortment of paper grains, many artists still choose to create their own surfaces. They draw from many sources: video grabs, scanned photos, texture collections on CD-ROM, scans of natural objects (leaves or richly grained wood), scans of papers or patterns and images drawn in Painter. They also generate their own seamless textures with Fractal's Make Paper and Make Fractal Pattern features.

When Corrine Okada first began using Painter, she began scanning her extensive paper collection, capturing the images in Painter and saving them into her own texture libraries. Her skill in applying these custom textures is evident in *Crane Maiden,* a CD-ROM cover commissioned by Silicon Graphics.

1 Scanning the papers. Okada scans her papers on a flatbed scanner in grayscale mode. She scans an 8 x 10-inch area at 300 ppi. If you're scanning a thin, light-colored sheet—like the piece of lacy rice paper that Okada scanned for this job—you may want to place a sheet of black paper behind it to create more contrast. Okada also scanned a sheet of Japanese maple leaf paper.

You'll have more flexibility when you apply the texture if the scan you apply has good contrast and a broad tonal range. So open your scanned texture and choose Effects, Tonal Control, Brightness/Contrast. Drag the top slider to the right to increase contrast. If necessary, adjust the lower slider (Brightness) and then click Apply.

2 Capturing the texture. Use the Rectangular Selection tool to isolate an area of your image. Start by selecting an area of about

Detail of the Rice Paper texture brushed behind the head

Detail of the Rice Paper texture brushed onto the kimono

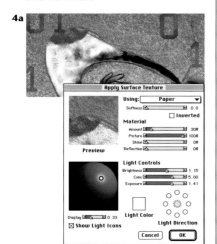
Applying a Surface Texture using Painter's Rice Paper texture

The Maple Leaf texture on the brushstroke (created with special effects) and the computer monitor (applied with the Soft Charcoal variant)

200 x 200 pixels (read the Width and Height dimensions in the Controls:Selection palette). The repetition of your pattern may be too obvious if your selection is much smaller. On the Art Materials:Paper palette, choose Paper, Capture Paper. Name your paper and click OK to accept (you'll get the smoothest results if you leave the Crossfade setting at 16), and a picture of the texture will appear in your current Paper library.

3 Applying grain with brushes. Painter lets you apply textures in two ways: with a brush or as a special effect. Okada used both of these methods (within selections and on floaters), in this piece. To brush the Rice Paper texture behind the woman's head, she first inverted the texture by checking the Invert Grain box on the front of the closed Paper drawer. She selected the area behind the head, then brushed the texture into the selected area using the Soft Charcoal variant of the Charcoal brush and a white color. Okada selected a purple color to brush the same texture (without inverting the grain) onto the woman's kimono. Near the end of the project, she used the same brush to apply the Maple Leaf texture onto the computer screen in blue, yellow and white.

4 Special effects with grain. To create a subtle woven look across the entire image, Okada selected Painter's Rice Paper texture from the Wild Textures library found in Papers, in the Free Stuff folder on the Painter 5 CD-ROM. She selected Effects, Surface Control, Apply Surface Texture. In the Using menu she selected Paper, then she set the Amount at 30%, the Shine at 0 and clicked OK.

To add color, value and texture to the brushstroke that sweeps across the lower half of the image, Okada applied multiple special effects using the Maple Leaf texture. She selected, then floated the brushstroke, and used Color Overlay, Apply Lighting, and Apply Surface Texture (all under Effects, Surface Control) a few times each with various settings to get the effect she wanted.

Spontaneous Pastels

***Overview** Add texture to a new document; use variants of the Chalk brush to create a sketch; block in color; add detail.*

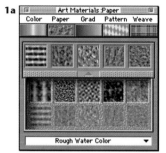

1a

Selecting the Rough Water Color paper

1b

The front of the Paper palette drawer

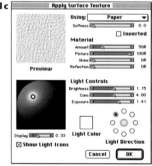

1c

Sammel's Apply Surface Texture settings

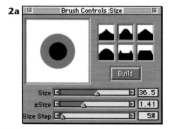

2a

Adjusting the settings for Tapered Chalk

THE CHALK BRUSH VARIANTS ARE AMONG PAINTER'S most responsive brushes, making them a natural match for artist Chelsea Sammel's spontaneous style. The Chalk family is also grain-sensitive—another good match for Sammel, who worked for many years with traditional pastels on rough paper. She began *Poppies* at a Macworld demonstration and finished it in her studio.

1 Preparing the drawing surface. Sammel created a rough, textured surface across her entire canvas. To do this, create a new document with a tan paper color. Choose a rough paper texture in the Art Materials:Paper palette. Click on the Paper drawer's push bar to reveal the Scale slider, and drag it to the left to make a finer grain. Sammel chose Rough Water Color from the Grains library (in the Free Stuff folder on the Painter 5 CDROM) and scaled it to 90%. To apply the texture, choose Effects, Surface Control, Apply Surface Texture. Choose Paper Grain from the pop-up menu and experiment with the settings. Click OK when you're done. Sammel set Amount to 50%, Picture to 100% and Shine to 0%.

2 Building brush variants. Sammel likes Painter's default Chalk brushes and makes only minor adjustments to their settings. She works quickly and spontaneously, creating a few variants on the fly and switching frequently among them. To create her Tapered Chalk, choose the Artist Pastel Chalk variant of the Chalk brush. On the Brush palette, choose Control, Size, In the Brush Controls: Size palette, set Size to 36.5 and ± Size to 1.41. Choose Control, Sliders to open the Advanced Controls: Sliders palette, and set Size to Pressure. This setting, combined with a

THE VANISHING SURFACE

Applying Surface Texture to an empty canvas is a good way to give an entire surface a texture, but it will be covered as you paint if the brush you're using doesn't show grain (doesn't have the word "grainy" in its submethod). Some artists apply Surface Texture before *and* after they paint.

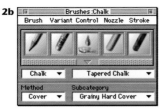

2b

The Tapered Chalk variant as it appears in the Brushes palette

3a

Drawing the poppy with the Conté variant over the ochre background

3b

The original finished poppy image, before the image was extended to incorporate the second poppy

4

Duplicating the poppy to balance the composition

moderate ± Size setting, creates more taper at the end of each stroke. Build the brush (press Command-B). To save the variant, from the Brushes palette, choose Variants, Save Variant, then name your brush and click OK. To create Sammel's Conté Crayon, start with the Sharp Chalk variant. In the Size palette, change Size to 9.4 and ± Size to 1.41. In the Sliders palette, set Size to Pressure, and build the brush. For a grainier stroke, drag the Grain slider in the Controls palette to 13%. Save the variant.

BRUSH SIZING SHORTCUT

Save a trip to the Art Materials: Size palette by resizing brushes while you paint: Hold down Command-Option, click and drag until the circle that appears (representing brush size) is the size you want, release and keep painting.

3 Sketching the first poppy. Sammel brushed a warm ochre onto the background using the Tapered Chalk, adding a few strokes of complementary blues and greens. She switched to the Conté variant, chose black, and sketched loose, dynamic shapes. She switched back to Tapered Chalk and began to block in areas of color, starting with the large poppy. She wanted an active, random look to the color, so she placed varying colors next to each other. Once she had blocked in the major areas, she chose the Frosty Water variant of the Water brush and smudged her strokes into the background. She switched to the Grainy Water variant in areas where she wanted to preserve the textured look.

4 Adding the second poppy. To balance the composition, Sammel decided to add another poppy, so she needed to enlarge her image. If you need to make more room in an existing image, choose Canvas, Canvas Size, and enter the number of pixels you want to add to each edge of your image.

Sammel created a duplicate poppy by floating a copy of the original. To do this, she carefully selected the large poppy with the Lasso, switched to the Floater Adjuster tool, held down the Option key (to copy) and clicked on the selected area. While the copy was floating, she scaled it smaller, flipped it horizontally, and rotated it slightly to distinguish it from the original (all of these effects are found under Effects, Orientation). When she was satisfied with floater's position in the composition, she dropped it by clicking on the Drop button in the Objects:Floater List palette.

Finalizing the image. Sammel extended the petals of the small poppy with the Tapered Chalk, blending and adding fresh color where needed. To further define the shapes, she added dark green line work with the Conté Crayon set to Buildup method, Grainy Hard Buildup submethod. (The Buildup method lets the color darken to black as strokes overlay each other.) She switched back to Cover method, Grainy Hard Cover submethod to finish the image by adding lighter complementary hues over the dark ones. 🐾

Cloning and Tracing

Overview *Open a reference image, make a clone; delete the contents of the clone; use tracing paper to aid in tracing the original image; add detail using Cloning brushes.*

CHER THREINEN-PENDARVIS

The original photo

PHOTO: DIGITAL STOCK

Sketching in the clone using Tracing Paper

Selecting the sky with the Magic Wand

WHEN THERE ISN'T TIME to draw from scratch—or if drawing from life isn't your fancy—Painter's cloning and tracing paper features make it easy to use a photo or other existing art as a reference for a new illustration.

1 Selecting an image and making a clone. In Painter, start by opening a reference image (such as a painting, or photo). To make a clone, choose File, Clone. The new clone will be linked to the original file—its clone source. The cloning process maps the clone (the destination image) directly to the original (the source image), pixel-by-pixel. Leave the original image open.

2 Tracing and sketching. Working with Tracing Paper in Painter is similar to using a conventional light table. In preparation for using the Tracing Paper function, select all (Command-A), and delete the contents from the clone canvas (Delete). Turn on Tracing Paper by clicking the Tracing Paper icon in the upper right scroll bar or choose Canvas, Tracing Paper (Command-T). The original image will appear "screened back," ready to be traced with a brush.

Choose a paper texture (Window, Art Materials), and click on the Paper icon to open the paper drawer. Click on a paper texture to choose it. We alternated between Basic and Smooth textures. Open the Colors palette (Art Materials, Colors), click in the hue bar to choose a hue, and in the color triangle to select a tint or shade of the color. We chose a warm gray for our sketch.

Open the Brushes drawer (Window, Show Brushes), and click on a brush to select it. (You do not need to use a cloning method brush to sketch using tracing paper.) Begin painting using the clone source image as a guide. To toggle Tracing Paper on and off as you work press Command-T.

3b

Filling the sky with imagery from the source image

3c

Adding grainy strokes to the sky and foliage using the Chalk variants

4

To add crispness to the soft illustration we cloned in a few details from the original.

5

Cloning the border. Notice the crosshair denoting the sampled area.

3 Making a selection and filling. After we had drawn a solid line to outline the building, (using the Fine Point Pen variant), we selected the white sky above the solid line with the Magic Wand. (In the Controls:Magic Wand palette, we first set the Tolerance to 1, so that only white pixels would be selected.) We saved the selection (Select, Save Selection, New), then loaded it and chose Effects, Fill, Clone Source to bring the color from the original image into the selected sky. (For more information about selection, turn to Chapter 4. Using shades of blue, we painted grainy strokes over the filled sky with the Chalk brushes.

> **USING CLONE COLOR**
>
> To paint with your own strokes in an illustration with color from another image, check the Clone Color checkbox on the Color palette.

4 Adding details with brushes. After painting the foreground foliage with the Pen and Ink variant of the Pens brush using greens and black, we switched to the Large Chalk to add loose curved strokes of white to denote highlights on the foliage. Using the Chalk brushes, we added more strokes to the foliage in various shades of green, some imported from the original image using Clone Color.

To brush detail from the original image onto your illustration, choose a cloning brush variant. We used the Chalk Cloner variant to add detail to the door of the mission. You can change any Painter brush into a cloning brush by switching its method to Cloning. Try cloning using the Soft Cover Cloning submethod available on the Brush palette for a smoother look.

5 Cloning a border with a chalky edge. In preparation for adding a rough-edged border, we increased the canvas size of the file (Canvas, Canvas Size) by 20 pixels on all four sides. (When you change the size of your image, Tracing Paper will no longer be available unless you also change the source image to the same pixel size.) We added the border by sampling imagery and making rough strokes along the edge using the Chalk Cloner. To clone from one point to another within an image, (much like using the Rubber Stamp in Photoshop), select a source point in your image (Control-click; Shift-click in Windows). Reposition the cloning brush in your document, stroking with the brush to bring the imagery into the area. Reload the cloning brush as necessary as you work around the edge.

> **CLONING FROM ONE IMAGE TO ANOTHER**
>
> To clone from one unrelated image to another (to map pixel for pixel, or to use the tracing paper function), the two images must have exactly the same pixel dimensions. Open two images that are the same size and choose one image for your destination image. Choose File, Clone Source, and designate the second image as the clone source. Use a Cloning brush to bring imagery into the destination image. To continue to clone or use tracing paper, the source image must be left open.

Painting with Pastels

Overview *Rough out a composition in gray; add color with a custom Chalk variant and fills; blend colors with a Water brush; use "scrumbling" for texture to finish.*

CHER THREINEN-PENDARVIS

An original "sketchbook" pencil sketch

Sketching in gray with the Chalk brush

Adjusting the settings in the Control:Brush palette

INSPIRED BY THE SOFT, WARM LIGHT of a sunrise in Baja California, *Punta San Antonio* was painted primarily from memory with Painter's Chalk brushes, although we occasionally referred to pencil sketches made on location. To achieve the soft atmosphere, we blended colors with a Water brush, and added a few accents of broken color to finish the piece.

1 Selecting a reference and opening a new file. Choose a photo or a sketch to use as a reference and open a new file. We started with an 11.5 x 7.5-inch file at 144 ppi and later doubled the image's resolution (using Canvas, Resize) midway through the painting process so it could be printed larger.

2 Choosing a gray color, a texture and a brush. It's often easier to work out the artwork's light and dark values in a neutral gray. Choose a gray tint from the Colors palette and a paper from the Paper palette. We chose Rough paper (Grains library in Free Stuff, Papers on the Painter 5 CD-ROM). Select the Chalk brush, choose one of the variants and begin sketching. We used Artist Pastel Chalk to create the thick, flowing lines of the landscape. To keep the freshness and energy of a sketch while you draw, don't get bogged down with details.

3 Building a custom Pastel variant. When you're done sketching and you're ready to add color, create a midsized, soft Pastel brush: First choose the Large Chalk variant and change the submethod to Grainy Soft Cover. In the Controls:Brush palette, set the Size to 12.0, and lower the Opacity to 30%. A lower opacity will allow you to build up color slowly with more sensitivity. To save this custom brush as a variant, from the Brushes palette choose Variant, Save Variant, name your variant and click OK. The new name will appear in the Brushes palette. Choose a color and begin painting. We adjusted our new variant's size and opacity as we worked, switching to a 50% opacity, for instance, when creating the gold lighting effect on the water.

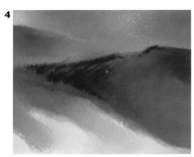

Blending with the Just Add Water variant of the Water brush

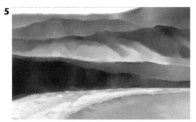

Selecting the sky with the Lasso tool

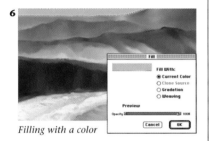

Filling with a color

Scrumbling on the white water

Adding texture to the foreground foliage

4 Blending colors. To achieve a smooth look with traditional pastels, you rub them with precise blending tools like a tortillion or a blending stump. Use the Just Add Water or Grainy Water variants of the Water brush to mimic these traditional tools. Choose Control, Size from the Brushes palette and in the Brush Controls: Size palette, choose the top left brush tip profile (the profiles are located above the Build button). Begin blending, and experiment with various brush sizes while you work.

5 Making selections for the underpainting. To quickly visualize color choices for the underpainting in the sky and the ocean, we made loose freehand selections of those areas using the Lasso tool. Select the Lasso, and on your image, drag around the area you want to select. If you want to edit the selection, hold down the Command key and redraw the marquee to take area away or hold the Shift key and redraw the marquee to add to the selected area. To slightly soften your selection, give it a small feather: From the Select menu, choose Feather, and type a number in the field (we used 2 pixels). Chapter 4 contains more information about selections and shapes.

6 Underpainting with fills and brushwork. Choose a color to fill the selection. If you want to use a color from your artwork, select the Dropper tool and click on your painting to sample color. To fill the selection, select Effects, Fill (Command-F), choose Current Color and click OK. After filling, deselect—choose Select, Deselect (Command-D). To avoid a static, flat look, you'll want to lightly brush over the filled areas to create movement and variation in tone. Choose a color that blends well with the fill color, then select the Chalk variant you created in step 3 and apply strokes over the fill. We switched to a very rough paper texture (Big Canvas, Grains paper library), then added darker orange strokes to the center of the sky, and darker and lighter blues to the water. We covered most of the filled areas with brushstrokes.

7 Finishing with scrumbling. Artists using traditional media will often finish a pastel drawing by brushing the side of the pastel lightly along the peaks of the rough art paper. This technique, called *scrumbling*, causes colors to blend optically and adds texture. To scrumble electronically, select the Large Chalk variant and adjust Opacity to 25% (Controls palette). Choose a rough paper (such as Big Canvas from the More Paper Textures library in Free Stuff, Papers on the Painter 5 CD-ROM). In the Brush Controls:Size palette, move the ± Size slider all the way to the right (for maximum pressure sensitivity), and select the lower left brush tip profile. Build the brush (Command-B) and apply strokes lightly using a color sampled from your image with the Dropper. We used scrumbling to add density to the shadows on the hills and to show wind activity on the water. To add a semi-transparent texture to the plant life in the foreground, we switched to the Grainy Soft Cover submethod.

Drawing with Colored Pencils

Overview *Create a sketch with the Colored Pencils variant; customize the brush to further develop the drawing; adjust Color Variability settings for a more active color effect.*

CHER THREINEN-PENDARVIS

1

The line sketch drawn with Colored Pencil

2a   **2b**

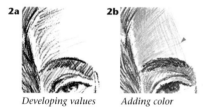

Developing values   *Adding color*

3

Building dimension using increased Color Variability settings and strokes that follow the form

YOU CAN MODIFY THE COLORED PENCILS variant and get a broken color effect (where the color only partially covers the background or underdrawing) by brushing lightly across a textured surface.

1 Starting with a sketch. Open a new, 4 x 2.5-inch, 225 ppi file with a white background, then choose the Plain Grain texture (Drawing Papers library). Choose a dark brown color, select the Colored Pencils variant of the Pencils brush and sketch the portrait.

2 Developing value and adding color. Change the Colored Pencils's method to Cover and the submethod to Grainy Edge Flat Cover. In the Size palette, set Size to 3.4 and ± Size to 1.54. Use this brush and a lighter brown to develop values throughout the sketch. Choose a skin color (we chose a tan for this portrait of Steve Pendarvis) and apply strokes with a light touch to partially cover some of the brown sketch. Follow the form with your strokes, switching colors and brush sizes as you draw.

3 Building dimension. To give a shimmery look to the color as it's applied, drag the Hue (± H) and Value (± V) sliders in the zoomed-out Color palette to 3%. Use this new pencil to apply a fresh layer of strokes in the areas of strongest color (in our drawing, the forehead and nose shadows and the hair). Remember to use a light touch to allow the under-painting to show through. 🖌

COLORED PENCIL WASHES

If you're using Colored Pencils on grainy paper, you can create a wash effect. Choose the Grainy Water variant of the Water brush, reducing Opacity and Grain penetration in the Controls:Brush palette to 40% or less. Stroke over your pencil work to blend colors while maintaining texture on the "peaks" of the paper grain.

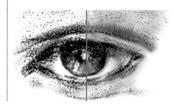

Blending and Feathering with Pastels

Overview Create and soften a sketch; build color and form; blend the painting; add feathered strokes to finish.

CHER THREINEN-PENDARVIS

Creating a loose sketch with Sharp Chalk

Smudging with the Grainy Water variant

Roughing in color and value with Chalk

Blending the underpainting with Water

Finishing with feathered Chalk strokes

FEATHERING—THIN, PARALLEL STROKES over a blended underpainting—is a traditional pastel technique that yields texture and freshness. Because the feathered finishing strokes remain unblended on the painting's surface, the viewer's eye must work to blend the colors. Here is an example of optical color blending.

1 Starting with a sketch. Open a new file with a white background—our file was 3 x 3.3 inches and 225 ppi. Select a rough paper texture from the Papers palette such as Sandy Watercolor (Drawing Paper Textures), a neutral color (we chose a red-brown), and select the Sharp Chalk variant of the Chalk brush. To get a more sensitive response, we moved the ± Size slider in the Brush Controls:Size palette to 1.54, and in the Advanced Controls: Sliders palette (choose Control, Sliders from the Brush palette menu), we set Size to Velocity. Use this brush to create a sketch.

2 Softening the sketch. Select the Grainy Water variant of the Water brush and blend your sketch, allowing your strokes to follow the direction of the form.

3 Building the underpainting. Use the Artist Pastel Chalk variant of the Chalk brush and add color and value to your sketch. To blend your strokes, switch to the Grainy Water variant of the Water brush; we lowered our variant's Opacity setting (Controls:Brush palette) to 40%. Add layers to the underpainting with these two tools until you're pleased with the form.

4 Adding feathered strokes. To create thin, textured strokes on top of the blended form, decrease the Size of the Artist Pastel Chalk variant to 4.2, increase the ± Size to 1.54, and in Advanced Controls:Sliders, set Size to Pressure. Stroke with this brush in the direction of the form. In our example, feathering is most noticeable in the upper portion of the apple. Finish the piece by using Grainy Water to soften the feathering in the shadow areas.

Glazing with Watercolor

Overview *Make a pencil sketch; apply layers of color to the sketch with Water Color brushes, drying the image between applications of color; add final highlight detail to the dried image with an Eraser brush.*

MARY ENVALL

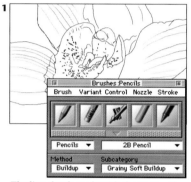

The line sketch made with the 2B Pencil

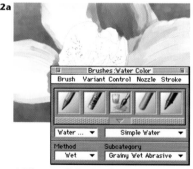

Adding very light tinted washes to the pencil sketch with the Simple Water brush

Adding slightly darker washes after drying

TWO COMMON TRADITIONAL WATERCOLOR techniques that are easily emulated with Painter are *wet-into-wet* and *glazing.* Wet-into-wet creates a softer-edged look—the painting surface is kept wet as new color is applied, so new paint blends easily with old. Glazing involves applying transparent washes of watercolor, drying the painting between successive washes; colors are usually built up in layers from light to dark. Drying an image after applying each new layer of color allows crisper rendering than is possible with the wet-into-wet technique.

Mary Envall frequently paints a close-up view of her subject to emphasize subtle details. Before beginning *Cymbidium Orchid,* one of a series of watercolor flower studies, Envall shot photos to use for reference. She began this image with a tight pencil sketch in Painter and used transparent glazes to build layers of color and value, progressing from light to dark.

1 Starting with a sketch. Open a new file with a white background (Envall's file was 1593 pixels wide); then choose a texture from the Papers palette. Envall chose Plain Grain (from the Drawing Paper Textures library) because she felt its natural-looking fine grain would complement her watercolor rendering. Choose a neutral gray color, select the 2B Pencil variant and draw your line sketch.

2 Adding the first washes. Using highlight colors for the first glaze layer, Envall added washes to her pencil sketch. Choose light colors and block in the large areas with the Large Simple Water and Simple Water variants of the Water Color

USE THE OPACITY KEYS

To change the opacity of your brushstrokes without using the Controls:Brush palette's Opacity slider, use these keyboard shortcuts: Press 1 for 10% Opacity, 2 for 20%, and so on (press 0 for 100% Opacity).

3a

Applying long strokes of color from the center of the flower toward the petals

3b

Adding midtone detail with the Diffuse Water and Simple Water brushes

4

Adding final details with the Simple Water brush

Brittany in Sailor Hat was painted using the Simple Water variant and a freer wet-into-wet style (the painting was kept wet—saved in RIFF format—throughout the painting process). Paying careful attention to her light source, Envall applied washes of highlight colors and the lightest skin tones, then added detail overall, varying color in the shadows.

brush. (Selecting a Water Color brush automatically activates Painter's Wet Layer.) With conventional watercolor, you can't paint on areas that you want to keep white, but Painter lets you lighten or remove color: Use the Wet Eraser variant of the Water Color brush.

If you want to erase linework on the background, do so with a "dry" Eraser variant before you dry the Wet Layer, since drying the Wet Layer drops it permanently to the background. Envall kept the pencil lines she needed for emphasis and erased others with the Ultrafine Eraser.

To complete the first glaze, choose Canvas, Dry to dry the Wet Layer, then start the next glaze by choosing a Water Color brush and continuing to paint. Select the Simple Water variant, for example, and add a slightly darker series of washes with more detail, as Envall did before developing the midtones in the next step.

3 Building form and midtone values. Choose medium-value colors and develop your midtones, applying lighter colors first, then darker ones to create form. Keep your light source in mind and let your strokes follow the direction of the forms.

Envall added the larger intermediate-value shapes and some of the shadows. She applied darker fuschia, mauve and gray colors to the interior of the orchid (to help make it appear to recede), and used the Diffuse Water variant of the Water Color brush to paint long, soft strokes from the interior of the orchid toward the tips of the petals. She also used the Diffuse Water variant to paint bright red spots on the interior of the orchid. She defined the petal edges and added shadows with a small Simple Water brush. To lighten areas of color in the Wet layer, she used the Wet Eraser Water Color variant. Changing brush sizes intuitively as she worked, she painted and dried her image, developing subtle layers of color and contrast.

4 Adding final details. Using a tiny Simple Water brush, Envall sharpened areas in the image that needed definition. After drying the image again, she defined highlights along the edges of the petals with the Ultrafine Eraser variant. Finally, to add texture to the flower petals, she sprayed soft wet spots onto the flower with the Spatter Water variant of the Water Color brush. 🖌

COMBINING WET AND DRY

You can easily switch between working in the Wet Layer and painting on the "dry" background: Switch to a "non-wet" brush to add linework or erase lines on the background, then return to the Water Color brushes to continue your work in the Wet Layer.

USING POST-DIFFUSE

To soften the edges of brushstrokes in the Wet Layer only, press Shift-D— Painter's Post-Diffuse command. Repeat the key combination to increase the effect.

Mixing Media

Overview *Create a sketch with the Pencil and the Pens brushes; add color with the Chalk and the Airbrush brushes; finish the piece with Chalk, Charcoal, Liquid and other brushes.*

PHILIP HOWE

1

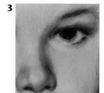

Sketching with the Sharp Pencil (left); then adding value with the Loaded Oils

2

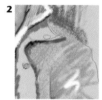 

Laying in loose color with Chalk (left); then airbrushing with color on the face

3

Adding detail with pencil and charcoal (left); then blending an area with Just Add Water and the Distorto variant

EASIER TEXTURE ACCESS

To make it easier to switch textures quickly, use the Paper Mover (choose Paper, Paper Mover from the Art Materials palette) to combine several papers from different libraries into single Paper palette. To read about libraries, see "Libraries and Movers," in Chapter 1.

TO CREATE *PORTRAIT OF SEAFTH,* Philip Howe combined no fewer than seven digital brushes—many of which would not mix well in conventional media—yet his finished piece retains the freshness of a sketch. You may want to loosely follow Howe's steps and experiment with your own "media mixing."

1 Sketching and adding value. Howe selected Surface 2 from the More Paper Textures library (in Free Stuff, Papers on the Painter 5 CD-ROM) and used the Sharp Pencil to create the sketch. He switched to the Fine Grain texture (More Paper Textures) and added detail to the eyes with the Fine Point variant of the Pens brush. To establish values, Howe chose the Loaded Oils variant of the Brush and painted loose, gray strokes on the hair, face and jacket.

2 Laying in color. To stroke color onto the jacket and background, Howe chose Eggscape from the Paper Textures library and the Large Chalk variant of the Chalk brush. He used a low-opacity Fat Stroke Airbrush to sculpt the boy's face with soft color.

3 A veritable brush frenzy. Using the Just Add Water variant of the Water brush, Howe softly blended selected areas of the image. He added more color to the face with the Large Chalk, blended it with Just Add Water, then darkened detail in the eyes and nose with Gritty Charcoal. Howe chose the Brushy variant of the Brush and painted loose strokes onto the background, hair and jacket. Using tiny strokes with the Thick & Thin Pencils brush, he redefined and enhanced the boy's facial features. He used the Distorto variant of the Liquid brush to smear areas of the hair and to create a soft, irregular edge on the background and jacket to make the boy appear to emerge from the paper's surface.

Expressive Custom Brushes

Overview _Create black-and-white art and import it into Painter; build custom brushes; create a new brush library for the brushes; paint soft lines and fills with custom brushes; add more color and texture._

AYSE ULAY

The black-and-white logotype

AYSE ULAY PREFERS TO NOT INTERRUPT the creative process by building variants as she works, so she prepares them in advance. Her _Harlequin_, painted from her imagination, was created for the California Institute of Technology's Beckman auditorium for their seasonal program cover and promotional posters.

1 Beginning with black and white. Ulay's client requested two renditions of the illustration—a black-and-white logotype and a full-color illustration. Because the logotype would be used in several sizes, Ulay built it in Macromedia Freehand. She began by drawing a sketch using pencil and paper, then she scanned the sketch and saved it as a TIFF file and placed it in Freehand to use as a template. Working in Freehand, she used the Pen tool to draw black-and-white Postscript art using the sketch as a guide. She saved the art as an EPS file and used Adobe Photoshop to rasterize it; then she saved the converted image as a TIFF file for import into Painter.

You can also import Postscript art directly into Painter by pasting through the clipboard or by dragging and dropping while both applications are running. Begin by selecting the illustration elements in Freehand (or Adobe Illustrator), copy the items to the

2a

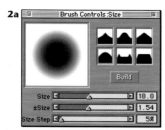

Ulay's settings in the Brush Controls:Size palette showing a "soft view" of the Dull tip profile and brush dab

2b

Testing the Light Fills (upper left) and Grainy Light Fills (right) brushes on a sample image

3

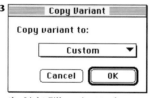

Copying the Light Fills variant to the custom brush style

4a

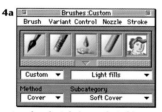

The custom brush style icon selected in the default Painter Brushes library

4b

Dragging the new custom style from the Painter Brushes library into a new library

clipboard, switch to Painter and paste. To drag and drop, select the elements in the Postscript program and drag them into an open Painter file window.

2 Creating variants. Using the Artist Pastel Chalk variant of the Chalk brush Ulay created seven custom variants. The Light Fills, Medium Light Fills, Thick Lines and Thin Lines variants were built using the Soft Cover submethod (subcategory), and were intended to apply soft lines and graduated fills. The Grainy Light Fills, Grainy Thick Lines and Grainy Thin Lines variants were built to interact with the paper texture on the image canvas.

To build Ulay's Light Fills variant, start with the Artist Pastel Chalk variant. In the Brush Controls:Size palette (found under the Control pull-down menu on the Brushes palette) set the Size to 18.8. Set the ± Size slider at 1.54. Change the Brush Tip Profile from the default Medium profile (top center) to the Dull profile (bottom left). To view the brush dab using the "soft" view click in the brush dab window to switch from "hard" view to "soft" view.

In the Controls:Brush palette, set the Opacity at 14% and Grain at 9%. To create a brush that would not be grain-sensitive, she changed the submethod from Grainy Hard Cover to Soft Cover. In the Brushes palette's submethod (subcategory) menu switch to Soft Cover. Save the variant by choosing Variant, Save Variant from the Brushes palette. Name it and click OK.

To create the Grainy Thick Lines brush, she began with the new custom Light Fills variant. She changed these settings in the Brush Controls:Size palette: Size: 15.4, ± Size, 1.31. In the Controls:Size palette, she set Opacity at 68%, and Grain at 38%. To allow interaction with grain on the image surface, she switched back to the Artist Pastel Chalk's default submethod, Grainy Hard Cover.

> **BRUSHES FROM SCRATCH**
>
> If you want to create custom brushes from scratch instead of basing them on pre-existing brushes, begin by making an icon for the brush. Select a square area of your image with the rectangular selection tool. Now, from the Brushes palette menu choose Brush, New Brush. Name your brush style and click OK. You'll see your selection appear in the Brush palette with no variants below it. You've just created an empty "variant holder," ready to be filled with custom variants.

3 Storing variants in a custom brush style. Once you've created a number of variants, you can create a brush style just for them. This is handy if you use certain brushes for specific jobs (as Ulay did here). And Painter 5 offers a variant mover (Variant, Copy Variant) that allows you to swap variants between brushes.

You'll create an icon for your brush in the process, so begin by using the Rectangular Selection tool with the Shift key to select a square area of an image that you want to represent your brush. On the Brushes palette choose Brush, New Brush. In the Save Brush

5

A flat color fill applied to a section of drapery

6a

Adding soft shadows and highlights to the drapery with the Light Fills variant

6b

Adding more colored elements and dimension to the illustration

6c

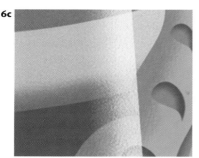

Painting textured highlights onto the light beam with Grainy Light Fills variant

Style dialog box, name the new style, and click OK. (Ulay named hers Custom). Having the selection ready on the image canvas will automatically give the new brush style an icon.

To copy your custom variant from the Chalk brush style to your new brush style, select it and choose Variant, Copy Variant. In the Copy Variant dialog box menu choose your new brush style, and click OK.

4 Making a new brush library. For optimal performance, it's a good idea to keep brush libraries small. Brushes will build more quickly and it will be easier to find a brush if the list is shorter. (A Painter library can hold a maximum of 32 variants.) So it's better to create new libraries for your custom brushes rather than storing them in Painter's default library. To move your new brush style to a new library of its own, from the Brushes palette's menu choose Brush, Brush Mover. Click the New button to create a new brush library, and in the New Brush File dialog box, name the new library and click OK. Select the new brush style on the left side of the mover that contains your new variants and drag and drop it into your new Brush library palette on the right side of the mover. To remove the original copy of the Custom brush style from your default Painter Brushes library (in the Painter 5 folder on your hard drive), select it and click the Delete button. Click Quit to exit the mover. Now—for some good housekeeping—back in the Brushes palette, remove the custom variants you added to the Chalk brush. Select the Chalk brush and choose one of the custom variants. From the Brushes palette's Variant menu, choose Delete Variant. Repeat the process to remove the other added variants from the list of Chalk variants.

Open the palette you just created by choosing Load Library from the Brush Style list. Navigate to your custom library. Select it in the directory and click Open to display it.

5 Making selections and adding flat color. Using the rasterized line art as a template, Ulay used the Pen to make selections of the important elements in the image. She saved each selection into the Mask List as a user mask by choosing Select, Save Selection. Then she loaded each selection (Select, Load Selection) and used the Paintbucket to fill areas of her image with flat color.

6 Adding more color, tone and texture. Ulay continued to lay down flat color within selected elements in her image. Next, she selected Basic Paper in the Paper palette and used the Light Fills and Medium Fills brushes to add smooth dimension and contrast to the drapery, columns, foliage, harlequin and stage. She added smaller details with the Thin Lines and Thick Lines variants. Finally, she added touches of grainy texture to the highlighted and shadowed areas of the image using the Grainy Light Fills and Grainy Thin and Grainy Thick Lines variants. 🖌

Gouache and Opaque Watermedia

Overview _Create a finely grained surface; build custom variants of the Camel Hair Brush, Cover Brush and Huge Rough Out; begin with a line sketch on a dark background; sculpt highlights and details using the custom variants; blend colors with a Liquid brush._

NANCY STAHL

Scaling the Micro Grain texture to 25%

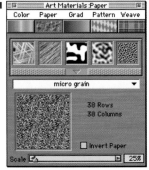

Sketching with the Cover Brush variant

ARTIST NANCY STAHL HAS WORKED WITH TRADITIONAL gouache on illustration board since 1976. When she began to work with the computer, her clients would accept her digital art only if the quality matched her conventional style. After much experimentation with Painter's brushes and surfaces, she has been able to fully re-create the effect of traditional gouache. Her self-promotional pieces _Woman with Braid_ (above) and _Tennis Woman_ (at the bottom of page 66) were juried into the _Communication Arts Illustration Annual_.

1 Emulating a traditional gouache surface. Create a new file. Stahl created a 5.7 x 8-inch file at 300 ppi with a white background color. Stahl's favorite traditional gouache support is a Strathmore kid finish illustration board. The kid finish is soft and allows for a smooth application of paint. To create Stahl's surface for gouache, begin by choosing Load Library (it's located at the bottom of the pop-out list of papers on the Art Materials:Paper palette) to retrieve the Micro Grain paper texture from the More Wild Textures library (located in Papers, in the Free Stuff folder

3

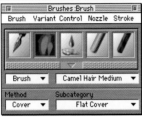

Sculpting facial features with Stahl's custom Camel Hair variant

4a

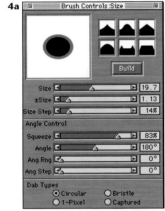

Four of the palettes used to create Stahl's No. 3 Gouache brush

4b

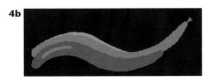

Layering strokes using the No. 3 Gouache brush

on the Painter 5 CD-ROM). To make the surface even smoother, scale it to 25%. This surface is most noticeable when using Stahl's No. 5 Brush in step 5.

2 Starting with a sketch. After roughing a dark brown into the background with the Huge Rough Out brush variant of the Brush, Stahl modified the Cover Brush variant and used it to create an outline sketch. Begin by selecting the Cover Brush variant of the Brush and set the Size to 2.0 in the Controls:Brush palette. Choose a russet color and begin sketching.

3 Sculpting teardrop shapes. To paint teardrop-shaped highlights in the hair and to sculpt the facial features, Stahl created a new variant based on the Camel Hair Brush variant of the Brush. Choose the Camel Hair Brush variant and change the submethod to Flat Cover; this will give your strokes the crisp edge that you would get using conventional materials. In the Controls:Brush palette, increase the brush size to 9.6. From the Brushes palette's Variant menu, choose Save Variant, name your variant (Stahl named hers Camel Hair Medium) and click OK. Stahl varied the size of her brush while she worked.

4 Building Stahl's No. 3 Gouache brush. To build Stahl's No. 3 Gouache brush, first take a deep breath—it's a complex brush. Start with the Camel Hair Brush variant and change the submethod to Flat Cover.

Now start making choices from the Control menu in the Brushes palette. In the Brush Controls: Size palette: set Size to 19.7; set ± Size to 1.13; set Squeeze to 83% (giving the brush a slightly oval shape); set Angle to 180. Build your brush (you can do it now or later) by clicking the Build button. To make the brush faster and smaller, choose Control:Spacing and

---

NOT JUST FOR GOUACHE

If you use Painter to emulate oils or acrylics, you may find it beneficial to use brushes with slight modifications. For example, you can get a multi-colored, multi-bristle "oil" brush using these Color Variability settings (in the zoomed-out Color palette) for Stahl's No. 3 Gouache brush: ± H, 3%; ± S, 5%; ± V, 3%. Apply paint with short, dabbing strokes.

---

change the Stroke Type from Rake to Single. (Don't worry about the Bristles setting; after you've set the Stroke Type to Single, the program ignores this slider.) Set Spacing/Size to 70%, and move the Minimum Spacing slider all the way to the left. Choose Control, Well, and reduce Resaturation to 66% (so brushstrokes run out of color sooner) and increase Bleed to 2% (to let colors mix a bit more). Choose Control, Sliders, and drag the Size slider to Pressure (this makes stroke size dependent on pressure, not velocity) and set Opacity to None (to make strokes more opaque). Save your variant as in step 3. Stahl used this brush to make linear strokes in the hair and on the blouse.

5a

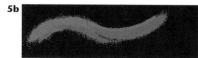

Size, Opacity and Grain settings for the No. 5 Gouache brush

5b

Stroking with the No. 5 Gouache brush

6

Pulling one color into another with the Coarse Smeary Mover variant

7a

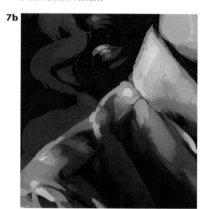

Line work on the lips using the Cover Brush Small variant

7b

Adding details with a modified Oil Paint variant

5 Building Stahl's No. 5 Gouache brush. Stahl wanted a fast, sensitive brush with grainy edges to use on the blouse and the background. To build her variant, start with the Huge Rough Out variant of the Brush. In the Brush Controls:Size palette, change Size to 25.3; drag the ± Size slider all the way to the right; click the Build button. In the Controls:Brush palette, set Grain to 100%. Save the variant.

6 Pulling color. To blend the opaque colors in the background and in the shadows on the blouse, Stahl used varying sizes of the Coarse Smeary Mover variant of the Liquid brush. Since this brush uses a Grainy Hard Drip submethod, she was able to soften color transitions with texture.

7 Finishing touches. Using the modified small Cover Brush variant from step 2, Stahl enhanced detail on the woman's profile and hair. She used a low-opacity version of the Oil Paint variant of the Brush to add texture on the blouse and collar.

Stahl painted Tennis Woman *with the same set of Gouache brushes used for* Woman with Braid. *To soften the background and focus more attention on the figure, she used the Smeary Mover variant of the Liquid brush on the background. To soften it further, she selected the background with the Lasso, she feathered the selection a few pixels to create a smooth edge (Select, Feather), then she used Effects, Focus, Soften.*

Painting with Oils

Overview *Create a sketch with a Pencils variant; add color to the underpainting with an Artist Pastel Chalk variant; use the Liquid brush to create the look of oils.*

DENNIS ORLANDO

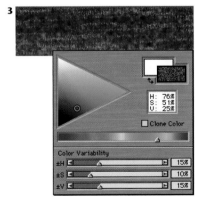

Sketching the canoes and shoreline

Switching to Grainy Soft Cover submethod

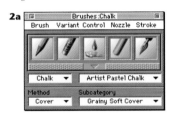

Roughing in the beach with the Artist Pastel Chalk variant

Painting the water (detail) with the Artist Pastel Chalk variant, using Color Variability settings in the Color palette

ARTIST DENNIS ORLANDO CAPTURES an exquisite harmony between man-made and organic elements in his *Canoe Trip at Cedar Water*. A strong composition, deft modeling of shapes, sensitivity to light and shadow and his unique electronic oil painting technique all combine to give the piece its power. Orlando used a photograph taken on a camping trip in the New Jersey Pine Barrens as a reference for the painting.

1 Sketching the canoes. Orlando set up a new 8.25 x 3.5-inch document with a resolution of 150 ppi and a white Paper Color. He placed the reference photo under the clear plastic flap of his drawing tablet, then he modified a Pencils brush variant and used it to trace the four canoes and the shoreline. To create his custom variant, select the Thick & Thin Pencils variant of the Pencils brush. Change to Cover method and Grainy Soft Cover sub-method. In the Brush Controls:Size palette (under the Control pull-down menu on the Brushes palette), drag the Size slider to 2.0. Select Basic Paper in the Paper palette, choose a color (Orlando started with a gray-blue), and begin sketching.

2 Beginning the underpainting. To help define the exterior shapes of the canoes, Orlando roughed in the beach with a Chalk brush and a rough texture. To do this, select the Artist Pastel Chalk variant of the Chalk brush. Change the submethod to Grainy Soft Cover—this gives softer brushstrokes than Grainy Hard Cover. In the Paper palette, load the More Paper Textures library from Papers inside the Free Stuff folder on the Painter 5 CD-ROM, and choose Big Canvas paper texture (Orlando used this paper on the rest of the piece). He chose a creamy tan tint and quickly blocked in large areas of the beach around the edges of the canoes.

3 Using Color Variability in the water. One of Orlando's "electronic oil" trademarks is activity in the color. He achieves this by adjusting the Color Variability settings for certain brushes. To re-create the active color look he achieved in the water, start with the same Chalk brush that you created in step 2. Choose a dark gray-green, then zoom-out the Color palette and adjust the Color Variability sliders: set Hue (± H) to 10, Saturation (± S) to 5,

4

Establishing values

5a

Choosing the Total Oil Brush variant

5b

Pulling color along the canoe with the Total Oil Brush variant

5c

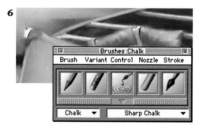

Detail of the foreground sand painted with the Artist Pastel Chalk and Total Oil Brush variants

6

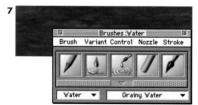

Painting crisp, final details on the boat with the Sharp Chalk

7

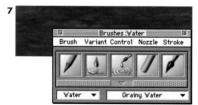

Using the Grainy Water brush to blend areas of the water

and Value (± V) to 10. Name and save this variant (on the Brushes palette, choose Variant, Save Variant, enter a name and click OK) or you'll lose these settings when you switch brushes. Begin painting. Orlando changed to a smaller brush size when working close to the canoes in order to preserve their shapes.

4 Establishing values and adding details. Use a smaller version of the same Chalk brush (Orlando resized his to 7.1) to rough in color and value details. Keep the same Color Variability settings. Orlando used a blue-gray color to paint the dark, recessed areas inside the canoes, then switched to a lighter value of the same color to paint the metallic hulls of the boats.

5 Simulating traditional oils. Painter's Liquid brushes let you smear existing "pixel paint" to get the same look that you would get by pushing conventional oils around a canvas. The Total Oil Brush variant, which Orlando used, also paints with the current color in the Color palette. Choose the Liquid brush, Total Oil Brush variant. In the Brush Controls:Size palette, drag the Size slider to 18.5 (Orlando varied his brush size slightly as he painted.) With the Dropper tool, sample a color from the area you want to paint, or hold down the Command key while you're using the brush to temporarily switch to the Dropper. To maintain the modulated color of the underpainting, give this brush the same Color Variability settings used in step 3. Save this variant.

Use this brush and short, crisp strokes to pull color from one area of your painting into another. Orlando switched between this brush and his Chalk variant to work over the entire surface of the painting, including the shadow areas on the sand and the detail in the canoes. He created the reflection of the sand on the canoes by sampling color from the sand and painting short, curved strokes on the canoes with the Total Oil Brush variant.

6 Defining the details. Orlando used the Sharp Chalk variant of the Chalk brush to define surface edges and to add color details on the sand and boats.

7 Blurring the water. The Grainy Water variant of the Water brush is perfect for blending and softening areas, making them appear to recede. Orlando dabbed this brush on the water, using short strokes to preserve the modulated color.

Output. Orlando typically makes proofs of several versions of a piece on a Canon Color Laser Copier with an EFI Fiery RIP. He then picks a favorite to send out to be printed with an Iris inkjet on archival paper. This image was printed by Cone Editions Press on Somerset, a softly textured, handmade English paper. (To read how to contact Cone Editions Press turn to Appendix C in the back of this book.) 🖌

Colorizing Pencil Illustrations

Overview *Scan a pencil sketch; clone it; tint it and add texture; restore from the original; add color with the Airbrush, Chalk and Water Color brushes.*

PHILIP HOWE

1

The original pencil illustration, scanned

2

Adding a tint and a texture to the clone

3

Using a Cloning method brush to partially restore the gray tones of the original

MUCH OF THE BEAUTY of illustrator Philip Howe's work lies in his seamless, creative blending of the traditional with the digital. In a spread for *Trailblazer* magazine—a detail of which is shown here—Howe used Photoshop to combine hand-drawn calligraphy, a photo of two slides, a photo of a watercolor block (for the background), and his own pencil sketches, colorized in Painter to simulate traditional watercolor.

1 Starting with a sketch. Howe began by sketching the various birds in pencil on watercolor paper. He scanned the images on a flatbed scanner, saving them as grayscale files in TIFF format. Each bird image was 4 to 5 inches square and 300 ppi.

2 Modifying a clone. Open a grayscale scan in Painter. Choose File, Clone, to clone your scan, giving you an "original" and a clone. Keep the original open—you'll want to pull from it later. Howe added a color tint and a texture to the clone of the scanned bird. To add a tint, choose a color in the Colors palette (Howe chose a reddish brown), then choose Effects, Surface Control, Color Overlay. Select Uniform Color from the pop-up menu, set Opacity to 30%, click the Dye Concentration button and click OK. To add texture, select a Paper texture (Howe chose Basic Paper) and choose Effects, Surface Control, Apply Surface Texture. Select Paper from the Using menu, set Amount to 50% and set Shine to 0%. Click OK.

3 Restoring from the original. Howe used Painter's cloning capabilities to replace most of the tint and texture in the bird's body with the light gray tones of the original. You could use a standard cloning brush to do this, but Howe chose the Fat Stroke variant of the Airbrush, changed the method to Cloning and the submethod to Soft Cover Cloning. Once you've changed methods, paint on the portion of your image that you want to restore. The original will automatically be revealed in the area covered by your strokes. Try lowering this cloning brush's Opacity in the Controls palette for more sensitivity.

Applying color tints with the Fat Stroke Airbrush in Buildup method

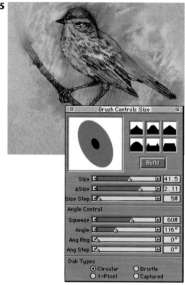

Using a modified Chalk brush to add color to the background

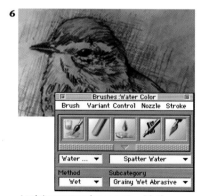

Applying watercolor accents with the Spatter Water variant

4 Adding color tints with the Airbrush. To achieve an effect of traditional airbrushing with transparent dyes or watercolor pigments, Howe used two versions of the Fat Stroke Airbrush variant. He switched back to Cover method, Soft Cover submethod, and reduced the Opacity setting in the Controls palette to between 5% and 10%. He used these settings to carefully lay in the golden brown tones on the bird's back. Next, he switched to the Buildup method, Soft Buildup submethod, and added the more saturated yellow and rust hues. The Buildup method allowed him to use a slightly higher Opacity (between 10% and 20%) to achieve richer color while preserving the intensity of the pencil sketch.

5 Cloning again and brushing with Chalk. Howe uses the Clone feature like a flexible "Save As" command. When he's ready to move on to the next phase of an illustration, he often makes a clone and uses the original as "source material." Here, when he had colorized the bird to his satisfaction, he chose File, Clone and saved the clone. If he over-worked an area, he restored it by cloning in imagery from the previous version. He opened the saved version of his file and designated it as the "source" by choosing File, Clone Source, then painted with a cloning brush to restore the area.

Howe switched to the Large Chalk variant of the Chalk brush and began to paint loose, gestural strokes on the image background behind the bird using two similar green hues. He modified the brush as he worked by making frequent adjustments in the Brush Controls:Size palette as he worked, changing Size, ± Size, Angle and Squeeze. (To open the Brush Controls:Size palette choose Control, Size from the Brushes palette menu.)

6 Adding a watercolor look. To add a finishing touch without muddying his existing color work, Howe used the Water Color brush. He used the Simple Water variant to add more depth to the color on the bird's head and other areas. He switched to the Spatter Water variant to add a "water drop" effect on the background, sampling color from the bird and background using the Dropper tool. When he finished, he chose Canvas, Dry to drop the color from the Wet Layer onto the background.

Another spot illustration from the Trailblazer *spread. Howe used the same brushes and technique for all illustrations.*

Merging the file. Howe opened the bird file and the 17 x 11-inch main image in Photoshop. He drew a selection around the bird, feathered it to 30 pixels, then copied it and pasted it into the main image. He used Photoshop's Multiply compositing command to blend the two images.

Lifelike Commercial Illustration

Overview *Sketch an object from life; add color; select the object to isolate it; add detail, shading, blending and type.*

The Photoshop sketch

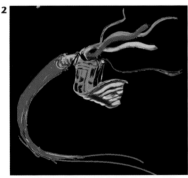

Using the Rough Out variant to add color

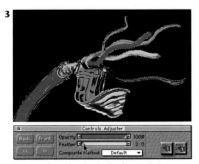

Setting the selection's feather to 2.0

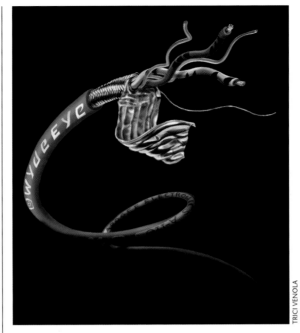

TRICI VENOLA

WHEN TRICI VENOLA WAS COMMISSIONED BY APOGEE—a manufacturer of sound equipment for the music industry—to illustrate an audio cable, she sold the client on a realistic, painterly approach to the product rather than a flashy airbrush illustration with exaggerated metallic highlights. Inspired by the Dutch master Jan Vermeer's simple and direct treatment of common household objects, Venola paid special attention to the lighting, rendering and composition of this piece. The finished illustration was a hit with the client and the audience: The ad featuring it won "Best Return Ad" award in the industry publication *Mix*.

1 Setting up the model. Choose an object and place it near your monitor for easy viewing. Set the lighting so it won't change, and begin sketching in Painter. Since Apogee's president Bruce Jackson had told Venola that the cable looked like a striking cobra, she propped up the cable, cobra-like, next to her monitor. He also wanted to feature the cable's patented braid design, so she positioned it to emphasize that aspect of the product. She covered the windows in the studio and lit the subject. To create the sketch, Venola used Photoshop's Airbrush tool and a small brush size, paying special attention to the subject's proportions.

2 Coloring with Soft Cover brushes. After the client approved the sketch, Venola opened it in Painter and chose Effects, Tonal Control, Negative (to create a black background and a white cable) and brushed in color. To recreate the custom brush she used, select the Rough Out variant of the Brush and change the submethod to Soft Cover. Block in areas of color using this

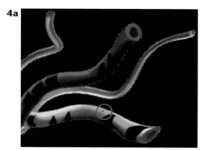

4a

Airbrushing inside the active selection

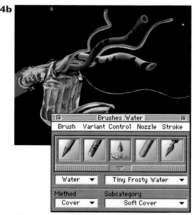

4b

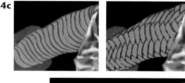

Changing the Tiny Frosty Water to Soft Cover to blend areas of the foil

4c

Adding detail and form to the cable

5

Hand lettering with the Scratchboard tool

brush. Venola also used the Artist Pastel Chalk variant of the Chalk brush to rough in the exposed wires.

3 Selecting the cable. To give the product a distinct edge and isolate it from the background, Venola selected the roughed-out cable, drawing around it with the Lasso tool. Then she softened the selection edge by applying a subtle feather of 2 pixels. To feather your selection, from the Select menu choose Feather, and type a number in the field. Click OK. The feather you use will depend on the size of your file. (Turn to Chapter 4 to learn more about working with selections.)

4 Rendering the cable. Starting with the exposed wiring and working down the cable, Venola rendered her image. Since every detail of the product was important to the client, she carefully studied the ends of the wire—even using a hand-held magnifying glass at one point—while zoomed in at 400%. To get the smooth look of Vermeer on the wiring and the rest of the cable, Venola used brushes with the Cover method, Soft Cover submethod. She added detail with the Scratchboard Tool variant of the Pens brush; added shading, highlights and reflected lighting with several variants of the Airbrush and the Dodge and Burn brushes (at 10–15% opacities); and blended the foil and other areas with a modified Tiny Frosty Water variant of the Water brush. To get a slightly coarser look in certain areas, she switched to the Artist Pastel Chalk. Venola changed brush sizes frequently as she worked.

5 Adding type. Mechanically setting curved lines of a custom typeface to fit the coiled cable would have been difficult and time-consuming; it was much easier for Venola to draw it by hand. She referred to a printout of the logo and sketched the type and the other lettering directly on the rendered cable using the Scratchboard variant.

Finishing in Photoshop. It's a rare client who's satisfied the first time around, and Venola's was no exception. He wanted the foil to look gold on both sides, he wanted to emphasize the hand lettering, and he wanted the tips of the wires to look less frayed. In Photoshop, Venola used the Airbrush in Color mode to tint the silver portion of the foil gold; she used a large, low-opacity airbrush to darken the lower right portion of her image; and she cleaned up the wire tips with a tiny Airbrush.

HOMEMADE COLOR SETS

For quick access to colors in Painter and to keep consistent color when you switch from Painter to Photoshop, you can place dots of solid color at the edge of your image. You can then sample color using either program's Dropper tool. (In Painter, turn any brush into the Dropper temporarily by pressing the Command key.)

Advanced Painting with Impasto

Overview *Open an image; make selections and save them; generate dynamic Impasto floaters for the selections; paint with relief and color on the floaters; add more texture with special effects.*

CHER THREINEN-PENDARVIS

The study for new cover illustration was based on the original cover

The completed flower selection

FOR THE FIRST TIME, LUSCIOUS THICK PAINT is available at the tip of your digital brush. Painter 5's Impasto brushes and floaters give you the ability to paint with exciting, realistic three-dimensional brushstrokes that leave bristle marks and paint texture on the surface of the image as you paint.

When it came time to update the illustration for the cover of this book, we knew Impasto was the tool for the job. It would create the look of thick paint as new colors were added to the illustration.

1 Starting with a color study. Open an existing image you wish to turn into an Impasto painting. (Our file was 2400 pixels wide).

2 Selecting the flower. To make it easier to paint the flower and then paint larger, looser brushstrokes on the background, we isolated the flower by making a Lasso selection.

To make a selection, choose the Lasso and drag around the area you want to isolate. (To read more about making selections and editing them, turn to the beginning of Chapter 4.)

After the selection is complete, store it as a user mask: In the Objects:Mask List palette, click the Save Selection button and accept the default choice "New" in the Save To pop-up menu in the Save Selection dialog box. Click OK. If you like, name your selection (as we did), by clicking in the Mask List to select the name of the mask, choosing Mask Attributes from the Mask palette menu, and typing a name in the Field. After naming, target the RGB canvas again by clicking on RGB Canvas in the Mask List.

For a subtle transition edge between your selection and the surrounding area, it's a good idea to apply a small feather to the selection. The feather you use will depend on the size of your file (ours was 2 pixels). To load the Selection, click the Load Selection button on

3

Applying the Impasto floater to the selection

4

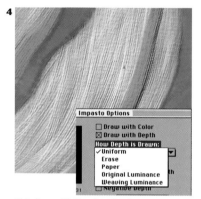

Painting with Depth only, drawn uniformly

5

Adding color details to the impasto layer with a small Soft Oil brush

6

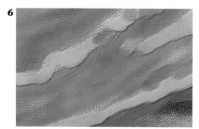

Painting larger strokes on the background

the Mask List palette and select the Replace Selection button and click OK. To feather the selection, choose Select, Feather, then type a number into the field, and click OK.

3 Making an Impasto floater. To make an Impasto plug-in floater from the selection after you've loaded and feathered it, switch to the Objects:Plug-In Floater palette by clicking on the Plug icon under the P. Float name in the Objects palette. From the pop-up menu on the bottom of the drawer, choose Impasto and click the Apply button. Painter will generate a *dynamic plug-in floater* based on the active selection. The dynamic floater will be a floating copy of the selection, and will appear at the top of the Objects:Floater List. Click OK to close the Impasto Options dialog box. (To learn more about dynamic plug-in floaters, turn to the beginning of Chapter 5.)

4 Adding the brushstrokes in the Depth layer. Choose a texture from the Paper palette. We used Raw Silk because its natural-looking fine grain would complement the soft bristle brushes we planned to use, Soft Oil from the Wow! Permanent Media brush library (on the CD-ROM that accompanies this book), and Thick Oil, which we chose from the Impasto Brushes library (located in the Extra Art Materials folder on the Painter 5 CD-ROM).

Impasto lets you separate color and thickness, or depth. To paint the first Impasto strokes over the entire flower, we painted with Depth only, maintaining the existing color. To do this, open the Impasto Options dialog box, choosing Options from the P.Float pull-down menu. Uncheck the Draw with Color checkbox. In the How Depth is Drawn menu we chose Uniform, because this option brings out the soft striations of bristle brushes, and we chose Opacity Controls Depth, which bases the dimension on the Opacity set in the Controls:Brush palette. For softer, richer relief in the strokes, we increased Smoothing by moving the slider to the right. When you have the settings the way you like them, click OK to close the dialog box and continue painting. For more information on the Impasto Options dialog box, turn to the beginning of this chapter, and to Chapter 12 of the *Painter 5 User Guide*.

5 Adding colored detail to the flower. To paint with both color and depth on the flower floater, in Impasto Options we checked the Draw with Color checkbox, and we increased the

7

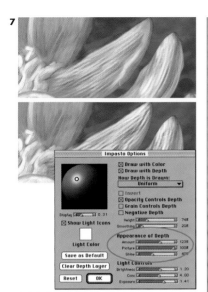

Subtle (85%) Appearance of Depth settings (top); moving the Amount slider to 123% (bottom).

8

Applying subtle Surface Texture to bring out the weave of the Raw Silk texture

ERASING IN THE DEPTH LAYER

If you're not satisfied with the look of relief after you've applied depth, you can erase with one of these two methods (while the floater is dynamic): To erase the entire depth effect, click the Clear Depth Layer button in the Impasto Options dialog box. To use a brush to erase depth from one area, open Impasto Options, uncheck Draw with Color and from the How Depth is Drawn menu, choose Erase. Brush over the area you want to smooth.

amount of Smoothing to 150% to enhance the blending of the strokes as they overlapped. We closed the Impasto Options dialog box so we could sample color from the image as we painted, using the Command key to temporarily switch from the Brush to the Dropper. We used the Soft Oil brush again, and a light touch on the stylus to make long strokes from the center of the flower out to the ends of the petals. When we were finished, we deselected the flower floater by clicking on a blank area below its name in the Floater List.

6 Painting the background. In preparation for painting the background, we made a second Impasto floater. Begin by loading the flower selection again; then choose Select, Invert, and save this selection as a user mask, naming it "Background." Target the RGB canvas again after naming the selection. To generate the second Impasto floater, follow the process described in step 3. To paint on the new floater, we used larger brushstrokes on the background, drawing the depth uniformly, and again drawing on the Impasto floater with both color and depth. In the Impasto Options dialog box we adjusted the Height to make the appearance of the strokes shallower, so as not to compete with the flower. To apply shallower strokes, move the Height slider to the left. To intermix shallower and deeper strokes, leave the dialog box open and continue to adjust the Height slider as you work.

7 Making adjustments to depth. To bring out texture in the flower and make the depth in the background more subtle, we changed the Appearance of Depth on each Impasto floater. This control affects the entire selected floater. And because the controls are dynamic, you can experiment, previewing settings as many times as you like before you make a decision.

To make an overall depth adjustment, select the floater by clicking on its name in the Floater List, and choose P. Float, Options to open the Impasto Options dialog box again. Adjust the Appearance of Depth slider to increase the look of depth or to make it appear more subtle. We adjusted the depth of both floaters, increasing the Amount slightly in the flower floater to 123%, and decreasing the Amount in the background to 70%. The Light Controls also apply globally to the selected floater.

8 Adding final effects. Before applying final special effects, we flattened the illustration by Shift-selecting each floater name in the Floater List and clicking the Drop button. Then, to blend the Impasto areas of the piece with areas not painted over with Impasto and to subtly bring out the weave of the Silk texture used when painting the image, we applied a subtle texture over the entire image. We chose Effects, Surface Control, Apply Surface Texture, Using Image Luminance. We set Amount at 22% and Shine at 0% (using the upper left light button). To compensate for the slight darkening of the image caused by the default lighting settings, we increased the Brightness of the light from 1.15 to 1.25. 🎨

■ Since buying her first Macintosh in 1984, **Trici Venola** has used the computer as her primary medium for fine art and commercial illustration. *Vincent's Room* (right) was commissioned for a poster by Media 100 and *Videography* magazine as a tribute to Vincent Van Gogh. Venola researched the Impressionist master's composition theory and application of oil paint. She used two Van Gogh masterpieces as reference for the illustration, *Bedroom at Arles* and *Vincent's Room at Arles.* To imitate Van Gogh's painting style in Painter, Venola used the Oil Paint, Loaded Oils and Cover Brush variants of the Brush on Basic Paper texture. Her clever screen saver pays homage to Van Gogh's famous painting *Starry Night.*

■ Location sketches made while traveling in the Southeast provided inspiration for **Margaret Sweeney** while painting *Cracker House.* Sweeney roughed out the composition using the Oil Paint and Loaded Oils variants of the Brush. Then she painted over some areas, adding more detail and movement with the Sargent Brush variant from the New Paint Tools library, one of Painter 5's new brush libraries. She finished by pulling and blending color with the Dry Brush variant (New Paint Tools).

■ Artist **Chelsea Sammel** is at home in both the fine art and commercial art worlds. She painted *Le Can de Triomphe* (left) for the Painter 5 promotional poster. Her vision was to create an Impressionistic look of thick paint using Painter 5's new Impasto feature. Sammel began the illustration by composing a reference image consisting of scans of bits of photos and Impressionist paintings. When she had finished the reference image, she cloned it (File, Clone) and selected the entire clone canvas. Then she generated an Impasto floater from the active selection by choosing Impasto from the Objects:Plug-in Floater palette and clicking the Apply button. To paint textured brushstrokes while retaining the color from the clone, she used several brushes from the Impasto brush library to paint only texture (Depth) without color. Specifically, to gouge into the paint on the image she used Negative Depth and turned off Draw With Color. Then, to add final details, she painted with both color and depth by choosing the Draw with Depth and Draw with Color options.

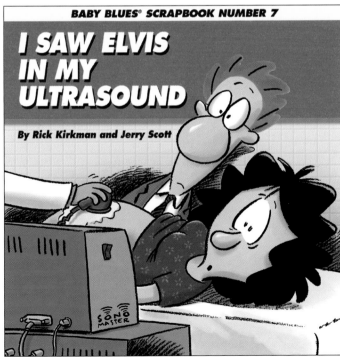

■ A freelance illustrator for the past 13 years, **Rick Kirkman** divides his time between producing cartoons for commercial clients and creating the King Feature Syndicate comic strip *Baby Blues* (with partner Jerry Scott). Kirkman began *I Saw Elvis in My Ultrasound* (left) in Painter with black linework using Colored Pencils on Basic Paper texture. He switched to a rougher paper and added color washes using the Simple Water variant of the Water Color brush. After the Painter Illustration was complete, he saved it as a TIFF file for import into Photoshop, where he made an RGB-to-CMYK-conversion. Finally, he placed the TIFF file into Adobe Illustrator 6.0, where he added the red panel and type. (Illustrator 7.0 accepts RGB TIFF files which makes direct import from Painter possible.)

■ **Nancy Stahl** created *Premiere*—two celebrities caught in the glare of the paparazzi—for the cover of New York City's *Premiere* magazine. She started by photographing herself in all of the figures' positions, then assembled the photos into a rough composition in Photoshop. She used the composite image as a reference for her work in Painter and brushed a dark green color onto the background of a new document using one of her gouache brushes. (See "Gouache and Opaque Watermedia," earlier in this chapter for a complete description of her custom brushes.) Stahl painted the lower left area first—without the photographers—then chose Effects, Surface Control, Apply Lighting to create a slight gradation over the entire image. She then painted the figures in the upper right. To get the flashbulb effects perfectly positioned underneath the photographers, she began by painting the photographers in another document. She selected them, then dragged them into her main image and positioned them. (To read more about floaters see the beginning of Chapter 5.) She saved the image as a TIFF file, opened it in Photoshop, and created the flash effects by drawing paths and stroking them with the airbrush. (To accomplish this in Painter, choose the Oval Selection tool, make a circular selection and choose Select, Feather, typing a number in the field. Now choose the Airbrush, and choose Selection, Stroke Selection. Stahl opened the image in Painter, and again dragged in the photographers. She positioned them precisely atop the original photographers (now covered by the glowing circles), gave them a low feather setting to soften the edges, then dropped them to the background.

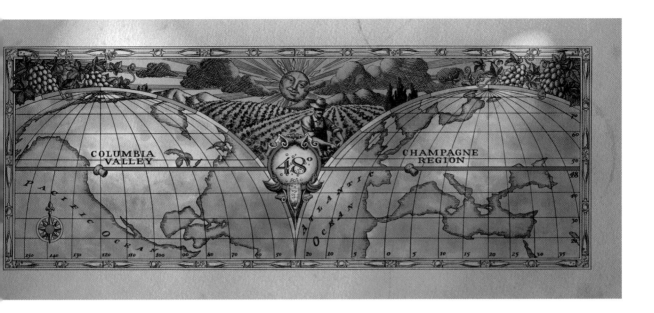

■ Although he has been a successful commercial illustrator for 20 years using conventional materials, **John Fretz** has happily set them aside for Painter's more exciting electronic tools.

Fretz created the **Domaine St. Michele Champagne Winery Map** (top) for an ad campaign. He began by drawing a detailed pen-and-ink map, which he scanned along with a painted, distressed piece of Arches cold-pressed watercolor paper. (He scratched the paper and made marks on it to make it look "aged.") Fretz pasted the line drawing into the paper background image, then used the Broad Water Brush, Simple Water, and Pure Water Brush variants of the Water Color

brush to paint and blend tints of color on the map. Other color was added with the Fat Stroke Airbrush, and spotlights were created with Apply Lighting. To further blend the pen-and-ink illustration with the background, Fretz used Effects, Surface Control, Color Overlay using Paper, and Mottled texture from the More Wild Paper Textures in Free Stuff on the Painter 5 CD-ROM.

Fretz created the **Microsoft Natural Keyboard Package** (bottom) using three layers of scanned images: a background of wood-flecked oatmeal-colored paper, a pen-and-ink line drawing of the hands and keyboard, and a pencil schematic. Fretz pasted the pen-and-ink drawing

onto the background as a floater, changed its compositing method to Gel in the Controls:Adjuster palette and painted the keyboard and hands using a low-opacity Fat Stroke Airbrush and the Fat Bleach variant of the Eraser (to remove color and create highlights). Fretz made the soft, irregular edges around the keyboard using a large, low-opacity Fat Stroke Airbrush, and added texture around the edges of the vignette using the Scratchboard Rake variant of the Pens. He added the pencil schematic as a floater (also composited with the Gel method), then added Effects, Surface Control, Color Overlay using Paper, and Mottled texture to unify the piece.

■ **Cher Threinen-Pendarvis's** experience with traditional style in pastel, watercolor and acrylic translates easily to digital pastel in Painter. *Paths to Water 1* (right), is one in a series of paintings of Sunset Cliffs Natural Park in San Diego, California. She began by making a color location study with Sharp Chalk on a beige background paper color using a Powerbook 1400cs, Painter 5 and Sandy paper from the Drawing Paper Textures library. Later, on her studio computer she added layers of color using modified Square Chalk and Large Chalk variants, working over the entire piece. She blended areas with the Frosty and Grainy Water brushes and added more directional strokes with the Chalk brushes. As a last step, she used Effects, Surface Control, Apply Surface Texture to apply Sandy paper texture to the entire painting, using subtle settings.

Intense, late-afternoon sunlight on a Northern California hillside inspired *Coastal Meadow* (below). Threinen-Pendarvis sketched on location with colored pencils and paper. In Painter, she used the Colored Pencils variant and a rough paper texture to sketch a composition. She blocked in areas of color with a modified Artist Pastel Chalk variant, then applied directional strokes on top with a smaller brush size. She finished the painting by alternating between the Artist Pastel Chalk and Grainy Water variants, first adding, then smudging color.

■ To create the vibrant look of oil paints, **Dennis Orlando** uses the Artist Pastel Chalk and the Total Oil Brush variant of the Liquid brush. He modifies the brushes by increasing their Color Variability settings (in the expanded Color palette), allowing him to paint with modulated color.

Inspired by a gift of flowers, Orlando painted *Flowers in Light and Shadow* (left). This piece was begun in MetaCreations Dabbler as a low-resolution painting. Orlando then opened the image in Painter and increased the image size. He tightened up details with a modified Artist Pastel Chalk, and used the Grainy Water variant to blend the painting. To add color and blend colors into each other he used the Total Oil Brush variant of the Liquid brush.

Willow Pond (below) is based on a photograph taken by Orlando. He blocked in colors with the Artist Pastel Chalk (with increased Color Variability settings). He finished by applying layers of color with the Total Oil Brush variant, using the Liquid brush variants to blend and move color within the willow tree and water reflections.

■ **Dennis Orlando** began *White Flowers* (left), with the Chalk brushes. Using many grays and purples, he developed a value study for the composition in Painter, then he added more color to build up an underpainting. Continuing to finesse the overall composition, he used the Sharp Chalk and a purple color to redefine the edge contours of the flower petals and leaves. Switching back and forth between the Artist Pastel Chalk and the Grainy Water brushes, he continued to add color and smudge it. Finally, to add more color and blend colors into each other he used the Total Oil Brush variant of the Liquid brush.

■ To paint *Still Life* (left), **Chelsea Sammel** took full advantage of Painter's "digital oils." Sammel began by applying Effects, Surface Control, Apply Surface Texture using Paper and Canvas 2 texture (More Paper Textures library). She sketched the composition on this surface using the Colored Pencils variant. To establish a warm, dark tone in the underpainting, she used the Coarse Hairs variant of the Brush, Grainy Soft Cover submethod (to allow more brush interaction with the canvas). To create a more opaque layer of paint, Sammel painted with the Loaded Oils variant, switching back to her custom Coarse Hairs variant where she wanted to add texture. For a dramatic effect, she used Effects, Surface Control, Apply Lighting, then added more strokes with the Coarse Hairs variant. She finished the image with another application of Surface Texture (again using the Canvas 2 texture) and added a few more brushstrokes using the default Coarse Hairs brush.

■ For many years, **Margaret Sweeney** worked with traditional watercolor and graphics media. Today, Painter is her favorite tool. To begin *Skipping Stones* (left), she used the Oil Paint and Loaded Oils variants of the Brush to paint a quick color sketch in Painter. Then she developed an underpainting with several additional Brush variants (the Small Loaded Oils, Brushy, and the Sable Chisel Tip Water), painting over custom-made paper textures. She finished the painting using brushes from Painter 5's Impasto Brush library on top of an Impasto floater. To arrive at a more natural look, Sweeney made modifications to the Impasto Brushes using the Impasto Options dialog box. (To access the dialog box, she selected the Impasto floater, opened the Objects palette and chose Options from the pull-down menu). For instance, to avoid a plastic look, she set the Shine lower and she decreased the overall depth of relief using the Appearance of Depth slider.

■ Art director, fine artist and nature-lover **Ben Barbante** had achieved a high level of skill with a traditional airbrush long before he discovered Painter. *Stalking on Still Water* is part of a series of wildlife illustrations that Barbante created for a show of his work. Inspiration for this piece came during a hike when he observed a great blue heron stalking and fishing. He later made a pencil drawing of the heron and scanned it. He tinted the scan in Painter using the Simple Water variant of the Water Color brush, switching to the Pure Water Brush variant to blend and the Wet Eraser variant to remove color. He "dried" the painting (Canvas, Dry) at various stages when he did not want new color to mix with the old. He created the water background in a separate file using Kai's Power Tools and Painter's Dodge and Burn brushes (located in the Photo brush library in the New Brush libraries folder). He selected the heron, then copied it and pasted it onto the background image. To create the bird's reflection in the water, Barbante copied the bird, flipped it, and reduced the copy's opacity, then used the Distorto variant of the Liquid brush to give the reflection a ripple effect. Final output was to an Iris inkjet printer, 24 x 36 inches, on archival paper.

■ **Jack Gold** often paints using location sketches for reference or scanned as a basis for painting. To begin *Lobster Buoys* he scanned a 30-year-old black-and-white sketch drawn in Maine. He opened the scanned sketch in Painter, and using the Chalk brushes and rough paper textures, he worked directly on the sketch, brushing layers of color over the line work. While painting with color he worked to preserve the texture of the aged original. When the underpainting was finished, he painted details with the Loaded Oils and Oil Paint variants of the Brush. Before finishing the piece, Gold customized the Oil Paint brush to increase the textured look by enhancing the interaction between the brush and paper grain. He made changes to the Opacity and Grain settings in the Controls:Brush palette: He set the Opacity of the brush to about 10%; and to further increase the interaction with the Grain, he set the Grain penetration to about 5%. Then, using a very light touch on the stylus, he brushed over areas of the underpainting to add more texture, while carefully preserving the underlying painting.

■ Commercial illustrator and fine artist **Kerry Gavin** frequently paints from memory. He first creates a pencil sketch, then uses the Pastel and Water brushes to create an oil pastel look.

Basic Blues began as a pencil sketch in Painter. Gavin loosely selected areas of the image—like the ashtray, the bass fiddle and the musician's shirt—with the Lasso. He also made selections for areas behind the figure. He roughed color into the selected areas and the background with a Chalk brush, then smudged the color with Water brushes to give volume to the flat color shapes. Gavin used Dye Concentration to intensify color in the foreground elements and to deepen the shadows behind the bassist, he also used Dye Concentration.

■ When he's not creating art for TV commercials, polishing an animation, drawing innovative characters or directing, **Dewey Reid** dusts off his traditional art tools and attends a life drawing class. Here are two images from his "still" portfolio.

Reid began *City Night* (above) and *City Day* (left), two in a series of images for Colossal Pictures, with traditional pencil sketches on paper and photos shot for "scrap" by designer Cindy Reid. He scanned the final sketch and photos, opened them in Photoshop and assembled them using the sketch as a guide. Beginning with *City Day*, he painted over the scanned imagery using Grainy Water, blurring and mixing the colors. Reid used the Airbrush Cloner to clone rust texture from a photo onto the car, and cloned masonry textures from another photo onto the buildings. At this point, he made a copy of the image and using Effects, Tonal Control, Adjust Colors, adjusted the Hue slider to change the colors in the image to a night scene. He added painterly details (reflections on the buildings and grill of the car) in both images using the Artist Pastel Chalk and Airbrushes, and blended the brushstrokes with Grainy Water. Finally, he painted the light beams and steam with the Airbrush and added highlights to the image using the Small Eraser. The lens flares in *City Night* were added later in Photoshop.

■ Although fine artist and illustrator **Francois Guérin** still works with conventional media, most of his commercial illustrations are created in Photoshop, Painter, or a combination of the two. Guérin painted *The Strawberries* using Painter's Water Color brushes exclusively. He used a modified Simple Water for most of the piece, adjusting the size of his brush as he painted. Guérin started with large areas of wash, then built volume and added detail. He liked the look of color pooled along the edges of his strokes, so as he blended the image with the Pure Water Brush variant, he left a few areas untouched. Guérin switched submethods frequently as he worked: To pull color out of tones that had become too dark, he changed to Wet Remove Density. He switched to Grainy Wet Buildup to add crisp details.

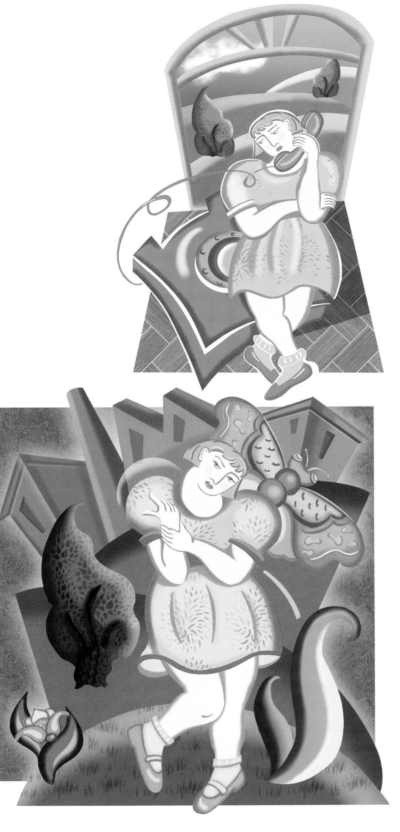

■ **Ayse Ulay** has been working in commercial illustration since 1985 and has used digital media since 1987. She loves Painter because she can achieve textural quality reminiscent of her favorite conventional medium: pastel. The two illustrations at left were created as part of a series of images to illustrate the children's book *The Magic Finger,* written by Roald Dahl.

Hello (top left) began as a conventional pencil sketch. After scanning her sketch, Ulay opened it in Painter. Working on the scanned sketch, she made selections of major elements in her composition and saved the selections into the Mask List. To begin the underpainting, she loaded each selection and filled it with a color using the Paintbucket. To define highlights and shadows on top of the fills, she used a custom brush based on the Artist Pastel Chalk variant. Next, she added subtle colored textures to a few areas using Effects, Surface Control, Color Overlay using Paper and Dye Concentration. Ulay created the wood floor with the Parquet Floor texture (from the Miles of Tiles library) applied with Color Overlay using Paper. Finally, she added more texture using a custom Grainy Light Fills brush based on the Artist Pastel Chalk variant. Her brush incorporates a lower Opacity and lower Grain penetration setting in the Controls:Brush palette which brings out the paper grain. To create soft light borders between colors, she used the Bleach variants of the Eraser.

The cover illustration for the book, *The Magic Finger* (bottom left), was painted using the same techniques and brushes as *Hello* above. The tree in the front and the heroine's dress were further enhanced with the Leaf, Grass and Sprigs paper textures from the Trees and Leaves library applied with Color Overlay using Paper and Dye Concentration.

SELECTIONS, SHAPE PATHS AND MASKS

Lighthouse. *Artist Chet Phillips drew paths around each of the elements, then he converted the paths to selections that he could use to modify the background canvas. He created letter shapes using the Text tool, then he rotated and resized them. After converting each letter to a selection, he filled each one with a different color. With all text selections active, he clicked and dragged using the Floater Adjuster tool to offset the letters slightly from the background, leaving a white "highlight" around the lower right side of each letter.*

IF YOU WANT TO GET THE MOST FROM PAINTER, you need to invest some time in understanding how the program isolates portions of images so that you can paint them, apply special effects or otherwise change them without affecting the rest of the image. Much of the program's power is tucked into the complex area of *selections*, *shape paths* and *masks*.

A *selection* is an area of the image canvas that has been isolated to allow changes to be made to the contents only, or to protect the area from change. Selections can be made with the Rectangular Selection, Oval Selection, Lasso, or the Magic Wand tools. The perimeter of a selection is indicated by an animated border—the selection marquee. There can be only one active selection at a time. Selections are temporary—if you accidentally click outside the selection marquee or choose Select, Deselect (Command-D), the selection will be lost—unless you have dragged it into the Selection Portfolio, or have saved it as a user mask in the Mask List by choosing Select, Save Selection (or clicking the Save Selection button on the Mask List palette).

A *shape path* is a mathematically described outline that can be stroked and filled. Shape paths can be created with the Rectangular Shape, Oval Shape, Text, Pen or Quick Curve tool. Because shapes exist as floating objects above the image canvas, they are automatically stored in the Floater List. Shapes can be used as independent elements in an illustration, or they can be converted to selections and used to isolate areas of the image canvas. When you convert a shape

SELECTING THE CANVAS

Selections are typically used to isolate areas of the image canvas. However, they can also be used in conjunction with floaters and transparent layers. To learn about how to use selections with floaters, turn to Chapter 5.

The selection and shape tools are grouped on the right side of the Tools palette.

STORE SELECTIONS AND SHAPES

Painter 5 offers several palettes for storage of selections and shapes: to open the Selection Portfolio choose Select, Selection Portfolio (Command-8); open the Objects palette and click on the Mask icon to open the Mask List—and click on the Floater icon to open the Floater List.

PHOTO: PHOTODISC

Type on a curve is most easily set in a drawing program. Convert the type to paths and save the file in either EPS or Illustrator format. To import the outlines into Painter, copy them to the clipboard in your drawing program, and paste them into your Painter image, or choose File, Acquire, Adobe Illustrator file.

To isolate areas of the canvas for filling, the Oval Selection tool was used to create an antialiased selection (left); the selection made by the Rectangular Selection tool needs no anitalising (right)

to a selection, (Shapes, Convert to Selection), its name disappears from the Floater List and an animated marquee appears on the image canvas. **Beware:** If you convert a shape to a selection using Painter 5.0, it will be permanently lost if you deselect it before you convert it back to a shape, save it as a user mask, drag it into the Selection Portfolio, or choose Undo (Command-Z). (Learn more about drawing shape paths and their relationship with selections in this chapter. The stroke and fill attributes of shapes, their layering capabilities and their relationship with image floaters, are covered in Chapter 5).

A *user mask* is pixel-based information. User masks can store grayscale information so that a painting, a photo, or a complex graphic can be used as a selection. Painter's 8-bit user masks allow 256 levels of protection, from fully opaque (which completely protects the pixels underneath from change) to fully clear (which fully exposes them to brushstrokes). The protective mask can be thinned or even completely removed pixel by pixel. Painter 5 allows up to 32 user masks in a single document, automatically stored in the Mask List palette. Besides allowing complex image information to be used as a selection, user masks provide a way of converting selection information to "permanent" storage until you need to use it.

The Mask List and Floater List palettes store user masks and shapes and control operations such as choosing them and turning them on and off. (The Mask List is described on page 98, and the Floater List is described in Chapter 5.) And the Selection Portfolio—available under the Select menu—is useful for storing path-based selections. (The Selection Portfolio is described on page 91.)

TWO KINDS OF SELECTIONS

The tool used to make a selection determines whether the selection is path-based or mask-based. Selections made with the Lasso, Rectangular, and Oval selection tools, as well as selections converted from shapes, are path-based selections. (For more information about path-based selections, turn to "Creating Selections and Shapes" on the following page.) Two procedures under the Select menu—Color Select and Auto Select—can be used to create mask-based (or 8-bit) selections. Painter 5's Magic Wand tool can also be used to create either a mask-based selection or a user mask. (To read about the Magic Wand, turn to "Selecting and Masking by Color," on page 93).

Using antialiasing. *Antialiasing* renders a smooth selection edge by making the pixels along the selection boundary semi-transparent. The semi-transparent edge is especially useful when

HIDE THE MARQUEE

To enable a quicker screen redraw when illustrating, hide the active selection border while keeping the selection itself active: Choose Select, Hide Marquee; choose Show Marquee to display it again.

To vignette this photo, we began by making an Oval selection. We scaled the selection using the Selection Adjuster tool, then applied a feather of 20 pixels (Select, Feather). Next, we clicked on the active selection with the Floater Adjuster to float it. To clear the background behind the floater, we deselected the floater by clicking on the image canvas, and chose Select, All and pressed the Delete key. To flatten the image, we chose Drop All from the Floater List palette's Floater menu.

WHERE'S THE PATH?

If you switch from the Pen to another tool (such as the Brush), and your paths seem to disappear, choose the Pen, the Direct Selection tool, the Whole Shape Selection tool or a Shape Edit tool to see them again.

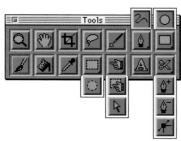

The selection and shape tools are located in the four right columns of the Tools palette. Some tools share a space in the palette with other tools as shown here in pop-out view: (in columns from left to right): Lasso; Rectangular Selection and Oval Selection; Magic Wand; Floater Adjuster, Selection Adjuster and Direct Selection; Quick Curve, Pen and Text tool; Oval and Rectangular Shape; Scissors, Remove Point (or Delete Point), Add Point, and Convert Point tool.

making selections or masks for collaging images because the selected material blends with the image it's placed in preventing jagged, pixelated edges. All selection tools make antialiased selections except the Rectangular Selection tool (which doesn't need antialiasing, because all its edges are either horizontal or vertical, and these are inherently smooth) and the Magic Wand which gives you a choice—just uncheck the Antialiased checkbox on the Controls:Magic Wand palette if you want to make a jaggy-edged, aliased selection.

CREATING SELECTIONS AND SHAPES

Because selections and shape paths come from outline information, we'll discuss them together first, then talk about masks later.

You can make selections and shape paths in a number of ways: Create them with one of the selection tools (the Lasso or the Oval or Rectangular Selection tool) or the shape design tools (Pen, Quick Curve, or Oval or Rectangular Shape tools) or with the Text tool; drag an existing path from the Selection Portfolio palette into your image; import EPS paths from a Postscript drawing program as shapes and convert them to selections. You can also convert masks to outline selections by loading a mask as a selection (Selection, Load Selection). To change a mask-based selection to an outline-based selection, choose Select, Transform Selection.

Rectangular and Oval selection tools. Drag to make selections with these tools. To constrain the oval or rectangular selection tools so they select perfect squares or circles, hold down the Shift key and drag.

Lasso tool. The Lasso tool is good for making quick, freehand selections. Choose the Lasso and carefully drag around the area that you want to isolate.

Rectangular and Oval Shape tools. Drag with these tools to create rectangular and elliptical shape objects. Press the Shift key and drag with the tool to draw a perfect square or circle shape.

Text tool. As you type with the Text tool, each letter appears as a shape; the name of each letter also appears in the Floater List palette. Make corrections as you type by using the Delete key, and press Return or Enter to start a new line of type.

Pen and Quick Curve tools. Choose the Pen tool for precise drawing using a combination of straight lines and curves. Click to

SAVE SELECTIONS!

If you've spent time making a careful selection, it's a good idea to store the selection for future use. To save an active selection as a user mask, choose Select, Save Selection, or click the Save Selection button on the Mask List palette. To save a path-based selection to the Selection Portfolio, choose Select, Selection Portfolio, or press Command-8, and using the Selection Adjuster, drag the selection directly into the palette.

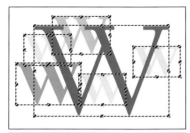

These type shapes were set with the Text tool and then selected with the Floater Adjuster tool (top), converted to active selections (Shapes, Convert to Selections) and then used to fill areas of the image canvas (bottom).

SHAPE PATH MANIPULATION

To manipulate a shape path while drawing it, press the Command key to switch from the Pen to the Direct Selection tool and adjust the anchor points and control handles.

These shapes were created with the Text tool. The shape path, (top, with no fill or line and selected with the Direct Selection tool) shows selected Bézier anchor points and curves. The lower letter shape, not selected, has been given a white fill using the Fill checkbox in the Shapes, Set Shape Attributes dialog box.

create straight line segments; to draw curves, press and drag to pull out handles that control the curves. Drag with the Quick Curve tool to draw freehand shapes. To complete an outline drawn by the Pen or Quick Curve tool, close the shape by connecting to the origin point or by pressing the Close button on the Controls:Shape Design palette. To convert a shape drawn with the Pen or Quick Curve tool to a selection, click the Make Selection button on the Controls: Shape Design palette, or choose Shapes, Convert to Selection.

Selection Adjuster, Floater Adjuster and Direct Selection tools. These tools share a space in the bottom row of the Tools palette. Use the Selection Adjuster to move or transform selections. Read more about this tool in "Transforming Selections," on page 95.

The Floater Adjuster tool is useful for working with shapes and floaters. Read more about it in the beginning of Chapter 5.

The Direct Selection tool (hollow arrow) allows you to select and adjust individual anchor points and control handles to modify shapes. This tool works much like its counterpart in Illustrator or like the Pick and Shape tool in CorelDraw.

Shape Edit tools. The Scissors, Add Point, Remove Point (or Delete Point) and Convert Point tools will also be familiar to Illustrator users. Like the Direct Selection tool, they are used for changing shape paths. The Scissors tool allows you to cut a line segment of a shape path selected with the Direct Selection tool. To add a new anchor point, select a path segment with the Direct Selection tool and click with the Add Point tool. To delete an anchor point, click on it with the Remove Point (or Delete Point) tool.

The Selection Portfolio. In Painter 5, the Selection Portfolio, (known as the Paths palette in earlier versions) can be chosen from the Select menu: Choose Selection Portfolio to open the palette, or press Command-8. To use a stored outline selection, drag an item from the front of the palette, or from the Selection Portfolio palette drawer into your image. If you use a lot of custom paths in your work, use the Selection Mover, (also found under the Select menu), to create custom libraries (see the "Libraries and Movers" section in Chapter 1).

PRECISION DRAWING SETUP

When you're drawing shape paths and you find the default stroke and fill on the path make it hard to see your path outline and to draw precisely, change the Shape Attributes to a skeletal line: Under Edit, Preferences, Shapes, check the Big Handles drawing option, Uncheck the Fill and Stroke preferences. You'll be able to see the path outline with anchor points and handles so you can draw more precisely.

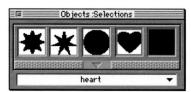

Choosing a heart-shaped path in Painter's Selection Portfolio, available from the Select menu

When these fish, drawn in Adobe Illustrator, were copied and pasted into Painter, they came in as compound shapes. To recreate this look, turn to "Dropping a Shadow," in Chapter 5.

Killdeer *by Mary Envall. To create this wildlife illustration—featuring a black and white ink drawing floating on top of colored, textured paper—Envall began by making a black and white scratchboard drawing in Painter. To drop the white background out behind the drawing she made an automatic selection, choosing Select, Auto Select using Image Luminance. She floated the active selection by clicking on it with the Floater Adjuster and then deselected the floater by clicking in the blank area below its name in the Floater List. Next, she filled the background with a colored texture, using Effects, Surface Control, Color Overlay using Paper and Dye Concentration.*

Importing EPS outlines. Painter 5 supports three ways to import shape paths, such as type on a curve created in a Postscript drawing program, or preexisting EPS clip art. The first option (File, Acquire, Adobe Illustrator file) creates a new file, importing the EPS outlines—with their strokes and fills—into Painter as shapes. To use the shapes in a composite file, copy and paste the shapes from the new file into your working composition. The second option allows you to copy outlines with strokes and fills from a Postscript program to the clipboard and paste them into your Painter file; the third option allows you to drag from a Postscript program (Illustrator 6 or 7 is recommended) and drop into Painter. The outlines will import into your document as shapes and will appear in the Floater List palette. Objects such as the letters "O" and "A" have a *counter,* or hole, cut in them and will come into Painter as compound shapes. Like other shapes, you can convert imported EPS shapes to selections (Shapes, Convert to Selection) to use the outlines to modify the image canvas.

> **EPS IMPORTING ALERT!**
>
> A word of warning: As of this writing, we encountered problems when importing some EPS files created in earlier versions of Freehand and Illustrator using both of the import methods. When importing compound objects, we obtained the best results with drawings completely created in Illustrator 5 or newer (simply resaving an older file created in the new format resulted in some compound objects not making the transition).

AUTOMATIC SELECTING AND MASKING

Two powerful functions—Auto Select and Auto Mask—create a selection or mask based on the criteria that you choose to sample, such as Paper, 3D Brushstrokes, Image Luminance, Current Color, Original Selection or Original Mask. The two dialog boxes are identical, with the exception that one creates a selection whereas the other creates a mask. Auto Select is located under the Select menu; to use Auto Mask, open the Objects:Mask List palette and choose Auto Mask from the Mask pull-down menu.

To generate a mask based on the brightness values in the image, try this: Create a new file with a white background. In the Art Materials:Color palette, select black, and from the Brushes palette choose the Scratchboard Tool variant of the Pens brush. Make a sketch, and generate a mask for your sketch by choosing Auto Mask (Command-Shift-M) using Image Luminance. In the Objects:Mask List, click on the mask name to target the mask, and open the eye icon to the left of the mask name to view the mask as a red overlay. Highlighting the mask name will target the mask, allowing you to paint on it using any brush. For an example of Auto Mask using Current Color—the only one of these automated masking methods that produces an aliased, jagged-edged mask—turn to "Isolating Color with Auto Mask," later in this chapter.

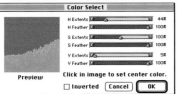

Generating a selection based on color for the sky in this Digital Stock image. Choose Select, Color Select and click in the image to sample the color you'd like to isolate. Adjust the H, S and V sliders until you see the red mask cover only the sampled color in the preview window. You can use Color Mask (located on the Mask List palette under the Mask pull-down menu) in the same way, and the mask will automatically be stored in the Mask List.

MASK VIEWS

To view the mask and image canvas simultaneously, open the eye icon representing the mask and the eye icon representing the RGB Canvas. To view the mask alone in black-and-white, toggle the RGB canvas eye icon closed. To hide the mask, close its eye icon.

SELECTING AND MASKING BY COLOR

Painter 5 offers useful new tools and procedures with which you can make selections and masks based on color.

Magic Wand. Painter 5's Magic Wand is greatly improved, and is a production time-saver. The Magic Wand lets you select an area of your image based on color similarities of contiguous pixels. This is especially useful for selecting a uniformly colored element in an image, without having to draw around the area with the Lasso or Pen tool. You can choose to build a user mask or a selection using the Magic Wand by checking the appropriate radio button. To select a wider range of color, move the Tolerance slider to the right. To smooth the edge of the mask or selection, check the Antialias checkbox. To add soft, or partially opaque values to the mask, increase the Feather by moving the slider to the right.

To add areas of similar adjacent color to the selection or mask, (like Select, Grow in Adobe Photoshop), Shift-click on the existing selection with the Magic Wand. To remove colors, Command-click on an area. To add areas of similar color that are not adjacent (like Select, Similar in Photoshop), press the Control and Shift keys together, and continue adding areas of non-contiguous color by pressing the Shift key as you click on the image. To turn off the non-adjacent mode, press the Control and Shift keys again.

DYNAMIC TOLERANCE

The Controls:Magic Wand palette features a dynamic Tolerance slider. Click once in an image to begin a mask. Move the Tolerance slider to the right to expand the masked area; move to the left to reduce the masked area.

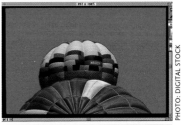

We clicked the Magic Wand in the sky area and began with a Tolerance of 3 and Feather of 2. Changing the Tolerance to 8 and leaving the Feather set at 2 covered most of the sky.

Using Color Select and Color Mask. Painter 5 offers two closely related, automated features that are useful for isolating images based on color. Use Select, Color Select to generate a mask-based selection based on the color you sample from an image. Adjust the H (Hue), S (Saturation) and V (Value) extents sliders to control the amount of each of these properties sampled in the image. Experiment with adjusting the Feather sliders to improve the edge of the selection. Save the new selection as a mask to make it permanent. Color Select is closely related to Color Mask; both dialog boxes

To make a selection isolating the large dahlia in this photo we used Select, Color Select, then used the Lasso to change the selection border—pressing the Command key to subtract from the selection—to exclude the smaller flower.

function essentially the same. Color Mask is found under the Mask pull-down menu on the Mask List palette. Masks generated using Color Mask are automatically saved into the Mask List. To learn more about Color Mask, turn to "Using Color Mask," later in this chapter.

Many artists begin the process of isolating complex areas of an image using Color Select or Color Mask, then finish a selection by editing it using the Lasso and the Command key to subtract from the selection and the Shift key to add to the selection. To convert a mask generated with Color Mask to a selection for editing, choose Select, Load Selection, and choose it from the menu in the Load Selection dialog box.

CONVERTING SELECTIONS, SHAPES AND MASKS

Path-based and mask-based selections have entirely different origins, but there is some degree of interchangeability. For instance, you can turn a *user mask* into a *selection* so you can isolate an area of the image canvas (see the "Masks" section later in this introduction) and then into a *path-based selection* using the Select, Transform Selection command, so you can move or modify the outline without editing the canvas.

To convert a user mask into a path-based selection, so you can transform the outline (scale, skew or rotate) using the Selection Adjuster tool, choose Select, Load Selection, and when the marquee is active, choose Select, Transform Selection.

To convert an active path-based selection into a user mask, so you can save the selection permanently into the Mask List without path-based information, choose Select, Save Selection.

To convert a shape to an active selection, so can you use it to isolate an area of the image canvas, select the shape by highlighting its name in the Floater List, and choose Shapes, Convert to Selection. An added bonus, the Pen and Quick Curve tools offer a Make Selection button on the Controls: Shape Design palette, allowing quick access to the command. **Beware:** If you convert a shape to a selection using Painter 5.0, it will be permanently lost if you deselect it before you convert it back to a shape, save it as a user mask, drag it into the Selection Portfolio, or choose Undo (Command-Z).

To convert an active selection into a shape, so you can edit it using its outline (using anchor points and control handles), or fill and stroke it—choose Select, Convert to Shape. A word of warning: Counters in text selections (such as the hole in the letter "O"), can be lost when converting from selections to shapes. To restore the counter in a letter, Shift-select the shape and its counter with the Floater Adjuster tool and choose Shapes, Make

We set this Adobe Woodtype Ornament shape using the Text tool—and Option-dragged with the Floater Adjuster to make a copy of the shape. We converted the copy into an active selection for treating the image canvas (Shapes, Convert to Selection.

To move a selection border without moving the image contents within the active selection, choose the Selection Adjuster. This tool operates on selection borders only. Transformations using the Selection Adjuster will not affect the image contents.

An active selection (left) ready to accept brushstrokes within its boundary; and an active, selected selection (right) ready to be moved using the Selection Adjuster tool. When the Selection Adjuster is chosen, an active, selected selection displays 8 square handles in addition to the marquee.

With the first release of Painter 5.0, you can't directly feather a rectangular selection, as you can selections made with the Lasso or the Oval Selection tools. If you try it, the corners will round as if it were feathered, but it you try Effects, Fill, you'll see that the edges are still unfeathered. Good news: Version 5.03 fixes the problem.

When you want to *paint* inside or outside of a selection, you can use the Drawing icons to quickly invert the selection without forcing the whole image to redraw every time you switch. However, *to invert the selection if you are applying a special effect*, you must use Select, Invert which forces a complete screen redraw.

Compound. To learn more, turn to "Making a Compound," on page 124, in the introduction of Chapter 5.

TRANSFORMING SELECTIONS

Painter 5 offers great flexibility, allowing path-based selection borders to be scaled, skewed or rotated without altering the image canvas. Selections made with the Lasso, Rectangular, and Oval selection tools, as well as selections converted from shapes are automatically path-based. Selections saved as user masks must be converted to path-based information before they can be scaled, skewed or rotated. To convert a selection stored in the Mask List to a path-based selection, load the selection (Select, Load Selection), when the selection marquee appears, choose Select, Transform Selection. (When a selection is loaded from a user mask and transformed, the user mask in the Mask List remains unmodified until it is replaced by another selection using the Save Selection, Replace Mask command.)

An important concept to understand when working with path-based selections is that of *active* vs. *selected*. An *active* selection displays an animated marquee, sometimes referred to as "marching ants." As soon as you've drawn a complete boundary with a selection tool, dragged a selection into your image from the Selection Portfolio, loaded a user mask as a selection or converted a shape to a selection, you will see a marquee letting you know it's active. The image canvas within the boundary can now be painted into, filled or treated with an effect.

A *selected* selection displays eight bounding box handles around its edges—the handles are visible only when the Selection Adjuster tool is chosen. You select selections in order to move them, scale, skew, rotate their outlines, or change them using commands under the Modify menu to widen, contract, smooth, or border them.

The distinction between "active" and "selected" gives you great flexibility. Both Painter and other image editors let you convert selections to paths in order to modify individual Bézier control points, *but Painter lets you scale, rotate and skew the selection outline without affecting the pixel information within it*. You can do these operations and more by applying the Selection Adjuster tool to the interior or to the bounding box handles of a selected path-based selection.

Working with the Selection Adjuster tool. Since path-based selections are based on mathematical information, they can undergo all of the following transformations, carried out with the Selection Adjuster tool, with no loss of edge quality and without moving the pixels within the selection boundary. To *move* a selection,

Use arrow keys to move selected selections or shapes one screen pixel at a time. Since the distance moved is a screen pixel and not a fixed width, zoom out from the selection or shape if you want to make coarse adjustments and zoom in for fine adjustments. Arrow-key nudging is especially useful for kerning type shapes.

Option-dragging a selection to make a copy

Dragging a side handle to scale horizontally

Shift-dragging one of the corner handles to scale proportionally

Using a corner handle and the Command key to rotate

PAINTER 5 TIMESAVERS

Use these Shift-key shortcuts to switch among the three Drawing icons to determine how the painting tools work with active selections:

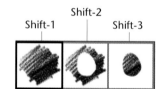

Shift-2

Shift-1   Shift-3

The Drawing icons are (from left to right): Draw Anywhere, Draw Outside and Draw Inside.

SELECT, INVERT—BEWARE!

Instead of using the Drawing icons, you can invert a mask by using the Select, Invert command. But *beware,* combining use of the Draw icons and the Select, Invert command can be confusing. At least through the initial release of Painter 5.0, when Select, Invert is chosen, the Draw icons do not change to reflect the new mask coverage.

position the Selection Adjuster over it and press; when you see the four-arrowed cursor, dragging will move the selection. To *duplicate*, hold down Option, drag and release. To *scale*, first select a path or selection by clicking on it once; position the tool over one of the corner handles; when the cursor changes, drag the handle. Use the Shift key to *resize proportionally*. If you want to *resize only horizontally or vertically*, drag on a center handle, side handle, top or bottom handle. To *rotate*, use a corner handle, adding the Command key as you position the cursor before dragging. To *skew*, press Command while positioning over a center handle on the side, top or bottom, then drag.

SAVING SELECTION OUTLINES

Use the Selection Adjuster tool to drag path-based selections to the Selection Portfolio to store them. If you want to save shapes into this library, first convert them to selections (Shapes, Convert to Selection) and then drag them to the Selection Portfolio. If you're very organized, you might create multiple selection libraries for different jobs. To swap outlines between libraries or to set up a new, empty palette, you can use the Selection Mover, found in the Select menu.

Use File, Export Adobe Illustrator file to export images to Postscript drawing programs. We successfully exported simple shape objects and more complex objects that included blends and compounds, opening them in Illustrator 6 and 7.

SELECTIONS AT WORK

Once you've activated selections, you can choose to draw outside of them instead of inside, or use them to isolate areas of the image canvas when applying special effects procedures found in the Effects menu.

Using the drawing icons. The Drawing icons are found in the bottom left corner of an active document's window. Take the name "Drawing icons" literally; they affect drawing and painting actions only, not fills or other effects. A fill or effect is always constrained to the inside of an active selection, regardless of which drawing icon you choose. Several of the techniques in this chapter demonstrate how these icons work, and you can refer to "Drawing Modes" in Chapter 9 of Painter's *User Guide* for a detailed explanation.

Inverting a selection. If you want to apply a fill or effect to the *outside* of your active selection, use Select, Invert. This procedure selects the inverse of the current selection. It's often useful to save a selection as a user mask into the Mask List, then save the inverse of it; for instance, save an element, then save the background, also as a user mask.

Stroking a selection. In Painter, you can use any brush variant *to stroke a selection marquee*. Begin by making a selection using any

To create a light-valued border for an image, make a rectangular selection, and choose Select, Modify, Border and set the radius for the border. (We used 30 pixels for this 750 pixel-wide image). With the border selection active (as shown here), choose Effects, Tonal Control, Adjust Colors. Move the Value slider to the right to lighten the values within the selection.

PAINTER AND PHOTOSHOP

To save Painter selections into the Mask List and use them in Photoshop 4.0 as channels, save a Painter file in Photoshop 3.0 format. When you open the file in Photoshop, the named user masks will automatically appear in the Channels palette. To learn more about using Painter masks and paths with Photoshop (and vice versa) turn to Chapter 8, "Using Painter with Photoshop."

Multiple applications of the Smooth function (Select, Modify, Smooth) can turn a perfectly good typeface (Stone Sans, left) into a trendy, avant-garde one. Set type shapes, convert them to selections (Shapes, Convert to Selections), apply the Smooth operation and fill them with a color.

of the selection methods. The effect is more fun to observe if you choose one of Painter's grain-sensitive brushes. In the Brushes palette, click on the Chalk brush and the Large Chalk variant. Next, open the Paper palette and choose a texture from the default paper library. With the selection still active, use the Drawing icons (located at the extreme bottom-left of the image window) to choose whether you want your stroke inside (Draw Inside), outside (Draw Outside), or centered directly on top of the selection border (Draw Anywhere), then go to the Select menu and choose Stroke Selection.

EDITING SELECTIONS

Painter 5 offers methods for finessing path-based and mask-based selections that will be familiar to Photoshop users. To read about editing masks, turn to "Masks," later in this introduction.

Expanding a selection. To add to an existing selection marquee, press the Shift key and drag outside of the existing marquee with the Lasso, Rectangular or Oval Selection tool. The Add to Selection command is also useful—it is described on page 99.

Subtracting from a selection. To remove a portion of an existing selection, press the Command key and drag inside of the selection marquee with the Lasso, Rectangular or Oval Selection tool. The Subtract from Selection and Intersect commands are also useful—they are described on page 99.

The modify menu. Four commands under the Select, Modify menu—Widen, Contract, Smooth and Border—allow you to change existing path-based selections. Widen and Contract allow you change the size of a selection by a specified number of pixels. The Smooth command is useful for rounding corners and softening jagginess in a selection. The Border function adds a second selection marquee (based on a specified number of pixels), outside the existing marquee, selecting only the area between the two.

Feathering. Feathering a selection softens its edge. To see feathering at work, drag a selection from the Selection Portfolio into your image. Choose Select, Feather, and type 20 in the field to define the pixel radius of the feather. Now choose Effects, Fill, select one of the options and click OK. Note the soft edges of the filled selection. The feather is always built both inward and outward from the path-based selection. At least with the first release of Painter 5.0, the Select, Feather command will change a path-based selection to mask-based, though Painter "remembers" the original path. To refeather the selection using a new setting, the path-based

Anderson Valley Apples. *To paint a resist for the trees with the Scratchboard Pen variant on the user mask, the mask was set at 100% opacity in the Mask Attributes dialog box (top left); washes were painted on the background using a Water Color brush (top right). The finished artwork included brushstrokes inside of the mask (above), made by reversing the mask after the other painting had been done.*

CHER THREINEN-PENDARVIS

selection information must first be restored—use Select, Transform Selection to restore it.

MASKS

You can create masks in Painter in several ways: by making a selection and saving it as a user mask, by painting directly onto a new blank mask with brushes, by generating masks with procedures such as Auto Mask or Color Mask, or by using Boolean operations to calculate new masks from existing ones.

Painting a resist using a mask. Instead of making masks by using Bézier curves to draw selections, artists with experience in drawing often feel more comfortable using brushes on the mask to paint the areas they want to isolate. One of the best ways to get acquainted with painting a mask is to paint a *resist*.

A traditional resist involves applying a protective substance to define an area and to prevent paint from being applied to it. To create a *resist* in Painter, begin with a new file and open the Objects:Mask List palette. From the pull-down menu choose New Mask. Target the new mask by clicking on its name in the Mask List to highlight it with blue. To see the red-tinted mask as you paint it, open the "eye" icon next to its name. Choose black to paint a solid mask, white to erase your work, and any color in between if you want varying levels of mask transparency. When you're done, select the image background by clicking on the RGB Canvas in the Mask List, and begin painting broad strokes across the image canvas. All red areas that you painted on the mask with black paint are protected from these strokes. To "reverse" the mask so you can paint with a brush on the areas covered by your mask, select the far right Drawing icon on the lower left corner of the image window. To view your work without the mask layer, choose the far left Drawing icon, or in the Mask List, target the mask and wink the eye icon shut.

NOW YOU SEE IT...

In the Mask List, make sure to click on the item's *name*—and not the eye icon—to select it.

USING THE MASK LIST PALETTE

The Mask List palette lists all the user masks in your file by name. A Painter file can contain a maximum of 32 user masks. If you'll be doing a lot of work with masks, it's a good idea to get on friendly terms with this palette. Here are some basics:

To view a mask as an overlay on top of the RGB image canvas, select the mask name, highlighting it with blue, and open the eye icon to the far left of its name.

To hide a mask, toggle its eye icon shut.

To view a mask alone in black-and-white, without the RGB Canvas, open the mask's eye icon and close the RGB canvas eye icon. The mask name will be highlighted in blue. Edit the mask by painting on it with any brush.

Several useful commands are found in the Mask List pull-down menu.

To change the mask overlay to a color easier to see while making a mask for an orange Garibaldi fish, we changed the overlay color from the default red to yellow using the Mask Attributes dialog box.

PHOTO: DIGITAL STOCK

INACTIVE, BUT USEFUL

Although the user masks stored in the Mask List don't affect brush-strokes (if they are dormant), they can be used to isolate areas of an image when using functions under the Effects menu such as Tonal Control, Adjust Color and Surface Control, Apply Surface Texture, Color Overlay, Dye Concentration or Express Texture.

We used Intersect with Selection to create the filled half circle (above right). Begin by making a square selection with the Rectangular Selection tool and Shift key and save the selection by choosing Select, Save Selection, or choosing Save Selection on the Mask List. View the mask as an overlay (above left) by clicking its eye icon open in the Mask List. Select the RGB canvas again, and make a new selection partially overlapping the square, with the Oval Selection tool. With the oval selection active, click the Load Selection on the Mask List, in the Load From pop-up menu choose the square mask, and click the Intersect With Selection button.

To view a mask as an opaque overlay, choose Mask, Mask Attributes, and move the opacity slider to 100%. Viewing a mask as an opaque overlay can often help to see defects in the mask. Adjusting this slider changes the overlay appearance only, and does not affect the actual density of the mask.

To apply a paper grain to a mask, use Effects, Surface Control, Express Texture, using Paper. Experiment with the Gray Threshold and Grain sliders.

To copy mask information to another mask, select a mask in the mask list and choose Mask, Copy Mask. From the Copy Mask To pop-up menu, select a destination mask, and click OK.

To feather a mask, select the mask in the mask list and choose Mask, Feather Mask, and type a number in the field.

CALCULATING AND OPERATING

Painter 5 offers Boolean operations, useful functions that help generate new masks that fit perfectly against existing ones. Skillful use of these techniques will save time and effort. To see these functions at work, turn to "Making Masks for Embossing," on page 100.

To edit a mask using a selection, create a selection marquee, and choose Select, Save Selection. In the Save Selection dialog box, choose the mask you wish to edit from the Save To pop-up menu, and the operation you wish to perform.

To replace a mask with the active selection, create a selection marquee and choose Select, Save Selection. In the dialog box, from the Save To menu, choose the mask you wish to replace, then click the Replace Mask button. This choice makes the original mask permanently unavailable.

To add to a selection, create a selection marquee surrounding the area you want to add. Choose Load Selection. In the Load Selection dialog box, choose the mask you want to add to and click the Add To Selection button.

To subtract from a selection, make a new marquee around the area you want to take away. Choose Load Selection, in the Load Selection dialog box select the mask you want to subtract from and click the Subtract From Selection button.

To intersect with a mask, creating a new selection isolating only the overlapping area of the new selection and the mask, begin with a marquee. Choose Load Selection, and in the Load Selection dialog box, choose the mask you want to use to make the intersection and click the Intersect With Selection button. 🐾

Making Masks for Embossing

Overview *Open a new file with a colored background; set a type shape; convert the shape to a selection; save the selection as a user mask; use the selection to build bevel and background masks; apply special effects to create three-dimensional looks.*

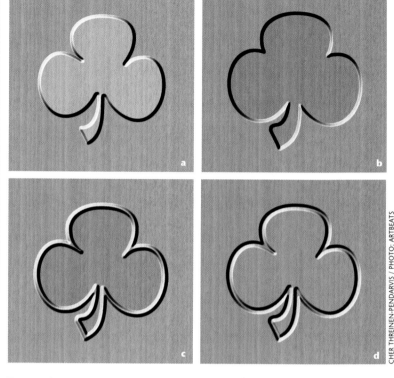

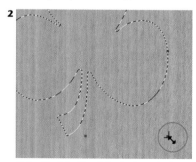

The shape before converting to a selection

Using the Selection Adjuster to scale the selection

PAINTER'S EFFECTS, SURFACE CONTROL MENU hides powerful features for creating the dimensional artwork needed for an embossed look or for interactive buttons. These features are most effective when combined with a skillful use of selections and user masks. To create these tooled wood reliefs, we began with a graphic shape for the face of the graphic. Then we created a series of masks based on the original graphic—a widened face, a bevel and a background—to isolate areas for special effects application. Preparing the masks up front allowed quick previewing of a variety of effects.

1 Setting a shape and converting it to a selection. Create a new file with a light background color, or open a textured background image (we chose Beechwood from the ArtBeats Wood and Paper CD-ROM). Click in the image with the Text tool and type a letter. (Using a 500-pixel-wide file, we set an ornament using the Adobe Wood Type Ornaments font.)

Before you can use the graphic shape to isolate areas of the image canvas, you'll need to convert it to a selection. Select the shape in the Objects:Floater List, or click on it in the image with the Floater Adjuster tool and choose Shapes, Convert to Selection.

2 Moving and scaling. Choose the Selection Adjuster tool (it shares a space in the Tools palette with the Floater Adjuster). Press inside the active selection with the Selection Adjuster tool, and

Typing a descriptive name for the mask

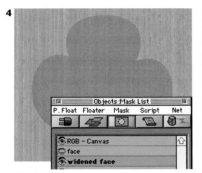

Viewing the widened face mask on top of the RGB Canvas

Loading the "widened face" mask

Subtracting the "face" mask

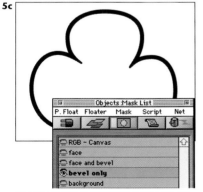

Viewing the bevel mask without the canvas

when you see the four-arrow cursor, you can safely move your selection without distorting it. To scale, drag on one of the selection handles; to scale proportionately, press Shift and drag one of the corner handles.

3 Saving and naming the selection. Saving a selection permanently stores it in the Mask List as a user mask. The first selection will be the top face of the bas relief, and we used it to create three user masks. To save a selection, choose Select, Save Selection, or click the Save Selection button on the Mask List palette. When the Save Selection dialog box appears, accept the default in the pop-up menu—Save to New. Click OK. To rename the user mask, double-click its name in the Mask List palette. We named ours "face."

4 Widening the selection. When you rename the mask, the naming process converts the selection from path-based to mask information and the selection ceases to be active on the image canvas. Load the "face" selection (Select, Load Selection, Load From "face") and choose Select, Transform Selection. You can use the transformed selection to create a wider boundary around the graphic. Choose Select, Modify, Widen and set the radius by typing a number in the field (we used 10 pixels). Save this new widened selection into the Mask List, naming it "widened face."

5 Creating new masks using calculations. Next, we created a bevel mask describing the thin area between the outside widened boundary and the original face boundary. Painter 5 offers Boolean operations, calculations in the Save and Load Selection dialog boxes to make the job easier. To build a mask for the bevel, choose Select, Load Selection and from the Load From pop-up menu choose the "widened face" mask. Now choose the Replace Selection radio button. When the marquee appears, choose Load Selection again, this time choosing "face" from the pop-up menu. Under Operation click the Subtract From Selection radio button to subtract the original face area from the widened face area, resulting in a user mask for the bevel. Save and name the mask.

We also built a mask isolating the image area outside of the widened face mask. To do this, load a selection using the "widened face" mask, and then choose Select, Invert. We saved this selection as a user mask, naming it "background."

QUICKER LOADING

To save a visit to the Select menu or Mask List palette when you'd like to load a selection—press Command-Shift-E to display the Load Selection dialog box.

MODIFYING SELECTIONS

Only path-based selections accept commands from the Modify menu such as Widen and Contract. To convert a mask-based selection to path-based information so you can modify it, choose Select, Transform Selection. For more information, turn to "Editing Selections," on page 97.

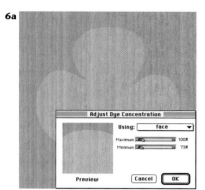

6a

Using Dye Concentration in conjunction with the face mask

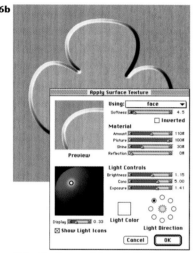

6b

Using the face mask to apply Surface Texture to create the embossed face

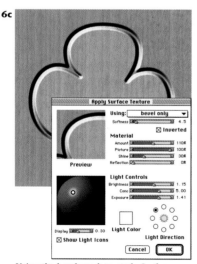

6c

Using the bevel mask to apply Surface Texture for the cut bevel effect

6 Putting the masks to work. Many operations available under the Effects menu in Painter 5—for instance, Tonal Control, Adjust Color; Surface Control, Apply Surface Texture; and Focus, Glass Distortion—offer a pop-up menu allowing you to apply the effect using any user mask saved in the Mask List.

To **emboss** the face, creating the bas relief look in image "a" at the top of page 100, you can use the "face" mask to isolate an area of the image. Lightening the face of the graphic will enhance the illusion of relief. With no selection active and the RGB-Canvas active in the Mask List, choose Effects, Surface Control, Dye Concentration and in the Using pop-up menu, choose the "face" mask. To lighten the area, set the Minimum slider to 80%. Click OK. Now, for the relief effect: To "pop" the graphic face out (creating a convincing 3D effect), choose Effects, Surface Control, Apply Surface Texture. In the Using menu choose "face." Set Softness to 4.5, reduce the shine to 30%, click the top left Light Direction button and click OK.

To **deboss** the face, of the graphic in image "b" with no selection active and the RGB Canvas active in the Mask List, choose Effects, Surface Control, Dye Concentration. In the Using pop-up menu choose the "face" mask. To darken the area, set the Minimum slider to 125%. Click OK. Then choose Effects, Surface Control, Apply Surface Texture. Click the Inverted checkbox to turn it on. In the Using menu choose "face." Set Softness to 4.5, reduce the shine to 30%, choose the top left Light Direction button and click OK.

To create the **beveled** look in image "c," begin by lightening the bevel area: With no selection active and the RGB-Canvas active in the Mask List, choose Effects, Surface Control, Dye Concentration and in the Using pop-up menu, choose the "bevel" mask. To lighten the area, set the Minimum slider to 80%. To emboss the bevel, making the face and background appear to recede, choose Effects, Surface Control, Apply Surface Texture. In the Using menu, choose "bevel." Set Softness to 4.5, reduce the shine to 30%, and click the top left Light Direction button. Be sure the Inverted box is not checked and click OK.

To **carve out the beveled area** leaving the face and background flat (image "d"), begin by darkening the bevel area. With no selection active and the RGB-Canvas active in the Mask List, choose Effects, Surface Control, Dye Concentration and in the Using pop-up menu, choose the "bevel" mask. To darken the area, set the Minimum slider to 125%. To deboss the bevel, making the bevel appear to be carved out of the wood, choose Effects, Surface Control, Apply Surface Texture. Click the Inverted button. In the Using menu choose "bevel." Set Softness to 4.5, set the Shine at 30%, and click the top left Light Direction button. Click to turn on the Inverted feature and click OK. 🖐

Working with Bézier Paths and Selections

Overview *Use the Pen tool to create shape paths of straight and curved lines; convert the shape paths to selections; use a custom pencil to draw inside and outside of selections.*

The logo sketch, including a rough grid

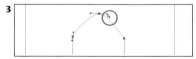
Pulling a handle from an anchor point to prepare for a curved path segment, then pressing and dragging to create the curve

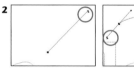
Dragging on a control handle to change the path's shape

CHANGING DIRECTION

While drawing with the Pen, Option-click on an anchor point to create a cusp and establish a new direction for the following curve. A cusp is a corner point between two curved line segments, such as the "dent" at the top of a heart shape.

JOHN FRETZ

TO DESIGN A LOGO FOR THE 100-YEAR-OLD Bethany Church in Seattle, John Fretz used a custom pencil to draw inside and outside of selections to create a hard-edged, graduated look similar to his conventional colored pencil illustration style.

1 Sketching the logo. Fretz created a 4 x 4-inch pencil drawing of the logo that included a rough grid aligning the roofs of the houses. He scanned the sketch at 300 ppi and opened it in Painter to use as a template.

2 Creating a path with Bézier curves. The most efficient way to create a combination of curve and straight-line path segments is with the Pen tool. Set up shape attributes (with no fill and stroke) to produce a skeletal line that will help you see precise lines and curves while you draw: Choose Edit, Preferences, Shapes to open the Shape Preferences dialog box. Under Drawing Options uncheck all the Fill and Stroke checkboxes. To make the anchor points and control handles easier to see and work with, check the Big Handles checkbox. Click OK. Now, choose the Pen tool and click to place anchor points for straight-line segments, and press, hold and drag to create anchor points with control handles that control curve segments. When you want to close a path, place the cursor over the starting anchor point, and click when you see a small circle designating the origin point, or press the Close Button in the Controls:Shape Design palette.

3 Changing the path shape. You can fine-tune a path during or after the drawing process with the Direct Selection tool. (While drawing with the Pen tool, press the Command key to temporarily change from the Pen to the Direct Selection tool.) Move the Direct Selection tool over an anchor point, a control handle, or a curve segment and drag to reposition it.

Click on the Make Selection button to change the shape path into a selection

Selections stored in the Mask List

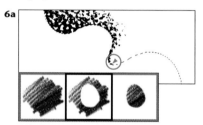

Scaling the Basic Paper texture in the Paper palette

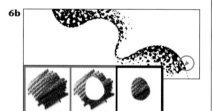

Painting outside of the cloud selection using the custom black pencil

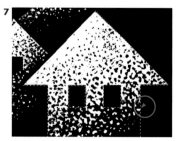

Painting inside of the cloud selection

4 Changing the path to a selection. Shape paths must be turned into selections before you can paint inside or outside of them on the image canvas. You can convert a path drawn with the Pen or Quick Curve tool to a selection immediately after drawing it by pressing the Make Selection button in the Controls: Shape Design palette. You can also change a shape path into a selection by selecting the shape in the Floater List on the Objects palette and choosing Shapes, Convert to Selection. In your image, the Bézier curves will turn into a black-and-white selection marquee. To save the selection as a user mask in the Mask List for future use, choose Select, Save Selection. To name a selection double-click on its name in the Mask List to open the Mask Attributes dialog box. Type a new name in the field. Click OK. The naming process will select the black-and-white view of the mask. To return to the image canvas, click on RGB-Canvas in the Mask List.

5 Creating the pencil and surface. To re-create the graduated effect he gets with conventional colored pencils on rough illustration board, Fretz built a heavy, grainy pencil based on Painter's 500 lb. Pencil variant. He modified the variant by switching to the Grainy Hard Cover submethod and increasing Size to roughly 200 pixels in the Brush Controls:Size palette, found under the Control pull-down menu on the Brushes palette. (You might also experiment with a brush that uses Grainy Edge Flat Cover method with a 10% Grain setting in the Controls:Brush palette; it will give you an even coarser texture—black-and-white, with no grays.) Fretz chose Basic Paper because of its even texture, and scaled it to about 300% using the Scale slider in the front of the Paper drawer.

6 Drawing in and out of selections. Fretz used the Drawing Modes, three icons located in the bottom left corner of the image window, to paint inside and outside of selections. Begin by loading a selection (Select, Load Selection). (You can also use the Select, Invert command to invert an active selection.) To protect the area inside an active selection, click on the middle Drawing button; to protect the area outside the selection, click on the far right Drawing button. Fretz switched back and forth between these two options as he rendered a graduated, even texture using his custom pencil.

7 Subtracting from a selection. To fill each house with white and leave the windows black, Fretz loaded each house selection and subtracted the window selection from it. Choose Load Selection again and in the Load Selection dialog box, choose a selection that you'd like to subtract from the original selected area. Fretz filled the resulting selection with white, then he added black texture to the house with his custom pencil. He continued to add textured, even tone with the black and white pencils until he completed the logo.

Fretz saved the finished image in TIFF format, and to eliminate all grayscale information, he opened the image in Photoshop and converted it from grayscale to a 600 ppi bitmap image.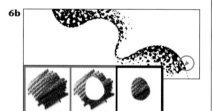

When the house is filled with white, the subtracted selection around the windows protects the area, keeping them black. Fretz used his custom pencil to add black texture over the white fill.

Selections and Airbrush

Overview *Create a pencil sketch; add Postscript outlines in a drawing program; import outlines and template into Painter; add texture and gradient fills within the selections; use the Airbrush to create a metallic look.*

JOHN DISMUKES, CAPSTONE STUDIOS

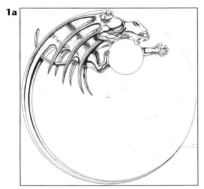

The original pencil sketch

Copying the selected and grouped panther outlines to the clipboard in Illustrator

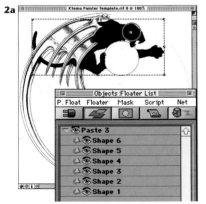

The pasted shapes selected with the Floater tool on the image and their names in the Floater List palette

ARTISTS USING TRADITIONAL AIRBRUSH technique cut friskets out of paper, film or plastic to protect portions of their artwork as they paint. For complex jobs this can become quite a task. That's one of the reasons why John Dismukes of Capstone Studios traded in his traditional tools for electronic ones. For this logo for Ktema, a manufacturer of promotional clothing for the entertainment industry, he started with a pencil sketch from memory, added Postscript paths and brought both into Painter. He painted inside and outside of the selections as he would with traditional friskets.

1 Creating the EPS paths. Dismukes scanned his pencil sketch and used it as a template as he drew the elements to fit using Adobe Illustrator. He drew Postscript outlines for the panther, the wing ribs and membrane, the large and small globes, and the Ktema nameplate. Painter 5 can recognize fill and stroke attributes and groups when Postscript art is imported, so you may find it helpful to fill and group certain elements as you draw them. This will help you identify elements so you can move and scale them. To prepare a document for importing into Painter 5, save a version in Adobe Illustrator 5 (or later) or EPS format.

2 Importing, positioning and scaling. Dismukes opened the original pencil sketch in Painter and begin importing the paths into the document. There are three ways to import Postscript outlines into a Painter file: using File, Acquire, Adobe Illustrator file (which creates a new file); copying from the Postscript program to the clipboard and then pasting into Painter; or dragging from Illustrator and dropping into Painter. For the second and third methods to work, both applications have to be running at the same time. All these alternatives import the outlines as shapes into your Painter file, but pasting through the clipboard is fairly fast and always reliable. To do this, select the outlines in Illustrator and copy,

2b

The Floater Adjuster tool changes to an arrow cursor when scaling the panther shapes to fit the template.

3

The named selections in the Mask List

4

Cloning texture into the membrane selection

5

Airbrushing highlights on the panther

6

Applying the shadow

then switch to Painter and paste. To drag and drop, select the outlines in Illustrator and drag them into an open Painter file window. You'll see a closed group of shapes appear in the Floater List palette. Move the shape group into position on the template using the Floater Adjuster tool or the arrow keys on your keyboard. To scale shapes proportionally, choose the Floater Adjuster tool, hold down the Shift key and drag on a corner handle.

3 Converting, saving and naming. If you have a complex graphic with overlapping shapes, you may want to ungroup the shapes before converting them to selections. This will enable you to save each selection as a user mask in the Mask List that can be used individually, or added to or subtracted from using the other selections. To ungroup, click the Ungroup button on the expanded Floater List palette. To convert shape to a selection so that you can paint or fill it, select a shape in the Floater List and choose Shapes, Convert to Selection. The selection will disappear from the Floater List and will become an active marquee on the image canvas. Store the active selection in the Mask List as a user mask by choosing Select, Save Selection. To name it, double-click on its current name. Type a name for the mask in the Mask Attributes dialog box and click OK. Click the RGB-Canvas in the Mask List to see the image again.

4 Filling selections. Dismukes created texture within the membrane selection using a Cloning brush and a modified paper texture from a second document. He filled the large globe with a maroon gradient and the small globe with a green gradient.

5 Airbrushing. Dismukes's template showed good shadow and highlight detail. Using it as a guide, he began by laying down dark colors, gradually building forward to the white highlights. He used the Airbrush, Feather Tip variant, adjusting only the Size and ± Size in the Brush Controls:Size palette, found in the Control, Size menu on the Brushes palette.

6 Floating a shadow. Dismukes used a floater to create the panther's drop shadow on the maroon globe. Use the Create Drop Shadow command to do this: Load the selection by choosing Select, Load Selection. To load more than one user mask at a time as a single selection, load the first selection, then choose Select, Load Selection again and in the Load From menu, choose a second selection and Add To Selection. Continue to Load and Add to your selection until you have all of the elements active. Store this complex selection as a new user mask by choosing Select, Save Selection.

Float the new selection by clicking on it in your image with the Floater Adjuster tool. Choose Effects, Objects, Create Drop Shadow. Use the default settings or experiment with other settings, then click OK to create the shadow.

As a final touch, Dismukes opened the image in Adobe Photoshop and applied the Lens Flare filter to the green globe. The 40 MB logo was output as a 4 x 5-inch color transparency at 762 ppi. 🐾

Working with Freehand Selections

Overview *Open a scanned drawing as a template; select areas of the image using the Lasso; use selections to constrain brushstrokes, fills and effects.*

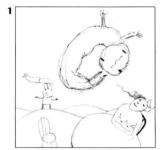

The original pencil sketch

An active selection around the girl and hills

Adding to a selected area

Subtracting from a selected area

Painting within a selection

TO ISOLATE AREAS FOR PAINTING, FILLING AND LIGHTING effects in the whimsical *Ægypt*, artist Steve Campbell used the Lasso tool. He painted and applied special effects within each selection, then he unified the piece by applying effects across the entire image.

1 Sketching and scanning. Campbell started with a pencil sketch, which he scanned and opened in Painter.

2 Creating selections. Select the Lasso tool, and in your image, drag carefully around the area you want to select, dragging the Lasso precisely to the origin point. You may find it helpful to zoom in on your image while making detailed freehand selections: Click with the Magnifier tool to zoom in, press Option/Alt and click to zoom out.

Painter 5's Lasso tool lets you add to or subtract from the currently *active selection*. To add to the currently selected area, hold down the Shift key and drag with the Lasso to reshape an area of the border to increase the selection. To subtract from the currently selected area, hold down the Command/Control key and drag with the Lasso tool.

Saving the completed selection as a user mask will store it permanently with your image in the Objects:Mask List. To save a selection, choose Select, Save Selection, or click the Save Selection button on the expanded Mask List palette. Campbell created selections for every object in the drawing.

3b

Painting brushstrokes using clone color

4

Adding lighting and texture to the sky

5a

Painting details within the face selection

5b

Adding paper grain texture to the face

5c

Applying lighting to the tumbler's back

3 Painting inside selections.
To paint within a selection, first make it active: Choose Select, Load Selection (or click the Load Selection button on the expanded Mask List). Campbell loaded individual selections and used the Simple Water variant of the Water Color brush to lay in color washes within each selection.

To begin painting the graduated sky, Campbell made a clone of the underpainting file (File, Clone), and filled the clone with the Night Sky gradation from the default Painter Grad library (Effects, Fill, Gradation, with an angle of 90° in the Grad palette). Then he selected the underpainting file and designated the filled clone as the clone source (File, Clone Source). In the underpainting file, he loaded the sky selection. He chose the Loaded Oils variant of the Brush and changed it into a cloning brush by switching its method to Cloning. To sample color from the graduated image—while painting in the destination file—he checked the Clone Color checkbox on the Color palette. Using the new Loaded Oils "cloner," he painted angled and curved strokes into the sky selection.

4 Adding effects to the sky. To add a graduated golden tint within the sky selection, Campbell used Effects, Surface Control, Apply Lighting (using a custom version of the Splashy Colors light), then he used Surface Texture to build up "thick paint." To give your image realistic "thick paint" highlights and shadows based on dark and light values in the brushstrokes, choose Effects, Surface Control, Apply Surface Texture, using Image Luminance.

5 Finalizing the image. To paint the central figure's face, Campbell used the Artist Pastel Chalk variant (on top of Basic Paper texture) to paint soft shading within the face selection, then he blended areas using the Just Add Water variant of the Water brush.

After painting the face, he changed its appearance dramatically by applying custom colored lighting and a paper grain effect within the active selection. To apply lighting within a selection, load a selection (Select, Load Selection) and choose Effects, Surface Control, Apply Lighting. Set up a light, and click OK. Campbell used similar procedures to add rich textures and complexity to other elements in the image—including the foreground, the table and the tumbling figures on the horizon.

To apply a paper texture within a selection, load the selection, and choose Effects, Surface Control, Apply Surface Texture using Paper. If you want, you can choose a different paper texture from the Papers palette with this dialog box still open.

Finally, to further unify the image, Campbell applied Surface Texture using Image Luminance to the entire image—this time using very low settings—moving the Amount slider to approximately 20 to 30%, and the Shine slider to about 20%. 🖌

A LASSO WITH A CLUE

As a reminder of how the existing selection will be edited, a plus sign (Shift key) or minus sign (Command key) appears next to the Lasso.

Using Color Mask

Overview *Use Color Mask and Masking brushes to mask an area of an image; convert the mask to a selection; use Adjust Color to shift the color of the selected area.*

1a

The original photo

1b

The default Color Mask dialog box

1c

Adjusting the sliders to isolate the leaf

2a

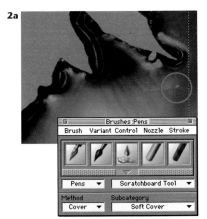

Using the Scratchboard Tool and white paint to erase an area of the mask

COLOR MASK IS ONE OF PAINTER'S most powerful features, letting you create a mask based on a specific color in an image. In the example above, we used a combination of Color Mask and editing with brushes to create masks for individual leaves. We saved the masks in the Mask List, then used Adjust Color to change the hue and saturation of the individual leaves and the background.

1 Sampling color and adjusting the mask. Open and image an open the Objects:Mask List palette and from the Mask pull-down menu choose Color Mask. When the dialog box appears, click in your image (*not* in the preview window) on the color you want to sample (the "center color"); the arrow will momentarily turn into a dropper as you do this. We selected a color on the tan leaf in the center of the image. To narrow the range of selected colors, drag the H (Hue) Extents slider to the left (we set ours to 10%). Press and drag to scroll the image in the Preview window so you can see how your settings are affecting other parts of the image within the marquee. Experiment with the S (Saturation) and V (Value) Extents sliders; we got the best results when we reduced the V Extents to 30% to isolate the leaf from darker tan colors in the background water. You may also want to adjust the three Feather sliders to create harder transitions in your mask. When you're satisfied with the preview of your mask, click OK. Painter will generate a mask based on the sampled color. The mask will automatically appear in the Mask List.

2 Cleaning up the mask. To view the mask as a red-tinted overlay on top of the image canvas, in the Mask List palette click the mask's name to select it, and open its eye icon. (Make sure the RGB-Canvas eye icon is also open.) To edit the mask, choose any brush from the Brushes palette; we used the Pens, Scratchboard Tool variant because it allowed us to paint smooth opaque "paint." Choose black and paint on the mask to add to your mask; paint with white to remove portions of the mask. The interior of your mask must be opaque to completely cover your subject, so unless you want some degree of transparency, use the brush to paint over any thin spots.

2b

Using the Scratchboard Tool to erase the mask from an overlapping leaf. The mask is viewed at a reduced opacity, making both the mask and the image beneath it visible.

2c

The finished mask of the center leaf viewed at 100% opacity

2d

Replacing the original mask

3

Adjusting color within the center leaf selection

You'll need to view the mask at full opacity to identify areas where coverage is not complete. To adjust the opacity of the mask overlay, display the Mask Options dialog box by double-clicking the mask name in the Mask List. Move the Opacity slider to 100%. The Opacity slider has no effect on the actual density of the mask, it is for viewing only.

As a final check for your mask, turn the mask into a selection by choosing Select, Load Selection. You can use the Lasso to select any areas that you'd like to add to the selection: Press the Shift key, then use the Lasso to draw around the area you want to add. To remove an area of the selection, hold down the Command key and use the Lasso to draw around the area. If you use this method, make sure you replace the original mask in the Mask List with the edited one: Choose Select, Save Selection, in the Save To menu choose the mask name and select the Replace Mask button.

3 Colorizing with Adjust Color. To make changes to the color within a selection, begin by loading a selection (Select, Load Selection). With the selection active, choose Effects, Tonal Control, Adjust Colors. Use this feature to change the hue, saturation or brightness in the selected area. If you prefer more radical changes, you can also paint within your selection or apply any of the commands under the Effects menu. To view your image without the mask, click the mask eye icon shut and target the RGB-Canvas by clicking on its name in the Floater List.

CLEANING UP MASKS WITH BRIGHTNESS AND CONTRAST

Here's a useful method for cleaning up masks that can save lots of time and effort. Open an image and make a mask using Color Mask. Click in the image to sample the color you need to mask. In the dialog box, adjust the H (Hue), V (Value) and S (Saturation) Extents sliders to create the best mask you can. To select the mask so you can view it in black-and-white, paint directly on it or manipulate it using commands under the Effects menu, click on the mask name in the Mask List palette. Now, click the RGB-Canvas eye icon closed. With the mask selected, we used a brush and white paint to touch up the mask of the bird. When we finished the bird, we were left with many tones of gray in the water area of the mask (below left). We used Effects, Tonal Control, Brightness/Contrast, to bump up the contrast and make the variegated water areas solid black (below right).

Adjusting settings in the Brightness/Contrast dialog box

The mask before (left) and after (right) adjusting Brightness/Contrast.

Isolating Color with Auto Mask

***Overview** Use Auto Mask to generate a mask based on a selected color; load the mask as a selection; fill the selection with a color.*

The black-and-white comp

Choosing Auto Mask from the Mask List

Viewing the new current color mask

PAINTER'S AUTO MASK FEATURE IS A QUICK WAY to isolate an area of an image; once the mask has been created, you can load the mask as a selection and fill the area with color or paint into it. Susan LeVan of LeVan/Barbee Studio did both while creating a series of three collectible phone cards for AT&T commemorating the 1996 Olympics in Atlanta. (The first two images of the triptych are shown above, the third is at the end of this story). She used Auto Mask's Current Color setting to create jaggy white "halos" around the background scratch marks, giving her piece texture, lightness and air.

1 Beginning with black and white. Because it's often easier to resolve a design without the added complexity of color and texture, LeVan built the initial sketches using only black and white. She opened a new document with a white paper color and chose Basic Paper from the Paper palette. She used variants of the Chalk brush to sketch the basic shapes of the image in black, gray and white and added linear details using the Scratchboard Tool variant of the Pens brush. As an added bonus of this technique, LeVan/Barbee

3

The Mask List showing the mask name

3a

Choosing Replace Selection in the Load Selection dialog box

3b

Preparing to fill an active selection behind the woman's shoulder

4

Filling the selection with golden yellow, the Current Color

already had black-and-white art on hand for cleaner faxing when the art director requested the sketches be faxed.

2 Generating and viewing a mask. To create a mask that would allow her to fill areas in her image based on a specific color, LeVan used Auto Mask's Current Color option. To do this, first sample a color from your image with the Dropper tool, making that color your Current Color. (LeVan clicked the Dropper on a gray area in her image.) To generate the mask, open the Objects palette, and from the Mask menu choose Auto Mask (or press Command-Shift-M), using Current Color and click OK. In your image, you'll see all instances of the current color masked in orange. The mask name, by default, New Mask 1, will appear in the Mask List.

Since Auto Mask using Current Color lacks the feathering capabilities of Painter's Color Mask (see "Using Color Mask," earlier in this chapter), you'll notice rough, aliased areas around the unselected portions of your image. LeVan likes the white "halos" that result when she uses Auto Mask for color fills because they accentuate the texture on the background.

3 Viewing the mask as a selection. If you want to apply an effect to the image canvas using a mask, or fill it with a color, load an active selection from the mask: Select the mask name in the Mask list, and choose Select, Load Selection (or click the Load Selection button on the expanded Mask List palette), and choose the Replace Selection button. To view RGB canvas and the active selection without the orange mask, click the eye icon to the left of the mask name shut.

4 Filling the selection. To fill the selected area of the image canvas with a color, first choose RGB-Canvas in the Mask List to target the image canvas. Choose a color in the Color palette. Then choose Effects, Fill, and when the dialog box appears, click the Current Color button and OK. The color you've chosen will fill the selected area. 🖐

The completed third image of the triptych

■ For an interactive children's book commissioned by Josten's Learning, **Beth Shipper** started *Castle* (left) with a tight line sketch, then colorized the image using Water Color brush variants. She used the Lasso tool to isolate areas and applied various textures using Effects, Surface Control, Apply Surface Texture. To add a sense of depth to the image, she scaled up textures to use in the foreground and scaled them down for use in the background (using the Scaler slider on the Paper palette). Shipper increased contrast in her image (using Effects, Tonal Control, Brightness and Contrast) and emphasized the texture using the Dodge and Burn brushes and the Ultrafine Bleach variant of the Eraser brush. Finally, she activated specific selections again (Select, Load Selection), and applied low-opacity Airbrush strokes in saturated hues, taking care not to cover the texture.

■ **John Fretz** began *Man at Crossroads* (below), an illustration commissioned for an investment brochure, on conventional black-and-white scratchboard using a very fine croquill pen for the hatching and line work. He scanned the scratchboard art, opened it in Painter and used the Pen tool to make curved and straight line selections on the scan. Using a low-opacity Fat Stroke Airbrush, Fretz painted colored tints into the selections. He used the Scratchboard Rake variant of the Pens brush in various sizes to add color and texture to the image and to weave the traditional scratchboard pen work smoothly into the digital illustration.

■ Although **Sharon Steuer** still works with traditional oils on canvas, she has used the computer as her primary illustration tool since 1984 because of its unlimited editing capabilities. *Eagle and Chick* (left) is one of a series of wildlife illustrations that Steuer created for a book proposal for the Smithsonian Institution. Starting in Macromedia Freehand, she drew the shapes that make up the larger eagle using the variable stroke Freehand tool and filled the shapes with colored gradients, then rasterized the file by opening it in Photoshop, where she roughed in the rest of the composition. Steuer opened the file in Painter and applied lighting effects (using Effects, Surface Control, Apply Lighting) to the eagle. She painted masks (which she later loaded as selections) for the sky, the water, the hills and the foreground grass. She worked within individual selections, applying lighting effects and painting with several Brush and Airbrush variants to add detail and create a dramatic, sculptural look.

■ **James D'Avanzo** created *Deep Love* (left) using saturated, complementary colors to help communicate the powerful healing of love. To create the background, he used the Lasso, then feathered and painted into the selection to create the illusion of a horizon. He used the same technique for the hand and figure. D'Avanzo worked from background to foreground, painting into the selections with low-opacity Thin Stroke and Fat Stroke Airbrush variants.

■ To create *Beatles*, an illustration for a two-page spread in *Live!* magazine (top), **Susan LeVan** used the Pen and Ink variant of the Pens brush to sketch loose black-and-white portraits of the Beatles in four separate source files. She copied the drawings and pasted them into a large image file with an orange-tan background color, then she flattened the image by clicking the Drop button on the Floater List. LeVan made rough-edged masks for areas of the image with Auto Mask Using Current Color. (Open the Objects:Mask List menu and choose Mask, Auto Mask, using Current Color.) She loaded each rough-edged selection (Select, Load Selection), and with RGB-Canvas selected in the Mask List, filled it with color using the Effects, Fill, With Current Color command or she added colored brushstrokes. For instance, LeVan selected a white area on the left side of George's face and used the Square Chalk variant of the Chalk brush and a green color to draw loose, textured strokes within the selection. She added final details with the Fat Stroke Airbrush variant, Pen and Ink and Square Chalk brushes.

■ **Susan LeVan** began the cover illustration for *Outlook Magazine* (left), by drawing in Painter using the Default Crayons variant over a rough paper texture. Then, she made a mask for the line work. From the Objects:Mask List menu she chose Mask, Auto Mask, using Current Color. She also made masks for areas of the man's face and shirt. Working with the RGB-Canvas chosen in the Mask List, she loaded individual selections from the masks and filled them with color. She made a current color selection for the background and filled it with an orange color which left white "halos" around the existing color. LeVan built the symbols for the head top in a separate file, copied them, and pasted them into her image. Then she added a drop shadow to each one using the Effects, Objects, Create Drop Shadow command.

■ To create *Swami's* (right), **Mary Envall** began by scanning a pencil sketch, and importing it into Painter. Using the Pen tool and Lasso she made selections for nearly every element in the illustration and saved them as user masks in the Mask List. Working within one selection at a time, she used the Felt Pens variant of the Marker brush to paint soft, luminescent color. To add activity to the color, she varied the opacity of the Felt Pens using the Opacity slider on the Controls:Brush palette. She also used Effects, Tonal Control, Brightness/Contrast to make subtle color adjustments within selections on the domes and on the front of the building. To finish, she blended areas using the Just Add Water variant of the Water brush.

■ **Cher Threinen-Pendarvis** began *Mendocino Point* (below), with a pencil-and-paper sketch made on location. She scanned the sketch, opened it in Painter, and using the Smaller Wash Brush variant of the Brush, painted washes of color onto the sketch. Then she used the Lasso to make selections of the major elements—the landscape, ocean and sky—on the underpainting. To speed up the compositional process, she used the selections to isolate areas of the composition while previewing variations in color. For instance, she loaded the "ocean" selection and used Effects, Tonal Control, Adjust Color to increase the Saturation, deepening the blue in the water. She also loaded a selection of the distant coastline, and used Adjust Color to lower its saturation. She used a custom Soft Oil brush to paint small strokes over the entire image, to blend the color adjustments into the image and to modulate the color. To finish, she sharpened details with a smaller version of the Soft Oil brush.

■ **John Fretz** began *Doctor's Game* (above), an illustration commissioned for Physician's Insurance Company's annual report, on conventional black-and-white scratchboard using a very fine croquill pen for the hatching and line work. He scanned the scratchboard art, opened it in Painter and used the Pen tool to make curved and straight-line selections on the scan. Using a low-opacity Fat Stroke Airbrush, Fretz painted colored tints into the selections. He used the Scratchboard Rake variant of the Pens brush in various sizes to add color and texture to the image and to weave the traditional scratchboard pen work smoothly into the digital illustration.

■ To create *Airbrush Head* (left), a self-promotional illustration, **Nancy Stahl** began by importing EPS outlines of the woman and background from Adobe Illustrator into Painter. She resized the outlines to fill her image, then she used the Mountains texture from the Texture Sampler library (found in Papers, in the Free Stuff folder on the Painter 5 CD-ROM), and chose the Fat Stroke Airbrush, Grainy Soft Cover submethod. Working with one selection at a time, she used various sizes and opacities of the Airbrush to fill each selection with soft, textured color.

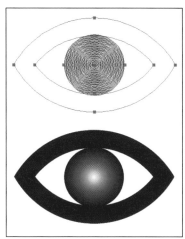

Viewing shape paths (top) and finished objects (bottom). For this filled compound outer object with blended interior object, we began by making a blend. To blend the interior blue circle with a very small white circle in its center, we selected both circles, then chose Shapes, Blend and specified 50 steps. To build the compound of the two outer shapes, we selected them both with the Whole Shape Selection tool and chose Shapes, Make Compound. (Choose the Direct Selection tool and press the Command key to switch to Whole Shape Selection mode.) The compound cut a hole with the smaller eye shape, allowing only the outer fill to be visible.

SHAPES OF A CURRENT COLOR

To automatically fill or stroke a shape with the Current Color chosen in the Color palette as you draw it, set up your Shape preferences: Choose Edit, Preferences, Shapes, check the appropriate checkboxes and click OK.

Setting up the Shape Preferences to automatically fill with the Current Color

shape—rather than simply changing its stroke and fill—it will be automatically converted into an image floater. When this happens, shape attributes (such as resolution independence, stroke and fill) are lost.

Blending between shapes. To blend between two shapes, select both shapes with the Floater Adjuster and choose Shapes, Blend. Make choices in the dialog box and click OK. The *Painter 5 User Guide* contains a complete explanation of the Blend dialog box.

Here's a useful application for Painter 5's Blend command: If you've imported an image created in Illustrator that has blends and they don't make the transition successfully into Painter, zoom in and delete the interior objects inside the blend using the Direct Selection tool and Delete key. Shift-select the two outside objects using the Floater Adjuster, choose Shapes, Blend and specify the number of steps to regenerate the blend.

Making a compound. To cut a hole in a shape and reveal the underlying image, make a compound using two shapes: Place a small shape on top of a large one, select both of them, and choose Shapes, Make Compound. The top shape will cut a hole in the bottom shape to reveal the underlying image. Compounds are made automatically to create counters in letters when the type is set or type outlines are imported.

Applying automatic drop shadows. Selecting a closed group of shapes and choosing Effects, Objects, Create Drop Shadow will apply an automatic drop shadow to each of the individual shapes in the group and will convert the shapes to image floaters as well!

USING DYNAMIC PLUG-IN FLOATERS

Dynamic plug-in floaters are special devices that allow you to create a variety of effects. To keep a plug-in floater dynamic (allowing changes to be made and previewed on the image without becoming permanent), the file must be saved in RIFF format. Saving in Photoshop format preserves the dynamic plug-in floaters as layers, but the effects will be frozen and the floaters' dynamic plug-in capabilities will be permanently lost.

Plug-in floaters fall into three basic categories. The first kind is similar to a lens or an adjustment layer in Adobe Photoshop. It allows you to set up a procedure such as a brightness and contrast correction or a posterization of the underlying image, without changing your image surface. Image correction tools such as

A HIDDEN RASTERIZER

You can rasterize Postscript art from Illustrator in Painter. Choose File, Acquire, Adobe Illustrator File. Select the shapes and convert them to floaters using Shapes, Convert To Floater. To flatten the image and make a selection, select each floater by choosing its name in the Floater List and use the Drop and Select command in the Floater List palette menu. And a bonus: If you'd like to store a selection for use later, choose Select, Save Selection to save it as a user mask in the Mask List.

Detail from Hot Beveled Metal. *Beginning with type shapes, we used the Bevel World dynamic plug-in floater to create a 3D type effect. Then we layered two more copies of the bevel—we painted on the first copy and we created the glow using the second copy. To read how to build the look step-by-step, turn to "Creating Hot Beveled Metal," in Chapter 7, "Exploring Special Effects."*

PHOTO: DIGITAL STOCK

Cool Water Drops. *To add a water droplet effect to this photo (simulating water drops on a camera lens), we used the Liquid Metal plug-in floater. First we made a clone of the image (File, Clone). In the Objects:Plug-in Floater palette we chose Liquid Metal and clicked Apply, using the Clone Source Map type and a high Refraction setting to make the "water" translucent with a blue reflection. We used the Circle tool to place the drops.*

Equalize, Brightness and Contrast and Posterize and special effects floaters such as Glass Distortion, Kaleidoscope and Liquid Lens fall into this category. To generate a "lens type" plug-in floater (such as a Posterize floater), open the Objects:P. Float palette, choose Posterize from the pop-up menu and click the Apply button. (To read more about Painter 5's image-correction plug-in floaters, turn to Chapter 6. For more information about creating special effects with this series of plug-in floaters, turn to Chapter 7.)

The second kind of plug-in floater applies procedures to a selected floater, the "source image floater." Because of the plug-in's dynamic capability, you can preview changes and then return the source image floater to its original condition if you like. Bevel World, Burn and Tear plug-in floaters require a source image floater to perform their magic. To make this kind of plug-in floater, select an area of your image with *any* selection tool, or select a floater in the Objects:Floater List, and choose Bevel World, for instance, from the pop-up menu on the Objects:P. Float palette, then click Apply. (If you make a selection on the image canvas, the plug-in will automatically generate a dynamic floater from the selection.) Read more about these plug-in floaters in Chapter 7.

The third type of plug-in allows you to build entirely new imagery. Impasto and Liquid Metal fall into this category. To read about techniques using Impasto turn to the introduction of Chapter 3 and to "Advanced Painting With Impasto," also in Chapter 3. Liquid Metal is covered in Chapter 7, "Exploring Special Effects."

To change a dynamic plug-in floater's options, begin by opening the Objects:Floater List palette, and select the dynamic plug-in floater by clicking on its name in the Floater List. From the P.Float palette menu choose Options to open the Options dialog box for the selected floater. Make changes in the dialog box and click OK.

To convert a plug-in floater to an image floater, so you can edit the floater's mask, or convert it into a reference floater (to scale it using Free Transform, for instance), from the Objects:Plug In Floaters palette menu, choose P. Float, Commit. The following actions will automatically convert a plug-in floater to an image floater: Transforming using Effects, Orientation (to scale, rotate or skew), applying an effect from the Effects menu (such as Effects, Surface Control, Apply Surface Texture); painting on a plug-in floater (with the exception of Impasto); applying one plug-in floater to another plug-in floater (such as applying the Tear plug-in to an active Burn plug-in floater); or collapsing a group that includes a plug-in floater.

Detail from Floating Still Life, *painted by John Derry, who achieves the look of 3D paint on layers of glass by turning a transparent layer into an Impasto plug-in floater*

To paint with both "impasto and transparency," begin by opening a new document and adding a transparent layer that covers the entire image (from the Objects:Floater List palette menu, choose Transparent Layer.) Now, for the Impasto effect: Switch to the Objects:Plug-in Floater palette and choose Impasto from the pop-up plug-in floater list. Click the Apply button to apply the Impasto plug-in to the transparent layer.) Load the Impasto brush library (from the bottom of the Brush list on the Brushes palette choose Load Library and navigate to the Extra Art Materials folder). Choose a brush (Derry used the Big Thick Impasto variant), and change its method to Plug-in and submethod to Transparent Layer Brush. Now, paint some strokes—and like magic, the textured paint stokes appear. When finished painting, choose P. Float, Commit to convert the plug-in floater back to a transparent layer. To create the look of painting on glass, use several layers and apply a drop shadow to each layer (as Derry did), allowing each brushstroke to cast its own shadow. The Effects, Objects, Create Drop Shadow command will base the new shadow floater on the transparent layer selected in the Objects:Floater List when generating a second transparent floater for the shadow.

To select and move a locked item or group, click on its name in the Floater List, then move it using the arrow keys on your key board. (See "Organizing with the Floater List" for information about locking and unlocking floaters and shapes.)

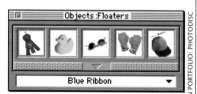

Create an empty Floaters palette by opening the Objects:Floater List and choosing Floater Mover from the pull-down menu. You can fill the portfolio with floaters while you're in the Floater Mover, as follows: Open the portfolio by choosing the Objects:Floater List palette, Floater menu, Floater Portfolio (or by typing Command-7). Drag floaters from your image directly into the portfolio, or drag floaters out of the Floaters Portfolio into another image.

IMAGES IN PORTFOLIO: PHOTODISC

ORGANIZING WITH THE FLOATER LIST

In the Floater List palette, Painter assigns sequential names to floaters and shapes (such as Floater 1, Floater 2 and so on) in the order they were created. **Rename** them by double-clicking on a name (or select the name and press the Enter key) to bring up the appropriate Attributes dialog box. Enter the name and click OK. **Grouping** floaters is an ideal way of connecting related elements—for instance, grouping a floating image and its drop shadow. To group floaters or shapes, Shift-select the elements in the Floater List and click the Group button or press Command-G. To **ungroup**, click the Ungroup button or press Command-U. If you want to apply effects (other than Scale and Create Drop Shadow) to a group of floaters or shapes, you'll need to open the group, select individual items, then apply the effect. You can **hide** floaters or shapes by clicking to close the eye icons next to their names, so that you can more easily work with underlying items. Click the eye open to **show** an item again. To **lock** an item or group (keeping it from being selected in the image window), click the lock icon to the left of its item name in the Floater List. To **unlock**, click to toggle it open. For the ultimate in floater management, see how Rick Kirkman did it in "Working With Shapes and Floaters," on page 130.

Using the Floater Portfolio. Open the Floater Portfolio by opening the Objects:Floater List and choosing Floater Portfolio from the Floater menu (or type Command-7). To remove floaters from your image, but store them for later use or for use in another document, use the Floater Adjuster tool to drag them into the Floater Portfolio palette. Hold down the Option key if you want to leave a copy of the floater in your document.

We made a luminosity mask in the cloud image source file and imported it as a reference floater with its mask into the image with the type, creating semi-transparent clouds over the letters.

USING WHITE TO ERASE

A good analogy to help you remember whether to use black or white when painting on a floater visibility mask (or any other mask), is to think of using white as an eraser on the mask and black as applying paint to the mask. To actually view and edit a floater mask in black-and-white, select the floater and open the floater mask eye icon in the Floater List.

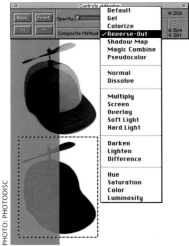

PHOTO: PHOTODISC

We applied two of Painter's Composite Methods to these beanies floating over a blue and white background. The top beanie uses Gel and the bottom one uses Reverse-Out.

FLOATERS AND THEIR MASKS

Just as the background canvas uses 8-bit background masks (see Chapter 4's introduction), each floater also has an 8-bit mask—the visibility mask—that allows for transparent effects. You can also add custom masks directly on a floater, using either brushes or automatic mask-generating commands (from the Objects:Mask List palette menu choose Mask, Auto Mask or Color Mask). View a mask on a selected floater by selecting it in the Mask List and opening its eye icon. For more information turn to "Floater Mask Visibility" on the following page.

Importing a reference floater with its mask. Because it's faster to work with small files than to manipulate large files, many artists assemble source files, then import them into a final composite file. Consider preparing a mask in a smaller source file that you plan to import as a reference floater (using File, Place). In the Place dialog box, check the Retain Mask checkbox, and click OK to place the reference floater in your document.

A VERSATILE MASK EXCHANGE

If you've made a mask for a floater and want to use it on another floater or on the background canvas, here's a way to trade masks back and forth. To copy a user mask and turn the copy into a floater visibility mask, begin by selecting the floater in the Floater List. Switch to the Mask List and select the user mask you want. From the Mask List palette menu choose Copy Mask. In the Copy Mask dialog box menu select the floater visibility mask as the destination and click OK. This action replaces the original floater visibility mask you selected with the user mask. To copy a floater visibility mask to a user mask in the Mask List, select the floater, switch to the Mask List and select the floater visibility mask. Choose Copy Mask from the Mask List palette menu. This time choose "New" to create a new mask for the image canvas based on the floater mask, or select an existing user mask you want to replace from the menu as the destination and click OK.

DROPPING AND SAVING A FLOATER VISIBILITY MASK

If you want to drop a floater and its visibility mask so it becomes part of the image canvas, choose Drop and Select from the Floater List palette menu. The selection will be temporary, and will be lost unless you save it as a user mask. To save the selection as a user mask in the Mask List, choose Select, Save Selection.

COMPOSITE CONTROLS

Painter's composite controls can give you nifty special effects with very little effort. With a floater and the Floater Adjuster tool selected, choose from the Composite Method pop-up menu in the Controls:Adjuster palette. The scrolling list includes many of Photoshop's blending modes (except Color Dodge, Color Burn and Exclusion) underneath Painter's native ones. "A Visual Display of the Compositing Methods" on the next page shows the Composite Methods in action. For more about using Photoshop and Painter together see Chapter 8, "Using Painter With Photoshop." ⅏

FLOATER MASK VISIBILITY

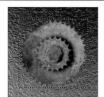

Floater Visibility Mask: ○ Disabled ● Normal ○ Inverted

Floater Visibility Mask: ○ Disabled ○ Normal ● Inverted

Floater Visibility Mask: ● Disabled ○ Normal ○ Inverted

You can use controls in the Floater Attributes box to determine which part of a floater is masked. To see how they work, press Command-7 to open the Floater Portfolio and drag a floater onto a colored background. In the Floater List double-click on the name of the floater to open its Floater Attributes box. Since the floaters in the Floater Portfolio have had masks already created for them, in the Floater Attributes dialog box the Normal button should be chosen, meaning that everything in the floater outside of the mask is invisible. To reverse the effect, click the Inverted button and click OK. Now the masked area will be invisible and the surrounding area will be visible. Clicking on the Disabled button in the Floater Attributes box will show both areas. Keep in mind that these modes affect visibility only; any painting or effect applied to the floater will be applied to the entire floater, not just the visible areas.

FLOATER AND SELECTION INTERACTION

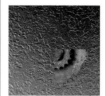

Selection Interaction: ● None ○ Selection Reveals Floater ○ Selection Conceals Floater

Selection Interaction: ○ None ● Selection Reveals Floater ○ Selection Conceals Floater

Selection Interaction: ○ None ○ Selection Reveals Floater ● Selection Conceals Floater

Floaters and selections can interact. To see how this works, start with any image in the background and make a selection on the image canvas using the Rectangular Selection tool. Press Command-7 to open the Floater Portfolio. Now drag a floater from the Floater Portfolio into your image. In the Objects:Floater List, double-click on the floater name to access the Floater Attributes dialog box. The default choice for Selection Interaction is None (the selection has no effect on the floater). Choose Selection Reveals Floater and click OK to display only the portion of the floater within the selection. Choose Selection Conceals Floater and click OK to display only the portion of the floater outside the selection. Any selection saved into the Mask List can be loaded (using Select, Load Selection) and used to operate on a floater if the Floater Attributes is set up for interaction.

A VISUAL DISPLAY OF THE COMPOSITE METHODS

Painter's Composite Methods (from the Controls:Adjuster palette, with the Floater Adjuster selected) change how a floater interacts with the image underneath. Here a leaf floats over a two-part background. The Default and Normal methods give the same results, as do Shadow Map and Multiply. For complete descriptions of what the modes are doing, refer to Painter's *User Guide, The Photoshop 4 Wow! Book* or Photoshop's *User Guide.*

Default / Normal

Gel

Colorize

Reverse-out

Shadow Map / Multiply

Magic Combine

Pseudocolor

Dissolve

Screen

Overlay

Soft Light

Hard Light

Darken

Lighten

Difference

Hue

Saturation

Color

Luminosity

Dropping a Shadow

Overview *Convert a shape to a floater and fill the floater; make the shadow by copying the floater, filling the copy, feathering it and reducing its opacity.*

CHER THREINEN-PENDARVIS

Background modified with Apply Surface Texture and Apply Lighting

Converting the pasted shapes into a floater

Filling the fish floater with a color

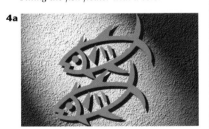

Filling the shadow floater

Selecting the floater shadow mask in the Mask List prior to feathering the mask

THERE ARE A NUMBER OF WAYS to create a drop shadow in Painter. Here's one that uses floaters, feathering and transparency.

1 Preparing a background. Create a new document: Ours was 788 pixels wide with a tan Paper Color. To add a "cave wall" appearance, in the Art Materials:Paper palette choose Sandier paper from the Drawing Papers library (located in the Extra Art Materials folder). Select Effects, Surface Control, Apply Surface Texture using Paper, and experiment with the settings until you get a look that you like in the Preview. Click OK. To create a spotlight effect, choose Effects, Surface Control, Apply Lighting. Choose Slide Lighting, lower the Distance and Spread settings, increase the Brightness and click OK.

2 Importing and converting. You can float any active selection or convert any shape to a floater. For this image, we imported fish drawn in Adobe Illustrator. With both Illustrator 6 and Painter 5 running, we copied the fish from Illustrator to the clipboard and pasted them into the cave wall image in Painter. Objects that have holes cut in them in Illustrator, such as the openings in the fish, or letters such as "O" or "A" converted to outlines, will import into Painter as compound shapes. Select the shape with the Floater Adjuster tool and choose Shapes, Convert To Floater.

3 Filling the floater. To apply a fill to the floater, choose a color from the Art Materials:Color palette, then select Effects, Fill, Current Color (100% Opacity) and click OK.

4 Creating the shadow. Use the Floater Adjuster tool to duplicate the floater to use for the shadow: Hold down the Option key, drag on the floater, and release when the copy is slightly offset from the original. In the Floater List, double-click on the copy's name and rename it "shadow"; then drag its name below the original floater's name. Fill the shadow as you did in step 3, using black or a dark color sampled from the background image. To soften the shadow's edge by feathering it (with the floater still selected), switch to the Objects:Mask List palette and select the mask for the shadow floater. From the Mask menu choose Feather Mask and set the radius for the feather. Finally, to make the shadow more transparent, select the RGB-Canvas for the floater and lower the Opacity in the Controls:Adjuster palette.

Working with Shapes and Floaters

Overview *Draw Bézier shape paths in Painter; fill and name the shapes; convert the shapes to floaters; paint details on the floaters with brushes; apply textured special effects with Color Overlay and Glass Distortion.*

RICK KIRKMAN

1

Kirkman's pencil sketch

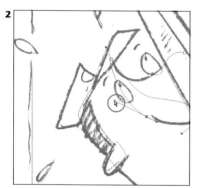

2

Dragging with the Direct Selection tool to adjust a control handle on a path

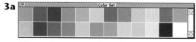

3a

The custom magazine color set

SHAPES BRING NEW POWER to Painter, saving many illustrators a trip to a draw program to create Bézier paths for import. With the expanded Pen tool (now similar to Illustrator's) you can completely create and edit Bézier paths, add a stroke and fill, name them, and organize them in the Floater List. After you draw shapes, you can convert them to floaters and add paint and special effects. Rick Kirkman created the illustration above—one in a series of editorial illustrations for the "Ideas That Work" column in *Professional Speaker* magazine—entirely within Painter.

1 Setting up a template. Kirkman began by scanning a pencil sketch, saving it as a TIFF file and opening the scan in Painter.

2 Creating shape paths. To create your outlines, you can work either in Painter or in a Postscript drawing program. If you plan to trace a template—as Kirkman did—set up shape attributes so that you can draw with a precise skeletal line. Choose Shapes, Set Shape Attributes and uncheck the Fill and Stroke checkboxes. Using the Pen tool to carefully draw Bézier shape paths, Kirkman traced his sketch. To make adjustments on the fly while drawing a path with the Pen tool (like adjusting a control handle or anchor point), press the Command key to temporarily switch to the Direct Selection tool. To easily select an entire path, choose the Direct Selection tool, press the Command key to temporarily switch to the Whole Shape Selection tool and click the path.

3 Coloring, naming and converting. Kirkman built a Color Set containing favorite basic colors for the series of magazine illustrations. (Read more about color sets in Chapter 2.) To name and

3b

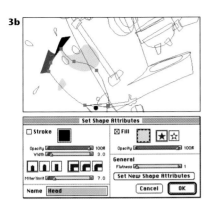

Preparing to fill the selected Head shape with a flesh color (selected here using the Whole Shape Selection tool)

3c

The layered floaters in the Floater List

4

Shading the left side of the machine (under the long stem) using the Spatter Airbrush

5

Detail showing the filigree design

add a colored fill (or stroke) to a shape, double-click on the shape's name in the Floater List. Rename the shape in the Set Shape Attributes dialog box and check the Fill checkbox. With the Fill field active, click in the Color palette, or click a color in your Color Set to update the color in the Fill field. After he had filled shapes with basic colors from his color set, Kirkman Shift-selected them in the Floater List and chose Shapes, Convert To Floater.

4 Shading individual floaters. To paint on an individual floater, select it in the image with the Floater Adjuster tool. To create a nice grainy look—similar to colored pencil on kid-finish illustration board—Kirkman chose Basic Paper texture and added shading to the machine and clothing using the Spatter Airbrush variant, switching between the Cover and Buildup methods in the Brushes palette. He also added strokes with the Fat Stroke Airbrush for a smoother look on the skin and eyes.

Layering the floaters helped Kirkman create the cast shadows. For example, to paint the shadow under the gauge and long stem, he deselected them and selected the underlying machine body floater and then airbrushed the shadow directly on it.

5 Adding details and texture. To see the template as he drew the delicate filigree design, Kirkman selected all the floaters and temporarily reduced their opacity (Controls:Adjuster palette). Then, using a tiny Feather Tip Airbrush variant, he added the dark gold and white filigree design to the sides and nozzle of the espresso machine and carefully painted the black notches on the gauge.

To create the subtly textured blue background, Kirkman selected the floater and applied a blue color with Effects, Surface Control, Color Overlay using Paper, and choosing Dark Cork texture from the Sensational Surfaces CD-ROM (available from MetaCreations). Before applying Color Overlay again (using a greenish-gray color), he checked the Invert Paper checkbox in the Paper palette. Next, he added a swirly, marbled effect to the colored background using Glass Distortion and Nature Spots (Wild Texture library, found in Papers, in the Free Stuff folder on the Painter 5 CD-ROM).

Finally, Kirkman built an irregular, textured edge for the background. He began by selecting the background and floating it (Select All and click with the Floater Adjuster). He created a luminosity mask for the background floater. (From the Mask palette menu, choose Mask, Auto Mask, Using Image luminance). To give the floater a soft edge, he feathered the floater mask 16 pixels by selecting the mask in the Mask List and choosing Feather Mask from the palette's Mask menu. To add texture to the soft edge, he viewed the floater mask in black-and-white (by opening its eye icon in the Mask List) and applied Express Texture using Paper (using Halftone 2 texture from the More Paper Textures library located in Papers, in the Free Stuff folder, on the Painter 5 CD-ROM). To flatten the image, he dropped all floaters (choose Drop All from the Floater List palette's Floater menu). 〰

Melting Text into Water

Overview *Use the Text tool to set text shapes over a background; convert the shapes to selections; float two copies of the text; use feathering and Dye Concentration to add dimension to the type; paint on the floater masks to "melt" the bottoms of the floaters.*

Selected text shapes on the background and in the Floater List palette

Option-clicking with the Floater Adjuster tool on the text selection to make the two floaters

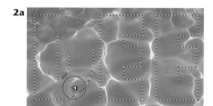

The Floater List palette after naming the two floaters

Selecting the text floater mask in the Objects: Mask List

YOU CAN ACHIEVE A DRAMATIC TRANSLUCENT EFFECT using Painter's brushes to partially remove the visibility mask of a floater. In the image above, we used the Fat Stroke Airbrush on the lower part of two floaters—the text and the feathered shadow behind it—to create the illusion of type melting into water. You can get a similar result using other backgrounds such as clouds, stone or wood.

1 Setting type shapes and converting to selections. Open an image to use as a background; our photo was 3 inches wide and 225 pixels per inch. Choose the Text tool and select a font in the Controls: Text palette. We chose 90-point Futura Extra Bold Condensed. Click in the image and begin typing. If the Floater List palette is open, you'll see each letter shape appear as you type. Use the Floater Adjuster tool to select individual letterform shapes and use the arrow keys on your keyboard to kern the type. To achieve the result in the above image, using the text outlines to float portions of the background, it's necessary to convert the text shapes to selections. With the Floater Adjuster tool chosen, and all the shapes selected, choose Shapes, Convert To Selection. The text shapes will disappear from your image and will reappear as black-and-white animated marquees. Save your selection as a user mask, in case you need to use it later. Choose Select, Save Selection.

2 Using selections to make floaters. To turn the type selection into the two floaters needed for this technique, choose the Floater Adjuster tool, press the Option key and make two separate clicks on the active text selection. (Holding the Option key makes a copy of the selection, leaving the background intact.) Open the Objects:Floater List palette. You'll see two items named Floater, followed by a number. Double-click on the top name (or select the name and press the Enter key) and rename it "text" in the Floater Attributes dialog box. Do the same for the floater below it, naming it "shadow."

3 Distinguishing the floaters. Use feathering and Dye Concentration to make the floaters stand out from the background and from each other. In the Floater List palette, click once on the text floater to make it active. Now, click the Mask icon to switch to the Objects:Mask List, and target the text floater visibility mask by

3b

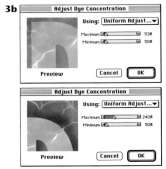

Using Dye Concentration to lighten the text (top) and create the shadow

4

Skewing the shadow to add a look of depth

5

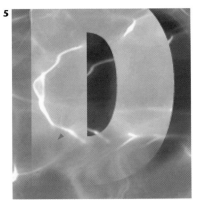

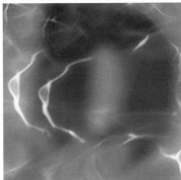

Using the Masking Airbrush variant on the text floater (top) and the shadow floater (with the text floater hidden) to reveal the underlying image

clicking on its name. From the Mask palette menu choose Feather Mask. When the dialog box appears, set the feather to 1 pixel to slightly soften the text's edge. Click OK. Now switch back to the Floater List, target the shadow floater by clicking on its name (follow the same procedure), this time setting the feather to 15 pixels.

Now, change the color of each floater by adding Dye Concentration. In the Floater List, target the text floater by clicking on its name. Choose Effects, Surface Control, Dye Concentration, using Uniform Adjustment and drag the Maximum slider to 53%. Click OK. To create a soft, saturated shadow, select the shadow floater in the Floater List and again choose Dye Concentration. This time experiment with setting the Maximum slider to a high value (we chose 240%). When you like the result you see in the Preview, click OK. A dark shadow should now surround the lightened type.

4 Offsetting the shadow. Give a greater illusion of depth to the type by nudging the shadow up and to the right using the up and right arrow keys on your keyboard. If you want to make the type appear to stand at an angle to the background, as we did, skew the shadow. With the shadow floater selected, choose Effects, Orientation, Distort. Drag the top center handle of the bounding box down and to the right, check the Better box (if you don't mind waiting a little longer) and click OK. There's no preview of this effect, so it may take a few tries to get the look you want.

5 Painting into the floater masks. To "melt" the lower portions of the letterforms into the water, use a brush to partially erase the mask layer of both the text and shadow floaters. Choose the Fat Stroke Airbrush variant of the Airbrush, and reduce its opacity in the Controls:Brush palette to 10% for more sensitivity. Choose white in the Color palette. Now select the text floater in the Floater List and select the text floater mask in the Mask List. To view the floater while editing its mask, keep the mask eye icon shut. Brush along the bottom of the letters to make the lower part of the text floater disappear. If you need to restore part of the text, switch to black paint. Then complete the effect by selecting the shadow floater in the Floater List and the shadow floater mask in the Mask List and brushing along its bottom, revealing the background. (You may find it easier to work on a shadow floater if you hide the text floater temporarily. To temporarily hide the text floater, select it in the Floater List and click to shut its eye icon; when you're finished working on the shadow, click the text's eye icon open again. To restrict mask changes to the area inside the shadow floater, double-click the floater's name in the Floater List to open the Floater Attributes box. Under Selection Interaction choose Selection Reveals Floater and click OK. Now load the selection you saved at step 1 (Select, Load Selection). Choose the floater, then switch to the Mask List and select the floater mask. Now paint on the mask.) 🖌

Using Transparent Layers

Overview *Begin with a blank image, or open a reference photo; clone it and make tracing paper; make a transparent layer; modify brushes to paint on layers; add more layers; paint on the layers and apply effects.*

CHER THREINEN-PENDARVIS

The reference photo with canvas added

PHOTO: DIGITAL STOCK

A transparent layer in the Floater List

Using Tracing Paper while sketching

The player selection saved as a mask. To see the mask in black-and-white, open the mask eye icon and close the RGB-Canvas eye icon.

PAINTER 5'S TRANSPARENT LAYERS bring more versatility to the program, allowing you to see underlying floaters and the background canvas as you paint or apply effects. See "Painting With Layer Brushes" at the beginning of Chapter 3 and "Working With Transparent Layers" earlier in this chapter for more information about transparent layers. To create *Diving Catch*, we painted onto several transparent layers with custom transparent layer brushes, then added a bit of texture.

1 Opening an image, extending the canvas and cloning. You can begin with a new blank file or start with a reference photo, as we did. Our reference photo was 883 pixels wide. In our image, the player's feet were very close to the edge of the frame, so we added 50 pixels to the right side of the image to enhance the speed of the flying jump (choose Canvas, Canvas Size). Next, we made a clone of the image. (Choose File, Clone). Prepare to use tracing paper by deleting the contents of the clone (select all and press the Delete key, leaving the original clone source image open.

2 Making a transparent layer. In the Objects palette click on the Floater icon, and from the palette's Floater menu choose Transparent Layer. You'll see the transparent layer appear in the Floater List. To name the layer, double-click its name in the Floater List. Type a name in the Floater Attributes box and click OK.

3 Modifying a brush to draw on a transparent layer. Painter provides several transparent layer brushes (located in the New Brush Libraries folder.) Brushes using the Transparent layer submethod apply colored paint and the floater mask with each stroke. For the image above, we modified a Pencil, an Airbrush and a Chalk to paint on transparent layers. Choose the Sharp Pencil variant of the Pencils. Change its method to Plug-in and its submethod (subcategory) to Transparent Layer Brush. To save the new variant, choose Save Variant from the Brushes palette's Variant menu. Name your variant and click OK. Now choose the Square Chalk variant of the Chalk brush, and repeat the process of modifying the variant and saving it.

To turn on Tracing paper press Command-T. Choose a dark

5

Painting brushstrokes on the fence and grass

Choosing the floater mask in the Mask List

7

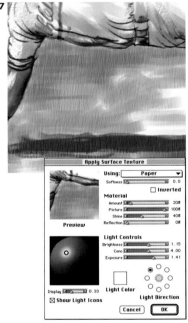

Applying a Paper texture to the grass layer

color in the Color palette, your new Sharp Pencil layer brush and draw or trace to make a line sketch.

4 Making a selection. To isolate the player we made a selection with the Lasso and saved it as a user mask. After making a selection, choose Select, Save Selection. (You'll use the selection in step 6.)

5 Painting elements on the layers. Add more transparent layers as you need them using the process described in step 2. We created layers for the fence, grass, shadow and ball player. We used a custom Square Chalk layer brush (adjusting the size in the Controls:Brush palette) to paint the fence, grass, shadow and ball player. You can paint up to the subject on the top layer or correct the edge later by masking it in step 6.

6 Correcting errors. To erase paint on a transparent layer, we erased a portion of the floater mask. Target the layer you'd like to correct by selecting it in the Floater List and select its mask in the Mask List. (To view the color image while you work, keep the mask eye icon closed.) Switch to the Thin Stroke Airbrush or another brush that is *not* a plug-in method brush (layer brushes use a plug-in method) and paint with white to erase the mask. Then switch back to the RGB-Transparent layer.

To mask any strokes that overlapped the player while painting the fence layer, we used the saved selection to mask it. We set the fence layer Floater Attributes to recognize the saved selection as follows: Double-click the floater's name to open its Floater Attributes box and under Selection Interaction choose Selection Conceals Floater. Then choose Select, Load Selection. (See "Floater and Selection Interaction" earlier in this chapter for more information about how this works.)

7 Adding texture. Transparent layers have a smooth surface; they do not interact with paper chosen in the Paper palette, but you can add texture using special effects such as Apply Surface Texture. When you apply an effect to a transparent layer, the effect is applied only to areas of the layer that contain brushstrokes. To apply a paper texture to a transparent layer, first select the layer in the Floater List, then choose Effects, Surface Control, Apply Surface Texture using Paper. To apply the texture to the Grass layer we used a low Amount setting (about 20%), and we used Grass texture from the Wild Textures library (Free Stuff, Papers on the Painter 5 CD-ROM.) 🖌

CLONING ONTO TRANSPARENT LAYERS WITH CUSTOM LAYER BRUSHES

In this example, we "painted" the photo into the face using a tiny Airbrush layer cloner.

You can use cloning to "paint" photo imagery onto transparent layers. Begin by opening an image and cloning it (File, Clone), then select all and Delete. Turn on Tracing Paper (Command-T). Next, add a transparent layer (from the Objects palette's Floater menu choose Transparent Layer). To clone imagery crisply, select the Thin Stroke Airbrush variant and make the brush very small (we used a 2–3 pixel brush on a 600-pixel-wide file). Change its method to Plug-in and the subcategory to Transparent Layer Brush. In the Color palette, check the Clone Color box. Save the new brush variant so you won't have to build it again, as follows: From the Brush palette's Variant menu choose Save Variant. Name your variant and click OK. Paint with the brush onto the transparent layer and watch the imagery appear. Larger brushes (such as the Square Chalk variant of the Chalk brush) yield less detail, but they can be used with the Transparent Layer Brush method and Clone Color for some beautiful painterly cloning. A bonus: The custom brushes described here are located in the Wow! Brushes folder on the Painter 5 Wow! CD-ROM that accompanies this book.

■ **Lorenzo Paolini** created *Giordano Bruno* as a tribute to the great 16th Century Italian monk and philosopher, jailed for many years for advocating personal and intellectual freedom and finally burned (with his mouth wired shut) in Rome at Piazza di Campo de' Fiori. To begin the painting, Paolini drew sketches with pencil and paper. Then he used Strata Studio Pro to create several elements in source files—for instance, the foreground desk still life. He copied and pasted the source files into Painter as floaters, using the Floater Adjuster tool to reposition the elements and Effects, Orientation, Scale to resize them. For the embossed calligraphy background, Paolini began by opening a black-and-white scan of calligraphy and cloned it (File, Clone), then he deleted the contents of the clone, leaving a blank clone image. To carve out the dark areas in the calligraphy, he chose Effects, Surface Control, Apply Surface Texture, Using Original Luminance, checking the Inverted box. When the relief was in place, he copied and pasted the calligraphy into the composite file and dropped it to the background (Drop button, Floater List). Then he used custom-made brushes to paint shadows on the background behind the floating figure of Bruno and to paint final details on the figure and still life elements.

■ **Ben Barbante** relied on the flexibility of Painter's floaters and brushes to create *Orcastration*, and to transform flat color shapes into a silent, mysterious environment. He began by creating basic colored shapes in Adobe Illustrator, rasterizing the files in Photoshop and opening them in Painter. He created selections for the colored areas and floated the selections, then he dragged and dropped the floaters into a new file. Barbante painted on the floaters. The Dodge and Burn brushes (Photo brush library) and the Airbrush variants are ideal for image-blending tasks like making the large whale's fin and back appear to break the water's surface. Barbante blended the images by dragging a second copy of the water's surface into the image, placing it on top the original surface and the whale, but below the background whales. Then, working on the surface water floater mask, he "erased" the water that covered the back and fin, revealing more of the whale. After flattening the image, he used the Distorto Liquid variant to create the bow waves in front of each whale and the trailing fin reflections. He painted the white foam around the whales and the puffs of mist coming from the blowhole using the Feather Tip variant of the Airbrush.

■ Bear Canyon Creative commissioned illustrator **Cecil Rice** to paint *The Green Hornet*, one in a series of illustrations for a set of audio book covers entitled *The Golden Age of Radio,* published by Dove Audio. An expert draftsman, Rice painted the portrait in Painter from start to finish using traditional painting theory. He began by gathering references from movies done in the 1930's and 1940's, then he did three portrait sketches in Painter, and presented them to his client. The chosen sketch was based on a still from an old Alan Ladd movie. For the final art, Rice used Canvas,

Resize to enlarge the sketch to the finished size plus bleed; then he made selections and clicked with the Floater Adjuster to float each element. While painting, he blended the colors from the sketch (with Water brush variants) and applied color with various brushes. Rice continued to refine the shapes of elements, for instance, the ascot and coat, by painting into the masks of the floaters. When he was pleased with the figure, he painted the background using the Artist Pastel Chalk variant. To blend the background, he used Effects, Focus, Soften.

ENTROPY

■ **Jeff Brice** began *Entropy*—an exploration of the similarities between manmade objects and nature—by selecting images from his photo archive. As a backdrop for these, he scribbled purple, beige and other hues (sampled from the photos) on the background using the Oil Paint Brush variant. He smudged colors using various Water brushes, then added more color using the Chalk and Water Color brushes with Medium paper texture (from the Drawing Papers library in the Extra Art Materials folder).

In Photoshop Brice created masks for the photos. His masks are quite complex and frequently include gradients. The main bone image, for instance, has a modified gradient mask that allows the background to show through the less important areas. He also created a gradient mask for the flower

image to make it blend more smoothly with the surrounding elements.

In Painter Brice positioned the floaters using the Default Composite Method in the Controls:Adjuster palette. When the arrangement was complete, Brice selected Drop All from the Floater List palette menu. He sampled dark colors from the image and used the Large Chalk variant—with very low Opacity and Grain settings (Controls:Brush palette)—to apply two custom textures that he had previously scanned: a crackled texture (applied to the instrument, skull and horns) and a crumpled-paper texture (to fade and blend the edges of the images). Finally, he created drop shadows on the sign and behind the instrument by making selections with the Lasso tool, then using the Fat Stroke Airbrush variant inside the selections.

■ **Chet Phillips** begins his illustrations with a black-and-white drawing made with white paint and the Scratchboard Tool variant of the Pens brush on a file with a with a black background. When the scratchboard drawing is complete, he selects the entire image and floats it. To see through the white areas of the floater, he changes the floater Composite Method to Gel in the Controls:Adjuster palette. Then he deselects the floater. To finish, he uses Airbrush variants to paint the background. (See page 00 for a step-by-step description of his technique.)

For *Horsepower Heart* (top), Phillips began by making a pencil drawing on paper. He scanned the drawing and made a clone (File, Clone). He deleted the contents of the clone file, and turned on Tracing Paper (Command-T). Using the sketch as a guide, he made a drawing with the Scratchboard Tool variant. Then (working on top of the scratchboard drawing), he used the Pen and Lasso tools to create shapes and converted each shape to a selection (Shapes, Convert To Selection). After he converted each selection, he saved it as a user mask (Select, Save Selection). Then Phillips floated the entire scratchboard drawing and set the Composite Method to Gel, then deselected the floater. Working on the image canvas, he loaded each selection (Select, Load Selection), and applied colored tints to the selected areas using Effects, Fill. Then he painted colored details with the Airbrushes. To finish, he applied subtle colored textures to selected areas of the background using Effects, Surface Control, Color Overlay.

Nortel Gridlock (below), a brochure cover illustration for Northern Telecom, was created by Phillips to illustrate DCR (Dynamically Controlled Routing). To paint *Nortel Gridlock*, he used the same painting and compositing techniques as for *Horsepower Heart* above. When Phillips was finished with the image he saved a RIFF file (with floaters) in case the client needed to make any color changes. Then he saved another copy of the file and flattened it (dropping all of the floaters) by selecting Drop All from the Floater List palette menu.

■ For *Meteor Man* (above) **John Dismukes** of Capstone Studios began with a tight visualization of the typography on paper. The pencil sketch was scanned and used as a template in Macromedia Freehand to create Postscript outlines. The team at Capstone extruded the outlines in Adobe Dimensions and opened them in Painter using File, Acquire, Adobe Illustrator file. Dismukes converted the shapes to two floaters (the two words). He began by Shift-selecting the letter shapes in each word and grouping them (Command-G). Then he chose Shapes, Convert To Floater and clicked the Collapse button on the Floater List palette to collapse the group into a single floater. He used the Thin Stroke and Fat Stroke Airbrush variants to complete the logo.

To create the *Miami Dolphins* program cover (right), Dismukes began with a composition sketch, then built the graphic elements and typography using Macromedia Freehand. He saved the file in EPS format. All elements were brought into Painter as shapes via File, Acquire, Adobe Illustrator file and converted to floaters. Dismukes painted on individual floaters using the Thin Stroke and Fat Stroke Airbrush variants. He applied texture to the background using Effects, Focus, Glass Distortion.

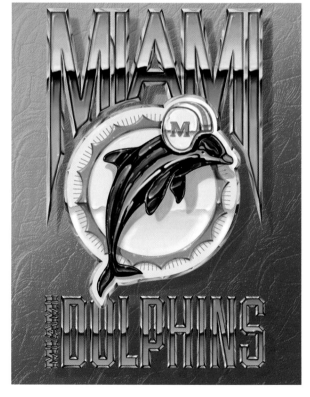

■ **John Derry** constructed the *Winter of Love 3* poster (left) almost entirely with resolution-independent shapes. He began by scanning a photograph of a Gretsch 6120 (Brian Setzer's favorite model of guitar). Then he made a clone of the scan (File, Clone), selected all and deleted the contents of the clone file. Derry turned on Tracing Paper (Command-T), and used the scan as a reference for drawing the silhouette of the guitar with the Pen tool. Next, using the guitar silhouette as a reference, he drew freehand Bézier curves for the red flame shapes with the Quick Curve tool. He also drew two more shapes for the orange and yellow flames surrounding the guitar.

Next, Derry set and distorted the "Brian Setzer Orchestra" type in Adobe Illustrator. Then, with both Illustrator and Painter running, he copied the type in Illustrator and pasted it into Painter as shapes. After positioning and scaling the shapes, he filled them with color by selecting them and using Shapes, Set Shape Attributes to define the colored fills. Derry created darker purple flame shapes under the type to "pop" the "Brian Setzer" type and make it stand out against the guitar silhouette. He set the "Winter of Love 3" headline type on a curve in Illustrator. All of the other type shapes were created in Painter.

To build the wavy graduated background, Derry filled the background canvas with a custom gradation and used Effects, Focus, Glass Distortion to warp it.

■ For this illustration for *America West* magazine (left), **Rick Kirkman** began with a pencil sketch on paper. He scanned the pencil sketch and used it as a template in Painter to draw shape paths with the Pen tool. He selected each shape path and applied a flat color fill by checking the Fill checkbox in Shapes, Set Shape Attributes. To convert all of the shapes to floaters at once, he selected all of the floaters (by Shift-selecting them in the Floater List) and chose Shapes, Convert To Floater. Working on each individual floater, he painted with the Airbrushes to create form. As a finishing touch, he applied textures to a few areas—the woman's hair, the dog's fur, and the floor—using Effects, Surface Control, Apply Surface Texture Using Paper.

6

ENHANCING
PHOTOS,
MONTAGE
AND COLLAGE

We used several features to enhance this portrait: We painted a mask to isolate the dancers; and to create a shallow depth of field, we used Effects, Tonal Control, Adjust Colors to desaturate the background and Effects, Focus, Soften to blur it.

PHOTO: DIGITAL STOCK

PHOTO: PHOTODISC

To isolate the sky from the buildings in this photo we made a Color Mask for the sky. (From the Mask menu in the Objects palette choose Color Mask.) Then we used the Pens, Scratchboard Tool variant and white paint to remove masked areas in the photo's foreground that had also been selected with the Color Mask command.

ALTHOUGH PAINTER BEGAN as a painting program, the features that have been added over the years have turned it into a powerful image processor as well. And with the release of Painter 5, many new tools designed *just* for photographers have been added, for instance, dynamic plug-in floaters that allow you to adjust brightness and contrast, perform posterization, apply special effects with Glass Distortion and more! (For the basics of how to work with plug-in floaters, see the introduction of Chapter 5.) The new release also adds 16 brush variants specifically designed for photographers such as the Scratch Remover brush and Saturation Add brush found in the Photo brush library (located in the New Brush Libraries folder). And, of course, when it comes to achieving painterly effects with photographs, Painter has no peer. If you're a photographer, a photo-illustrator or a designer who works with photos and you want to get the most out of Painter, you'll want to pay attention to the following areas.

The Effects Menu. Most of Painter's image-altering special effects can be found in the Effects menu. The features under the sub-heads Tonal Control, Surface Control and Focus are loaded with creative promise for the adventurous digital photographer.

Selections and Masks. To alter only a portion of an image, you'll need to become acquainted with Painter's shape paths, selection and masking capabilities. If you're not familiar with the Pen and Lasso tools, turn to "Working with Bézier Paths and Selections" and "Working with Freehand Selections" in Chapter 4.

Painter's powerful automatic masking features—under the Mask menu in the Objects:Mask List palette—give you a big jump on the tedious process of creating masks to isolate parts of your image. And a bonus: All of Painter's brushes (except plug-in

To add a palette knife paint effect to this photo we used the Glass Distortion plug-in floater and River Map texture from the Branched Textures library (from Papers, in Free Stuff on the Painter 5 CD-ROM). To read about the technique step-by-step, turn to "Adding Diffusion and Relief," in Chapter 7.

Correcting the tonal range in an overexposed image using Effects, Tonal Control, Equalize

brushes) can be used to paint directly on a user mask. For an in-depth look at combining automatic and painterly masks, turn to "Using Color Mask," in Chapter 4.

Floaters. Chapter 5 gave you an overall look at techniques using floaters; this chapter focuses on using floaters and masks for photo-compositing and other photo effects—for example, in "Simulating Motion," "Selective Coloring" and "Creating a Montage Using Masks and Floaters," later in this chapter.

New plug-in floaters. Painter 5 offers dynamic plug-in floaters that are useful for making adjustments to images. They are: Brightness and Contrast, Equalize and Posterize. You'll find these versatile tools in the Objects:P. Float palette. Several of the techniques described later in this chapter use plug-in floaters. To read more about plug-in floaters and how they relate to other elements in Painter, turn to the beginning of Chapter 5.

Cloning. A very powerful and versatile feature—cloning (File, Clone)—lets you make multiple copies of an image, alter each of them, then recombine them in various ways while preserving access to the original. Several of the techniques described in this chapter use this or another kind of cloning method.

IMAGE-PROCESSING BASICS

With its strong focus on *creative* image manipulation, Painter has left some *production*-oriented tasks such as color-correcting CMYK images to Adobe Photoshop. But there's no need to move an image from Painter to Photoshop to perform the basic image-processing tasks such as sharpening and adjusting brightness and contrast, because Painter has tools that can be set to emulate many of Photoshop's.

Equalizing. Choosing Effects, Tonal Control, Equalize (Command-E) produces a dialog box with a histogram similar to Photoshop's Levels dialog box—except that the image is automatically equalized (an effect similar to clicking on the Auto button in Photoshop's Levels). Move the triangular sliders toward the ends of the histogram to decrease the effect.

Painter 5 also features an Equalize plug-in floater that operates like Effects, Tonal Control, Equalize, but on a floating copy of your image so you can easily try out different tonal adjustments. To make an Equalize floater, open an image and choose Objects:P. Float to open the Plug-in Floaters palette. From the palette menu, select Equalize and click the Apply button to generate the floater. When the Equalize dialog box appears, set the controls as you would for Effects, Tonal Control, Equalize. Using an Equalize plug-in floater you can preview as many changes as you like. Click the Reset button to return your image to its original condition, then apply a new correction.

PHOTO: DIGITAL STOCK

Using a feather setting of 15 pixels, we created a textured edge for this 500-pixel-wide photo. (To make a soft-edged vignette around an image, turn to page 90, in the introduction of Chapter 4).

For the image above we created a textured vignette as follows: Begin by making a selection with the Oval Selection tool. Use the Selection Adjuster (Tools palette) to position and scale the selection. Next, apply a feather (Select, Feather). Save the selection (Select, Save Selection). Now for the textured edge: In the Mask List, open the mask eye icon and close the RGB-Canvas eye icon to view the mask in black-and-white. Select a rough paper texture in the Paper palette (we used Hatching), and choose Effects, Surface Control, Express Texture. Adjust the sliders to confine the texture to the soft edge. Click OK. In the Mask List, click the mask eye icon shut and select the RGB-Canvas. Load the selection (Select, Load Selection). Next, click on the active selection with the Floater Adjuster to float it. To clear the background behind the floater, deselect the floater by clicking on the image canvas, choose Select, All and press the Delete key. To flatten the image, choose Drop All from the Floater List palette's Floater menu.

Adjusting brightness and contrast. Painter 5 offers two ways to change image brightness and contrast. The first—Effects, Tonal Control, Brightness and Contrast—applies a correction directly to an open image or selection. But if you'd like to preview several Brightness and Contrast options, consider making a Brightness and Contrast plug-in floater. In the Objects:Plug in Floater palette, select Brightness and Contrast. Click the Apply button to generate the plug-in floater. When the Brightness and Contrast dialog box appears, continue to adjust the settings as you preview the corrections in your image. Turn to "Making a Selective Correction" on page 152 to see a Brightness and Contrast plug-in floater in action.

Stripping color from an image. There are several ways to turn a color image into a grayscale one in Painter. The quickest way is to desaturate the image using the Adjust Color dialog box. Choose Effects, Tonal Control, Adjust Colors and drag the Saturation slider all the way to the left.

Changing color. While you're using the Adjust Color dialog box, experiment with the Hue Shift slider to change the hue of all of the colors in an image (or a floater or a selection). You can get greater control in altering specific colors (turning blue eyes green, for instance) by using Effects, Tonal Control, Adjust Selected Colors. Click in the image to select a color, then drag the Hue Shift, Saturation and Value sliders at the bottom of the dialog box to make the changes. Fine-tune your color choice and the softness of its edge with the various Extents and Feather sliders.

To repair a white scratch on this photo we used a two-step process, beginning with Painter 5's useful new Scratch Remover brush (located in the Photo brush library, in the New Brush Libraries folder). Choose the Scratch Remover variant. Open a photo you'd like to repair and for the best results, use a small brush size (we used a 1.7 pixel brush on this 350-pixel-wide image), and a low Opacity setting in the Controls:Brush palette. (We used 9%.) Zoom in to a magnification where you can see the scratch in detail, and carefully paint to blend the scratch into the image. This first step is usually sufficient for images with even color. But the sky in our image was graduated and required more repair. Next, we used a Soft Cloner variant of the Cloners brush (from the Painter Brushes library) with a small brush size and a very low Opacity. Set the clone source to a point near the repair by Control-clicking, then gently paint over the repaired area to bring back appropriate colors.

PHOTO: DIGITAL STOCK

The scratched image (left) and the repaired image (right)

Using the Saturation Add brush from the Photo brush library to "pop" the color on the red raincoat, umbrella and reflection

We applied Micro Grain (from the More Wild Textures library, in Free Stuff, Papers, on the Painter 5 CD-ROM), to this photo with Effects, Surface Control, Dye Concentration using Paper with the Maximum slider set to 200%.

To "age" this photo giving it a crackled texture, we painted with the Add Grain Brush using Crackle texture from the Painter Brushes library.

The image above was sharpened to produce the result on the right using these settings: Radius, 2.15; Highlight, 90%; Shadow, 80%.

Painting saturation with brushes. To "pop" the color in a specific area, use Painter 5's new Saturation Add brush from the Photo brush library (located in the New Brush libraries folder).

Adding film grain. Photoshop's Noise filter is a good way to emulate film grain. To get a similar effect in Painter, choose a fine Paper grain like Fine Grain, Micro Grain, or Synthetic Super Fine from the More Paper Textures library (located in Free Stuff, Papers, on the Painter 5 CD-ROM), and select Effects, Surface Control, Dye Concentration. Scale the texture in the Papers palette until the grain in the Preview window is barely visible—try 50% as a starting point. Try minor adjustments to the Maximum and Minimum sliders in the Adjust Dye Concentration dialog box.

Adding grain with a brush. Painter 5 offers an exciting new pressure-sensitive brush—the Add Grain Brush—that allows you to paint grain onto your images. To begin, load the Photo brush library by choosing Custom palette, Shortcut to New Brushes from the Window menu. Click on the Camera icon to quickly load the library, and select the Add Grain Brush variant. Choose a texture in the Paper palette and brush lightly onto your image. For a more subtle effect, reduce the Opacity of the brush in the Controls:Brush palette.

Creating a shallow depth of field. By softening the background of an image, you can simulate the shallow depth of field that you'd get by setting your camera at a low *f*-stop. Select the area you want to soften and feather the selection by choosing Select, Feather to avoid an artificial-looking edge. Then choose Effects, Focus, Soften.

Smudge and Blur tools. To get an effect similar to Photoshop's Smudge tool, choose the Just Add Water variant of the Water brush, varying Opacity (in the Controls:Brush palette) between 70% and 100%. For a more radical effect, try the Distorto variant of the Liquid brush. To emulate Photoshop's Blur tool, use the Blur brush variant (located in the Photo brush library) set to a low Opacity (about 20%).

Sharpening. Painter's Sharpen feature (Effect, Focus, Sharpen) gives you control equivalent to unsharp masking on a drum scanner. Use it to give definition to a selected area of interest, or to an entire image as a final step in preparing for output. To sharpen the highlights and shadows of an area in an image using a brush, choose the Sharpen brush from the Photo brush library. This brush puts sharpening (very similar to Photoshop's Unsharp Mask filter) on the tip of a brush.

Retouching. The Straight Cloner and Soft Cloner variants of the Cloners brush work like Photoshop's Rubber Stamp tool in Clone Aligned mode; use the Control key, as you would Photoshop's Option key to sample an area (even in another image), then reproduce that image (centered at the point of sampling) wherever you paint. The Straight Cloner variant reproduces imagery without changing it; to clone imagery with a soft edge and low opacity (like an Airbrush) use the Soft Cloner variant.

After changing this color photo to a sepia-tone, we used Effects, Tonal Control, Equalize to increase the contrast.

To add a mysterious gold spotlight to this photo of an Indian woman, we used Effects, Surface Control, Apply Lighting. We modified the Center Spotlight by changing the Light Color from white to gold. To make the spotlight softer, we decreased the Exposure from 1.00 to .85.

A classic solarization, created by merging positive and negative clones of the same image. The purple tone was added with Effects, Tonal Control, Color Overlay.

ADVANCED TECHNIQUES

It often takes a lot of time and trial-and-error to get cool effects in-camera or in the darkroom. Some third-party plug-in filters do an adequate job of replicating these effects, but Painter gives you more control than you can get with filters alone.

Here's a short guide on how to use Painter to re-create traditional photographic techniques, starting with simpler, in-camera ones and progressing to more complex darkroom procedures.

Motion blur. You can use the camera to blur a moving subject by using a slower shutter speed or jittering (shaking) your hands while you hold the camera, or you can blur the background by panning with the subject. See "Simulating Motion" on page 150 to read about a versatile motion blur technique that incorporates a floater.

To create the look of "camera jitter," just as if you had moved the camera while taking a picture, choose Effects, Focus, Camera Motion Blur. When the dialog box appears, drag in the image (not the Preview), to specify the camera's direction and distance of movement. Dragging further in the image will create a wider blur. To move the origin of movement along the path of motion, adjust the Bias slider.

Creating a sepia-tone. Sepia-tones get their reddish-brown color cast in the darkroom when the photographer immerses a developed photo in a special toner bath. You can use Painter's gradation and tonal control features to quickly turn color or grayscale images into sepia-tones. Begin by opening an image. Select the Sepia grad in the Art Materials:Grad palette and choose Express in Image from the palette's Grad menu. If the image looks muddy, use Effects, Tonal Control, Equalize (or apply an Equalize plug-in floater as described on page 137) to restore the bright highlights and deep shadows.

Lens filters and special film. To re-create in-camera tinting effects achieved with special films (like infrared) or colored filters, use Effects, Surface Control, Color Overlay. If you want to mimic the effect of a graduated or spot lens attachment (partially colored filters), choose a gradation and fill your image (Effects, Fill) with the gradation at a reduced opacity. (You may need to add contrast to your image afterwards with Effects, Tonal Control, Equalize.)

Shooting through glass. With Painter's Glass Distortion effect or Glass Distortion plug-in floater you can superimpose glass bas relief effects (using a paper texture or any other image) on your photo. A small amount of this feature adds texture to an image; larger amounts can make an image unrecognizable! To apply the procedure directly to your image choose Effects, Focus, Glass Distortion. To generate a Glass Distortion plug-in floater for your image, click the plug icon in the Objects palette and select Glass Distortion from the plug-ins palette. (See Phil Howe's work with Glass Distortion in the gallery at the end of this chapter).

Using Effects, Surface Control, Express Texture to get the effect of a line conversion using a straight-line screen. We used Line 40 from Simple Textures in Free Stuff, Papers on the Painter 5 CD-ROM.

We posterized this Craig McClain photo using a Color Set of "desert" colors and Effects, Tonal Control, Posterize Using Color Set.

The original photo of a kelp frond had strong contrast, giving good detail for this embossing technique (created on a clone of an image using Effects, Surface Control, Apply Surface Texture with 3D Brushstrokes).

Lighting effects. Use Painter's Apply Lighting feature (under Effects, Surface Control) to add subtle or dramatic lighting to a scene.

Multiple exposures. Whether created in camera (by under-exposing and shooting twice before advancing the film) or in the darkroom (by "sandwiching" negatives or exposing two images on a single sheet of paper), it's easy to reproduce the effect using floaters or clones in Painter.

Solarization. Painter's Express Texture (Effects, Surface Control) command is a great way to re-create darkroom solarization. Read about a Painter version of a "classic" solarization on page 158.

Line screen. Instead of developing your image in the darkroom onto high-contrast "line" or "lith" paper, try getting a similar effect in Painter. Choose a lined paper texture from the Simple Textures library (in Free Stuff, Papers on the Painter 5 CD-ROM), or make your own using the Make Paper dialog box found under the Paper menu on the Art Materials palette. (Read more about the Make Paper feature in Chapter 7's introduction.) Next, choose Effects, Surface Control, Apply Screen, using Paper to get a two- or three-color effect with rough (aliased) lines. Or try Effects, Surface Control, Express Texture, using Paper to get more subtle control and smoother, anti-aliased lines. Turn to "Toning with Textures," on page 159 to read about using Express Texture to apply colored, textured effects to an image.

Posterizing an image. Like other image processors, Painter lets you limit the number of colors in your image via posterization. To apply a posterization directly to your image choose Effects, Tonal Control, Posterize and enter the number of levels (usually 8 or fewer). With Painter 5 you can also perform a posterization using the Posterize plug-in floater. In the Objects palette, click the plug icon and select Posterize from the palette menu. Click Apply and enter the number of levels. Because the Posterize plug-in floater is dynamic, you can continue to preview the effect on your image until it's the way you like it.

You can get creative posterization effects by making a Color Set (see "Capturing a Color Set" in Chapter 2) and selecting Effects, Tonal Control, Posterize Using Color Set. This is a great way to unify photos shot under a variety of conditions.

Embossing and debossing. To emboss an image, raising its light areas, choose File, Clone; then Select All and delete, leaving a blank cloned image. Now choose Effects, Surface Control, Apply Surface Texture, and choose 3D Brush Strokes from the Using pop-up menu. To get a debossed look—where light areas recede—click the Invert box *or* change the Using menu choice to Original Luminance. Images with a lot of contrast give the best results, and busy images work better if less important areas are first selected and softened using Effects, Focus, Soften. 🖌

Putting Type over a Photo

Overview *Set headline type shapes and adjust their opacity; draw a rectangular shape and use it to lighten an area of your image to make the body copy on top of it more readable.*

Exploring the **EAST CAPE**

The East Cape of Baja California Sur offers crystal clear waters, white sand beaches and a lush tropical desert along the Sea of Cortez.

CHER THREINEN-PENDARVIS / PHOTO: DIGITAL STOCK

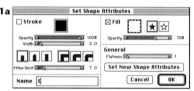

The settings in the Set Shape Attributes dialog box

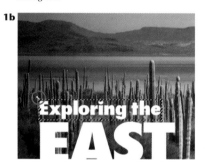

Scaling a shape group proportionally by Shift-dragging on a corner handle

Positioning the text bar using the Floater Adjuster tool

Reducing opacity of the shapes

PAINTER OFFERS MANY TECHNIQUES to make text and other objects stand out against a background. Here's one of our favorite (and fastest) methods, applied to a comp for a magazine layout.

1 Preparing the type. Open your photo and select the Text tool. Choose a typeface and size from the pop-up menu in the Controls:Text palette (we chose Futura Condensed Extra Bold). To fill the type shapes with white as you set them, select white in the Art Materials:Color palette and choose Shapes, Set Shape Attributes. In the dialog box, check the Fill checkbox and make sure that the Stroke checkbox is unchecked. Then click in your image and type your headline. Kern individual letterforms by selecting them in the Floater List palette and using the arrow keys to move them. After you've kerned the letters, group the letters in each word to make them easy to select and reposition as a unit, as follows: Shift-select the letters in the Floater List palette and Group them (Command-G.) When you're finished, use the Floater Adjuster tool to move or scale the type shape groups. (For more information about transforming shapes, see "Working With Shapes" in the introduction of Chapter 5.)

2 Adding the text bar. We wanted to be able to reposition the text bar to try out different layout options, so we drew a white-filled rectangle with the Rectangular Shape tool. After drawing your rectangular shape, use the Floater Adjuster tool to move or resize it.

3 Adjusting the opacity.
Finally, get the "screened-back" look by Shift-selecting the items in the Floater List and lowering the Opacity slider in the Controls:Adjuster palette. We set ours to 70%.

Selective Coloring

Overview *Open a color photo and float a copy; desaturate the floater; paint with a brush to erase areas of the floater mask and reveal the underlying color photo.*

The original color image

Using the Adjust Colors dialog box to desaturate the floater to black-and-white

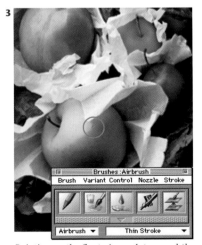

Painting on the floater's mask to reveal the color image underneath

IF YOU WANT TO FOCUS ATTENTION on a particular element in a color photo, you can turn the photo into a black-and-white image and then selectively add color back into it for emphasis. Here's a way to use Painter's floaters and brushes to "paint" color on an image.

1 Floating a copy of the image. Open a color photo and choose Select, All (Command-A). Choose the Floater Adjuster tool, hold down the Option key and click on the image. This creates a floater with the exact dimensions of the original image.

2 Desaturating the floater. Now use the floater to make the image appear grayscale: Choose Effects, Tonal Control, Adjust Colors, and drag the Saturation slider all the way to the left.

3 Revealing color in the underlying image. To allow parts of the color image to show through, use a brush to erase portions of the floater's mask. In the Brushes palette, choose an Airbrush variant and choose white in the Color palette. In the Objects:Mask List, select the floater mask. (To view the floater in color while editing its mask, keep the floater mask eye icon shut.) As you erase the mask on the floater in the area you wish to colorize, the color will appear. If you want to turn a color area back to grayscale, choose black from the Color palette and paint on the area.

FINE-TUNING YOUR MASK

It's difficult to tell if you've completely covered (or erased) areas when working on a mask with a brush. To view a floater mask in black and white, select the floater in the Floater List and in the Mask List, open the Mask eye icon. Choose any brush, and paint directly on the mask to clean up areas. (Black creates an opaque mask; pure white, no mask; shades of gray, a semi-transparent mask.) To switch back to color view, click the floater mask eye icon shut.

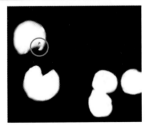

Painting on the floater mask using the Thin Stroke Airbrush

Simulating Motion

Overview *Open a color photo and float a copy; apply Motion Blur to the copy; paint with a brush to erase areas of the floater mask and reveal the original photo.*

CHER THREINEN-PENDARVIS / PHOTO: DIGITAL STOCK

The original photo

PHOTO: DIGITAL STOCK

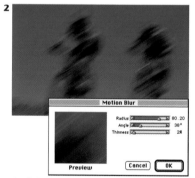

Applying Motion Blur to the floater

Erasing the floater mask on the face and arm

Adjusting the opacity of the blurred floater

CREATING A SENSE OF MOVEMENT for a subject *after* the film is out of the camera is easy with Painter's floaters and Motion Blur command. We blurred a floater, then erased some areas to reveal the untouched image underneath. The benefits of this method over applying effects to selections are that you can control the amount of the effect by adjusting opacity of the floaters, you can simultaneously add effects other than a blur (such as lighting and texture) and you are altering a floating copy leaving the original intact, and this makes it easy to correct errors.

1 Floating a copy of the image. Open a color photo and choose Select, All (Command-A). Choose the Floater Adjuster tool and Option-click on the image. This creates a floater with the exact dimensions of the original image.

2 Blurring the floater. Select the floater by clicking on its name in the Objects:Floater List and choose Effects, Focus, Motion Blur. To get a dramatic blur on our 1500-pixel-wide image, we set Radius to about 80, Angle to 31°, Thinness to 2%. Experiment with different Angle settings for your particular image. We set the angle to complement the direction the bikers were moving.

3 Painting on the mask. To allow parts of the original image to show through, use a brush to erase portions of the floater's mask. To give the leading rider an illusion of more speed we erased the frontal blur, leaving long trails of motion blur behind her. We erased most of the blur on the second rider to give the illusion of slower speed. In the Brushes palette, choose an Airbrush variant and choose white in the Color palette. Select the floater in the Objects:Floater List, switch to the Mask List and select the floater mask. As you paint the floater mask in the area you wish to erase, the underlying image will appear. If you want to restore an area of the blurred floater, choose black from the Color palette and paint on that area of the floater mask.

4 Adjusting the opacity. To make the floater slightly transparent, allowing the original image to show through the blur, we lowered the Opacity of the floater in the Controls:Adjuster palette to 75%. 🐾

Zooming and Solarizing

Overview *Float a copy of the image, use Painter 5's Zoom Blur feature to zoom-in on an area of the floater; paint the floater mask to accentuate the focal point; make a solarization by changing the Composite method.*

CHER THREINEN-PENDARVIS / PHOTO: DIGITAL STOCK

The original photo of the volleyball players

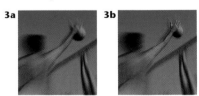

The Zoom Blur dialog box after clicking in the image

The zoom-blurred floater (left) and the mask retouched to reveal the underlying image of the hand and ball (right)

The Opacity and Composite Method settings for the solarization

WITH PAINTER 5'S ZOOM BLUR feature you can create zoom and pan effects that rival results you can achieve when shooting with a zoom lens. Here we used Zoom Blur to elongate the subjects, adding to the excitement and illusion of speed during a volley. Afterward, to add more drama we changed the photo into a mysterious "night scene."

1 Floating a copy of the image. Open a color photo and choose Select, All (Command-A). Choose the Floater Adjuster tool and Option-click on the image. This creates a floater with the exact dimensions of the original image.

2 Blurring the floater. Select the floater by clicking on its name in the Objects:Floater List and choose Effects, Focus, Zoom Blur. To get a moderate blur on our 600-pixel-wide image, we set Amount to 31%. Set the focal point of the zoom by clicking in the image (not in the Preview). To create the elongated, distorted effect of zooming in, check the Zoom In box. Click OK.

3 Painting on the mask. To enhance the focal point of the image, we erased areas of the floater mask to reveal the underlying image, for instance, the ball and hands. To allow parts of the original image to show through use a brush to erase portions of the floater's mask. Choose white in the Color palette and in the Brushes palette, choose an Airbrush variant. Select the floater in the Objects:Floater List, switch to the Mask List and select the floater mask. As you paint the floater mask, the underlying image will appear.

4 Making a solarization. Next, we created a solarized "night scene" from the image by selecting the floater in the Floater List, choosing the Floater Adjuster tool and changing the Composite Method to Difference in the Controls:Adjuster palette. To make the floater slightly transparent, allowing the original colored image to show through, we also lowered the Opacity of the floater to 85%.

Making a Selective Correction

Overview *Use a plug-in floater to adjust the brightness/contrast of an image; convert the plug-in floater to an image floater; make a selection; use the selection to reveal a portion of the floater.*

The original photograph

Generating a Brightness/Contrast plug-in floater

The completed active selection on the image canvas

HERE'S A USEFUL IMAGE-EDITING TECHNIQUE that combines a dynamic floating Brightness and Contrast adjustment and a selection. Using a plug-in floater has the advantage of being able to make a correction and dynamically preview the changes on the image without harming the image. To enhance the focal point of this image—shining more light onto the faces—we selectively lightened the shaded window area.

1 Editing brightness and contrast with a plug-in floater.
Open a grayscale or color photo. To generate a Brightness and Contrast plug-in floater for your image, begin by clicking the Plug icon in the Objects palette and choose Brightness and Contrast from the plug-ins menu. Click the Apply button on the Plug-in Floater palette to generate a dynamic floater covering your entire image. (Read more about plug-in floaters in the introduction of Chapter 5.)

When the dialog box appears, adjust the sliders and preview the correction in your image. To see more detail on the faces, we moved the Brightness (lower) slider to the right, making the image lighter. We also slightly increased the contrast by moving the Contrast slider (upper) to the right.

When you've finished making adjustments, convert the plug-in floater to an image floater as follows, so it will have the capability to work with selections. From the P: Float menu choose Commit. Then hide the floater temporarily before beginning the next step: Switch to the Floater List, click the floater eye icon shut, then deselect the floater by clicking in the blank area below its name.

2 Making a selection and saving it as a mask. In our example, when we were satisfied with Brightness/Contrast adjustment in the window area, the blue wall was too light and flat. In preparation for using only the window area of the adjusted floater, we made a selection of the window area on the image canvas and saved it as a user mask. Choose the Pen tool or Lasso and make a selection. (We drew a shape path with the Pen and converted it to a selection using

3a

Selecting the mask to view it as a red overlay

3b

Viewing the mask as a red overlay before editing and feathering

3c

The completed mask

4a

Setting up the Floater Attributes dialog box

4b

Detail from the final corrected image with more detail in the shaded areas

Shapes, Convert to Selection.) When you've completed the selection, choose Select, Save Selection to save it into the Mask List. Click the Mask icon in the Objects palette to switch to the Mask List.

3 Editing and feathering the mask. To get a clear view of the mask as we edited and feathered it, we worked back and forth between viewing it as a red overlay (on the image) and as a black-and-white mask. We used an Airbrush and white paint to spray soft edges along the top of the window and added a 3-pixel feather to the entire mask to give it a soft transparent edge. If your mask needs editing, select the mask name in the Mask List. To view your mask as a red overlay, click both the mask eye icon and the RGB-Canvas eye icon open. Then click back on the mask name to select the mask so you can paint or feather it. To view the mask in black-and-white, click the RGB-Canvas eye icon closed. For a soft edge, apply feathering as follows: Target the mask in the Mask List, then select the mask by clicking on its name and choose Feather Mask from the Object palette's Mask menu. Set the radius and click OK. Now shut the mask eye icon and click on the RGB-Canvas to prepare for the next step.

4 Setting up the floater and selection interaction. Now that your mask is complete, it's time to set up the Floater Attributes to recognize the selection you'll load from the mask. Switch back to the Floater List, and double-click on the Brightness/Contrast floater's name to open its Floater Attributes dialog box. Under Selection Interaction choose Selection Reveals Floater. Click OK to accept.

Now, choose Select, Load Selection and choose the mask that you wish to interact with the floater. Click OK to accept. Finally, in the Floater List, click the Brightness/Contrast floater eye icon open to display the floater masked by the selection. 🐾

SET UP YOUR WORKSPACE

To make it easier to access items stored in the Objects:Floater List and Objects:Mask List when working between both palettes, consider tearing off the palettes and displaying them side-by-side on your monitor. Begin by opening the Objects palette. To be able to tear off a palette, the palette must be inactive, so choose one you don't plan to tear off. Now touch a sub-palette icon and drag it off from the parent palette.

FLOATER AND SELECTION INTERACTION

You can have several selections saved in the Mask List and choose any one of them to operate on a floater in your image. Open the Objects:Floater List and double-click on the name of a floater to open the Floater Attributes dialog box. Hidden in this large dialog box are many powerful controls that pertain to the floater. Set up the individual Floater Attributes first for the operation you need (Selection Reveals Floater, or Selection Conceals Floater). Choose the Floater Visibility Mask option by clicking the appropriate button. (In most cases, you'll choose Normal.) If there is more than one mask in the Mask List or if you make a new selection on the image canvas, by default the floater will interact with the most recent selection. To choose another selection, choose Select, Load Selection and pick the selection you need from the menu.

Hand-Tinting a Photo

Overview *Retouch a black-and-white photo; use selection and masking tools to isolate areas of the photo; tint the image using Water Color brushes.*

1

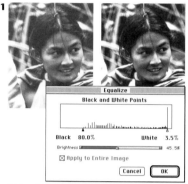

Using Equalize to adjust the tonal range of the black-and-white scan

2

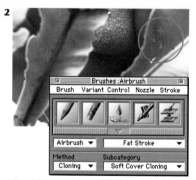

Repairing scratches with the Fat Stroke Airbrush, Soft Cover Cloning submethod

3a

Image with the background mask visible

CHER THREINEN-PENDARVIS

HAND-TINTING IS A GREAT WAY to give an old-fashioned look to a black-and-white print. It also gives the sensitive artist plenty of opportunities to add depth to an image using hues, tints and shades. To create *Rell with Bird's Nest Fern,* we hand-dyed a portrait of Hawaiian friend Rell Sunn using Painter's Water Color brushes, applying transparent color without disturbing the existing photo.

1 Equalizing the image. To preserve shadow detail during tinting, choose a light image without solid shadows or correct the tonal range after scanning as described below. We scanned our 8 x 10-inch print at 100%, 150 pixels per inch. The print was slightly overexposed, so we used the Equalize command to darken it, taking care to preserve detail in the shadows. If your image needs tonal correction, select Effects, Tonal Control, Equalize (Command-E). Your image will be automatically adjusted when the dialog box appears. To obtain a more subtle result, experiment with spreading the triangular sliders on the histogram; move them closer together for a stronger effect. Use the Brightness slider to make the graytones brighter or darker overall. Slider adjustments will be reflected in your image.

2 Retouching scratches. To touch up scratches, first use the Magnifier tool to enlarge the

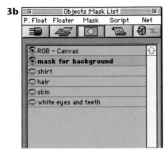

3b

The Mask List palette, showing mask visibility settings for Figure 3a

4a

Tinting the background with the Large Simple Water variant. The mask (green marquee) protected the foreground.

4b

Flat transparent washes on the foreground

5

Adding color and highlights to the shirt

area that needs retouching. Choose the Soft Cloner variant of the Cloners brush or switch the method on an existing brush (such as the Fat Stroke Airbrush) to Cloning method, Soft Cover Cloning submethod. Establish a clone source by Control-clicking (Shift-clicking in Windows) on your image near the area that needs touch-up, then begin painting. A crosshair cursor shows the origin of your sampling. If necessary, re-establish a clone source as you work.

3 Making selections and a mask. Before beginning the tinting process, make several selections to isolate areas of the image. Choose the Pen tool and draw a shape path around an area you want to isolate. When you've finished drawing the path, click the Make Selection button in the Controls:Shape Design palette. To smooth the edges of the selection, choose Select, Feather and set a 1-pixel feather. As you make each selection, it's a good idea to store it in the Mask List for future use. To save the selection as a mask choose Select, Save Selection.

To isolate larger areas you may want to paint a mask with a brush; to do this, choose New Mask from the Objects:Mask List palette menu. Now, choose black in the Color palette and select a brush. We used the Pens, Scratchboard Pen variant to isolate the background from the figure. To view the new mask as a red overlay on top of your image—as you paint it—select the mask in the Mask List and open its eye icon. When you're finished painting the mask, feather it 1 pixel to soften its edge, as follows: From the Objects palette's Mask menu choose Feather Mask and set the Feather. Click OK.

4 Applying transparent color. Turn off the mask eye icon and select the RGB-Canvas by clicking on its name. Choose a color and the Large Simple Water variant of the Water Color brush. (Simple Water variants are the fastest Water Color brushes.) Choose Select, Load Selection to activate a selection, then apply strokes to your image. The strokes are actually in the Wet Layer, which floats above the image. (The Wet Layer is turned on whenever you choose a Water Color brush.)

5 Emphasizing the area of interest. After you've added a layer of flat color, look at the overall balance and color density of your image. Add more or brighter color to the areas that you want to emphasize and apply darker or less saturated colors to make other areas appear to recede. Switch to the Simple Water variant for detail work. To remove color from oversaturated areas, use the Wet Eraser variant of the Water Color brush, adjusting its Opacity setting in the Controls:Brush palette as you work.

If you're coloring in more than one work session, save your image in RIFF format to keep the Wet Layer "wet," or separate from the canvas. Choosing Canvas, Dry drops the Wet Layer onto your image, so do this when you're finished tinting. If you dry your image and then want to add more color, you can add more Water Color brush strokes in those areas and chose Canvas, Dry again. For a complete example of this *glazing* technique, turn to "Glazing with Watercolor" in Chapter 3.

Blending a Photo

Overview *Open a photo and clone it; use the Just Add Water variant to smear pixels in the image; restore a portion of the original with the Soft Cloner variant.*

Hathaway's original photo of the dogs

Choosing the Just Add Water variant

Making loose strokes with the Just Add Water variant at 40% opacity

Partially restoring the dog's face using the low-opacity Soft Cloner variant

TO CREATE THE EXPRESSIONISTIC *DOGS OF THE SURF*, Andrew Hathaway used Painter's Water brush to paint directly onto a clone of one of his photographs, transforming it into an intense, emotionally charged abstract painting. He gave the piece a touch of realism with a Cloners brush, using it to restore a hint of the original photo to the clone.

1 Choosing a subject and making a clone. Open your photo in Painter, then choose File, Clone to make a copy of your image to alter. Hathaway chose a PICT file from a Photo CD—an image of two dogs running toward him on the beach—then cloned it.

2 Blending with a Water brush. Hathaway used the Just Add Water variant of the Water brush; since it uses the Soft Cover submethod and doesn't show paper texture, it's the smoothest of the blending brushes. You may want to adjust the brush Size or ± Size in the Brush Controls:Size palette (Brushes palette, under the Control pull-down menu) or the Opacity in the Controls:Brush palette for a more subtle smearing effect. Now, make some strokes on your clone. Hathaway painted energetic, diagonal, smeary strokes on the clone to emphasize the focal point and perspective in the fore-ground, then he smeared the background into more abstract shapes. He modified his brush as he worked, varying Size between 10 and 30 pixels, increasing the ± Size setting, and lowering the Opacity to 30–40%.

3 Partially restoring from the original. As a last step, Hathaway used the Soft Cloner variant of the Cloners brush with a very low opacity (5%) to subtly restore the foreground dog's face. Try this on your clone. Use the Soft Cloner brush to bring the original back into the blurred areas of your image. Experiment with the Opacity slider until you find a setting that suits your drawing style and pressure. 🖌

Cloning a Portrait

Overview *Retouch a photo and soften background detail; clone the image with brushes; paint details by hand; add texture.*

1a

The original photograph

1b

Using darker colors to paint over the busy flowers in the background

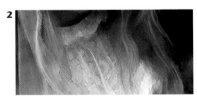
2

Adding hand-painted details to the hair

3

Adding relief to the brushwork with Surface Texture Using Image Luminance

LAUREL BECKER

PAINTERLY CLONING IS A GREAT WAY to add natural atmosphere to photos. To create *Flower Girl,* Laurel Becker began by retouching a photo. Then she enhanced a clone of the photo by painting expressive brushstrokes and adding texture. When cloning, you don't have to rely too much on the photo content; after blocking in the image, add hand-painted details, highlights and shadows.

1 Scanning, adjusting and retouching. Becker scanned an 8 x 10-inch photo at 100% and 150 ppi. Then she bumped up the image contrast using Effects, Tonal Control, Brightness /Contrast. To focus attention on the girl, she selected the background and "played down" the busy foliage details. If your background is busy consider making a selection and using Effects, Focus, Soften to blur details or paint over areas with darker colored brushstrokes, as Becker did. (For information about making selections, turn to Chapter 4).

2 Cloning and painting. Next, she cloned the photo (File, Clone). For this portrait, Becker chose Basic Paper texture and the Fine Brush variant of the Brush. Before beginning to paint, she checked the Clone Color box in the Paper palette (to sample color from the original image). Then she painted over the entire clone. As she worked, she sized the brush using the Size slider on the Controls:Brush palette. She used a larger brush while painting loose strokes behind the girl and a tiny brush to paint the details on the face, dress and hair. She turned off Clone Color, then painted brighter highlights on the cheeks, nose, eyes, chin and lips, her brush following the contours of the forms.

3 Adding texture. After she was finished painting, Becker added relief and texture to her brushwork using two applications of Effects, Surface Control, Apply Surface Texture: The first, Using Image Luminance, Amount 20% and Shine 0%; the second, Using Paper, Amount 20% and Shine 0%. She left other settings at their defaults.

Solarizing

Overview Use Express Texture on positive and negative clones of an image; merge the images by filling with a Clone Source.

1

The original image after equalizing (left), and the negative clone

2

Creating black-and-white positive (left) and negative versions of the clones using Express Texture

3

Merging the positive and negative images

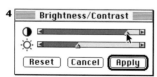

4

Adjusting the image's brightness and contrast

IN THE DARKROOM, SOLARIZATION OCCURS when a negative is exposed to a flash of light during the development process, partially reversing the photo's tonal range. To achieve this effect digitally, we tested other image-processing programs and filters, and found that we got the most control and detail using Painter's Express Texture feature. Our technique gives you a lot of control over the image's value contrast and it frequently creates a glowing edge-line effect where contrasting elements meet.

1 Making positive and negative clones. Open an image with good value contrast, then choose Effects, Tonal Control, Equalize (Command-E) to increase its tonal range. Choose File, Clone twice. Make one of the clones into a color negative by selecting Effects, Tonal Control, Negative.

2 Making black-and-white separations. Use Painter's Express Texture feature to convert both clones to black-and-white: Choose Effects, Surface Control, Express Texture, and select Image Luminance from the pop-up menu. Experiment with the sliders and click OK. Repeat the process for the second clone. We set Gray Threshold to 72%, Grain to 72% and Contrast to 160%. These settings helped emphasize the gradient effect in the sky.

3 Merging the two exposures. Choose File, Clone Source and choose the positive clone. Now fill the negative image with a percentage of the positive (the "flash of light"): With the negative window active, choose Effects, Fill, Clone Source. Set the Opacity slider between 40% and 60%.

4 Pumping up the tonal range. To achieve a broader tonal range while maintaining a silvery solarized look, we selected Effects, Tonal Control, Brightness/Contrast. We increased the contrast (the top slider) and decreased the brightness.

Toning with Textures

Overview *Use Painter's Express Texture feature to make two line conversions of a color image; colorize the two images and merge them into a single file.*

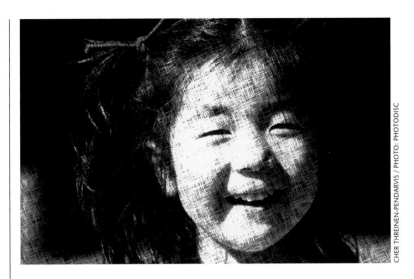

CHER THREINEN-PENDARVIS / PHOTO: PHOTODISC

The original photo

Scaling down the Angle Weave texture

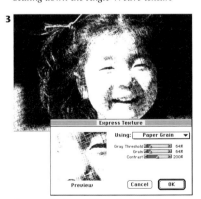

Express Texture settings for Light Exposure

CONVERTING CONTINUOUS-TONE PHOTOGRAPHS into custom line art effects—like mezzotints, etch tones and straight-line screens—can be accomplished either in the darkroom or with a graphic arts camera using a screen made of film printed with a textured pattern. There are digital plug-in filters that give similar results, although they usually eliminate much of the original's fine detail. By using Painter's Express Texture feature on two separate, textured exposures and then "sandwiching" them, you can retain more highlight and shadow detail during the conversion process than through any other digital means.

1 Selecting an image and cloning. Open a file with good tonal balance and contrast. Make two clones of this file—choose File, Clone twice. Save and name one clone "Light Exposure," and the other "Dark Exposure."

2 Choosing a texture. Select a paper texture that resembles the screen effect you wish to achieve. To get a random line effect, we chose Angle Weave from the Wild Textures library (located in Papers, in Free Stuff on the Painter 5 CD-ROM); to preserve detail in our 738-pixel-wide image, we scaled the texture to 50%.

3 Making a light exposure. To create a light, "overexposed" image that brings out shadow detail, click on the Light Exposure clone to make it active. Choose Effects, Surface Control, Express Texture, using Paper. Drag all three sliders to the left and experiment to see which settings bring out the most shadow detail: We got the best results in our image by setting Gray Threshold to 64%, Grain to 64% and Contrast to 200%.

4 Making a dark exposure. Next, create an "underexposed" image—dark, with texture visible in the midtones and highlights. Select the Dark Exposure clone and again choose Effects, Surface Control, Express Texture. Drag all three sliders farther to the right,

4

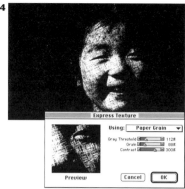

Express Texture settings for Dark Exposure

5

Applying a brown-to-white gradation to Dark Exposure (left) and a brown-to-tan gradation to Light Exposure

6

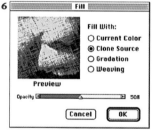

Filling Dark Exposure with Light Exposure

near their original (default) settings of 110%, 80%, 300%. We got good results by setting Gray Threshold to 112%, Grain to 88% and Contrast to 300%.

5 Coloring the clones. Using Art Materials, Grad, Express in Image to tint the two clones before merging them gives richer tonal depth to the final image than coloring it after merging the images. Start by selecting the Two-Point gradation in the Grad palette and choose colors for the front and back Color rectangles in the Color palette. Next, choose Express in Image from the Grad pull-down menu, and click OK. We applied a brown-to-white gradation to Dark Exposure, and a brown-to-tan gradation to Light Exposure.

6 Combining the images. Painter offers many ways to blend images; we got the best results on our example by filling with a Clone Source. Begin by making Light Exposure the Clone Source by choosing File, Clone Source, Light Exposure. Now fill Dark Exposure with Light Exposure: With the Dark Exposure window active, select Effects, Fill. Click the Clone Source button and experiment with a 40–60% Opacity setting, (we chose 50%). Click OK.

As a final step to increase the color and tonal range, we selected Effects, Tonal Control, Equalize (Command-E). The effect was too strong, so we selected Edit, Fade at a 50% setting. 🖌

TRADITIONAL LINE CONVERSION EFFECTS

Here's our best guess at the Painter textures required to emulate the look of a few traditional line conversions, using Express Texture on a single 553-pixel-wide color image. Use these examples as inspiration for your own experimentation. To give your image a greater tonal range before using Express Texture, you may want to use Effects, Tonal Control, Equalize.

Mezzotint: *Fine Grain (More Paper Textures library), scaled to 50%*

Dry brush: *Wheat String (More Wild Textures library), scaled to 65%*

Halftone: *Halftone 1 (More Paper Textures library), scaled to 40%*

PHOTO: PHOTODISC

Creating a Montage Using Masks and Floaters

Overview *Create masks for photos in Photoshop or Painter; copy them into a single document; use a brush to edit the floater masks when compositing them; paint on the final image.*

JOHN DISMUKES / CAPSTONE STUDIOS

The original photos

The cut-and-pasted comp ready to be scanned and used as a template

WHEN CONTINENTAL CABLEVISION asked John Dismukes of Capstone Studios to illustrate a direct-mail piece, he and his team turned to Painter. He combined photographs and splashy color with loose airbrush and chalk brushstrokes to illustrate the theme "Can Summer in California Get Any Better?"

1 Gathering illustration elements. Begin by collecting all of the individual elements that you'll need for your illustration. Dismukes and his associates photographed separate images of clouds, a pair of sunglasses, ocean foam, palm trees, and a television on the sand. The photo negatives were scanned in Kodak Photo CD format.

2 Making a template from laser prints. Many experienced artists and designers who honed their skills without the aid of a computer prefer to assemble their "comps" by hand rather than digitally. Dismukes' team created a traditional comp by printing the individual elements, then photocopying them at different scales and assembling them using scissors and adhesive. They turned the completed comp into a template by scanning it at 72 ppi, opening it in Painter and sizing it to the final image size of 4 x 5 inches at 762 ppi, using Canvas, Resize. The template would act as a guide for Dismukes to accurately scale and position the various elements. If you choose to include this step, don't be concerned about the "bitmapping" that occurs when scanning the comp at a low resolution; when the composition is finished, the template will be completely covered by the source images.

3

4a

Three of Dismukes' Photoshop masks

The glasses source file with active selection, ready to copy and paste or drag and drop into the background image

4b

Bringing the floaters into the composite file

5

Selecting the floater mask in the Mask List

6a

Using an Airbrush variant to erase the portion of the cloud floater's mask that covers the TV

3 Masking unwanted portions of the source images.

Working in Photoshop, Dismukes used the Pen tool to cut masks for the sunglasses, ocean foam, palm trees and television on the beach. He converted each path to a selection, saved the selection as Channel 4, then saved each image as an RGB TIFF file, including the alpha channel. You can accomplish the same result in Painter. Open one of your source photos and use the Pen or Quick Curve tool to draw a shape path around the desired portion of the image. When you're done, turn the path into an active selection by clicking the Make Selection button in the Controls:Shape Design palette. To save the selection as a user mask choose Select, Save Selection. View the selection as a mask by clicking the mask eye icon in the Objects palette and opening its eye icon in the Objects:Mask List. You should see your image covered by a red overlay—the default color for the mask. To view only the mask in black-and-white, click the RGB-Canvas eye icon shut in the Mask List.

4 Compiling the source files.

When you've finished masking the images, bring them into a single document. Open either the template or the photo that will become your background image. Choose the Floater Adjuster tool and click the Floater icon in the Objects palette to open the Floater List. Then open each of the source images and choose Select, Load Selection and Option-click on each selection to float it. Loading the selection and floating it prepares Painter to export the item from the source image with its mask.

There are three ways to import source images into a composite file: Copying and pasting through the clipboard, performing a drag and drop, or using the File, Place command to bring the source image in as a reference floater. To paste using the clipboard, select the floater in the source image with the Floater Adjuster tool, choose Edit, Copy, then make the background image active and choose Edit, Paste. To drag and drop items from one Painter image to another, select the floater in the source image with the Floater Adjuster. Now use the Floater Adjuster to drag the masked item to the background image.

If you're working with large files, positioning and scaling can be accomplished much more quickly using reference floaters. (For more

6b

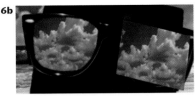

Compositing the clouds inside the glasses

6c

Revealing the cloud floater around the tree

7

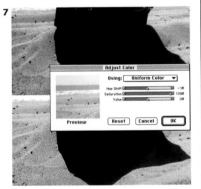

Using Adjust Colors to increase saturation in the image

8

Adding squiggles and lens glare (top) and smudges and blurs

information about reference floaters see "Using Reference Floaters," in the beginning of Chapter 5.) To import an image as a reference floater with a mask, save the source file in RIFF format (to preserve its mask), then choose File, Place, navigate to the source image and choose Open. In the Place dialog box check the Retain Alpha checkbox and click in the image to place the floater.

5 Putting the masks to work. To view the mask on a floater, select it in the Floater List, switch to the Mask List palette and open the floater's mask eye icon. To switch back to Color View, toggle the floater mask eye icon shut.

6 Positioning the floater and painting on its mask. First scale, rotate and position one floater on top of another and make sure that the top floater is selected in the Floater List. Now, fit one element inside of another by using a brush to erase a portion of the floater's mask, as follows: Switch to the Mask List and target the floater mask by highlighting its name. Select an Airbrush variant and choose white in the Color palette. Begin painting around the edge of the top floater to erase part of its mask, making it appear "inside" of the floater beneath it. Paint with black to restore the mask. You may find it quicker and easier to work without the Floater Marquee visible; if so, choose Hide Floater Marquee from the Floater List palette's Floater menu (or press Command-Shift-H).

When you've completed all compositing, make a copy of your image with the floaters dropped to the background by choosing File, Clone. This step gives you a lot of flexibility—you have an "original" with floaters intact, and a "working image" (the clone) on which you can paint and make other adjustments.

7 Shifting colors. To make the image "pop" a bit more, Dismukes increased the color saturation. Choose Effects, Tonal Control, Adjust Colors, and experiment with the Hue Shift, Saturation and Value sliders to shift the colors in your image.

8 Painting on the photo montage. To transform the television into a lively caricature in vivid color, Dismukes first used the Feather Tip Airbrush variant to add glare to the glasses and other details. He switched to the Impressionist variant of the Artists brush to paint on the sand and water, and then painted spontaneous, textured squiggles around the TV and on the sand and water with the Artist Pastel Chalk variant and the Big Canvas paper (from the More Papers library, located in Free Stuff, in Papers, on the Painter 5 CD-ROM). As a final touch, Dismukes switched to the Water brush, Grainy Water variant, Cover method and Grainy Hard Cover submethod to add the smudges and blurs on the sand and television.

Finishing the job. Using the same style, technique, tools and colors, Dismukes created similar illustrations on a smaller scale that were used throughout the brochure, as well as a border around the edge of the piece. 🖌

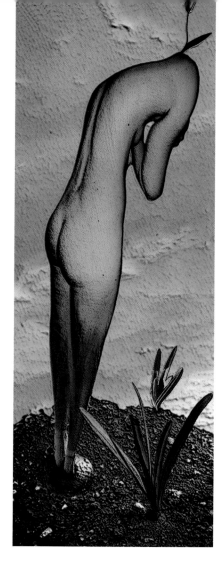

■ For this double-page illustration for IBM's *AS/400* magazine, **Jean Francois Podevin** began with conventional pencil sketches based on his own photographs. Podevin then collaborated with colleague **Larry Scher** on the computer. The team scanned Podevin's sketch and used it as a guide to position Podevin's Photo CD images. The image was composed and filter effects added in the DOS programs RIO and VIP, and then it was imported into Painter. Podevin retouched and painted on the image using the Airbrush, Water and Chalk brushes. To create the drop shadow of the final composite, the team selected the image, then floated and duplicated it. The duplicate was feathered, filled and moved behind the composite.

■ **Caty Bartholomew** created *Planted Nude* as a vivid symbol of personal growth. She envisioned a distorted nude that would express "growing pains" and incorporated a tulip as a symbol of hope. She began with some initial photo-compositing work in Photoshop, but wanted to avoid a slick, photographic look, so she imported the nude into Painter. Bartholomew retouched the legs and bulb with the Thin Stroke Airbrush variant, then stretched the figure disproportionately using Effects, Orientation, Scale. She cut and pasted the nude and other plants onto the dirt. To give texture and dimension to the piece, she used Effects, Surface Control, Apply Surface Texture twice: first with Original Luminance; then with Paper Grain and a medium-rough paper texture.

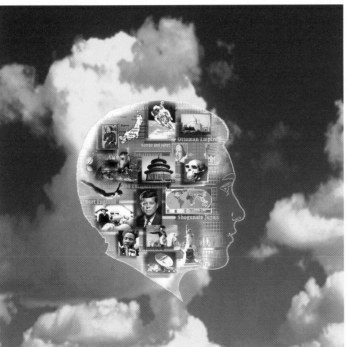

■ **Philip Howe** was commissioned by Harry Hansen to create *Police,* a photo collage painting to promote positive aspects of law enforcement. The final piece—printed on canvas and enhanced with oil paints—is part of a traveling show of police art touring the United States. To build the image, Howe began with two source photos: a brick wall with a cast shadow of a motorcycle rider, and a vertical photo of a policeman standing against a brick wall. Beginning in Photoshop, Howe copied the rider image and pasted it into a copy of the vertical wall image as a layer. He worked back and forth between Photoshop and Painter as he retouched the brick areas above the standing figure's head to match the bricks of the top image. When the retouching was complete, Howe began the process of building relief on the background wall image in Painter. He applied Effects Focus, Glass Distortion Using Image Luminance and the Refraction Map Type, using strong settings. Next, he opened the original vertical brick wall image and applied Effects, Focus, Glass Distortion, Using Image Luminance and the Refraction Map type, using subtle settings. Finally, he selected the composite file and defined the subtly distorted image as the clone source (File, Clone Source.) Using an Airbrush Cloner variant, he cloned the subtle distortion onto areas of the image canvas to softly smooth out areas of the relief.

When Microsoft commissioned **Philip Howe** to illustrate their *Encarta CD-ROM Interactive Encyclopedia* packaging, he created a photo montage that included a transparent glass effect. Howe began by building two source files of the same size, a montage that incorporated an illustrated background, a time line and several photos; and a second image, a retouched cloud photo. To begin the crystal effect, he opened both the cloud image and the montage and made the montage the clone source (File, Clone Source). Working in the cloud image, he applied Effects, Focus, Glass Distortion, Using Original Luminance and the Refraction Map Type to create the crystal. To combine both images, he cloned the montage into the crystal image, taking great care to preserve the crystal effect around the edges of the image. To further define the head against the clouds, he used white paint and the default Fat Stroke Airbrush variant to paint a glow around the inside edge of the back of the head. Finally, to increase the glass effect, Howe used Effects, Surface Control, Dye Concentration, using Original Luminance, keeping the montage as the clone source.

■ *Girl of Guadalupe* (top) and *Boy and Father* (bottom) are two works from a photo-essay by **Cher Threinen-Pendarvis** entitled *Children of Guadalupe.* Both images began with photographs shot in Mexico over a three-year period at the Virgin of Guadalupe celebration. Parents who had brought their children to church to be blessed were delighted to have their children photographed wearing Virgin of Guadalupe costumes. After the color photos from the shoot were processed in Photo CD format, she opened the images in Painter and performed the solarization procedure described on page 158, which converted the images to grays. She chose solarization for the photo essay because she felt the graduated tonal quality and glowing edge line effects complemented the spiritual purpose of the celebration. After solarizing, she "toned" the images by coloring them with custom multi-colored gradations using Express Grad in Image.

For *Girl of Guadalupe,* after solarizing and coloring the photo with a custom gold-red-black gradation, Threinen-Pendarvis painted into the image with several brushes. She used a small Diffuse Pull Brush (from the Gooey Brush library), to pull color and to enhance the granular texture produced by the solarization. As a last step, she used Effects, Tonal Control, Equalize to bump up the gradation's glow and enhance the "edge line" effect in the solarization.

Threinen-Pendarvis began the treatment for *Boy and Father* using the same solarization process. She then increased the contrast and value range using the Effects, Tonal Control, Equalize command. To color the image she applied a custom gradation that included purple, green, gold and red. To increase the saturation of a few colors, she used Effects, Tonal Control, Adjust Selected Colors.

■ The work of **Lawrence Gartel,** a pioneer of computer art and digital photography, has been exhibited in museums and galleries worldwide for over two decades. *South Beach* is one in a series of images commissioned by the Miami International Airport for the first major public art installation of digital photography. Gartel scanned each of the source photos into Photoshop and made selections to isolate a few of the subjects from their backgrounds. He opened a large new blank file, copied each source image and pasted it onto its own layer in the composite. Next, he opened the layered image in Painter and repositioned floaters (which Painter had automatically made from the layers) with the Floater Adjuster tool until the piece felt balanced. Gartel painted on many of the floaters. To emboss a few of the floaters, he applied Effects, Surface Control, Apply Surface Texture, Using Image Luminance. Then he changed the Opacity and Composite Method (Controls:Adjuster palette) of several of the floaters: the kids playing on the beach in the middle of the work, the motorcycle at the bottom and the Beach Patrol building in the middle right of the picture. Gartel feels that by combining images using different composite methods and opacities, an artist is sharing critical information—the image is in a translucent state, giving the viewer the opportunity to see each layer of imagery without losing the overall message. "Naturally, as a collagist, I like to pack an image with lots of pictures that add up to a full story. It's then up to the viewer to interpret," says Gartel.

Ellie Dickson created *Wright Brothers* for an advertisement for the U. S. Postal Service. She began the image with two black-and-white photos (the plane and the two Wright brothers) supplied by the client's ad agency. She retouched both images in Photoshop, colored them with light tints, then composited them into one image. She opened the composite in Painter and painted directly on the image using the Artist Pastel Chalk and the Just Add Water variants, building up multiple layers of colored strokes.

S. Swaminathan used Painter to combine and enhance two images, building this portrait of two friends—the dedicated Chicano Rights activist Caesar Chavez and Luis Valdez, the renowned film director of *La Bomba, Zoot Suit,* and *The Cisco Kid,* and director of El Teatro Campesino. (Swaminathan captured the portrait of Valdez, and Chavez was photographed by Lupe Valdez.) Swaminathan opened the Valdez image and used the curves in Effects, Tonal Control, Correct Colors to increase its brightness and contrast and to eliminate a yellow cast. He cloned the color-corrected image and used a large custom Fat Stroke Airbrush with high Color Variability settings (zoomed-out Color palette) to selectively lay down spattery, diffused brushstrokes in the clone. Using a tiny Airbush, he painted back into the blurred image to restore detail to Valdez's face, his clothing and his Aztec pendant. Swaminathan used similar techniques to enhance the image of Caesar Chavez, then copied and pasted it into the Valdez image as a floater. He painted on the floater mask to create an irregular transparent edge on the Chavez floater. To complete the dual portrait he adjusted the opacity of the floater in the Controls:Adjuster palette for a soft effect.

■ As part of an advertising campaign, Wacom Technology Corporation commissioned **Philip Howe** to create *Portrait of Harley*. Howe started by shooting a Polaroid of his brother Harley to use as a reference. In Painter, he used the 2B Pencil variant to create a freehand sketch, then rendered the photorealistic portrait using the Fat Stroke Airbrush. Howe scanned paintbrushes, pastel sticks and pastel dust and composited the objects atop the portrait in Photoshop. Back in Painter, he painted on the image using the Oil Paint variant of the Brush, the Flemish Rub variant of the Artists brush (to break up existing strokes) and Liquid brush variants (to pull color around). Finally, he used a light touch of Effects, Focus, Glass Distortion to emphasize the brushstrokes.

■ **John Derry** used photographs he took in Japan to build *Asakusa*, part of his ongoing *City Series*. The image illustrates religion intertwined with commercial culture in the Asakusa district of Tokyo, famous for its temple and marketplace. To isolate areas of the source photos, Derry made Bézier curve selections using the Pen tool. He copied and pasted the selected areas into the composite file, where he scaled and repositioned the floaters and gave them drop shadows. To blend the masks in the center of the image with the temple prayer card beneath, Derry filled the mask in the top floater with a custom gradient to reveal part of the underlying image (Effects, Fill, Fill With Gradation). He created an Asian-inspired pattern and used it as a background element, then added final painterly details using a modified Big Wet Oils variant and blended colors with the Just Add Water variant.

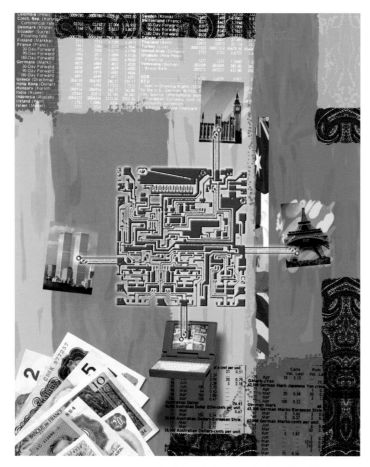

■ **John Derry** designed and assembled the cover illustration for the international banking book *Price Waterhouse Technology Forecast 1997*, entirely within Painter. Using the Big Wet Luscious brush from the New Paint Tools library, Derry began by painting a colorful "Robert Rauschenberg–inspired" background. Then he prepared several source files including scans of type and paisley fabric and photos selected from a photo CD-ROM collection. To isolate areas of the source photos (such as the money and the computer), Derry made selections using the Pen tool. Then he used the Floater Adjuster to drag and drop the selected areas into the background file. After scaling and positioning the elements, he applied a drop shadow to the image of the computer using Effects, Objects, Create Drop Shadow. Derry selected the shadow floater in the Floater List and used Effects, Orientation, Distort to exaggerate the perspective of the shadow. To drop the background out behind the scanned financial text, he made a luminosity mask. (From the Objects palette's Mask menu choose Auto Mask, Image Luminance.) He also modified the mask of the World Trade Center and Eiffel Tower images by selecting each floater mask in the Mask List and painting into it with a brush.

■ Photographer **Fred Gillaspy** shoots images with Painter in mind. For *Recuerdos de Sante Fe* (below), he used a 2¼-inch Ukrainian Kiev 88 camera (90 seconds at *f*32) to capture the soft glow of the *luminarias*—candles in brown paper bags—set out on Christmas Eve in Santa Fe, New Mexico. He scanned and cloned the photo, then used several Airbrush variants to retouch the image. He added brush strokes with the Just Add Water variant and retouched the foliage. To amplify the original photo's suggestion of heat, Gillaspy added brush strokes to suggest a lava flow along the driveway. Using a small Water brush and a tiny white Airbrush, Gillaspy burned out the center of every light source and reflection and added a light flare to each light source.

■ **Jeff Burke** and **Lorraine Triolo** of Burke/Triolo Productions created *Painted Sunflower* (left), as a promotional piece. The partners styled the still life, photographed it and scanned it. Then Burke opened the scanned photo in Painter. He used the Grainy Water variant of the Water brush (on top of Basic Paper texture) to smear and blend edges of the flower and its shadow. To add hand-painted detail and texture, he used the Chalk variants to paint subtle streaks and small dabs of color behind the stem and along the edge of the flower and shadow. To smoothly blend some areas, Burke used the Just Add Water variant.

■ A national news report of a white buffalo born in the Plains of the Midwest was the inspiration for *White Buffalo* (bottom), by **Gary Clark**. Clark shot the buffalo, figures and tree photographs with a digital camera. Then he assembled two more source files: a landscape generated in Vista Pro and a sky built in MetaCreations Bryce. He copied and pasted all four source files into a large composite file as floaters and made silhouette masks for the buffalo, tree and figures. Clark positioned the sky and landscape floaters with the Floater Adjuster, then dropped them to the image canvas using the Drop button on the Floater List palette. To add interest to the landscape and sky, he cloned texture from a photo of grass into the image using a low-opacity Straight Cloner variant. To add color to the tree, Clark cloned color from a scan of brightly colored paint swatches.

■ **Ellie Dickson** began each of these photo illustrations by scanning a black-and-white photo in RGB-mode. In Photoshop, she made loose freehand selections with the Lasso and filled the selections with tints of color (using Color mode). Dickson opened the tinted image in Painter and applied strokes with a low-opacity Artist Pastel Chalk variant, using Soft Cover submethod for a smooth look. She softened the Pastel strokes using the Just Add Water brush and intensified the image's watery look with the Distorto variant of the Liquid brush. Finally, she modified the 2B Pencil variant of the Pencils—changing its method to Cover so she could paint light over dark—and emphasized details in the images.

For *Warren* (top), Dickson's client requested a portrait print with a painterly look. She began by scanning the aged and torn photo: She opened the scan in Photoshop, extended the canvas on the left side, retouched it using the Rubber Stamp tool and applied color tints. In Painter, she painted over the image using a custom Artist Pastel Chalk brush. Facial details were important, so Dickson completed the faces of the subjects using a very small custom 2B Pencil variant. The final piece was output to an Iris 3047 ink jet printer as a 24 x 36-inch print on soft rag paper.

Psychology Today magazine commissioned Dickson to create *Rich, Mom and Ellie* (bottom), an editorial illustration to accompany a story on family dynamics. For this image, Dickson used contrasting values and deeper color. To paint loose, expressive brushstrokes on the image she used larger custom Artist Pastel Chalk, Water and Distorto brushes. Dickson sized the brushes as she worked using the Size slider in the Controls:Brush palette.

■ "Although the program is called Painter," says renowned photographer **Pedro Meyer**, "it's important not to exclude photography from its repertoire, given that the program can also be used effectively in that medium."

Eagles (above) and *Fear, Anger and Hate* (left) reflect Meyer's observation of the youth of Los Angeles and of how they deal with finding their identity. Although the need to belong is nothing new, what's different today is the form in which the ritual of belonging takes place. Meyer's photographic eye captures the call for unity with peers—the gang—as well the declaration of individuality and rebelliousness—for example, the upside-down flag in *Eagles* and the slogans on the wall in *Fear, Anger and Hate*.

EXPLORING
SPECIAL
EFFECTS

Special effects wizard Steve Campbell relied on Painter's selections, and Apply Lighting, Apply Surface Texture and Glass Distortion commands to add dimension to this piece, The Performance.

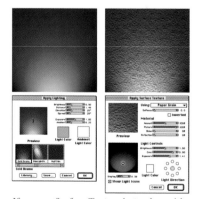

If you use Surface Texture in tandem with Apply Lighting, you'll get more dramatic results if you choose similar lighting directions for both commands.

PAINTER'S SPECIAL EFFECTS ARE SO NUMEROUS and complex that an entire book could be written about them alone. Because they're so powerful, there's much less need for third-party filters than with Photoshop or other image processors. But with that power comes complexity; some of these effects have evolved into "programs within the program." This chapter focuses on five of Painter's most frequently used "mini-programs"—Apply Surface Texture, Apply Lighting, Patterns, Glass Distortion and Mosaics plus several new special effect plug-ins—Bevel World, Burn, Tear and Liquid Metal, to name a few—along with a handful of other exciting effects.

ADDING EFFECTS WITH SURFACE TEXTURE

One of the most frequent "haunts" of Painter artists is the Effects, Surface Control, Apply Surface Texture dialog box. You'll find it used in a number of places throughout this book. The Surface Texture dialog box contains intricate, powerful controls, allowing you to apply paper textures to images, build realistic highlights and shadows for masked elements, and more. First, the Softness slider (located under the Using pop-up menu) allows you to create soft transitions, such as smoothing the edge of a mask or softening a texture application. Adding Softness can also increase the 3D effect produced when you apply Surface Texture Using Mask. And with the Reflection slider (bottom Material slider), you can create a reflection in your artwork based on another image or the current pattern.

Another very important Surface Texture control is the preview sphere, located below the image Preview. Think of the sphere displayed as a dome supporting lights above your image. Although the preview sphere seems to show a spotlight effect, any lights you set are applied evenly across the surface of your image. Experiment

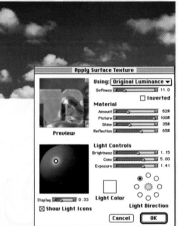

Creating the illusion of type under water (top), with Apply Surface Texture using Original Luminance and a reflection map. We applied the reflection using a clone source image of a cloudy sky (tinted red using Effects, Tonal Control, Adjust Colors to match the color in the type).

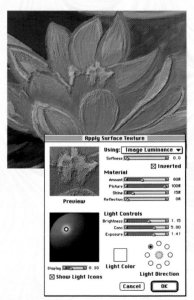

Creating textured, dimensional brush strokes with Apply Surface Texture using Image Luminance

with adding more lights to the preview sphere by clicking on the sphere. Adjust an individual light by selecting it, changing its color, and adjusting its Brightness and Conc (Concentration). Use the Exposure slider to control ambient light in the environment.

You can get some interesting effects by changing your color choices for the lights. For instance, if the area to be lit contains a lot of blue, you can add more color complexity by lighting with its complement, an orange-hued light.

Applying a reflection map. Reflections can add interest to type and to other shiny surfaces like glass or metal objects in your illustrations. The Reflection slider allows you to apply a separate image to your illustration as a reflection. Open an image and make a selection or mask for the area where you'll apply the reflection. You can use a pattern as a source for a reflection map or you can open an image the same size as your working file (the current Pattern is applied automatically if you don't choose another image as clone source). (Turn to "Making a Reflection Map" and Applying a Reflection Map," later in this chapter to read about how Michele Lill builds custom-made maps and applies them to her images. And for more inspiration, check out Michele Lill's E-Maps folder on the Painter 5 Wow! CD-ROM, and the Pattern libraries in the Free Stuff, Patterns folder on the Painter 5 CD-ROM).

Creating 3D effects. You can use Surface Texture to enhance the surface of your image and give dimension to your brushstrokes. Image Luminance, in the Using pop-up menu, adds depth to brushstrokes by making the light areas appear to recede or "deboss" slightly. If you want to bring the light areas forward, check the Invert box. Experiment with the sliders to get the effect you desire. You can get a stronger 3D effect by adding a second light (a bounce or a fill light) to the preview sphere with a lower Brightness or a higher Concentration (Conc) setting.

Combining Surface Texture with other effects. Apply Surface Texture works especially well when combined with other Painter tools. "Adding Diffusion and Relief" uses a Glass Distortion plug-in floater and Surface Texture to add brushstrokes to a photo; John Derry used a combination of Glass Distortion and Surface Texture to give the illusion of refracted water in "Creating a

> ### REFLECTING ANOTHER IMAGE
>
> To use a separate image as a reflection map, bend it using Effects, Surface Control, Quick Warp to achieve a spherical or rippled look. (Quick Warp is applied to the entire image, not just to selections or floaters.) Designate it as the clone source (File, Clone Source). Then (in the original image not the map image) choose Effects, Surface Control, Apply Surface Texture using Mask, (or Original Luminance to apply the effect to an entire image). To see the reflection, move the Reflection slider to the right and distort the reflection effect by moving the Softness slider to the right. Experiment with the other settings.

Detail from Ægypt by Steve Campbell. In several areas of the image—for instance, in the sunrise shown here—Campbell created atmosphere and dimension by applying custom lighting to selections and floaters. See "Working with Freehand Selections" in Chapter 4 to read more about Ægypt.

To create soft spotlights for a background, increase the Elevation setting and decrease the Spread of the lights in the Apply Lighting dialog box.

Tidepool"; "Draping a Weave" uses a powerful Glass Distortion displacement in combination with Surface Texture to achieve the look of draped fabric. And Steve Campbell used Surface Texture and Apply Lighting together to add gradations to textured areas while creating the illustration "Drummer Sam" in the gallery later in this chapter.

ADDING DIMENSION WITH LIGHTING

Painter's *User Guide* gives a good description of how to adjust the controls under Effects, Surface Control, Apply Lighting. Here are some tips and practical uses for the tool:

Applying Lighting to unify an image. Like most of the Surface Control effects, applying lighting across an entire image can help to unify the piece. (If the lighting effect is too dramatic, try using Edit, Fade immediately afterwards to reduce it.)

Preventing hot spots. You can avoid "burnout" of lit areas by increasing the Elevation of the light, reducing the light's Exposure or Brightness, or giving the light a pastel or gray color.

Lighting within selections or floaters. Add instant dimension to a selection by applying lighting within it. When lighting floaters, remember that the effect is applied to the entire floater, not just an area you may have masked. See Steve Campbell's work in this and other chapters for his use of this lighting technique.

Creating subtle gradient effects. To achieve colored gradient effects in an image, some artists prefer lighting with colored lights instead of filling with a gradient; they prefer the lighting command's smooth luminosity shifts over the more "mechanical" result usually achieved when using gradations.

Painting back into lit areas. For fine artists who want to achieve a more painterly effect, the Apply Lighting command can look a bit artificial. Artists Sharon Steuer and Chelsea Sammel (see Chapters 3 and 4) use Apply Lighting and then break up the lit area with brush-strokes, sampling color from the image as they work.

Creating softly lit backgrounds. On a white background, start with the Splashy Colors light effect. Increase the Brightness and Elevation on both colored lights until they form very soft-edged tinted circles on the white

Detail of the Carp source image for Corinne Okada's package created for The Digital Pond—notice the realistic fish scale texture (bottom). Okada scanned a photo of fish skin and used Art Materials, Pattern, Capture Pattern (top), to create a custom seamlessly tiling pattern. Then, to test her pattern, she used the Check Out Pattern command (Pattern, Check Out Pattern). Okada used the wrap-around image in the Capture Pattern Preview to scroll and look for edges in her pattern. She used cloning brushes to repair any edges that weren't seamless, and when it was complete, she saved the new pattern to the library (Add Image to Library).

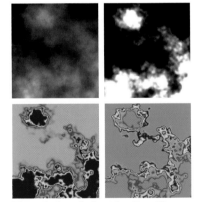

The evolution of a fractal pattern. The original pattern, made by choosing Art Materials, Pattern, Make Fractal Pattern (top left); a hard edge added with Effects, Surface Control, Express Texture Using Image Luminance (top right); the Earthen grad applied via Art Materials, Grad, Express in Image (lower left); adjusting the Bias to 46% in the Express in Image dialog box (lower right).

background. Add another light or two and change their colors. Move the lights around until the color, value and composition are working. Save and name your settings and click OK to apply the effect. Repeat this process two or three times, returning each time to your saved effect and making minor adjustments in light color, light position and other settings.

EXPLORING PATTERNS

Under Art Materials, Pattern, there are commands that let you make seamless wrap-around pattern tiles. Once a pattern has been defined and is in the Pattern palette, it becomes the default Clone Source when no other clone source is designated. You can apply a pattern to an existing image, selection or floater with Cloning brushes, with the Paint Bucket tool (by choosing Fill With: Clone Source in the Controls:Paint Bucket palette), with any of the special effects features that use a clone source (such as Original Luminance or 3D Brushstrokes), or by choosing to fill with a pattern or clone source (Command-F). (The Fill dialog box shows a Pattern button if no clone source image is designated; if a clone source *is* available, a Clone Source button appears.) Use the pattern feature to create multimedia screen design backgrounds, textile design, wallpaper—anywhere you need repeating images.

Defining a Pattern. When you choose Define Pattern, Painter creates a wrap-around for the selected image. Here's a great way to see it work. Make a new document that will become your pattern tile and select Define Pattern from the Art Materials palette's Pattern menu. Choose the Image Hose brush in the Brushes palette (or use any brush). Select an Image Hose nozzle as follows: From the Brushes palette's Nozzle menu choose Nozzles to open the Nozzle palette, or press Command-9, and click on a nozzle. Begin spraying across your image and beyond its edge. Notice how the hose images "wrap around" the edges of the pattern tile you've defined (so that when an area is filled with these pattern tiles, the edges match seamlessly).

Capturing a Pattern. To make and store a pattern image in the Pattern palette, select an area of your document with the Rectangular Selection tool (or press Command-A to select the entire image) and from the Art Materials palette's Pattern menu, choose Capture Pattern. To offset your pattern use the Horizontal and Vertical shift options and the Bias slider to control the amount of the offset. Experiment with these settings to get nonaligned patterns—for example, to create a brick wall look, wallpaper or fabric.

Making a Fractal Pattern. You don't need an open document to use Make Fractal Pattern because choosing Art Materials, Pattern, Make Fractal Pattern automatically creates a pattern as a new file when you click OK. If you have a lot of memory allotted to Painter, you'll be able to create larger tiles; if not, the larger size options will

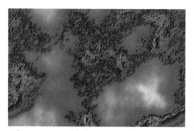

After creating this topographic map, we added clouds for more atmosphere by copying the Fractal pattern file and pasting it into the map image as a floater. We changed the Composite Method in the Controls:Adjuster palette to Screen to reveal only the light areas of the floater. Then we adjusted the Opacity slider to 90%.

MARBLED REFLECTIONS

The Effects, Esoterica, Blobs feature is commonly used to prepare a base image before using Apply Marbling. Designer Michele Lill creates environment maps from photos of nature and uses them with Blobs to build bases for marbling. Her secret is: Select an environment map for the current pattern (such as the Reflection Map from the Art Materials, Pattern palette), and in the Blobs dialog box, choose the current Pattern. Click OK. Choose Effects, Esoterica, Apply Marbling. (See "Applying a Reflection Map" later in this chapter.)

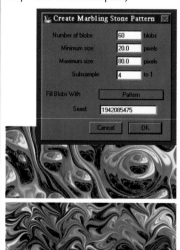

Michele Lill's settings for the Blobs (top); the blobs image (center), and the "marbled reflections" (bottom).

be grayed out. Some of the textures you can create with Make Fractal Pattern make very cool paper textures: Select the area of the fractal pattern that you want for your texture (or choose Select, All) and choose Art Materials, Paper, Capture Paper. Or, you may want to capture the texture after you've applied effects to the pattern using Grad, Express in Image, Express Texture, Glass Distortion, Image Warp or Quick Warp.

Enhancing fractal patterns. You can add any special effect to fractal (or regular) patterns and they still remain patterns. Here are two creative applications of fractal pattern.

To create a hard-edged fractal pattern with wild color, make a Fractal Pattern, setting Power to –150, Feature Size to 75 (for a relatively coarse pattern), and Softness to 0. Click OK. Select Effects, Surface Control, Express Texture using Image Luminance. Adjust the Gray Threshold and Grain sliders to about 80, and set the Contrast slider at 200 for a contrasty effect. Click OK. Now colorize the pattern by choosing the Brights gradation and selecting Art Materials, Grad, Express in Image. Experiment with shifting the image's hue by dragging the Bias slider.

To make an abstract topographical map image with color and relief, create a new pattern using Fractal Pattern's default settings. Give the image a "topographical" look by choosing Effects, Surface Control, Apply Surface Texture, using Image Luminance (Amount, 200; Picture, 100%; and Shine, 0%). Tint the image with Art Materials, Grad, Express in Image and the Earthen gradation. Now, add a little relief by applying a second pass of Apply Surface Texture, using Image Luminance (Amount, 100%; Picture, 100%; and Shine, 0%). To add a swirl to your "map" choose Effects, Surface Control, Quick Warp and click the Swirl button. Experiment with different Angle Factor settings in the dialog box.

CREATING REPEATING TEXTURES WITH MAKE PAPER

Using Art Materials, Paper, Make Paper you can generate seamless repeating textures to apply to your images. For the image below, Corinne Okada created her own repeating texture that resembled a grid of pixels to represent the digital output process. She generated the grid of beveled squares using Make Paper using the Square Pattern, then applied the texture to the central portion of her image using Effects, Surface Control, Color Overlay.

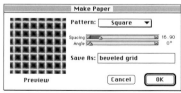

Left: Detail from The Digital Pond package design created by Corinne Okada. The complete illustration is featured on page 206. Above: Okada's settings for the grid of beveled squares

Use Effects, Tonal Control, Adjust Colors, then drag the Hue Shift slider to change the hue of your image. Use Uniform Color to shift the hue of the entire image, or use Image Luminance to change color properties only in the lighter areas.

Highpass (under Effects, Esoterica) acts like a color filter. It looks for dark areas with smooth transitions (as in a sky or shadowed background) and replaces them with abrupt edges or halo effects. It also emphasizes highlights in an image and lightens shaded areas. Keep the Radius slider to the left for a more pronounced halo effect. To further enhance Highpass, try using Effects, Tonal Control, Equalize.

The initial, unaltered photograph

PHOTO: CHER THREINEN-PENDARVIS

Adjust Colors, Uniform Color: Hue Shift, -44%; Value, 25%

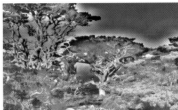
Adjust Colors, Image Luminance: Hue Shift, 20%; Value, 25%

Highpass: Radius, 26.05

PHOTO: DIGITAL STOCK

Conventional diffuser screens attach to the camera lens, breaking up or softening the image as it refracts through the screen. Painter's Glass Distortion plug-in floater works the same way but with more variety. To generate a Glass Distortion plug-in floater for your image, in the Objects palette click the plug icon, select Glass Distortion from the plug-ins palette and click the Apply button. From the Using menu choose Paper and experiment with refracting your image through different textures. On this photo, we used Diagonal 1 from the More Paper Textures library (in Free Stuff, Papers on the Painter 5 CD-ROM).

CREATING EFFECTS WITH GLASS DISTORTION

Try using another image as a "refractor" for your main image. With Painter 5's Glass Distortion features you can superimpose glass bas relief effects (using a paper texture or another image). To apply the procedure directly to your image choose Effects, Focus, Glass Distortion. A benefit of the Glass Distortion plug-in is that you can preview the effects on a copy of your image without changing the original image; however, the Effects, Focus, Glass Distortion features a dialog box with more controls. (To learn more about using Effects, Glass Distortion turn to "Diving into Distortion" and "Draping a Weave" later in this chapter. To read about using the Glass Distortion plug-in floater turn to "Adding Diffusion and Relief.")

WORKING WITH MOSAICS

Tile mosaics became a popular medium at about 200–300 BC in the Roman Empire and Greece; floors and walls of many building were decorated with mosaics made of small pieces of glass, stones and shells. They were most often built to celebrate a historic event or for religious purposes. And early Christians built mosaics from bits of sparkling glass, illuminating the walls and ceilings of their churches with biblical scenes designed to inspire the viewer.

Inspiration for mosaics. You can build mosaics using Painter 5's new Mosaic brush and dialog box—by drawing them from scratch, by basing them on a line drawing that you've scanned, or by creating a clone-based mosaic using an existing piece of art or a photo. Keep in mind that because of the nature of the Mosaic tool, your decorative design or photo reference should have a strong compositional focal point. If you want to use a photo that has a

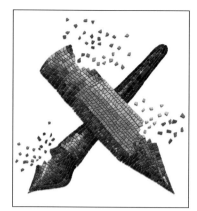

To create Pencil and Brush, *artist John Derry began by making a mosaic in Painter beginning with white grout. After the tiles were in place, he added realistic highlights and shadows to the tiles using Effects, Surface Control, Apply Surface Texture, Using Mask.*

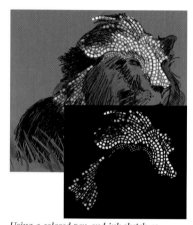

Using a colored pen-and-ink sketch as reference for a mosaic. Top: The cloned sketch (with tracing paper turned on) shows the mosaic in progress with recently applied tiles. Bottom: The same stage with tracing paper turned off. Click tracing paper on and off without closing the Make Mosaic dialog box by using the checkbox.

The default grout color is white, shown here (left) in the Select Grout Color dialog box, which uses the Apple color picker. Dragging the Lightness slider to the left darkens the color of the grout.

busy background, consider simplifying it first by desaturating or blurring. (For tips on neutralizing busy backgrounds, see the beginning of Chapter 6.)

Laying down tiles. Here's a way to try out Painter's Mosaics. Open a new blank file, or a reference on which to base your mosaic. Visualize the forms in your design before you begin laying down the tiles, and rotate your page by clicking on your image and dragging with the Rotate Page tool, (nested with the Grabber tool) to accommodate your drawing style so you'll be able to make smooth, controlled strokes to describe the forms.

Choose Canvas, Make Mosaic to open the Mosaic dialog box. Opening the dialog box will turn the background of the currently active image white, the default grout color. To change the grout color using the Apple color picker in the Select Grout Color dialog box, click in the Grout box, move the Lightness slider to the left to increase the value and click on a new color in the color picker. Then choose a contrasting color in the Color palette to paint some tiles. Switch colors again and continue to make tiles. Once you have tiles in place, you can sample color from an existing tile by pressing the Command key as you click on it. You can undo an action without closing the Mosaic dialog box by pressing Command-Z. To erase a tile, press the Control key and stroke with the Mosaic brush over the tile. While working on a mosaic, save it in RIFF format to preserve the resolution-independent nature of the mosaic. (Because mosaic tiles are mathematically described, a mosaic can be resized without loss of quality.) For an in-depth explanation of Painter's mosaic-building tools check out Chapter 6 of the *Painter 5 User Guide*. And to read about using a photo-reference for a mosaic, turn to "Building a Clone-Based Mosaic," later in this chapter.

SPECIAL EFFECTS USING PLUG-IN FLOATERS

Painter 5 features eight dynamic plug-in floaters that allow you to create exciting special effects quickly—they are—Glass Distortion, Kaleidoscope, Liquid Lens, Burn, Tear, Bevel World and Liquid Metal. In the paragraphs below, we focus on special effect applications for several of these plug-ins. (To read more about working with plug-in floaters turn to the introduction of Chapter 5; see Chapter 6 to see how plug-ins apply to image correction and photography; to read about painting techniques using Impasto plug-in floaters turn to the beginning of Chapter 3 and to "Advanced Painting with Impasto," also in Chapter 3. Turn to "Adding Diffusion and Relief" later in this chapter to read about using the Glass Distortion plug-in in combination with Apply Surface Texture. And the *Painter 5 User Guide* contains good descriptions for each of these plug-ins.)

Painting with metal and water. Painter 5's versatile Liquid Metal plug-in allows you to paint with bas relief and give it the look of several substances, such as chrome, steel, ice and water to name a few. The Liquid Metal plug-in works in an existing file to

To create the title T3, Jack Davis began by with a scanned image that he colored in Photoshop. He opened the image in Painter and made a Liquid Metal plug-in floater. In the Liquid Metal dialog box, he chose the Standard Metal Map type and the Brush tool, and these settings for the 800-pixel-wide file: Smooth 100%; Size, 10; Volume, 83; leaving other settings at their defaults. Then he painted on the floater to hand-letter the logo. To carve out areas in the metal he held down the Option key and painted with the Brush.

PHOTO: DIGITAL STOCK

Space Bubble. To add a bubble to this photo, we used the Liquid Metal plug-in floater. First we made a clone of the image (File, Clone). In the Objects:Plug-in Floaters palette we chose Liquid Metal and clicked Apply, using the Clone Source Map type. We used the Circle tool to place the bubble, then used the Metal Selector (arrow) to reposition the bubble. To make the "bubble" transparent, we chose a high Refraction setting. And to enhance the image refraction we increased the Smooth setting.

BURNED AND TEXTURED

By checking the Paper Texture box in the Burn plug-in dialog box you can apply the current Paper texture to the burned edge of a floater.

make a floater on which you create the metal. To make a dynamic floater, open an image, choose the Liquid Metal plug-in from plug-ins list on the Plug-In Floaters palette and click the Apply button. To paint with chrome, select the Brush in the Liquid Metal dialog box and choose Chrome 1 or Chrome 2 from the Map menu. Drag in the image with the Brush.

If you'd like to paint with bubbles or water drops that reflect your image, begin by making a clone of the image (File, Clone). Select the clone and make a Liquid Metal floater. From the Map menu choose Clone Source, choose the Circle or Brush and drag to paint on the floater. For flatter drops use an Amount of 0.5 –1.5. For the look of 3D water drops on a camera lens, move the Amount slider to between 3.0 and 4.0. For bubbles use an Amount of 5.0.

You can color the objects on a Liquid Metal floater based on a clone source or on the current pattern. Begin by using the Liquid Metal plug-in to make a floater. In the Liquid Metal dialog box, choose Clone Source from the Map menu. Select a pattern in the Art Materials:Pattern palette or open an image and define it as the clone source (File, Clone Source). Now use the Circle or Brush to apply metal to the floater.

Tearing, burning and beveling. The Tear, Burn and Bevel World plug-ins require a selected "source image floater" to perform their effects. To **Tear** or **Burn** an image's edges, begin by opening a file. You can select a floater in the image and apply the plug-in to it or you can reduce the image canvas to accommodate the torn or burned edge to come: Choose Effects, Orientation, Scale—we scaled our image at 80%. The Scale command will automatically create a "source floater." With the floater still selected, open the Objects:Plug-In Floaters palette by clicking the plug icon, choose the Tear or Burn plug-in from the plug-ins list and click the Apply button. To change the color of the torn (or burned) edge, click in the Color box and choose a new color from the color picker. Move the Lightness slider to the left to increase the value. **Bevel World** allows you to create complex bevels quickly. You can apply a bevel

A striking beveled button designed by Michele Lill. She captured a custom-made environment map as a pattern, and applied it to the button graphic using the Reflection Map slider in the Bevel World dialog box. To learn more about reflection maps turn to "Making a Reflection Map" and "Applying a Reflection Map," later in this chapter.

to a "source floater" in an image or make a unique beveled frame for an image using Bevel World. Open an image you'd like to frame, choose Select, All, and choose the Bevel World plug-in from the Plug-In Floaters palette plug-ins list and click the Apply button. Choose your settings and click OK. To read more about using the Bevel World plug-in floater, turn to "Creating Hot Beveled Metal," later in this chapter.

Diving into Distortion

Overview *Use Glass Distortion to displace an image using a clone source; then combine a dramatic distortion with a subtle one to create a water-stained effect.*

1a

The original photograph

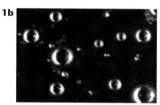
1b

The water image displacement map

2a

Settings for the subtle distortion

2b

The Extreme clone (left), and the Subtle clone (right)

3

Cloning in a dramatic water drop

PAINTER'S GLASS DISTORTION can move pixels in an image based on the luminosity of another image. We used it here to simulate water drops on a camera lens.

1 Choosing images and making clones. Choose an image for a displacement map (the water drops in this case) that has good contrast; both crisp and soft-focus images can give good results. Because you'll be applying the displacement map image to the original image as a clone source, you'll need to size the map image to the same pixel dimensions as the image you want to distort. (Our images were 883 x 589 pixels.) Make two clones of the image you want to distort by choosing File, Clone, twice. Save the clones, naming them Extreme and Subtle, then size and position them on your screen so that you can see both of them.

2 Applying the distortion. Open the displacement map image. Now, click on the Extreme clone, and designate the displacement image as the clone source (File, Clone Source). Click back on the Extreme clone and choose Effects, Focus, Glass Distortion, using Original Luminance, and chose the Refraction Map model. (Refraction works well for glass effects; it creates an effect similar to an optical lens bending light.) Our settings were Softness, 2.3 (to smooth the distortion); Amount, 1.35; Variance, 6.00. We left Direction at 0, because it has no effect when using a Refraction map, and clicked OK. Click on the Subtle clone, and apply more subtle settings. (Our settings were Softness 15.0; Amount, 0.06; and Variance, 1.00.) We wanted the diving board to curve, while preserving smoothness in the image.

3 Restoring from the extreme clone. We added several dramatic water drops from the Extreme clone to enhance the composition of the Subtle image. Click on the Subtle clone to make it active and choose the Extreme clone as clone source. Use the Soft Cloner brush variant of the Cloning brush to clone dramatic effects from the Extreme clone into your Subtle image. 🖌

Adding Diffusion and Relief

Overview *Combine Glass Distortion and Surface Texture special effects to transform a photo into a painting by creating brush-strokes and building up paint.*

CHER THREINEN-PENDARVIS / PHOTO: DIGITAL STOCK

The original photograph

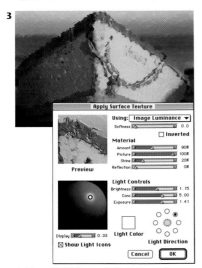

Applying Glass Distortion to the photo

Adding highlights and shadows to the distorted image with Surface Texture

BY COMBINING TWO POWERFUL EFFECTS, Glass Distortion and Apply Surface Texture, you can create a palette-knife paint with highlights and shadows—turning a photo into a painting. This effect can be applied to an entire image, a selection or a floater, giving you much more flexibility than you would have in the darkroom working with diffuser screens and masks.

1 Choosing an image and making a selection. Choose an image with a strong focal point and good highlights and shadows. You can achieve good results with either crisp or soft-focus images. In preparation for generating a Glass Distortion plug-in floater for the image in the next step, choose Select, All.

2 Initiating strokes. Choose a coarse paper texture—large organic textures with a broad tonal range help to emulate thick strokes made with a palette knife. We chose River Map from the Branched Textures library (in Free Stuff, Papers on the Painter 5 CD-ROM), and scaled it down to 68% to complement our 883-pixel-wide image. To diffuse or break up the image into strokes based on paper, apply the Glass Distortion plug-in. In the Objects palette click the plug icon to open the Plug-in Floaters palette. Choose Glass Distortion from the pop-up menu and click the Apply button. In the Using menu select Paper. Choose subtle settings—our settings were Amount, 0.75; Variance, 1.00; and Softness, 0. Click OK to apply your settings.

3 Adding texture and shadows. To add realistic relief to complete the painted effect choose Effects, Surface Control, Apply Surface Texture. When the Commit dialog box appears asking you if you'd like to convert the plug-in floater to an image floater, choose Commit. In the Using menu choose Image Luminance. Use subtle-to-moderate Surface Texture settings to avoid a harsh look and to preserve the original image. We used Amount, 90%; Picture, 100%; Shine, 20%; and Softness, 0. Choose a light direction that complements the existing light in your photograph. We chose the 1 o'clock Light Direction button to complement the overhead light source in the photo, and clicked OK.

Creating Hot Beveled Metal

Overview *Open a file and set type shapes; convert the shapes to a floater; bevel the floater and paint flames; make a glow and a gel; composite the floaters.*

CHER THREINEN-PENDARVIS

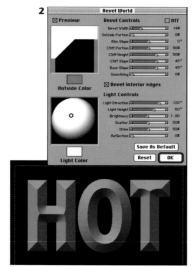

The selected, grouped text shapes

Applying a bevel to the floater

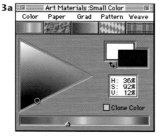

Lowering the value of the orange

TODAY'S MULTIMEDIA AND PRINT DESIGNERS need quick solutions for titles, and Painter 5 is just the tool for the job. The Bevel World plug-in allows you to create complex custom-made bevels on a selected floater quickly. To create this three-dimensional text effect, we applied the Bevel World plug-in to a floater, duplicated it, then used brushes and compositing effects on the layered floaters.

1 Setting up a file and creating the type. Create a new file with a black background (our file was 883 pixels wide). Choose an orange color in the Color palette to automatically fill the type shapes with color as you type. Select the Text tool, choose a font and size in the Controls:Text palette and set the type. We set 120-point type using Futura Extra Bold Condensed. Group the shapes (so you can work with the type shapes as a unit), by Shift-selecting them in the Objects:Floater List and clicking the Group button, or press Command-G.

2 Beveling the type. In preparation for using the Bevel World plug-in, convert the shapes to a floater by selecting the group with the Floater Adjuster and choosing Shapes, Convert to Floater. With the floater still selected, open the Objects:Plugin Floaters palette by clicking the plug icon; choose Bevel World from the plug-ins list and click the Apply button. To build a bevel effect without a flat face, we moved the Bevel Width slider to 14%, leaving the other settings at their defaults. Experiment with the sliders on your image.

3 Painting the flames. To paint semitransparent flames on the bottoms of the letters, we used the Fire brush from the F/X brush library. To quickly load the Fire brush, choose Window, Custom Palette, Shortcut to New Brushes, click the F/X icon and choose the Fire brush from the brush list. For a subdued fire effect that you can build up gradually, with a light pressure on the stylus, choose a very dark orange color with a value of l0–15% in the Color palette triangle. We reduced the size of the brush to 8.0 using the Size slider in the Controls:Brush palette, then painted brushstrokes using light pressure on the stylus. When you attempt to paint on a dynamic plug-in floater, you will be asked if you would like to commit the

3b

Painting flames with the Fire brush

The stacked floaters in the Floater List

dynamic floater to an image floater. Click Commit to accept, then begin painting.

4 Adding a glow and a gel. We wanted to add a glow, and the color of our type needed more richness. So we made two copies of the floater—the first to make a glow and the second for a gel (color filtered effect). Choose the Floater Adjuster and Option-click on your floater twice. In the Floater List you will see two more copies of your floater. Make the glow as follows: Select the bottom floater copy. Switch to the Mask List and select the floater mask. From the Mask menu choose Feather Mask (we typed in 30 pixels and clicked OK). Select the RGB-Floater then switch back to the Floater List. To give the feathered floater a yellow color, choose a warm yellow in the Color palette and then choose Effects, Fill, Current Color. Now, make the Gel as follows: Select the top copy and change its Composite Method in the Controls:Adjuster palette to Gel, then reduce the Opacity of the floater for a more subtle blending (we used an Opacity of 72%). ✍

BUILDING BEVELED CAST METAL AND CHROME

These two 3D type looks were created using Bevel World. We prepared a background file for the images by opening a new 1000 x 1000-pixel file and filling the background with a light blue (Effects, Fill). To add colored texture to the background, we chose a darker blue in the Color palette, selected the Hand Made texture in the Paper palette and chose Effects, Surface Control, Color Overlay, using Paper and Dye Concentration. Then we added a gradation with lighting by choosing Effects, Surface Control, Apply Lighting using a custom spotlight (beginning with the Plane Light). We chose the Text tool, selected 300-point Futura Extra Bold in the Controls:Text palette and typed a "G", then converted it to a floater (Shapes, Convert to Floater.)

The cast metal (top) and chrome (bottom) letters and their bevel profiles in the Bevel World dialog box

To build the cast metal (top), we began in the background file and filled the letter shape with a custom gold gradient built using the Grad Editor (Art Materials, Grad, Edit Grad), then choosing Effects, Fill, Gradation. We opened the Plugin Floaters palette by clicking the plug icon, chose Bevel World from the plug-ins list and clicked the Apply button to generate the dynamic floater. (At this point, we saved a copy of the file in RIFF format for use with the chrome image to follow.) To make a flat face on the beveled letter, we reduced the Bevel Width (in the Bevel World dialog box) by moving the slider to 8%. To make a dipped edge at the outside of the letter we reduced the setting for the Base Slope by moving the slider to −52°. For the drop shadow, we Option-clicked to make a copy of the selected floater, then dragged it below the plug-in floater in the Floater List. We chose Commit from the P.Float menu to convert the dynamic floater to an image floater. Next, we chose black in the Color palette and filled the floater (Effects, Fill, Current Color). To build the soft edge for the shadow, we gave the floater mask a 30-pixel feather. (Select the floater mask in the Mask List and choose Feather Mask, typing a number in the field.) Then we positioned the selected shadow using the arrow keys on the keyboard.

For the reflective chrome letter we opened the saved copy of the background image that included the plug-in applied to the type floater. To set up for the reflective chrome effect, we chose the Reflection Map pattern in the Art Materials:Pattern palette, then we double-clicked the floater's name in the Floater List to bring up the Bevel World dialog box. In the Bevel World Light Controls we used these settings: Reflection 100%; Shine 82%. We used these Bevel Controls settings: Bevel Width 28%; Rim Slope −3°; Cliff Portion 80% (for a wider distance between the base and the rim); Cliff Slope 44°; Base Slope 3° (for a gentler slope at the base); Smoothing 15% (to smooth the jaggies in the reflection); we left the other settings at their defaults. We built the shadow using the same procedure as for the cast metal.

Making a Collage with Eroded Type

Overview *Soften the edge of the type in source files; erode the type using Express Texture; apply a mask; collage the type in a composite file; add transparency effects.*

CHER THREINEN-PENDARVIS

1

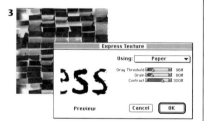

Filling Adobe Stone Sans type with black

2

Softening the edges of the type with a 5-pixel Super Soften setting. The gray information in the edges helps to create the eroded effect.

3

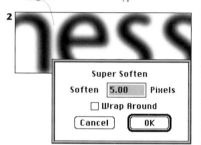

Using Express Texture with a custom paper texture to roughen the type edges

4

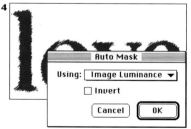

Applying a luminosity mask

YOU CAN USE PAINTER'S EXPRESS TEXTURE command to erode the smooth edges of a typeface, resulting in an organic, textured look. For the collage above, we eroded individual words in separate source files, then combined them in a composite image and added more effects. (If you're only interested in learning to erode type, follow steps 1–3 below.) A similar process might be used to erode photos and make them into a collage.

1 Setting the type shapes in small source files. Use Painter's Text tool to create type in individual source files. Choose black in the Color palette to automatically fill the type shapes with black as you type. Select the Text tool and choose a font and size in the Controls:Text palette. For each word we created a 400 x 200-pixel source file with a white background, then set 110-point type using various weights of Berkeley and Stone Sans typefaces. Some of the words were scaled down later in the compositing process.

2 Softening the type. In preparation for softening the letters, drop the type shapes to the background by choosing Drop All button from the Floater List palette's Floater menu. Now build a gray edge into the letterforms that you can manipulate in the "eroding" process in step 3, as follows: Choose Effects, Focus, Super Soften to bring up the Super Soften dialog box. We used a 5-pixel setting for the thin Stone Sans letterforms and a 10-pixel setting for Berkeley Black.

3 Eroding the type edges. To add an organic edge to the type's perimeter, choose Effects, Surface Control, Express Texture using Paper. The Express Texture dialog box is interactive, so you can test different paper textures or switch to a new paper library without needing to close the Express Texture dialog box. Change the shape of the type and the quality of the edge by moving the Gray Threshold, Grain and Contrast sliders. For the large "kindness" type, for example, we used the Globes texture (sized to 70% using the Scale slider on the Paper palette) from the More Wild Textures library (in Free Stuff, Papers, on the Painter 5 CD-ROM) and used settings of Gray Threshold, 80%; Grain, 64%; and Contrast, 300%.

5

Pasting type floaters into the composite

6

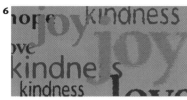

The rough composite showing flat color fills and approximate sizing

7

Applying the Overlay Composite Method to the large lavender "peace" (left), and the Multiply Composite Method to the small maroon "kindness"

8

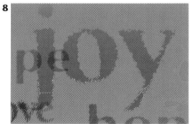

Filling the "joy" floater's mask with a gradation. Note how the type fades near the top (the lightest area of the gradation).

9

Using Color Overlay to add the Cloud texture and purple tint to the background

4 Making masks. To hide the white area of the image that surrounds the type, you need to make a luminosity mask. To do this, from the Objects palette's Mask menu choose Auto Mask (Command-Shift-M). Choose Image Luminance, leave the Invert box unchecked and click OK. Repeat this process for the other source files. The Auto Mask command automatically saves the masks to the Mask List. In the Mask List, click the New Mask eye icon shut to hide the mask, and then select the RGB-Canvas.

5 Copying and pasting into the composite file. Now choose Select, Load Selection. Copy the selection (Command-C), create a new file for your composite (ours was an 883 x 450-pixel file with a warm gray Paper Color) and Paste (Command-V) into the composite file. Use this copy-and-paste method to bring type from other source files into the composite.

6 Coloring, scaling and positioning. Fill each floater with a color by selecting it in the Floater List, choosing a color and pressing Command-F, using Current Color. Use Effects, Orientation, Scale to resize selected floaters and use the Floater Adjuster tool to reposition them.

7 Creating transparency effects. You can achieve dramatic transparent effects using Composite Methods with layered floaters. Select a floater using the Floater Adjuster tool; in the Controls: Adjuster palette, choose a Composite Method from the pop-up menu. We used Overlay on the large "joy," "kindness" and "peace" elements, and Multiply on the smaller elements. (Turn to the introduction of Chapter 5 for a visual reference of the various Composite Methods.)

8 Adding a gradation to a mask. Applying a light-to-dark gradation to a floater's mask will vary the type's intensity. When used on a few type floaters, this technique can add dynamic movement to the collage. We used the gradation editor (Art Materials, Grad, Edit Grad) to change the midpoint of a Two-Point, black-and-white gradation to 15%, making a predominantly black gradation that fades to white. (See Chapter 2 for more about the gradation editor.) To apply a gradation to the floater's mask, select the floater in the Floater List then switch to the Mask List and select the floater mask. Choose Effects, Fill, Gradation. To view the colored image again, turn off the floater mask by clicking the its eye icon shut. The type should fade out where the mask is the lightest.

9 Completing the collage. We chose a purple color and applied it to the image background (click in a blank area of the Floater List to deselect all floaters) using Effects, Surface Control, Color Overlay, using Paper Grain (the Clouds texture from the Texture Sampler library in Free Stuff, Papers on the Painter 5 CD-ROM) at 80% Opacity, with the Hiding Power button selected. As a final touch, we selected some of the floaters with the Floater Adjuster tool and adjusted their Opacity settings in the Controls:Adjuster palette.

Making a Reflection Map

Overview *Choose a file and resize it; make a selection; use Quick Warp to bend the image into an environment; capture it as a pattern.*

MICHELE LILL

YOU CAN USE PAINTER'S QUICK WARP FEATURE to bend any image into a useful environment map—or reflection map—an image that shows an environment as if it were seen through a fish-eye lens or reflected in a shiny metal sphere. Multimedia designer Michele Lill creates her own environment maps—like the one above on the left, and uses the maps to enhance images by applying them as she did in the image on the right. (To read more about applying environment maps in Painter turn to "Applying a Reflection Map" on the following page.)

1a

Michele Lill's original photo

1. Opening an image and making a selection. Open an image in Painter. To conserve disk space and optimize performance, Lill recommends that a reflection map image be a square that is 256 pixels or less. Using the Rectangle Selection tool, make a 256 pixel square selection, holding down the Shift key to constrain the selection to a square as you drag, as you check the Width in the Controls:Selection palette. If you need to move or scale the selection, use the Selection Adjuster tool. (Turn to "Transforming Selections" in Chapter 4 for more information about manipulating selections.) Copy the square selection (Edit, Copy), and paste it into a new file by choosing Edit, Paste, Paste Into New Image.

1b

Making a square selection on the image

2 Bending the image. To get the "fish eye lens" effect that adds realism to the map (since most surfaces that reflect their environment are not flat), Lill used Quick Warp, by choosing Effects, Surface, Control, Quick Warp and selecting the Sphere option. Lill used the default settings of Power 2.0 and Angle Factor 2.0. The effect applies to the entire canvas.

2

Applying the Quick Warp Sphere option

3 Saving the image as a pattern. To save the map into the current Pattern library, capture it as a pattern. With the environment map image open, select all and choose Capture Pattern from the Art Materials palette's Pattern menu. Name the map when prompted and click OK. The environment map is now a permanent member of the library. Now you can use the map to enhance special effects—as Lill did in her water illustration above. To read a description of how Lill used a custom environment map to enhance an image step-by-step, turn to "Applying a Reflection Map," on the following page. 🐾

3

Naming the water map in the Capture Pattern dialog box

Applying a Reflection Map

Overview *Open a file and set type shapes; convert the shapes into a floater; add a reflection map, dimension and a soft drop shadow to the type; add a border to the image.*

MICHELE LILL

Choosing a font and size in the Controls:Text palette

1a

Selected type shapes on the image

1b

2a

The selected type shapes in the Floater List

Grouping the type shapes

2b

TO CREATE THE TITLE DESIGN *RED ROCK*, multimedia designer Michele Lill used a custom-made environment map in combination with one of Painter's most powerful and versatile tools, Apply Surface Texture.

1 Opening an image and setting the type. For this example, Lill began by setting 60-point VAG Rounded BT type shapes on top of a photo. Begin by opening a background image (Lill's image was 889 pixels wide). Select the Text tool and choose a font in the Controls:Text palette. For the best results, choose a bold font with a broad face and rounded corners. Position the cursor in your image and type the text.

When you're finished setting the text shapes, select the Floater Adjuster tool and kern the type by repositioning the letters to your taste. To select an individual letter, click on its name in the Objects:Floater List. Move it using the arrow keys on your keyboard. (To read more about manipulating shapes, turn to "Working with Shapes," in the beginning of Chapter 5.)

2 Converting the shapes to a floater. If you'll be applying a series of effects to an entire word or block of text, it's most efficient to make the type into a single floater. To do this, select all of the type shapes by Shift-clicking on their names in the Objects:Floater List palette. Group them by clicking the Group button, or type Command-G. To turn the grouped shapes into one floater, click the Collapse button on the Floater List and when the Commit dialog box appears, click the Commit All button.

3 Selecting the reflection map. Open the Art Materials:Pattern palette and choose the Reflection Map pattern from the pattern drawer. Lill used an environment map made from the same Red

3

Choosing Lill's custom-made reflection map in the Pattern Library

4a

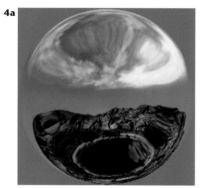

Michele Lill's Red Rock environment map

4b

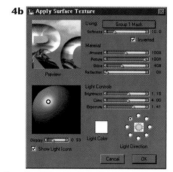

Settings for the second Surface Texture application showing dimension on the type

5a

Setting up an automatic drop shadow

5b

The Red Rock image with the drop shadow applied to the text floater

Rock photo she used for the background. (To read about how to make your own environment map, check out Michele Lill's method in "Making a Reflection Map," on the previous page.

4 Adding reflection and dimension to the type. To achieve a strong reflection in the type and a realistic 3D look, Lill used two applications of Apply Surface Texture. Begin by selecting the text floater with the Floater Adjuster tool, then choose Effects, Surface Control, Apply Surface Texture. To reflect the environment map onto your type, use these settings: In the Using menu choose the text mask to access the environment map. Move the Reflection slider to 100% (so the reflection map shows up) and move the Softness slider to the right (to scale the reflection map). Adjust the other settings to suit your image. Lill's Apply Surface Texture settings for the Red Rock image at the beginning of this story are as follows: Softness 40.0; Amount 200%; Picture 100%; Shine 40%; and Reflection 100%. The Surface Texture dialog box is interactive, so you can size your pattern while viewing the reflection map in the Preview window. When the reflection looks good, click OK in the Apply Surface Texture dialog box.

Now add a realistic 3D look to the text by choosing Apply Surface Texture a second time. This time, check the Inverted box (to add a second light source); decrease the Reflection slider to 0% by moving it all the way to the left; and decrease the Softness to about 10. Lill's second Surface Texture application settings are as follows: Softness 10.0, Amount 100%, Picture 100%, Shine 40% and Reflection 0%. Click OK.

5 Adding a shadow and a soft black border. Next, Lill added a black drop shadow to her text, adding to the 3D look and giving her image more contrast. To generate the shadow, she chose Effects, Objects, Create Drop Shadow. She specified settings in the dialog box for the X and Y coordinates to fit her image, and she increased the Opacity of the shadow to 80%, leaving the other settings at their defaults. Next, she checked the Collapse To One Layer box to combine the text and shadow into one floater and clicked OK.

Then, to finish the image with a more graphic look that would complement the shadow, Lill added a softly feathered black border to her image. To create her border effect, begin by choosing Select, All. Then from the Select menu choose Select, Modify, Contract. In the Contract Selection dialog box, type in 12 pixels. Now choose Select, Feather and set the feather to 24 pixels. Click OK to accept. Finally, Lill filled the selected, feathered edge with black using the Paint Bucket. Begin by choosing black in the Color palette. Open the Controls:Paint Bucket palette and from the What To Fill menu choose Image and from the Fill With menu choose Current Color. Click inside the active selection with the Paint Bucket tool. 🎨

Building a Terrain Map

Overview Create a terrain map from elevation data; make a custom gradation; color the map; use Apply Surface Texture to give it realistic dimension.

Kellogg Peak, Idaho

1

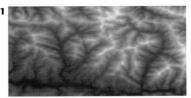

The grayscale image representing elevation

2a

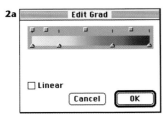

Edit Grad

☐ Linear
Cancel   OK

Building a custom gradation for the map

2b

The map with the custom gradation applied using Express in Image

3

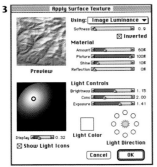

Apply Surface Texture

Using: Image Luminance ▼
Softness   0.9
                  ☒ Inverted
Material
Amount   60%
Picture   100%
Shine   10%
Reflection   0%
Preview
Light Controls
Brightness   1.15
Conc   2.00
Exposure   1.41
Display   0.32
Light Color
Light Direction
☒ Show Light Icons
Cancel   OK

Gordon's settings in Apply Surface Texture used to produce the terrain map

TO CREATE THIS REALISTIC MAP OF KELLOGG PEAK, IDAHO, Steven Gordon included color terrain backgrounds built from real data. A freelance cartographer and designer, Gordon produces many custom maps for electronic and print publication. His specialties include city maps and maps for tourism featuring relief renderings of the terrain.

1 Making a grayscale-to-height image. To begin the terrain map, Gordon downloaded a digital elevation model (DEM) file from the Internet (www.usgs.gov). He processed it using the shareware program DEM Reader (www.electiciti.com/~brianw/DEM_Reader.html), and the resulting PICT image contained grayscale values mapped to elevation values which Gordon used to build the map's terrain.

2 Coloring the image. Gordon opened the grayscale PICT file in Painter and built a custom gradient to color the map. To make your own gradation, open the Color palette and the Grad palette; in the Grad palette choose the Two-Point gradation. Now open the Grad Editor by choosing Edit Grad from the Art Materials palette's Grad menu. Using the Grad Editor, create a new gradation with color control points representing elevation zones (as Gordon did). Add two control points to the center of the grad by clicking in the Grad bar. Select each control point by clicking on it, and then click in the Color palette to choose a color. Gordon's gradation progressed from dark blue–green valleys to light tan mountain tops. When the grad looks good, save it by choosing Save Grad from the Art Materials palette's Grad menu. Apply the grad to your image by choosing Express in Image from the Art Materials palette's Grad menu.

3 Building terrain. To add realistic relief to your map, choose Effects, Surface Control, Apply Surface Texture Using Image Luminance. Click the Inverted box to make the light areas in the map "pop-up". To blur undesirable detail Gordon set the Softness slider to 0.7. Adjust the Amount to build dimension for the terrain. To prevent glare on the mountain tops, reduce the Shine to between 0 and 20%. In the Light Controls, Gordon decreased the Conc to 2.00 to lighten his image, keeping the Light Direction setting at a 11:00 to display the 3D terrain.

Building a Clone-Based Mosaic

Overview *Choose a photo reference and retouch it if needed; make a clone of the retouched photo; use the Make Mosaic dialog box to design and lay down colored tiles in the clone.*

S. SWAMINATHAN

1

The original photograph

Increasing the contrast in the source image

2b

Detail of the retouched source image

MOSAICS HAVE BEEN USED AS A NARRATIVE and decorative art form since Hellenistic and Roman times. Because of its graphic nature the mosaic is a medium that can be used to express strong emotion. S. Swaminathan created the digital mosaic *Soul of Homelessness*, based on his photograph of a homeless man. His vision was to create an abstracted mosaic portrait of the man that would portray the dignity he projected.

1 Selecting a source image. Choose a photo with a strong focal point and meaningful content, so the mosaic technique does not overpower the image. The photo should also have a broad tonal range and good color detail to help build value and color complexity into the tiles. Swaminathan began with a 675 x 920-pixel photo.

2 Retouching and cloning. To separate the subject from the background, Swaminathan used a modified Fat Stroke Airbrush to simplify the background of the photo, adding soft blue and white strokes. He also increased the contrast in the image using Effects, Tonal Control, Brightness/Contrast.

When he was satisfied with the retouching, he cloned the image. Choose File, Clone to make a clone of your source image. In preparation for laying down colored tiles in the clone based on the color of the clone source image, check the Clone Color checkbox in the Color palette.

3a

Designing a horizontal tile to use on the face

3b

Using Tracing Paper to view the clone source while positioning tiles on the clone

4a

Erasing a course of tiles in the hair

4b

Adding new irregular tiles in the hair

3 Laying tiles. With the clone active, open the Make Mosaic dialog box (Canvas, Make Mosaic), and check the Use Tracing Paper checkbox so you can see the source image while laying down the tiles. To design a custom tile, begin by setting Dimensions for the tile; choose a Width, Length and Grout size. Make a stroke on your image to test the settings. Press Command-Z to Undo a test stroke without closing the Make Mosaic dialog box. Experiment with the settings until you get just the look you want.

Swaminathan began with the face, which would become the focal point of the mosaic portrait. As he worked, he varied the size of the tiles, using larger tiles for the broader areas of the face (the forehead and cheeks), and smaller tiles to render detailed areas (the shadowed right side of the man's nose, eyes and eyebrows).

Generally, he worked from the center out, beginning with the face and hair and then rendering the shirt, shoes and background. To depict the long hair (and to contrast with the more uniform shapes of tiles on the subject's jacket) he designed narrow, irregularly shaped tiles. To customize the Randomness Settings of tile shapes and grout (as Swaminathan did), press the Settings pop-up menu to access the Randomness sliders. Begin by moving the Cut slider to the right to increase Randomness in the shape of the tile ends. To vary the spacing between tiles, move the Grout slider to the right. Experiment with each of the sliders individually until you arrive at the look you want.

4 Completing the image. To refine the tile design, Swaminathan sampled color from existing tiles (by pressing the Command key and clicking on a tile), and applied the color to other tiles. (Before sampling color from a tile, turn off Clone Color in the Color palette.) To erase tiles, click the Remove Tiles icon and drag the cursor over the tiles that you want to remove. Click back on the Apply Tiles icon and drag with the Mosaic brush to add new tiles.

Adding highlights and shadows. Finally, Swaminathan used a subtle application of Apply Surface Texture to add the realistic highlights and shadows you would see on the slightly uneven surface of handmade tiles. Choose Effects, Surface Control, Apply Surface Texture using Image Luminance. Try these settings: Softness, 0; Amount, 20; Picture 100; Shine, 25; and Reflection, 0. Click OK.

SAMPLE WITH A CLICK

To sample color from an existing tile in your mosaic (with Clone Color turned off in the Color palette), press the Command key and click on a tile. You won't see the Mosaic brush's crosshair cursor change to the Dropper tool when you're working with the open Make Mosaic dialog box, but you *will* be able to sample the color.

CORRECTION SHORTCUT

To remove tiles without clicking the Remove Tiles icon, press the Control key and drag the Mosaic brush over the tiles that you want to remove.

Creating a Tidepool

Overview *Create a sandy background; spray plants onto the ocean floor using the Image Hose; light the scene; combine special effects to "ripple the water."*

JOHN DERRY

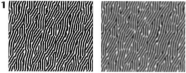

Wheat Stalks texture applied to the blank image (left), then Super Softened

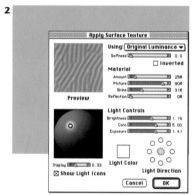

Applying Surface Texture with Original Luminance to the sand-colored clone

The Pressure Plant nozzle file with images from small to large size

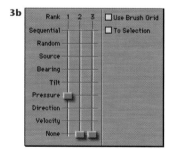

The zoomed-out Brush Controls:Nozzle palette showing Rank 1 set to Pressure

THE ILLUSION OF LIGHT REFRACTING through water is essential to creating a realistic underwater scene. In *Tidepool*, after using a variety of Image Hose nozzles to paint undersea plant life, John Derry engineered the look of rippling water by applying Lighting, Glass Distortion and Surface Texture to the image.

1 Creating a soft sandy bottom. To begin as Derry did, open a new 1200-pixel-wide image with a white background. Select black in the Color palette, choose Wheat Stalks paper texture from the Textures 1 library (in Free Stuff, Papers, on the Painter 5 CD-ROM) and scale it to 400% using the Size slider on the front of the Papers palette. Apply the black texture to your file with Effects, Surface Control, Color Overlay, using Paper and Hiding Power at 100% Opacity. Derry liked the Wheat Stalks texture but felt it needed softening to look like rippled sand. Soften the background by choosing Effects, Focus, Super Soften; enter 12 when the dialog box appears. Click OK.

2 Giving the rippled sand color and texture. To make the background look more like sand, you can combine a sand-colored file with the gray rippled image. First, clone the gray image (File, Clone), choose a sand color and fill the clone with the color (Command-F, Current Color, 100% Opacity). Next, combine the sand-colored clone with the gray image. Go to Effects, Surface Control, Apply Surface Texture, and choose Original Luminance. For a subtle effect use these settings: Amount, 25; Picture, 90; Shine, 30. Click the 11 o'clock Light Direction button, then move the Brightness slider up to 1.19 (to slightly increase the brightness), increase Concentration (Conc) to 5.00 (to decrease the spread of the light) and leave the Exposure at 1.41.

3 Loading a nozzle and spraying images. Most of the Image Hose nozzles that Derry used in this piece can be found in the Tidepool Nozzles library on the Painter 5 Wow! CD-ROM, in the John Derry's Nozzles folder. To choose an Image Hose nozzle from

3c

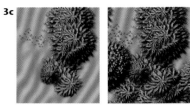

Using short spiral strokes to Spray plants and pebbles onto the sandy ocean floor

4

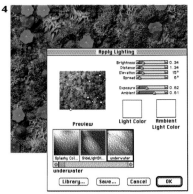

Creating a soft, diffused custom light

5a

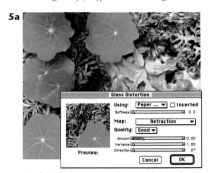

Applying Glass Distortion to initiate the ripple effect

5b

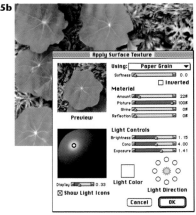

Adding Surface Texture to complete the illusion of rippling water

a Nozzle palette library, open the palette by pressing Command-9 and click on a nozzle. To load an individual nozzle that isn't part of a library, press Command-L (or choose Nozzle, Load Nozzle from the Brushes palette's menu), open a folder containing nozzle files and open a nozzle. Once you've loaded a nozzle, you can choose to add it to the current library (Nozzle, Add to Library) or view it (Nozzle, Check Out Nozzle). To paint with a nozzle, select the Image Hose icon in the Brushes palette and begin painting.

To make a nozzle spray in a specific way, change the hose variant (Method, Brushes palette) or use the controls in the Nozzle palette. For the undersea image, choose the Pressure Plants nozzle, select the Image Hose icon and paint with short, spiral strokes in your image.

Derry added strokes to the piece using a number of nozzles: Shadowed Coral, Pastel Coral, Shiny Coral, Pointed Plant, Nasturtium, Pressure Plants and Pebbles. Load the Tidepool library from the Painter 5 Wow! CD-ROM by choosing Load Library from the bottom of nozzle list on the Nozzle palette. See Chapter 7 in the *Painter 5 User Guide* to learn how to create your own Image Hose nozzle.

4 Applying Lighting. To create a diffused lighting effect with soft pockets of light and dark areas, Derry modified an existing light, copied it four times, then modified the individual lights. To create a look similar to the one he achieved, choose Effects, Surface Control, Apply Lighting, Slide Lighting. Reduce the Brightness, Distance and Spread settings, then click on two new locations in the Preview window to create two more lights with settings identical to the original. To reposition a light, click and drag on the large circle, and to aim the light in a new direction, click and drag on the small circle. Make further modifications to one of the three lights, then click in the Preview window two more times to create two more lights with those new settings, making a total of five lights. To create a softer effect on the whole scene, drag the Exposure slider to the left and the Ambient slider to the right. Store your custom light in the library by clicking the Save button, then click OK to apply the lighting to the image.

5 Creating a water ripple effect. Derry used a powerful but subtle combination of Glass Distortion and Apply Surface Texture to create a realistic water ripple effect. To ripple your image, in the Art Materials:Paper palette choose the Seismic texture (from the Wild Textures library in Free Stuff, Papers on the Painter 5 CD-ROM) and scale it to 400%. Now select Effects, Focus, Glass Distortion using Paper and accept the default settings of Amount, 0 and Variance, 1.00. To add a subtle bump to the transparent water ripple, choose Effects, Surface Control, Apply Surface Texture using Paper: Amount, 22%; Picture, 100%; and Shine, 0%. Click the 11 o'clock Light Direction button to set a general light direction. To fine-tune your Lighting, set Brightness at 1.15 and Concentration at 4.00, and leave the Exposure at 1.41.

Draping a Weave

Overview *Paint a grayscale file that will be your source image; fill a clone of that file with a weave; use a combination of Glass Distortion and Surface Texture to wrap the weave around the source image.*

CHER THREINEN-PENDARVIS

1

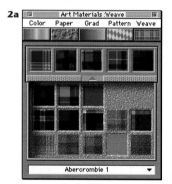

The grayscale form file with strong values

2a

Choosing a weave in the Weaves palette

2b

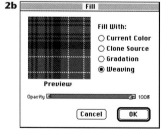

Filling the clone with the weave

YOU CAN USE PAINTER'S WEAVES FEATURE—located in the Art Materials palette—to fill any selection or document, using either the Fill command or the Paint Bucket tool. Weaves can be used in fashion design, and they make good backgrounds for scenes, but their flat look can be a drawback. To create the appearance of fabric—to hang behind a still life, for instance—we added dimension to a weave by "draping" it over a painted form using a powerful Glass Distortion displacement effect along with Apply Surface Texture.

1 Making the form file. Think of the form file as a kind of mold—or fashion designer's dress form—over which you'll drape your fabric. Create a grayscale form file that has strong value contrast and smooth dark-to-light transitions. As a reference for our 500-pixel-square form file, we draped fabric over a chair and sketched it in Painter, then cleaned up the sketch with the Fat Stroke Airbrush variant, working mostly with the Straight Lines Draw Style button checked in the Controls:Brush palette. Since any hard edges in the form file would make a noticeable break in the weave's pattern, we softened the image with Effects, Focus, Super Soften. We used a 7-pixel Super Soften setting on our file.

If you don't want to paint the form file, here's a fast, but less "organic" way to create it. Start by choosing one of the Line textures from the Simple Patterns paper library and drag the Scale slider in the Paper palette to 400%. (Alternatively, choose Art Materials, Paper, Make Paper, using Line and a high spacing setting.) Choose black in the Color palette, then select Effects, Surface Control, Color Overlay, using Paper and Hiding Power at 100% Opacity. Use Super Soften as you described above.

2 Making a clone and filling it with a weave. Choose File, Clone to make a duplicate of the form file with identical dimensions. Now choose a weave from the Weaves palette, and fill the

3

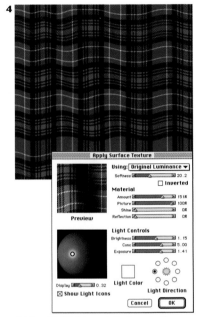

Applying Glass Distortion to the weave

4

Adding highlights and shadows to the distorted image using Surface Texture

clone with your weave (Command-F, Weaving, 100%). We used the Abercrombie 1 weave from the Scottish Tartans library (in Free Stuff, Weaves, on the Painter 5 CD-ROM).

3 Initiating the distortion. Here's where the movement begins. Choose Effects, Focus, Glass Distortion, using Original Luminance. Now let Painter know the direction that you want the fabric to go when it overlies the form file. When a clone image is displaced by Glass Distortion using Original Luminance, the distance each pixel moves is based on the luminance of each pixel in the source file. We chose Vector Displacement to move pixels in a specific direction, and used the Amount slider to get a moderate "ripple" effect in the Preview (we chose 1.54), leaving Variance at 1.00. To establish the direction (and make the light areas move up and to the right, dark areas move down and to the left—based on the form file), we moved the Direction slider to 80°. We added a Softness of 15.2 to smooth any rough edges that might be caused by the distortion of the weave. Experiment with your settings; the Softness, Amount and Direction may change based on the size of your file.

4 Adding highlights and shadows. Using Apply Surface Texture adds to the illusion of folded fabric by contributing highlights and shadows based on the form file. Choose Effects, Surface Control, Apply Surface Texture, using Original Luminance. Experiment with your settings—paying special attention to how the lighting controls affect the look—and click OK. We set Softness to 20.2 (to smoothe the image and slightly increase the depth of the folds), Amount to 151%, Picture to 100% (to make the image lighter while maintaining weaving detail), and Shine to 0%, then chose the 9 o'clock Light Direction button.

MOLDING A WEAVE OVER TYPOGRAPHIC FORMS

Try wrapping a weave (or other image) around type or a logo. Follow the same steps as in "Draping a Weave," and remember to use the Super Soften command on the type. For the "Wow!" image we chose Angle Displacement Map in the Effects, Focus, Glass Distortion dialog box (it makes the angle of the distortions vary based on luminance information in the form file), and we used a high Softness setting to compensate for the extreme wrap applied to the weave. This helped to smooth out the threads. In Effects, Surface Control, Apply Surface Texture, we set Softness at 2.2; Amount at 171%; Picture at 100%; Shine at 40%; and chose the 9:00 Light Direction with a Brightness of 1.19.

Type set in Adobe Reporter 2 (left), then given a Super Soften setting of 7 pixels.

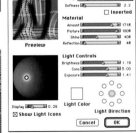

Using Glass Distortion and Apply Surface Texture to complete the "wrapped type" effect

■ *Drummer Sam* (right), the cover
illustration for the *Sacramento News &
Review* Sammie Awards issue, was created
by special effects genius **Steve Campbell**.
His inspiration for the illustration was the
original Sammie logo (shown on the
monitor) designed by Steve Barberia.
Campbell applied many textures and
special effects within the selections. To add
depth and movement to the stage floor
and wall—and to make the drums look
round—Campbell used Apply Lighting
within individual selections, increasing the
elevation and brightness of the lights to
achieve soft gradients on the surfaces.

■ DC Marketing commissioned
Beth Shipper to create the editorial
illustration *Bernard Smoking*. Shipper
began by making a tight line sketch in
Painter using the Colored Pencils variant
and a blue color, then she painted
transparent washes onto the image using
low-opacity Water Color brushes. When
she was finished, she dried the Wet layer
by choosing Canvas, Dry. To smooth a
few areas, she painted soft strokes with
the Airbrushes. Then she used the Lasso
tool to isolate some areas and applied
various textures using Effects, Surface
Control, Apply Surface Texture. To
emphasize areas of texture (such as
highlights on the pants and shirt), she
used Bleach and Darkener variants of the
Eraser. To "animate" Bernard's left hand,
Shipper selected the area with the Lasso
and Option-clicked to float several
copies, then she applied Effects, Focus,
Motion Blur (using varied settings) to
each floater. Then she lowered the
Opacity of each of the floaters
(Controls:Adjuster palette). She used the
same procedure to complete the blue
streamers on the fan.

■ **Susan LeVan** of LeVan/Barbee Studio
began the fine art work *Waiting Blue*, by
roughing the image in with the Large
Chalk variant of the Chalk brush. Then
she added transparent color with the
Simple Water variant of the Water Color
brush. After drying the image (Canvas
Dry), she used the Chalk brushes, Default
Crayons and Scratchboard Tool (Pens),
for the details. While painting, she used a
variety of subtle and coarse paper
textures to build complexity and richness.
LeVan effectively applied a special
effect—Effects, Surface Control, Apply
Surface Texture—to the right side of the
figure's face to enhance the strong
emotional quality of the piece.

■ **Phil Howe** collaborated with associate
Glenn Yoshiyama for the music CD cover
Feathers of Green and Gold. Yoshiyama
began by hand-lettering the calligraphic
title using traditional methods and tools.
Then Howe scanned the calligraphy and
the feather (placing the feather directly on
the scanner), and pasted them into their
own layers in Photoshop, where he colored
them. He also set the small type elements
in Photoshop on their own layer. When the
items were in place, Howe saved the file in
Photoshop format to preserve the layers as
floaters when he opened it in Painter.
Working in Painter, he used a combination
of Effects, Focus, Glass Distortion and
Effects, Surface Control, Surface Texture on
the individual elements to add rich texture
to the image. For instance, to define the
feather and emboss it, he applied Surface
Texture using Image Luminance. To
roughen the edge of the square element,
he feathered the mask and used Effects,
Focus Glass Distortion using Paper to
break up the edge. Then, to add a rough
watercolor paper texture to the
background, he used Apply Surface
Texture using Paper.

■ *Scenario Magazine* commissioned **Carol Benioff** to create *Donnie Brasco 1*, one of four editorial illustrations depicting scenes from the play *Donnie Brasco.* Benioff made sketches with pencil and paper, then she etched a copperplate (as shown on pages 262–263). After printing the plate she scanned the etching, cloned the scan, turned on Tracing Paper and painted the color illustration with custom Water Color, Chalk and Oil brushes. To add a colored gradation to the background wall, she applied custom lighting using Effects, Surface Control, Apply Lighting (using a method similar to the one described in the beginning of this chapter). Then she composited the scanned etching and color image using the Multiply Compositing Method.

■ The Navajo Hoop Dance served as the inspiration for **S. Swaminathan's** image *The Dance* (right). He composed the photomontage using three source photos—the sunset and skyline, the Navajo dancer and a photo of the Silicon Valley taken from a mountain peak. He began with the sunset and skyline as the base image, designated the hoop dancer as the clone source (File, Clone Source) and softly cloned the dancer into the image using a custom Oil Pastel Chalk brush (using Clone Color in the Color palette). Then he used Effects, Tonal Control, Adjust Colors to change the Hue and increase the Saturation in the image. To finish, Swaminathan cloned elements from the Silicon Valley photo into the foreground of the image.

■ "Discontinuity, wars that I did not participate in, but was affected by," provided inspiration for *Viet Nam* (above), by fine artist and multimedia designer **Patrick Litchy**. He began the work with four source photos—a rifleman, a boy and skull, a blind-folded prisoner and a photo of the Viet Nam War Memorial in Washington, DC. Litchy applied custom color gradations to the small source images using Art Materials, Grad, Express in Image and he used MetaCreations Convolver to filter the War Memorial background image, spiraling the type. Then he copied and pasted the three photos into the background file. For a subtle transition with the background, he feathered the edges of the floater masks to make them transparent. He used Effects, Surface Control, Apply Surface Texture, Using Image Luminance to add highlights and shadows to the floaters. To finish, he applied Apply Surface Texture to the background using more subtle settings.

■ **Bill Niffenegger's** illustration *AIDS* (right) for *Dentistry* magazine was honored with the APEX award for magazine covers. The piece reflects the devastating, yet sensitive, nature of the subject. Author of the book *Photoshop Filter Finesse*, Niffenegger painted the piece in Painter using a wide variety of brushes, custom paper textures, Apply Lighting and MetaCreations Texture Explorer and Gradient Designer.

■ *Seeking* (right), by photographer **S. Swaminathan,** was inspired by a photo of two figures temporarily stranded on a rock during an incoming tide. Swaminathan opened a scan of the photo in Painter, cloned the image (File, Clone) deleted the contents of the clone, and chose Canvas, Tracing Paper. Working in the clone, he painted with the Pencil and Watercolor brushes. He used Clone Color (Color palette) while painting to import color from the original image. To paint the moon he used the Dodge brush from the new Photo brush library and enhanced the color of the image using Effects, Surface Control, Dye Concentration using Image Luminance. Then, to finish the work, he used Effects, Surface Control, Apply Surface Texture, using Image Luminance to add realistic highlights and shadows based on the luminosity values in the image.

For *Hyakutake and the Moon* (below), Swaminathan began by taking a photo of the moon captured using an exposure time of 1.5 seconds and a photo of the Comet Hyakutake taken with an exposure time of 45 minutes, resulting in lovely curved lines that suggest the comet's movement through space. After color-correcting both images using Effects, Tonal Control, Correct Colors, he applied Effects, Surface Control, Apply Surface Texture to the moon to add texture. He used a custom Airbrush with enhanced Color Variability (Color palette) to paint brushstrokes onto the comet and stars. Then he copied and pasted the moon into the comet image. To create ice crystals in the star and comet trails, he floated two copies of the trails and composited them using the Dissolve and Darken Composite Methods (Controls:Adjuster palette).

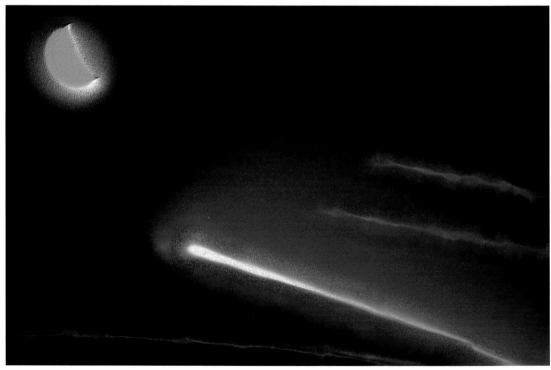

■ *Swami's* (left), by **Jack Davis,** was created with much the same style and brushwork as Davis's traditional oils on canvas, which incorporate brilliant colors painted onto a black "ground." Davis began the work by making sketches with pencil and paper, then took photos of the location. He scanned the photos into Photoshop, then copied and pasted bits and pieces of the photos into a reference file and increased the saturation of the images. When the composition looked right, he flattened the file and saved it in Photoshop format. Then he opened it in Painter and cloned it (File, Clone). Davis deleted the contents of the clone and filled the background with black. Next, he turned on Tracing Paper (Canvas, Tracing Paper) and chose the Big Wet Luscious Brush from the New Paint Tools library. To rough in blocks of color based on color in the reference collage, he checked the Clone Color box on the Color palette. After he had laid in the basic composition, he turned off Tracing Paper and the Clone Color option and completed the painting. As a last step, he added realistic highlights and shadows to the brushstrokes—building the look of thick paint—using Effects, Surface Control, Apply Surface Texture using Image Luminance with subtle settings.

■ To create *Dancers* (left), **Pamela Drury Watenmaker** began the image in Photoshop by painting flat color areas. She selected areas and saved them as channels. She then loaded each selection in turn, reversed the selection, and deleted the rest of the image, then saved under another name in Photoshop format. She opened each file in Painter and applied Effects, Focus, Glass Distortion and Effects, Surface Control, Apply Surface Texture—using Paper for both—to the selections. Back in Photoshop, she opened the textured files she had made in Painter one at a time and pasted them into the selections in her original file.

■ While creating *Kamakura,* an image in his on-going *City Series* (above), **John Derry** used photos he took in Japan. The photo-collage is inspired by a temple dedicated to children in the town of Kamakura near Tokyo. To isolate areas of the source photos, Derry made selections. Then he copied and pasted the selected areas into the composite file, where he scaled and repositioned the floaters. He built the soft, abstract background from photos of walls, trees and fabric. He copied and pasted the elements into the image. Then he selected each floater with the Floater Adjuster and lowered its Opacity (Controls palette) to 10–20%. For the irregular edge on the large photos, he erased areas of the floater masks. To create the water droplets, Derry used the Liquid Metal plug-in using the Clone Source Map type and a high Refraction setting. He used the Rain option to create drops in three different sizes. When the drops were complete, he used Effects, Tonal Control, Adjust Colors to increase the Saturation of the drops. Then added a shadow to add to their dimension (Effects, Objects, Create Drop Shadow). He painted the glow behind the dancing child with the Airbrushes and white paint. To finish, he painted over areas of the image background with a Big Wet Ink brush using a low opacity (Controls palette) and a light color.

■ **Abbie Rabinowitz** was commissioned to paint *Portrait of Stephanie* (right). To begin, she photographed her subject, scanned the photo, opened it in Painter and cloned it (File, Clone). The she applied Paint Alchemy's Cubist filter to the clone to build geometric planes. She made a second clone of the original photo, deleted the contents of the clone, and turned on Tracing Paper (Canvas, Tracing Paper). She roughed in the painting using custom Chalk and Oil brushes, with Clone Color checked in the Color palette. Then she designated the cubist image as the clone source (File, Clone Source), and added angles to her painting. She completed the portrait using the Chalk and Oil brushes with Tracing Paper and Clone Color turned off.

■ *This Town's a Gas,* by **Gary Clark,** portrays a fictional town that includes photos taken in several small towns throughout Pennsylvania. Clark built the composite image from many source files: photos of toys, figures and buildings shot with a digital camera and landscape elements created in MetaCreations Bryce. He assembled the collage in Photoshop and Bryce, then brought the image into Painter, where he added brushwork and texture. He used the Smeary Mover (Liquid brush) to paint and blend color and the Dodge and Burn brushes (Photo brush library) to add highlights and shadows. Then he used Effects, Surface Control, Surface Texture using Paper to apply a canvas texture to the image.

■ *Information Highway* was based on an illustration **Ayse Ulay** created for *Occidental* magazine. Eight figures were placed over filled circular selections, then distorted with a KPT Glass Lens filter to achieve a spherical effect. Ulay opened a second file—a black-and-white scan of a world map—in Painter and used Effects, Surface Control, Color Overlay and Apply Surface Texture to tint it and add dimension. She used a KPT Glass Lens filter to turn the map into a globe. Ulay created a background in a third file with Apply Surface Texture using Paper, then used Xaos Tools' Paint Alchemy to add more texture. She pasted the map and the other eight spheres into the background file and used Effects, Objects, Create Drop Shadow to make them appear to float above the canvas.

■ **Corinne Okada**, an innovative designer, illustrator and artist, designed *The Digital Pond* package (above) as a three-part image to illustrate services that The Digital Pond provides—communicating the transition from sketch through digital file to the final high-resolution image. After making sketches with pencil and paper, Okada began the image background and detail elements in Painter. Working in several small source files, she used brushes, her own custom paper textures and patterns, and Painter's special effects (such as Color Overlay and Surface Texture) to add color, texture and dimension to all of the elements. Finally, she opened the frog, carp, dragon fly and background files in Photoshop and completed the composition.

■ To create *Chocklit*, **Rhoda Grossman** began with photos of her niece Nesa, and of her mother, and scans of a paper bag and a handwritten note. Grossman colored the photos as sepia-tones using Art Materials, Grad, Express in Image. Then she built the "fudge" background starting with the scan of the paper bag. She applied Effects, Focus, Soften and then distorted it with the Bulge variant of the Gooey brush. She used the Burn plug-in floater to char the edge of the handwritten note. Next, she created the chocolate drops in a source file using the Liquid Metal plug-in floater, using the Clone Source Map type with the fudge file designated as the clone source. To paint the chocolate shapes, she used both the Brush and Circle tools. When the photos, chocolate pieces and burned note were complete, she copied and pasted the images into the composite file. To finish, she applied a drop shadow to the chocolate pieces using Effects, Objects, Create Drop Shadow.

■ *The Dallas Morning News* commissioned **Chet Phillips** to create *The Oasis Garden* to illustrate a story about drought prevention in the *House and Garden* section of the paper. Phillips began with an underpainting—he made selections for the sky, foreground, grassy mound, mountains and tree with the Lasso and Pen tools—then he filled each area with soft color (Effects, Fill). Next, he began the process of building two custom Image Hose nozzles. He created several small leaf illustrations of different shapes and sizes and saved them in RIFF format that he could load as a nozzle. (From the Brushes palette's Nozzles menu, choose Load Nozzle, select the RIFF file and click Open). Then he selected the Image Hose icon in the brushes palette and painted with the new nozzles to build the tree top and the grassy mound. He also used several of Painter's default nozzles to paint the grass. Afterward, he used the Airbrushes to touch up areas and blend shadows, then he painted the tomato plant, roses and squash. For the ferns in the shadows and the cracked ground he used the Scratchboard (Pens) variant. Finally, Phillips loaded the selection for the distant mountain range areas (Select, Load Selection) and used Effects, Focus, Glass Distortion using Paper and a linear texture to create the atmospheric heat ripple.

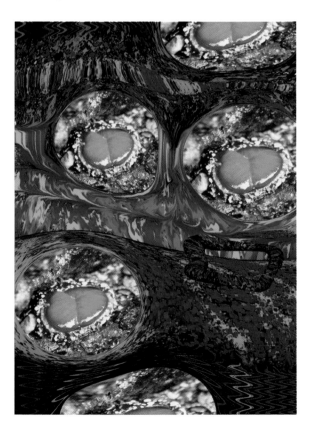

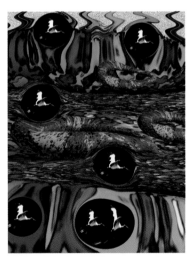

■ **Will Tait's** series of abstract images entitled *The Space Between* explores the dynamic energy that exists between varying forms of nature. Two of the images in the series (shown here) started as large, texture-mapped images in 3D Studio, which he saved as TIFF files and imported into Painter. To add blobs containing his own photos of tidepool and swamp life into the images, he copied each photo to the clipboard, then used Effects, Esoterica, Blobs. He touched up the image with Liquid brushes.

Using
Painter
With
Photoshop

Sungold, *one in a series of fruit label illustrations by Donal Jolley, was created for Michaeli's Nursery using Photoshop and Painter (turn to the gallery to see more of the series).*

A SINGLE MASK

Saving Painter images in TIFF format (with the Save Alpha box checked) will let you open the file in Photoshop and work with a single mask in Photoshop as Channel #4 in an RGB file. And a bonus: Saving as a PICT file also permits saving a single mask for import into Photoshop, even though the Save Alpha check box is not available.

WITH PAINTER 5 IT'S EASY TO MOVE FILES back and forth seamlessly between Painter and Photoshop. Images can be moved with their layers, masks and paths intact.

And what does Painter have to offer the Photoshop user? Fantastic natural media brushes that give your images warmth and a multitude of textures and fabulous special effects! In addition to the work showcased in this chapter, several of the artists whose work appears in this book have used both Painter and Photoshop in the development of their images. If you're an avid Photoshop user and would like to see more examples of how other artists have combined use of the two programs, check out the work of these artists for inspiration: Matthew Angorn, Gary Clark, Ellie Dickson, John Dismukes and Trici Venola. The index in the back of this book contains page references for each of their names.

PAINTER TO PHOTOSHOP

Here are some pointers to keep in mind for importing Painter 5 files into Photoshop 4 and presumably later versions.

• To preserve floaters (Painter's version of layers) when moving an image from Painter into Photoshop, save a Painter 5 file in Photoshop 3 format. Photoshop will open it and translate the floaters to layers with the names and layer hierarchy intact.

• If a Painter document contains floaters that extend beyond Painter's live image area, and that document is opened in Photoshop 4, areas outside of the live area are no longer trimmed off. (Photoshop 3 clipped the layer information outside the image window.)

• Painter offers all of the Photoshop 4 Blending modes—except three—Color Dodge, Color Burn and Exclusion, and it has seven

Sprawlers by Ellie Dickson. To see more of her work using Painter and Photoshop, turn to the gallery in Chapter 6.

To see more of her work using Painter and Photoshop, turn to the gallery in Chapter 6.

DYNAMIC FLOATERS

When a Painter dynamic floater such as Liquid Metal is opened in Photoshop the layers are preserved but the dynamic capabilities are lost. To keep their dynamic properties, save a copy of your file with live dynamic floaters in RIFF format.

PATHS TO PHOTOSHOP

Any Painter selection that includes path information will appear in the Photoshop 4.0 Paths palette. When you make a selection with the Lasso, Rectangular or Oval Selection tools or set type shapes and convert them to selections in Painter (Shapes, Convert to Selection), path information is automatically stored in the file. And if you paint a user mask or generate one with the Automask or Color Mask functions, you can build path information into the file: Convert this mask-based selection to outline information using Select, Transform Selection. Then if you save the Painter file in Photoshop 3.0 format, all of these kinds of outlines will appear in Photoshop's Paths palette.

Convert Paths?

This file contains paths. Paths are no longer supported in Painter. Would you like to convert these paths into shapes?

[Cancel]   [No]   [**Yes**]

To import Photoshop paths into Painter, open the file, and choose Yes in the Convert Paths dialog box. The Photoshop paths will convert to shape paths, which will appear in the Floater list.

---

additional Compositing Methods of its own. When Photoshop encounters a Painter-native Composite Method (like Pseudocolor or Reverse-out), it converts that layer to Normal. Photoshop converts Magic Combine to Lighten mode, Gel to Darken mode, Colorize to Color mode, and Shadow Map to Mulitply.

• To save Painter selections into the Mask List and use them in Photoshop 4.0 as channels, save a Painter file in Photoshop 3.0 format. When you open the file in Photoshop, the named user masks will automatically appear in the Channels palette.

• Painter's Shapes cannot be imported into Photoshop with their object-oriented information intact. Saving a Painter file with shapes in Photoshop 3.0 format converts shapes to Photoshop layers, which appear in the Layers palette using the compositing (blending) method you specified for the shapes in Painter.

• Bezier shape paths or type shapes set in Painter that are converted to selections (Shapes, Convert to Selection), and saved as masks (Select, Save Selection) in the Mask List in Painter will import into Photoshop and appear in the Paths palette with their names intact.

PHOTOSHOP TO PAINTER

Here are some pointers for importing Photoshop files into Painter 5.

• If you prefer to begin your file in Photoshop, you'll need to use Grayscale or RGB color mode for opening in Painter, as Painter does not open CMYK files.

• If you save your Photoshop 4 image with layers in Photoshop format, Painter 5 will open it and translate the layers to floaters. If you are using Photoshop 3, save the file in Photoshop 3 format.

• A Photoshop document made up of transparent layers only—that is, without a Background layer—will open in Painter as floaters over a white background.

• Painter can recognize all but three (Color Dodge, Color Burn and Exclusion) of Photoshop's Blending modes when compositing the floaters. Painter converts Color Burn, Color Dodge and Exclusion modes to Default Compositing method.

• Photoshop Alpha Channel masks will be recognized by Painter 5. The channels will appear in Painter's Objects:Mask List. To view a mask in black-and-white, make sure no floaters are selected, switch to the Mask List, click the mask eye icon open and shut the RGB-Canvas eye icon. And Photoshop layer masks convert to floater masks. To view a floater mask, select the floater in the Floater List, switch to the Mask List and click the floater mask eye icon open.

Collage Using Cloning and Layers

Overview *Scan photos into Photoshop and cut masks; use Painter's brushes and textures to clone a background image; complete the composite image in Photoshop.*

The four source images used in the composite illustration

The masks for the bottle and shears

BURKE/TRIOLO PRODUCTIONS IS FAMOUS for its unique food photography. When partners Jeff Burke and Lorraine Triolo conceived the studio promotion piece *Fruit Comp*, they turned to Photoshop for image compositing and to Painter for a textured, painted look.

1 Setting up, shooting photos and scanning. Lorraine Triolo began by building the fruit still life and cake arrangements. The team photographed the food and drum-scanned these two photos.

A very soft, even, flat quality of light can achieved with flatbed scanning that is hard to duplicate on a photography set. Burke and Triolo like this look, so they placed the cognac bottle and garden shears on the scanner bed and scanned each object directly.

2 Preparing the source files. Because he was familiar with Photoshop's compositing tools, Burke opened the scans of the bottle, shears and cake in Photoshop. To silhouette each object, he used the Pen and Lasso tools to make selections. Then he saved each selection as a channel in the source file by choosing Select, Save Selection. Burke planned to use the selections during the compositing process (step 4).

3 Building the background. Burke opened the fruit image in Painter. He made a clone of the image and filled the clone with a

3a

Using Tracing Paper while cloning

3b

Building up the image using the Chalk Cloner and rough textures

4

Using the Scatter and Long String Rice textures while cloning imagery into the edge with the low-opacity Chalk Cloner

5

Pasting the bottle into the background

warm cream background color. Choose File, Clone. Select a color in the Color palette, then choose Effects, Fill, Current Color to fill the clone canvas. To see the original image as you work, turn on Tracing Paper (Command-T). In the Brushes palette, select the Chalk Cloner variant of the Cloners brush. Before you begin to paint, adjust the size and opacity of your brush. Using the Size slider in the Controls:Brush palette, increase the size of the brush to about 45 pixels. (Burke's image was about 1700 pixels wide.) And you'll have more control while cloning if you use a brush with a low opacity. Set the opacity at about 30% using the Opacity slider. Save your custom cloning variant (so you won't have to build it again later) by choosing Save Variant from the Brushes palette's Variant menu. Now begin brushing the imagery into the colored background of the clone. While cloning the image into the background, Burke switched between Basic Texture and a few textures from the More Wild Textures library (located in Free Stuff, Papers on the Painter 5 CD-ROM). To load another library, choose Load Library from the bottom of the Paper palette's paper list, navigate to the library and click Open.

4 Making the textured edge. Using the custom Chalk Cloner Burke cloned a soft irregular edge, switching between the Scatter and Long String Rice paper textures as he worked. He finished by adding a few touches of brighter color with the Impressionist variant of the Artists brush. (The Impressionist brush includes Color Variabilty in the Color palette, which allows you to paint with a range of color.)

5 Compositing the images. Burke opened the finished background image in Photoshop to complete the composite. As described below, he loaded the selection, copied the contents of each selection, pasted the selected source image into the background image and repositioned it. To achieve a transparent effect for the bottle floater, he applied Luminosity Compositing Method and used an Opacity of about 80%. (The procedure is almost identical in Photoshop.) In Painter, select the source file and choose Select, Load Selection. Copy (Command-C), target the background image and Paste (Command-V). Reposition the pasted image using the Floater Adjuster. In the Controls:Adjuster palette, change the Compositing Method to Luminosity and lower the Opacity. To flatten your image, choose Drop All from the Objects palette's Floater menu. To prepare his final image for print, Burke used Photoshop to make a CMYK conversion.

MASK MAXIMUMS

A Painter file can contain up to 32 user masks. Photoshop's maximum is 24 channels in a RGB file, but three of the channels are taken up by the Red, Green and Blue color channels (leaving room for 21 masks). If you attempt to open a file with 32 masks in Photoshop, you will be greeted by a polite dialog box asking if you would like to discard the channels (numbers higher than 21 will be discarded).

⚠ This file contains more than 24 channels. Discard extra channels?

[Discard]   [Cancel]

Compositing, Painting and Effects

Overview *Scan a drawing and a sheet of paper into Photoshop and composite the scans; open the image in Painter and add color, texture with brushes and a colored lighting effect; open the image in Photoshop and convert it to CMYK.*

JOHN FRTEZ

The sheet of speckled Oatmeal paper

The pencil-and-charcoal drawing on paper

Compositing the scans of the Oatmeal paper and the sketch in Photoshop

JOHN FRETZ COMBINED TRADITIONAL DRAWING materials and digital ones in Photoshop and Painter to build the composite illustration *AM Exercise* for an American Lung Association calendar.

1 Drawing and scanning. As a basis for his illustration Fretz drew a black-and-white study using pencil and charcoal on a rough newsprint paper. Then he used a flatbed scanner to scan the drawing and a sheet of Oatmeal paper into Photoshop using RGB mode.

2 Compositing the scans. Fretz composited the image in Photoshop because he was more familiar with Photoshop's compositing procedures. (This compositing process that follows can be accomplished almost identically in Painter.) Fretz copied the drawing and pasted it as a new layer on top of the Oatmeal paper background. Then, to make the light values in the drawing transparent, he applied Multiply blending mode to the drawing layer using the menu on the Layers palette.

For the soft irregular edge on the background layer, Fretz first used the Lasso to draw a selection around the perimeter of the image. He reversed the selection by choosing Select, Inverse and feathered it 30 pixels (Select, Feather), then he filled the border area with 100% white. He saved the file in Photoshop format to preserve the layer for import into Painter.

3 Modifying brushes. At this point, Fretz opened the composite drawing in Painter where he planned to add color and texture. Before beginning to paint, he made two custom Soft Charcoal brushes. The first, for adding soft values, used the Soft Cover submethod; the second, for subtly darkening color, used the Grainy Soft Buildup submethod and a low opacity. To make Fretz's "darkener," in the Brushes palette, choose the Soft Charcoal variant

Building up color to the faces using the custom Soft Charcoal brushes

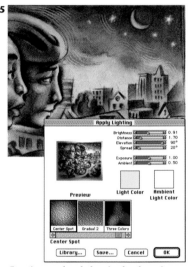

Creating a colored glow in the sky using Apply Lighting

Painting details on the foreground

of the Charcoal brush and change its method to Buildup and the submethod to Grainy Soft Buildup. A lower opacity will give you more control when building up color, so in the Controls:Brush palette change the Opacity to about 15%. Save your new variant by choosing Save Variant from the Brushes palette's Variant menu. Name it and click OK.

4 Adding color and texture in Painter. Fretz chose Basic Paper texture in the Paper palette. To enlarge the texture to complement the grain of the Oatmeal paper background, he used the Scale slider on the Paper palette. He brushed color onto his drawing using two grain-sensitive brushes, the Large Chalk and Square Chalk variants of the Chalk brush and used the custom Charcoals to deepen color saturation in some areas. Choose a Chalk brush and begin painting color onto your image background; switch to the custom Soft Charcoal variant using Grainy Soft Buildup to darken color. To change the brush size and the opacity while you work, use the Size and Opacity sliders in the Controls:Brush palette.

5 Emphasizing the sky with lighting. For a warm glow in the sky that faded across the people's faces, Fretz applied a colored lighting effect within a soft-edged selection. Begin by choosing the Lasso tool and making a loose freehand selection. Now give the selection a soft edge by applying a feather. Choose Select, Feather, type in 30 pixels, and click OK. Now apply the lighting effect to make the sky glow as Fretz did: Choose Effects, Surface Control, Apply Lighting. In the Lighting dialog box, choose the Center Spot light. To give the light a colored tint, click on the Light Color box to open the Select Light Color dialog box. Move the Lightness slider to the left to see color, then choose a color by clicking on it in the color picker. Click OK. To move the spotlight to a new location in the Preview window, click on the large end of the light indicator and drag the light. To save the custom light, click the Save button and name the light when prompted, then click OK to apply the light to your image.

6 Painting final details. To merge the floater and image canvas into one surface on which he could paint details, Fretz flattened the image by choosing the Drop All from the Objects palette's Floater menu. Then he chose the Scratchboard Rake variant of the Pens brush. Before painting, he modified the Scratchboard Rake, reducing the number of bristles on the brush. To do this, open the Brush Controls:Spacing palette by choosing Spacing from the Brush palette's Control menu. In the Spacing palette reduce the number of bristle to 5. Fretz added finishing strokes in various colors to several places in the foreground, the grass, and highlights on the cars. He also used a smaller brush and more subtle colors to add textured strokes to areas of the background.

Fretz saved a copy of the image as a TIFF file. He opened the TIFF file in Photoshop and converted it to CMYK for use in the calendar.

■ **Donal Jolley** created these four colorful fruit illustrations for *Michaeli's Nursery* as a part of a series of illustrations to advertise the nursery's hybrid fruit trees.

Jolley began each illustration in Adobe Illustrator by drawing the basic shapes with the Pen tool and applying flat color fills. When the basic shapes were complete, he opened the Illustrator art in Photoshop 4, used the selection tools to create masks for the fruit, leaves and background elements and saved them as channels. Then he saved each image in Photoshop format for import into Painter,

where he planned to render form and dimension. He opened each image in Painter and used the masks saved in Photoshop to isolate areas of his image. He loaded each user mask in turn (Select, Load Selection) and painted within the selections using the Chalk and Oil brush variants. He smoothed areas of the backgrounds using the Water brushes and added final colored details to the fruit and foliage using small Oil and Chalk brushes. To add a few more touches of texture (on the orange, for instance), he used Effects, Surface Control, Apply Surface Texture using Paper.

■ **Philip Howe** worked intuitively, back and forth between Photoshop and Painter while building the montage illustration *Banker's Life,* a promotional illustration for his studio. Many of the tasks (such as making masks or compositing) could have been accomplished with either Photoshop 4 or Painter 5. Howe is very comfortable with Photoshop's masking and compositing tools, so he chose to do most of these procedures in Photoshop. He turned to Painter for its brushes, and to add texture and special effects.

Howe began *Banker's Life* by making composition sketches. He designed the image to have four "planes of reference": the background elements (green texture and brown rectangle), individual elements (such as the photos and the painting of a building), and the accents (curved elements and dollar signs). After he worked out size relationships, he scanned the photos (a hand with a disc, a man with a brief case and a textured metal surface) into Photoshop. He also scanned a few large nails placed on a flatbed scanner. Howe began the building element by making a digital painting using both Photoshop and Painter. Then he exaggerated the perspective using the Distort command in Photoshop. To prepare the images for import into the montage, he used Photoshop to make silhouetting selections and saved them as masks by choosing Select, Save Selection. After loading the selections (Select, Load Selection) he copied and pasted the selected images from the source files into a composite image as layers. When the images were in position, Howe applied a motion blur on the image to the right of its center, and also to the hand holding the disc. At this point, Howe opened the file in Painter and added scratchy brushstokes on the background using Painter's Pen variants. He created a painted look on the scanned elements by targeting individual "planes" in the image and adding texture. To accomplish this, he used two procedures on each of the floating "planes": First he applied Effects, Focus, Glass Distortion using Paper; then he applied Effects, Surface Control, Apply Surface Texture using Paper. He blended areas of the image with the Grainy Water variant. To give the image more drama and depth, he added lighting to the image with Effects, Surface Control, Apply Lighting.

■ For *Swimmers 2*, one in a series of images inspired by the carefree feeling of weightlessness underwater, **Cher Threinen-Pendarvis** made grayscale scans of three source photos—a man, a woman and a fish—and solarized the man and woman (using the technique described on page 158). She selected the male figure and copied and pasted it into the woman image. The female figure was also floated, and the glows behind the figures were created by duplicating and offsetting the two floaters. Elements were activated one at a time and tinted using Art Materials, Grad, Express in Image. Threinen-Pendarvis moved the image briefly to Photoshop to apply an arbitrary color map (in the Curves dialog box) to add more complexity to the color. Back in Painter, she painted on the water with the Oil Pastel variant, Soft Cover submethod (to preserve the smooth, photographic quality), then she used a custom Distorto variant to pull one color into another and to add more detail and movement to the water. Painterly details were added on the figures with modified Coarse Distorto and Just Add Water variants. She dropped all floating figures, then pasted in multiple copies of the fish. She emphasized the solarized edge lines around the figures with a modified Sharp Chalk variant.

■ **Asye Ulay** created *Unitur* for a travel agency poster that was featured at a London travel convention. She began the illustration by making sketches, dividing the design into three sections. Before beginning to paint, she created several custom brushes based on Painter's Chalk variants. Then she painted each section of the image in a separate file in Painter. Ulay planned to assemble the poster image in Photoshop, because she was familiar with Photoshop's compositing tools. She saved the files in Photoshop 3 format for import into Photoshop, where she pasted the three source files into a composite image. She brought the Photoshop file back to Painter and gave it a yellow tint using Effects, Surface Control, Color Overlay, Using Paper, Dye Concentration and a crackle texture. To finish, she opened the image again in Photoshop, enlarged the canvas size to make room for the type and pasted in the type from a source file. To add the texture to the type, she applied a mosaic texture using an Auto F/X plug-in filter.

A fine artist and designer, **Debi Lee Mandel** brings over 20 years of traditional experience to digital art. Mandel used similar methods to create *I am the Sea* (top) and *Echo* (bottom). She began both images by making large, loose color sketches on paper. She scanned reference material into Photoshop and pulled other images (such as the sea fan in *I am the Sea*) from her own image stored on Photo CD. To build a reference that would inspire, but not overpower her brushwork, she softened some of the images using Photoshop's Gaussian Blur filter and others using Painter's Effects, Focus, Soften command. Mandel assembled the images into a Photoshop composite file. Then she opened the images in Painter, and used the soft imagery as a basis for the paintings. She painted over the images using several Oil Paint and Chalk variants and blended areas using the Water variants. She set type for *I Am the Sea* in Illustrator, pasted it into Painter as shapes and adjusted its Opacity in the Controls palette. When the images were near completion, she flattened them by choosing Drop All from the Objects palette's Floater menu. Then she cloned a few elements into each painting. For instance, she cloned imagery from a sea fan photo into *I Am the Sea* and foliage details into *Echo*.

■ To create *T-Rex*, one of a series of six dinosaur illustrations, **Richard Biever** began by sketching the dinosaur with pencil and paper and shooting landscape photos for the environment. He scanned all of the elements into Photoshop and began to assemble the photo-montage portion of the image. He copied each source photo onto a layer in a composite file. Once the environment was in place, Biever saved the file in Photoshop 3 format, then opened it in Painter. He also opened the scan of the drawing. He copied the photo-montage, made a clone of his pencil sketch, then pasted the photo into the clone and used the tracing paper feature to begin rendering the dinosaur. Using the Chalk brushes, he laid in color on the dinosaur, using the Water brushes to blend color. Biever took advantage of Painter's textures to create the look of dinosaur skin quickly—using Caviar paper texture from the Wild Textures library (located in Free Stuff, Papers, on the Painter 5 CD-ROM). As he painted, he varied the textured effect by using the Scale slider on the Paper palette to change the texture size. To complete the rendering of *T-Rex*, he used the Chalk and Airbrush variants.

■ **Dewey Reid** began *Juiceland*, an illustration for Hi-C and Colossal Pictures, with traditional pencil sketches on paper that were scanned into Photoshop. He opened the final scanned drawing in Painter and made masks for the building elements, sky and foreground using the selection tools. He painted the image using the Chalk variants and used Grainy Water to blend and mix the colors. He activated the selections (Select, Load Selection), and applied texture to areas using Effects, Surface Control, Apply Surface Texture using Paper. Next, Reid sharpened details in the image using a small custom Artist Pastel Chalk and a custom Airbrush. He applied a lighting effect within several selections to create spotlight effects at the tips of the juice straws. To finish, he opened the image in Photoshop and added a few small lens flares to the image.

■ **John Fretz** began *Fruitcakes*, a promotional illustration for his studio, by making a black-and-white drawing with pencil and charcoal on newsprint paper. Using Photoshop, he scanned the drawing and a sheet of Oatmeal paper. He pasted the scan of the drawing into the paper background file in Photoshop, and applied the Multiply Blending mode to the drawing layer. Then he saved the file in Photoshop format for import into Painter. Fretz added color and texture to the illustration using custom brushes built in Painter based on the Charcoal variants. (Fretz's brushes are described in detail on page 212–213.) He flattened the image by choosing Drop All from the Objects palette's Floater menu. To finish, he used a modified version of the Scratchboard Rake (Pens) variant to paint brushstrokes on the image, most noticeably on the sky, grass and dog house.

■ To create *Tomcats*, **Marc Brown** started out with a loose pencil drawing. He scanned the drawing and placed it into Adobe Illustrator as a template. In Illustrator he drew the background and midground on individual layers and filled the elements with flat color. To rasterize the image, he copied each Illustrator layer and imported it into Photoshop as a layer. (This process can also be accomplished in Painter by drawing shapes and filling them with color, or by importing Illustrator art into Painter. See Chapters 4 and 5 for more information about using shapes.) At this point, Brown opened the layered file in Painter. He used the Airbrush and Chalk variants to add colored detail to the sky and cityscape. Then he blended colors using the Water variants. Brown created each tomcat in a separate source file using several floaters: the cat's body, head sunglasses and instrument, for instance. When he finished painting each cat, he merged all the floaters by choosing Drop All from the Objects palette's Floater menu. Then he copied and pasted each cat into the composite image. After he had completed the composite, he flattened the image by choosing Drop All from the Floater menu. To finish, he painted over areas of the image to break up some of the smooth edges. To create the spotlights on the brick walls, he used Effects, Surface Control, Apply Lighting.

MULTIMEDIA AND FILM WITH PAINTER

Film artist Dewey Reid created this pre-production comprehensive for the Nike All Conditions Gear TV commercial using scanned images and Painter's brushes, effects and Scripts; he worked back and forth between Painter and Adobe Premiere, using Premiere for timing and transitions.

A Current Script showing the instructions for an application of Surface Texture

WHETHER YOU'RE AN ANIMATOR, film artist, designer, or 3D artist, Painter's multimedia capabilities offer you dozens of practical techniques. Multimedia artists appreciate the creative freedom offered by Painter's brushes, textures and effects. The ability to record painting scripts lets you make tutorials to show others how your painting was built and even lets you batch-process a series of images. If you're producing an animation or making a movie, many of the techniques and effects shown in this book can be applied to frames in a Frame Stack, Painter's native animation format, or to an imported movie clip. And Painter gives 3D artists a wide variety of choices for creating natural, organic textures to be used for texture mapping.

WORKING WITH SCRIPTS

Painter's versatile Script feature lets you record your work, then play the process back, either in Painter or as a Quicktime, AVI or VFW movie. If you use this feature a lot, you'll soon discover its limitations: for example, its inability to record some Painter operations can change the look of the image during playback.

How did I do that? With Painter 5's automatic script feature, you can reproduce what you just did using the Current Script. While you work, Painter transparently records your actions automatically—saving them as the Current Script in the Painter Script Data file in the Painter 5 folder. You can tell Painter how long to save scripts by specifying the number of days in the Preferences, General dialog box. (The default is one day.) A word of caution: Saving several days of scripts can use a lot of hard disk space!

To work with the Current Script, open the Objects palette, click on the Script List icon, and expand the Script List palette by clicking the grow box in the upper-right corner of the palette. From

To create this animated logo for Fox Television, Geoff Hull built text selections in Painter and used several Oil Paint brushes to add lively brushstrokes and saturated color to his design. Turn to the gallery to see more of Hull's work.

Use these buttons on the front of the Scripts palette to begin recording a single script (center red button) and to stop recording when you're finished (left square button).

The Wow! Effects Script library chosen in the Objects palette. Use these scripts to apply special effects to images and movies.

the Objects palette's Script menu select Open Script, choose Current Script from the Painter Script Data file list and click Open. The Current Script cannot be edited, but to use only a specific set of instructions from it, you *can* copy them to the clipboard and paste the instructions into a new script. Then you'll be able to use your new script to re-create just that series of actions. To do this, open the Current Script, Shift-select the instructions that you want to use (you may want to work backwards from the bottom of the list, where the most recent instructions are found), choose Copy from the Script menu, and then choose New Script from the Script menu. Type a name for your new script in the Name the Script dialog box, and click OK. The script will be saved into the current library visible in the Objects:Scripts palette. When the empty script window appears, choose Paste from the Script menu, and choose Script, Close Script. To play your new script, choose Script, Playback Script and select the new script by name.

Recording a planned script. To record a series of deliberate actions into a script (instead of copying and pasting from the automatically recorded script), choose Script, Record Script to begin recording. When you're finished working on your image choose Script, Stop Recording Script (or click the square Stop button on the left side of the Scripts palette). Painter prompts you to name your script. The new script will appear in the drawer of the Scripts palette, available for later playback. Choose Script, Playback Script, or click the forward arrow button to play the new script.

Recording and saving a series of scripts. If you want to record the development of a complex painting and you don't want to finish the painting in one sitting, you can record a series of work scripts to be played back, one on top of the other. From the Objects palette's Script menu choose Record Script, and begin your painting. When you want to take a break, stop recording (Script, Stop Recording Script). Include a number in the name of your script (such as "01") to help you remember the playback order. When you're ready to continue, choose Script, Record Script again and resume working on your image. Record and save as many scripts as you need, giving them the same name and numbering them so you can keep track of the order. To play them back, open a new file of the same dimensions as the original, then choose Script, Playback Script. Choose the "01" script, and when it's done playing, choose the next script: It will play back on top of the image created by the first script. Continue playing back scripts in order until the image is completed.

Automating a series of operations. A recorded series of actions can save you a lot of time when you need to apply the same effect to several images or to a frame stack. Test a combination of operations (such as a series of choices from the Effects menu) until you get something you like. From the Objects palette's Script menu,

To add lighting and a paper texture to this Mediacom video clip, we played a special effects script (using Effects, Surface Control, Apply Lighting and Apply Surface Texture) onto the frames.

choose Record Script and repeat the series. After you've stopped recording and have saved your script, you can apply the series of operations to a selection, a floater or a still image by selecting your script in the Script palette and choosing Script, Playback Script. To apply your script to a frame stack choose Movie, Apply Script to Movie, select your script from the Recorded Script lists and click the Playback button. Turn to "Automating Movie Effects" later in this chapter for a detailed explanation of this technique.

Playing a script back as a movie. This is a great option if you want to send your script to someone who doesn't have Painter. Quicktime movies can be played on Macintosh and PC/Windows computers with a freeware Quicktime projector such as Movie Player (included on the *Wow!* CD-ROM that accompanies this book).

Begin by choosing Script, Script Options. Check Record Initial State (otherwise Painter will playback the first few commands or brushstrokes of your script using whatever colors, brushes and textures are active, instead of the ones you actually used during the script). Check Save Frames on Playback, and leave the time interval Painter uses to grab frames from your script at 10, the default. (For future recordings, you may want to experiment with lower settings to get a smoother playback result.) Click OK.

Next, open a new file of the same dimensions as your eventual movie file. From the Objects palette's Script menu choose Record Script and make your drawing. When you're finished, choose Script, Stop Recording Script; name and save your script. Now here's when Painter actually converts the script to a movie. First, watch your recorded script played back as Painter Frame Stack by opening a new file (same dimensions) and choosing Script, Playback Script. Choose your script from the list, and Painter will prompt you to create a new movie file. Name it, then specify the number of layers of Onion Skin and color depth by clicking on the appropriate buttons. Click OK, and your script will unfold as a Frame Stack. When it's finished playing, save it in Quicktime/AVI/VFW (Video For Windows) movie format by choosing Save As, Save Movie as Quicktime. The Quicktime/AVI/VFW file will be smaller than a Frame Stack (if you use a compressor choice in the Compression Settings dialog box) and will play back more smoothly. (Because most compression degrades quality, compress only when you've completed the project. Film artist Dewey Reid suggests

Highly saturated colors can smear when output to video. Choose Effects, Tonal Control, Video Legal Colors to make the colors in your file compatible with NTSC or PAL video color. In the Preview, press and release the grabber to toggle between the RGB and Video Legal Colors preview, and click OK to convert the colors in your file.

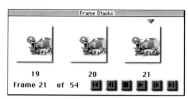

The Frame Stack palette for Donal Jolley's animation Turtle Rockets *showing movement in frames 19–21*

using Animation compression or None.) To read more about preserving image quality when working with movies, turn to "Importing and Exporting," later in this chapter introduction.

Making movies using multiple scripts. Save a series of successive scripts, then play back the scripts as frame stacks and save them as Quicktime movies without compression to preserve quality. Open the movies in a program such as Adobe Premiere, Adobe After Effects or Avid Video Shop and composite the movies into a single movie.

ANIMATING WITH FRAME STACKS

If you open a Quicktime or VFW movie in Painter, it will be converted to a Frame Stack, Painter's native movie format. Frame Stacks are based on the way conventional animators work: Each frame is analogous to an individual transparent acetate cel. You can navigate to any frame within a stack and paint on it or apply effects to it with any of Painter's tools (see "Animating an Illustration" later in this chapter).

Artists accustomed to specialized animation and video programs such as Adobe After Effects and Adobe Premiere will notice the limitations of the Frame Stack feature (there are no precise timing or compositing controls, for instance). If you use one of these programs, you will probably want to work out timing and compositing in the specialized program, then import your document into Painter to give it an effects treatment.

When you open a Quicktime or VFW video clip in Painter or start a brand-new movie, you'll specify the number of frames and color bit depth to be used in the Frame Stack. You will be asked to name and save your movie. At this point the stack is saved to your hard disk. A Frame Stack will usually take up many more megabytes on your hard disk than it did as a movie (depending on the kind of compression used), so have plenty of space available. Each time you advance a frame in the stack, Painter automatically saves any changes you have made to the movie. When you choose Save As, Painter will ask you to name the movie

When you're turning a script into a Frame Stack by checking the Record Frames on Playback box (Objects, Script, Script Options), a long script may result in a huge Frame Stack. There is currently no way to preview the number of frames that will be created when you enter an interval number in the dialog box, so you need to make sure you have plenty of hard disk space available.

To record the painting process of Mill Valley *(360 x 504 pixels, painted with Pastel and Water brushes), we made a movie using Save Frames on Playback and an interval of 10. The resulting movie was 100.6 MB with 142 frames.*

SAVING FRAMES ON PLAYBACK

To save a script as a movie, check Save Frames on Playback in the Script Options dialog box (Objects palette, Script, Script Options). Painter will grab a slice of your script as a frame at the interval (tenths of a second) that you set. A lower setting in the interval box (such as 1 or 2) results in smoother playback than the default setting of 10, but file sizes for lower settings are larger. For instance, a short script with an interval setting of 1 resulted in a 4.2 MB Frame Stack; the same script recorded with an interval of 10 produced a 1.4 MB file.

A storyboard frame from the MGM movie Stargate. *Peter Mitchell Rubin used Painter to build digital storyboard illustrations for the movie, saving them as numbered PICT files and animating them with Adobe Premiere.*

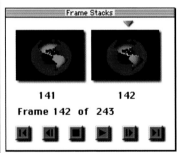

To change the continents from brown to green in this Cascom video clip, we recorded a script while performing the Color Mask procedure and Color Overlay tinting process on one frame, then stopped recording and saved our script. After undoing the effects applied to the first frame, we chose Movie, Apply Script to Movie and took a break while Painter completed the masking and tinting process on all 243 frames. Above: The Frame Stack palette showing frame 141 with the operations applied, and frame 142 as yet untouched.

again. This is not a redundant Save command, but an opportunity to convert the file to another format: Save Current Frame as Image, Save Movie as Quicktime or VFW format, or Save Movie as Numbered Files (to create a sequence of frames to composite in another program such as Adobe Premiere).

Creating animated comps. Painter provides a good way to visualize a rough animation. An animatic (a comp of an animation, consisting of keyframe illustrations with movement applied) can be comprised of images drawn in Painter; scanned elements; or numbered PICT files created in Painter, Photoshop or even object-oriented programs that can export PICT files (such as Illustrator). See "Making an Animated Comp" on page 231, featuring Dewey Reid's illustrations in a demonstration of an animatic technique. You can also alter individual frames in a movie with Painter's effects or brushes. For a demonstration of frame-by-frame painting, see "Animating an Illustration" on page 229.

Rotoscoping movies. There are numerous ways to rotoscope (paint or apply special effects to movie frames) in Painter. Many of the techniques in this book can be used for rotoscoping—brushwork, masking, tonal adjustment, filters, Effects, Surface Control, Apply Lighting and Apply Surface Texture or Effects, Focus, Glass Distortion, for example.

Reid used Apply Lighting and Apply Surface Texture (using Paper Grain) on the animated character Yuri the Yak *for Sesame Street (produced by Children's Television Workshop).*

A frame from an animation based on a video clip. We began by using Painter's Water Color brushes in the Wet Layer to illustrate the frames. Because the Wet Layer sits on top of the entire Frame Stack, we chose Canvas, Dry to drop the Wet Layer's contents onto every frame in the movie when we had finished painting all of the frames. As a final touch, we applied an effects script (with Apply Surface Texture using Paper Grain) to complete the piece.

EXPORTING A GIF ANIMATION

When your frame stack is complete, you can export it as a GIF animation for use on your web pages. Choose File, Save As, and when the Save Movie dialog box appears, choose Save Movie as GIF animation, name the movie and click Save. Make choices in the GIF Options dialog box, and click OK. A word of caution: Name the GIF animation a different name so you don't replace the original frame stack file. (When a movie is saved in GIF animation format, it is no longer possible to edit it as a frame stack in Painter). For more information about using Painter to generate Web graphics turn to Chapter 10.

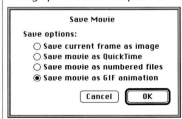

Choosing the GIF animation option in the Save Movie dialog box

USING A VIDEO CLIP REFERENCE

Painter's cloning function allows you to link two movies—a video clip and a blank movie of the same pixel dimensions—and use the video as a reference on which to base an animation. Open a video clip that you want to use as a reference, then make a blank movie (File, New) of the same pixel dimensions as your video clip. (The second movie doesn't need to have the same number of frames.) Under File, Clone Source, select the video clip. In the blank movie frame, turn on Tracing Paper (Command-T), and using the clone source as a guide, choose a brush and paint on the frame. To use the Frame Stacks palette to advance one frame in the original, click the appropriate icon (circled in the palette shown below), or press Page Up on your keyboard. Do the same to advance the clone one frame. Use Movie, Go to Frame to move to a specific frame in either clone or original. You can also apply special effects such as Effects, Surface Control, Apply Surface Texture and Color Overlay or Effects, Focus, Glass Distortion (all using Original Luminance) to your new movie using the clone source.

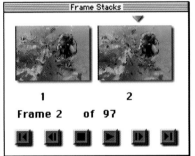

We opened a video clip (shown here in the Frame Stack palette) and a new frame stack, both using two layers of Onion Skin. Click on the circled icon to advance one frame in the Frame Stacks palette.

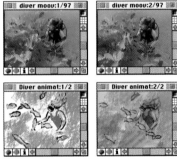

Frames 1 and 2 of the Diver video clip (top row), and corresponding frames in the animation (bottom row), painted with the Sharp Chalk variant. Tracing paper is active on the bottom right image.

Basing an animation on a movie. You can use Painter's Tracing Paper to trace images from a source movie to a clone to create an animation. This feature lets you shoot video and use it as a reference on which to base a path of motion.

IMPORTING AND EXPORTING

With a little planning and understanding of file formats, still and animated files can easily be imported into Painter and exported out of Painter to other programs.

Preserving image quality. Because compression can degrade the quality of image files, when you obtain source files to bring into Painter, choose uncompressed animation and video clips. And because quality deteriorates each time you compress (the degree of degradation depends on the compression choice), save your working files without compression until your project is complete. If you plan to composite Painter movies in another application, such as Adobe Premiere, After Effects or Avid Video Shop, save them without compression. For an in-depth explanation of compressors for Quicktime or for Video For Windows, see Chapter 14 in the *Painter 5 User Guide*.

Jon Lee of Fox Television used Painter's brushes and effects to progressively modify the logo from the comedy Martin, *creating numbered PICT files for an animated sequence. The files were animated on a Quantel HAL.*

Importing multimedia files into Painter. Painter can accept Quicktime and VFW movies from any source, as well as still image PICT files and numbered PICT files exported from Postscript drawing programs, Photoshop and Premiere. To number your PICT files so that they're read in the correct order by Painter, you must use the same number of digits for all the files, and you must number them sequentially, such as "File 000," "File 001," "File 002" and so on. With all files in a single folder, use the Open dialog box to select the first numbered file in your sequence and, when prompted, select the last file. Painter will assemble the files into a Frame Stack.

Exporting Painter images to multimedia applications. Since multimedia work is created to be viewed on monitors and the standard monitor resolution is 72 ppi, set up your Frame Stacks and still image files using that resolution. Most files used in multimedia have a 4 x 3 aspect ratio: 160 x 120, 240 x 180, 320 x 240 or 640 x 480 pixels. Television also has a 4 x 3 aspect ratio, but for digital television the pixels are slightly taller than they are wide. Artists and designers who create animation for broadcast usually prepare their files at "D-1 size," 720 x 486 pixels. Digital television uses a ".9" pixel (90 percent the width of standard square pixels). The narrower pixel causes circles and other objects to be stretched vertically. To create a file for D-1 maintaining the height-to-width ratio (to preserve circles), begin with a 720 x 540-pixel image. Then scale the image non-proportionally to 720 x 486. This will "crush" the image slightly as it appears on your computer screen, but when it's transferred to digital television it will be in the correct proportions.

Quicktime movie files can be exported from Painter into multimedia programs such as Premiere, After Effects and Macromedia Director. If you're using one of these programs to create an 8-bit color production, you'll save processing time if you start with an 8-bit Frame Stack in Painter: Choose the 8-bit Color System Palette

LIGHTS, CAMERA, ACTION!

When you recorded a *session* in previous versions of Painter only your actions were captured. But when you tell Painter 5 to record a script, your "thinking time" (the pauses between actions) is recorded. Keep this in mind if you plan to play back your script as a movie. Recorded "thinking time" can lead to series of "blank" frames. Plan to storyboard your moves so that you'll be able to execute the operations without long pauses. Here's another work-around: After you Record Frames on Playback, check out the Frame Stack, make note of any "blank" frames and use Movie, Delete Frames. Or you can save the Frame Stack as a Quicktime/VFW movie and edit it in Adobe Premiere or Avid Video Shop.

IMPORTING AND EXPORTING MOVIES WITH MASKS

You can create a mask in a Painter movie and use it in your Frame Stack, or export it within a Quicktime movie to another program such as Premiere or After Effects. To make a movie with a mask, choose one of the options with a mask in the New Frame Stack dialog box. (You can also make a Frame Stack from a sequence of numbered PICT files in which each file includes its own mask.) To export the movie from Painter as a Quicktime movie and include the mask, choose Save As and select the Quicktime movie option. When the Compression Settings dialog box appears, in the Compressor section, choose Animation or None from the top pop-up menu to make the mask option available, then choose Millions of Colors+ in the lower pop-up menu. Click OK.

We used a modified photo to create this repeating pattern. To generate seamless, tiled textures for 3D, use any of the commands under Art Materials, Patterns. Turn to "Exploring Patterns" in the beginning of Chapter 7 for more about working with patterns.

option in the New Frame Stack dialog box (after choosing File, New and naming your movie). If you don't set up your file as 8-bit in Painter, you should consider using Photoshop or Equilibrium Debabelizer—both offer excellent color conversion control.

Many experienced artists prefer to export their Painter images as PICT files rather than as movies because they have more control over the sequence of frames. To export Painter still images to applications such as Premiere and After Effects, or to other platforms, save them as single PICT images or as a series of numbered PICT files. You can include a single mask in a Painter PICT file that can be used in compositing in Premiere or After Effects. See "Animating a Logo," on page 233, for a demonstration of exporting Painter images to another platform.

You can also import Painter-created Quicktime movies and still PICT images into Macromedia Director. A Quicktime movie comes in as a single linked Cast Member in the Cast Window, which means it will be stored outside the Director file, keeping file size manageable. 🐾

CREATING TEXTURE MAPS FOR 3D RENDERING

A *texture map*—a flat image applied to the surface of 3D object—can greatly enhance the realism of rendering in 3D programs such as Strata Studio Pro, MetaCreations Ray Dream Designer or Infini-D. Many kinds of images can be used for texture mapping—scanned photographs, logo artwork or painted textures, for example. 3D artists especially like Painter's ability to emulate colorful, natural textures (such as painted wood grain or foliage) that can be used as color texture maps in 3D rendering. (A *color map* is an image that's used to apply colored texture to a 3D rendering of an object.) Other types of mapping use grayscale information; for instance, a *bump map* (a two-dimensional representa-

tion of an uneven surface), a *transparency map* (used to define areas of an image that are transparent, such as glass panes in a window) and a *reflectance map* (used to define matte and shiny areas on an object's surface). If you're applying more than one of these surface maps to a 3D object, you can keep them in register by using Save As or making clones of the same "master" Painter image to keep file dimensions the same. Remember to save your surface maps in PICT format so the 3D program will be able to recognize it.

These floating globes were rendered by John Odam in Studio Pro 1.5.2. He created a texture map in Painter using the Wriggle texture from the More Wild Textures library (in Free Stuff, Papers on the Painter 5 CD-ROM) and applied the texture to the objects as follows: color map (A), bump map (B), reflectance map (C) and transparency map (D). The Studio Pro document size was 416 x 416 pixels; the texture map size was 256 x 256 pixels.

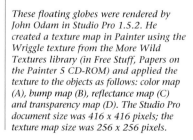

Automating Movie Effects

***Overview** Open a video clip; test a series of effects on a single frame; undo the effects; repeat the effects while recording; apply the session to the entire clip.*

1

Frame 1 of the original video clip

2

The Apply Surface Texture and Apply Lighting settings chosen for the movie

3

Choosing Movie, Set Grain Position to create a "live" texture on the movie

4a

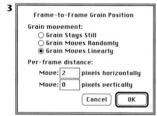

The Stop button (left) and the Record button (center)

4b

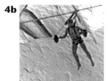

Detail of effects on Frames 35 and 50

WITH PAINTER'S SCRIPTS FEATURE, you can automate any series of recorded effects and apply them to each frame of an entire movie.

1 Starting with a video clip. Tests will be processed faster if you begin with a small video clip like the one we used—320 x 240 pixels with 67 frames. When you open a video clip, Painter converts it to a Frame Stack. (When you save the Stack, give it a new name so the original clip isn't replaced.)

2 Testing a series of effects on a frame. Before you test a sequence of effects on a single frame, set up multiple Undos so you can return the clip to its original state: Choose Edit, Preferences, Undo, and enter a number that exceeds the number of effects you plan to use. Choose a paper texture (we chose Painted Waves from the Nature library on the Wild Bundle CD-ROM, available from Metacreations on request) and apply it to Frame 1 in your movie with Effects, Surface Control, Apply Surface Texture, using Paper (we settled on Amount 22%, Picture 90% and Shine 12%). Next, we added a look of cloud-filtered sunlight by choosing Effects, Surface Control, Apply Lighting. We customized the Slide Light, named it "sunlight," and saved it. (See Chapter 7 for more about lighting techniques.) When you've finished testing, undo the effects you applied to Frame 1. (Painter will remember the last settings you used in the dialog boxes.)

> **HI-RES MOVIE EFFECTS**
>
> If you want to apply effects to a broadcast-quality (640 x 480 pixels) video, use an editing program (such as Premiere) to create a low-resolution version on which to test a combination of effects. Because it takes a higher setting to get a result in a larger file, you may want to adjust the settings before treating the larger file.

3 Moving paper grain in the movie. To add subtle interest to your movie, you can change paper grain position on a frame-by-frame basis by choosing Movie, Set Grain Position. We chose the Grain Moves Linearly button and a 2-pixel horizontal movement.

4 Recording and playing back the session on the movie. Begin recording the effects by clicking the Record button in the Scripts palette; then repeat your sequence of effects. When you're finished, click the Stop button on the palette. Give your script a descriptive name, and undo your effects again. To apply your script to the movie, choose Movie, Apply Script to Movie. When the dialog box appears, find your new Script in the list, click the Playback button, and watch as Painter applies the recorded series of effects to each frame.

Animating an Illustration

Overview *Create an illustration; open a new movie document; paste the drawing into the movie in each frame as a floater; position and drop the floater into a new, precise position in each frame; use brushes to paint on individual frames.*

DONAL JOLLEY

Jolley's finished Painter illustration

Beginning a new Frame Stack, 3 x 3 inches, 72 ppi, with 35 frames

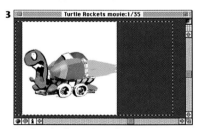

Pasting the floater into the movie

Entering coordinates for the second floater

CREATING AN ANIMATION—whether you use Painter or draw on traditional acetate cels—is labor-intensive because of the sheer number of frames required to get smooth motion. But working digitally does have advantages. You can save a lot of time by copying and pasting a single illustration onto multiple frames; corrections to digital art are easier to make than with conventional methods; and, thanks to the Frame Stacks player, you can see results immediately, instead of needing to film each individual cel in stop-motion.

To begin *Turtle Rockets*, a cartoon "teaser" used between segments of a youth outreach video, Donal Jolley painted and animated a not-so-pokey turtle with Painter's brushes. Once the basic animation was in place, Jolley painted speed blurs, flame, smoke, and even a wad of gum picked up by one of the skateboard's wheels.

1 Planning the animation and illustrating. It's a good idea to do a quick storyboard sketch on paper to visualize the path of motion for your animation. To keep the process simple, choose a subject that you won't need to redraw in every frame—such as a soaring bird without flapping wings or a speeding car. Jolley sketched a turtle on a skateboard moving from right to left across a 3 x 3-inch frame.

Create an illustration in Painter, choosing a file size no more than a few inches square at 72 ppi. Use Painter's brushes to paint just the essential image; you'll be adding the details to each individual frame later. When you've finished your illustration, choose Select, All, then copy it to the clipboard. It's now ready to be pasted into a movie. To fill his movie more completely with his image, Jolley created an illustration file two inches wider than the movie file would be (5 x 3 inches at 72 ppi). He rendered a line sketch of the turtle, rockets and flame using the Fine Tip Felt Pens variant. Jolley added color using the Oil Paint variant of the Brush, modeled forms with the Fat Stroke Airbrush, added linework and shadows using the Felt Marker variant and blended color with the Just Add Water variant.

2 Starting a new Frame Stack. To open a new movie file, choose File, New. Choose a small size so Painter will play the movie quickly, then click the Movie Picture Type, and enter enough frames to give you a smooth animation. Jolley created a 3 x 3-inch movie at 72 ppi with 35 frames to start, and added more frames as he needed them using Movie, Add Frames. His finished

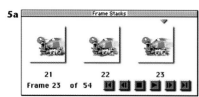
The red marker shows that Frame 23 is active.

Detail of Frame 25, showing motion blur

Frame 28 with Tracing Paper/Onion Skin (three layers) turned on

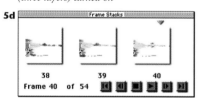
The Frame Stack palette, showing the movement in Frames 38–40

Shaping the flame and adding smoke on Frame 40

animation was 54 frames. Click OK, name and save your movie, and in the New Frame Stack dialog box, choose Jolley's options: three layers of Onion Skin and 24-bit color with 8-bit mask.

3 Positioning the first floater. Paste your illustration into the movie file—it will come in as a floater. Use the Floater Adjuster tool to move it into its starting position, then double-click on its name in the Floater List palette. Jot down the numbers that appear in the Top and Left boxes (Jolley's numbers were Top, 4 and Left, 200) and click OK. Click the Drop button in the Floater List palette (or press Command-Shift-D) to drop the floater onto Frame 1.

4 Offsetting floaters to create movement. To put a floater into the next frame, go to Frame 2 by pressing Page Up on your keyboard. Paste the illustration again, double-click on its name in the Floater List, and in the Top and Left boxes, add or subtract the number of pixels you want the character to move in the frame. Since Jolley wanted his turtle to move from right to left with no vertical variation, he entered 190 in the Left box for Frame 2, leaving the 4 in the Top box unchanged. When you've positioned the floater, drop it and advance to the next frame, continuing this paste-and-move process until you have filled all of your frames. To avoid a staccato effect, add or subtract the same number of pixels each time. (Remember to drop the floaters each time, too.) Jolley used a consistent, 10-pixel difference between frames, resulting in a smooth-moving image.

> **MOVIE AUTO-SAVE**
>
> Painter saves your movie every time you advance a frame.

5 Adding variety to the animation. When the illustration has been positioned and dropped into all of your frames, add to the feeling of motion by painting on individual frames. Look at the Frame Stacks palette to check your progress. You can also view previous frames "ghosted" in your main image—much like an animator's light box—by choosing Canvas, Tracing Paper (Command-T). The number of previous frames displayed is determined by the number of Onion Skin layers you chose when you opened the movie. To change the number of layers, close the file, reopen it, and choose a new number of layers. Use Command-T to turn the Onion Skin layers on and off as you work.

Jolley painted on individual frames to give more life to the animation. He used the Gritty Charcoal variant to paint the dirt—altering it slightly in each frame—and the Oil Paint variant to paint the gum picked up by the first skateboard wheel. He shaped the flame by adding white, then used the Just Add Water variant to smear the pigment. Jolley also created speed blurs by smudging the turtle's back using the Just Add Water variant. 🐾

Making an Animated Comp

Overview *Set up a layered illustration file with floaters; record the movement of a floater using scripts; play the script back into a movie.*

DEWEY REID

Reid's original street scene illustration

Painting the mask on the background

The topmost floater showing the dropped-out area that will reveal the background scene underneath

The Dino character showing the painted mask (left), and with the background dropped out

TO VISUALIZE MOTION in the early stages of creating an animation, Dewey Reid often makes an animated comp (a conceptual illustration with a moving element). Adding motion is a great way to help a client visualize a concept, and it's more exciting than viewing a series of still images. Reid's storyboard, above, shows frames from a movie created by recording a script of a moving floater.

Using scripts and the Record Frames on Playback feature, you can record a floater's movement. When you play the script back, Painter will generate a Frame Stack with the appropriate number of frames, saving you the tedious work of pasting in and moving the character in each frame. After you've made your Frame Stack, convert it into a Quicktime (or AVI/VFW on the PC) movie for easier and faster playback, using a freeware utility like Movie Player.

1 Beginning with an illustration. Begin with an image at the size you want your final movie to be. Reid started with a 300 x 173-pixel street scene illustration from his archives.

2 Setting up a layered file with floaters. Like conventional animation where characters are drawn on layers of acetate, this animation technique works best when all elements in the image are floated on separate layers. You may want to create masks for the various elements in separate documents, then copy and paste them into your main image. (For more about floaters and masking, turn to Chapter 5.) An easy way to try this technique is to drag items from Painter's default Floaters palette into your image—like the hand, the bicycle and the block, for example.

Reid envisioned three floating "layers" for this comp: a background image (the street scene), a copy of the street scene with a painted mask, and a dinosaur positioned between the two street scenes that would move from left to right across the "opening" created by the painted mask in the topmost street scene floater. Reid floated two copies of the image by selecting all and Option-clicking twice with the Floater Adjuster tool. To make it easier to see the top floater as you work, hide the bottommost floater by clicking its eye icon shut in the Floater List. Select the top floater. To remove an area of the floater's mask, select a brush that will

2d

The Dino floater, selected in the Floater List and in starting position (with the selection marquee turned off), ready to be moved by the arrow keys

3a

Setting up Scripts, Script Options to Save Frames on Playback

3b

Saving and naming the script

4

The Dino script selected in the Scripts palette

5

Choosing the Quicktime button in the Save Movie dialog box

apply opaque color (such as the Scratchboard Tool Pens variant) and choose white in the Color palette. In the Mask List, target the floater mask and paint with white to erase. When you're finished, select the RGB-Canvas. To see the background floater again, click its eye icon open in the Floater List.

In a separate file, Reid painted a mask to isolate Dino the dinosaur from the background and turned the mask into a selection by choosing Select, Load Selection. He copied Dino to the clipboard and pasted him into the street scene RIFF file. In the Floater List palette, Reid dragged Dino between the two street scene floaters. To hide the marquee (making it easier to see while you're positioning your character) choose Hide Floater Marquee from the Floater menu on the Objects palette. Using the Floater Adjuster and the arrow keys, Reid positioned the dinosaur so that only the red nose was visible behind the left front building, establishing Dino's starting position in the animation.

3 Recording the script. Choose Objects, Script, Script Options; uncheck Record Initial State, check Save Frames on Playback and enter a number for Every 1/10ths of a Second (Reid chose 5). Select the floater that will be moving by clicking on its name in the Floater List and toggle its marquee off (Command-Shift-H). Choose Script, Record Script and hold down an arrow key to move the floater smoothly in the RIFF file. When you have completed the path of motion, choose Script, Stop Recording Script and name the script. Return the character to its starting position using the Floater Adjuster tool or arrow keys.

4 Playing back the script into the movie. Choose Script, Playback Script and choose your script from the list. When prompted, name your movie a different name than the RIFF file. Click the Save button, and Painter will convert your RIFF image to a movie (leaving the original RIFF intact) and will add the movie frames needed.

As the movie is generated, you will see the frames accumulating in the Frame Stack palette, and corresponding movement in the movie window. When Painter finishes generating the Frame Stack, remove the floaters that are floating above the movie by selecting them in the Floater List and deleting them. (If you don't, you won't be able to see your movie.) Finally, press the Play button on the Frame Stacks palette to play your movie!

5 Converting the Frame Stack to Quicktime or VFW. To be able to play the movie without having Painter loaded, convert the Frame Stack to Quicktime or VFW format: Choose File, Save As, and when the dialog box appears, choose Save Movie as Quicktime/AVI/VFW. Give your movie a new name (such as "Dino movie.qtime"), and when the Compression Settings dialog box appears, select a choice from the top pop-up menu (Reid recommends Animation or None). 🎨

> **HIDE THE MARQUEE**
>
> Turn the marquee off (Command-Shift-H) before you record a script or the marquee will be recorded and will be visible when you play back your script.

Animating
a Logo

Overview *Make a clone of existing artwork and modify it with Painter's brushes and effects; save it, make another clone, and alter the new clone; continue to progressively make and alter clones, restoring the image when needed by pasting a copy of the original logo from the clipboard.*

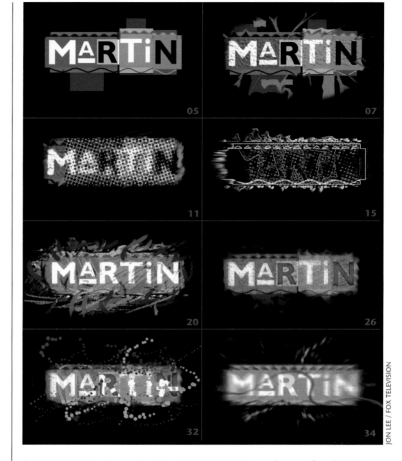

Starting with the existing Martin logo

Lee began manipulating the logo by selecting and scaling a portion of the cloned image (left). Then he selected and inverted a portion of the next clone in the sequence (right).

"IMPROVISATIONAL, FRESH, SPONTANEOUS, and very flexible!" says Jon Lee, Director of Art and Design for Fox Television, when describing his artistic experience with Painter. For the Fox TV program *Martin,* Lee built an animated title sequence like a painting, saving frames at different stages of development. He created a wild, hand-done, organic look to express the comedic street sensibility of the TV show.

Lee created a series of 35 keyframes in Painter (keyframes are the frames that establish essential positions in an animated sequence), eight of which are shown above. When he finished, he moved them from his Macintosh to a lightning-fast Quantel HAL system, where he added dissolves to blend one frame into the next. (Dissolves can also be achieved on the Macintosh desktop in Adobe After Effects or Adobe Premiere.)

1 Beginning with existing art. Lee began by opening the existing Martin logo in Painter. He copied and pasted it into a new file measuring 720 x 486 pixels (the aspect ratio of the Quantel HAL) with a black background, then dropped the floater by clicking the Drop button in the Floater List palette.

2b

Adding colored boxes to Frame 05 with the Rectangular Selection tool and the Fill command

2c

Using a variety of Liquid brushes to pull paint onto the background in Frame 07

2d

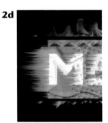 

A motion blur effect applied in 14 (left), and then cloned and filtered in 15

3a

(logo image)

Adding hand lettering and colored brush strokes to a clone of Frame 15 in Frame 16

3b

Restoring readability with a floater in 17

Choose an image that you want to manipulate in your animated sequence and open it in Painter. Name your file "01" and save it in PICT format. In order for a numbered sequence of files to automatically play in numerical order, the files must be named using the same number of digits, such as 01, 02, 03 and so on.

2 Manipulating progressive clones. After planning how many keyframes you'll need and how the artwork will progress through the frames, begin your manipulation. Clone the first document (File, Clone) and use Painter's tools and special effects on your clone. If you don't like the result of a brushstroke or applied effect, undo it and try something else. When you're satisfied with the result, name the file "02," and make another clone from it. The new clone will become the next canvas for your experimentation. Working quickly and intuitively, Lee treated the logo with a wide variety of brushes, filters and Effects, Surface Control effects, saving progressive versions in a numbered sequence.

3 Restoring the logo. After a few progressively altered clones, your image may become unrecognizable. To restore the original to some degree, go to your original file, select all and copy, then paste it into your current clone. Adjust the Opacity (Controls:Adjuster palette, Floater Adjuster tool selected) and drop the floater. Lee used this technique to periodically restore the readability of the logo, working it back into the progressive image.

Outputting the Painter files. When Lee was finished with the series of PICT frames, he used Electric Image Projector (a subprogram within Electric Image) to automatically shuttle the files over to the Quantel HAL platform for compositing and output to Beta videotape for broadcast. The workstation is set up with the Quantel HAL and Mac systems side-by-side; they're connected with an Intelligent Resources card that helps convert the digital imagery from one platform to another. Part of the translation process involved converting RGB color to the NTSC video color system for television.

On the HAL, Lee "stretched" the 35 original frames to 90 frames; the HAL added the appropriate number of dissolves between each pair of keyframes to make the animation even and smooth. To create a 10-second title sequence at 30 frames per second, Lee needed 300 frames total. He made a loop of the 90-frame sequence and let it cycle until it filled the necessary frame count. 🖌

Marc Brown created the splash screen for *The Adventures of Pinocchio Activity Center CD-ROM*, which was based on the 1996 movie *Pinocchio*. Brown began the illustration in Adobe Illustrator. To rasterize it, he pasted each Illustrator layer onto a layer in Photoshop and saved the file in Photoshop format. He opened the file in Painter and used Painter's brushes to render details on each floater, working from the background to the foreground. He laid in color details in the bluish-gray trees in the background using the Camel Hair Brush variant. To blend color, he used the Just Add Water variant. To build the shafts of light, he activated a selection (Select, Load Selection) and feathered it (Select, Feather). Then he filled the selection with yellow (Effects, Fill using a 30% Opacity). To paint the midground and foreground, the yellow forest floor, the green bushes and the red trees, he used the Camel Hair Brush. For Pinocchio, Brown referred to reference photos from the movie while painting with the Oil Paint and the Just Add Water variants.

Lawrence Kaplan of Hot Tech Multimedia turned to Painter 5's special effects to "make a painting come to life," in a music video. Working with the New York artist **Crash**, Kaplan co-directed the four-and-a-half minute animated music video *What She Wants* for Warner Bros. Reprise Records. For a series of frames early in the video, he created a "morphing" animation using Painter 5's Liquid Metal. He began by opening a new movie with one frame and made a Liquid Metal plug-in floater. Using the Brush in the Liquid Metal dialog box (and the Standard Metal Map type), he painted a quantity of Liquid Metal into the first frame and clicked OK to close the dialog box. He copied the Liquid Metal plug-in floater to the clipboard, then dropped the floater (Command-Shift-D) into the first frame. Kaplan added a new frame, pasted the plug-in floater into the new frame and pressed the Enter key to open the Liquid Metal dialog box again. Using the Arrow tool, he selected areas of the metal and deleted them, then added more metal and clicked OK. Kaplan repeated the process of adding frames and editing the plug-in floater to complete the series of frames, morphing the dancing figure into a heart that changes into two figures and fades away into the bottom of the frame, then saved the file.

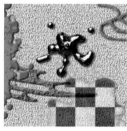

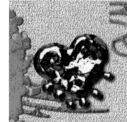
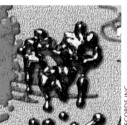

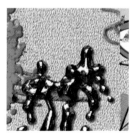

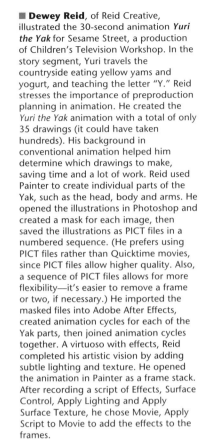

■ **Dewey Reid**, of Reid Creative, illustrated the 30-second animation *Yuri the Yak* for Sesame Street, a production of Children's Television Workshop. In the story segment, Yuri travels the countryside eating yellow yams and yogurt, and teaching the letter "Y." Reid stresses the importance of preproduction planning in animation. He created the *Yuri the Yak* animation with a total of only 35 drawings (it could have taken hundreds). His background in conventional animation helped him determine which drawings to make, saving time and a lot of work. Reid used Painter to create individual parts of the Yak, such as the head, body and arms. He opened the illustrations in Photoshop and created a mask for each image, then saved the illustrations as PICT files in a numbered sequence. (He prefers using PICT files rather than Quicktime movies, since PICT files allow higher quality. Also, a sequence of PICT files allows for more flexibility—it's easier to remove a frame or two, if necessary.) He imported the masked files into Adobe After Effects, created animation cycles for each of the Yak parts, then joined animation cycles together. A virtuoso with effects, Reid completed his artistic vision by adding subtle lighting and texture. He opened the animation in Painter as a frame stack. After recording a script of Effects, Surface Control, Apply Lighting and Apply Surface Texture, he chose Movie, Apply Script to Movie to add the effects to the frames.

■ *Snuffy 1 and 2* are two compositional layout illustrations by **Cindy Reid** of Reid Creative for a proposed Sesame Street production of Children's Television Workshop. The animation was conceived to accompany the children's song "I Wish I Were Small." In frame 1 Snuffy (who is normally mammoth-size) becomes small enough to fit into a bird's nest; in frame 2, small enough to fit in a buttercup. To create both frames Reid shot photos of a bird's nest, the sky and clouds, foliage and buttercup flowers for "scrap." She scanned the photos into Photoshop and pasted the images onto layers to build two composite files. When the elements were in place, she opened the layered composite file in Painter, where she added painterly brushwork to each floater using the Grainy Water variant. She added details using a small Chalk variant. When the brushwork was complete, she flattened the image by choosing Drop All from the Objects palette's Floater menu.

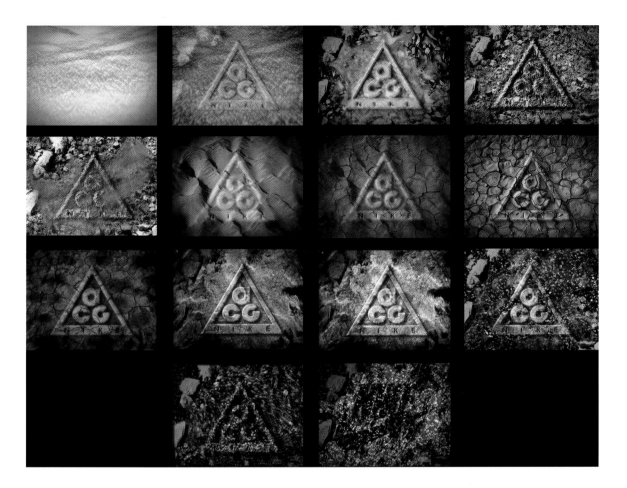

■ Creative director and film artist **Dewey Reid,** working with Colossal Pictures, engineered the preproduction for the *Nike All Conditions Gear* TV commercial. To begin the preproduction visualization, Reid scanned a variety of images. Then he used Painter to create keyframes to establish the essential positions in the animated sequence. He imported the Nike logo (by copying it from Illustrator and pasting it into the Painter file as shapes while both applications were running), converted the logo shapes to selections (Shapes, Convert to Selection) and applied a feather to the selections. He embossed the artwork in stages, with Effects, Surface Control, Apply Surface Texture (using Mask), creating the illusion that the logo pushes up through the scanned images. Reid saved the keyframes as numbered PICT files, then used

Adobe Premiere to create transitions (such as Cross Dissolves) between the keyframes. He manipulated a few of the masks in Adobe After Effects.

Back in Painter, Reid painted clouds of dust with the Fat Stroke Airbrush variant and used Effects, Surface Control, Image Warp to subtly change the shape of the clouds. He imported the dust image into Premiere and moved the dust across one series of frames.

After working out the timing in Premiere, Reid used Painter to add special effects to the entire movie to increase the 3D look. A whiz with scripts, he opened the movie as a frame stack and treated it with an effects script that included third-party filters; Effects, Surface Control, Apply Lighting; and Apply Surface Texture (using Image Luminance).

■ Peter Mitchell Rubin, a
gifted and innovative storyboard
artist, used a variety of Painter's
brushes and compositing
controls to create the storyboards
for the MGM movie *Stargate.*
The Giza, Egypt, sequence is
shown here. Rubin outputs his
illustrations from Painter as
numbered PICT files, then
animates them in Adobe
Premiere.

Rubin's love of drawing shows in
his storyboards. He works very
quickly, in gray, at 72 ppi. His
document size depends on the
amount of detail needed, but is
usually under 600 pixels wide.
The aspect ratio depends upon
how the film is shot. Rubin
organizes the thousands of
drawings that he creates for a
film in folders according to
scene. He sets up Quickeys
macros to automate actions
wherever possible.

When Rubin adds other elements
to an image, he pastes the
element, drops it, then paints
into it to merge it seamlessly into
the composition. He also uses
Painter's Cloners brushes. For
example, he created the texture
in Frame 15 (left column, third
frame down from top) by
photographing the actual set
sculpture used in the movie,
scanning it and cloning the scan
into his drawing.

■ As both a broadcast designer for Fox Television and a freelance graphic designer, **Geoff Hull** employs a spontaneous, progressive approach when designing with type.

Hull began the *Fox Logo Pattern* with a black background. He imported a solid and an outline version of the Fox logo (using File, Acquire, Adobe Illustrator file—which creates a new file). He copied the shapes from the new file and pasted them into the larger background file, then converted the two logo shape groups into two floaters. Working quickly and intuitively, he painted on the logo floaters with various Oil Paint brushes and saturated color. To build a layered look, Hull made additional copies of the floaters and added more brushstrokes. In busier areas, he erased portions of floaters by painting the floater masks with white paint.

To create the animated title sequence for the TV show *Wild Oats*, Hull envisioned a hand-done calligraphic look. He began the image with a white background and set type in Painter using the font Earthquake, a typeface from the T26 foundry. After setting type shapes filled with black, he made a clone (File, Clone) and erased its contents. He chose Canvas, Tracing Paper and expressively traced the letterforms. Hull made a series of progressive clones, switching clone sources (File, Clone Source) among the original and several later versions of the title sequence.

Hull created *The Crossing Guard* storyboard for a Miramax Films movie title and trailer. He began with a black background and set individual letterform shapes in Painter using Mason from the Emigré font library. After converting the shapes to floaters, he filled them with color and erased portions of the letters by painting the floater masks with white paint. He also used Effects, Orientation, Scale on the floaters to vary the size of the elements.

USING
PAINTER FOR
WEB
GRAPHICS

Matthew Angorn illustrated Ruben, a regular character featured in the late-night Insomniacs Asylum™ *suite created by the Warner Bros. Online team. To see more work from the* Insomniacs Asylum™, *turn to page 247.*

©1996 WARNER BROS.

© 1998 WARNER BROS.

WHAT DOES PAINTER OFFER AN ARTIST who designs graphics for the World Wide Web? In addition to its powerful natural media painting and compositing tools, image hose brushes, mosaics and floaters with masks, Painter can help you with image prep for Web screens. For example, use shapes to set type for titles or draw polygons, convert the shapes to a floater and define the area as a clickable region for use on your screen. You can open source video in Painter as a frame stack and grab stills to use as graphics or as references for your screen illustrations, or export the frame stack directly from Painter as a GIF animation. (If you need help with the painting techniques or selection methods referred to in this chapter you can find more information in Chapters 3, 4 and 5. Turn to Chapter 9 for information on scripts and frame stack animations. And see Appendix E for recommended books relating to Web design.)

CREATING GRAPHICS FOR THE WEB

Painter has tools that make it easy to adapt graphics for the World Wide Web: For instance, you can save in GIF and JPEG (the two most popular image formats used on the Web). And you can tell Painter to do some of the coding to help you set up image maps or linked graphics. Here are some tips for creating Web graphics in Painter.

First, there are two basic uses for images on a Web screen. One is an in-line graphic or "static" image embedded in the page without a link to another location—for example, an embedded background graphic. The second use for graphics is as a "hot spot," or "button." A hot spot is a clickable region on your artwork that will allow the user to hyperlink (or travel) to another location on the Web, either within the same Web site or at another site. There are two general types of hot spots. The simpler one is a button that links to one location (URL, or Uniform Resource Locator). The

To help create an image with a reduced palette that would load more quickly, Dewey Reid used a solid black background when painting The Storyteller. *He saved valuable colors for the characters' clothing and skin tones. Turn to this chapter's gallery to view the entire image.*

Painter offers two imaging methods in the Save as GIF dialog box: Quantize to Nearest Color and Dither Colors. Quantize to Nearest Color uses areas of solid color, picking the colors in the current palette that are the closest match to the color you're trying to convert. Dither Colors converts colors using a random pattern (giving a less banded result or a better visual color match), but dithering generates a file that can't be compressed as small as one with solid colors.

Detail from the Sequoyah Online *hub screen, designed by Lynda Weinman, shows the use of a subtle background.*

second is an image map—an image that has been divided into regions, each of which lets you link to a different URL.

Making an image map. You can choose any kind of graphic as an "image map": title type or a particular word in a sentence, a photograph or an illustration you've painted. Define an image map by selecting all or part of an image (by dragging around it with a selection tool and floating it). Double-click on the floater name in the Floater List to access the Floater Attributes dialog box. Use the checkbox to make it a WWW map clickable region.

Using Web-friendly file formats. The JPEG and transparent GIF formats that Painter supports are the most popular file formats used in Web page design. Transparent GIF files make use of the mask you've saved with the file, allowing a graphic to be placed on the page with an irregular edge or with holes cut into it to reveal the background underneath. Make a transparent GIF by choosing File, Save As, GIF. In the Save As GIF Options dialog box, use the Output Transparency checkbox. Click the Preview Data button to make sure your mask is working.

We suggest using GIF format to save simple line art and flat-color graphics without gradations and soft edges. Save photos and painted artwork in 24-bit JPEG format. When you Save As GIF or JPEG, choose the server type (CERN or NCSA) that your service provider recommends. Painter will create the map definition file for you, writing a text file that defines the hot spots.

Building small files that load fast. Many Web-savvy designers recommend making graphics files small, between 20 and 30K, because most folks surfing the Net will not wait for images that take a long time to load. The average modem speed is 14,400 baud and graphics of 20–30K will load within about 30 seconds. To make GIF images small, use Painter's Save As GIF Options dialog box to compress the number of colors from millions to 256 (8-bit) or fewer. Save as GIF in the exact pixel dimensions needed for the page design. When you use JPEG format to preserve the 24-bit color of an image, experiment with the JPEG Encoding Quality settings to determine how much compression an image can withstand. JPEG is a lossy compression (it removes information, which can't be restored when the image is compressed), so make sure to use File, Save As to create the new JPEG file with a different name, preserving your master file.

Creating a subdued background. Painter has tools for creating exciting patterned backgrounds, but a busy, contrasty pattern can take attention away from the subject of the screen and overwhelm your audience. Here are two suggestions that will help you make a background pattern more subtle: Turn down the contrast using Effects, Tonal Control, Brightness and Contrast. Or desaturate the background (using Effects, Tonal Control, Adjust Colors) to call attention to brighter-colored content. To desaturate, move the

A row of interactive buttons on the Lenny Kravitz *Web site* Music *screen designed by Hugo Hidalgo with BoxTop Interactive for client Virgin Records. The center button features a colored animation, inviting the viewer to click there first.*

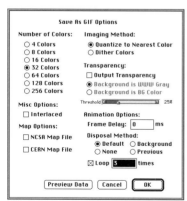

Hugo Hidalgo created buttons, patterns, type and glows in Painter for the Lenny Kravitz *site. Click the glowing button (above), and Netscape boots Simple Player. Click the forward arrow to play the Quicktime movie. See more work from the Kravitz site in this chapter's gallery.*

Saving a GIF animation and reducing the number of colors from millions to 32 colors. To create a looping animation, choose the Loop box and specify the number of times you want the animation to repeat.

Saturation slider to the left. Click OK when you see the look you want in the Preview window.

Adding movie stills and video to your page. You can open a movie in Painter and capture frames for static images or hot-spots. And you can save a Quicktime or AVI/VFW movie using very small compression such as Adobe Premiere's Cinepak, so it can be played within the Netscape 2.0 (or newer) browser. Clicking on a button that's linked to a movie causes Netscape to boot Simple Player, and you can click the forward arrow to play the movie with sound.

Exporting a movie as a GIF animation. Painter 5 makes it easy to add movement to your Web pages with GIF animations! You can open a Quicktime/VFW/AVI movie as a frame stack (or create your own animation in Painter) and export it directly from Painter as a GIF animation. Here are some tips to help you make a GIF animation that loads quickly and plays smoothly on your Web page: Make movies with a small frame size (such as 160 x 120). Painter 5 doesn't permit movies to be resized. So if you plan to import video into Painter, reduce the frame size in a video editor such as Adobe Premiere before opening it in Painter. Use as few frames as possible. (You can use the Movie, Delete Frames dialog box to remove any unnecessary frames.) Reduce the number of colors—using black-and-white or just 3 to 4 colors, for instance, will help to make a smaller animation file.

To save a completed frame stack as a GIF animation, choose File, Save As, and choose Save Movie as GIF Animation. In the Save As GIF Options dialog box, make choices that you need. **Beware:** Save your GIF animation as a new name so you don't replace your frame stack. Painter 5 will not open a GIF animation as a frame stack. ✍

WEB-FRIENDLY COLOR

Painter 5 ships with several color sets built for Web graphics. To load a Web-friendly color set, from the Art Materials palette's Color menu choose Load Color Set. Navigate to the Painter 5 CD-ROM, open the Free Stuff folder, then open the Colors folder. Select a "Hex" Color Set, the Netscape 216, Macintosh default 256 or Windows Default 256 Color Set and click Open. David Siegel, author of the book *Creating Killer Web Sites*, has discovered that Photoshop and Painter subtly shift the browser-safe color palette. He recommends Equilibrium Debabelizer for making final color reductions.

SHRINKING A COPY

If you're doing detailed painting to be displayed on the Web at 72 ppi, you may want to create your art at a higher resolution so you can zoom in and paint the details. Then use Canvas, Resize to shrink a copy of your image down to 72 ppi. Sharpen areas that become soft (Effects, Focus, Sharpen).

A MASTER TIME-SAVER

To make Web page updates easier, save a master RIFF file with live floaters for each screen design. To replace an image, clear the old one and paste in the new (double-click the floater's name in the Floater List and enter specifications in the Floater Attributes dialog box). Save As in GIF format using a new name.

Creating a Web Page with an Image Map

Overview *Scan elements; build a patterned background using the scanned elements; create floaters and designate an image map in Painter; finish the HTML.*

The grayscale scan of a hand graphic

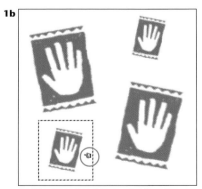

Positioning a hand floater by dragging with the Floater Adjuster tool

LYNDA WEINMAN, AUTHOR OF THE BOOK *Designing Web Graphics,* creates graphics and animation for movies, TV commercials, music videos and World Wide Web sites. To build the Web site *Sequoyah Online* for an alternative elementary and junior high school in Pasadena, Weinman used Painter to create a background pattern, a logotype, graphics, and image map buttons. She designed the site to be viewed with any browser and used her own site, http://www.lynda.com. to develop the prototype.

1 Laying out the pattern tile. As the basis for the background, Weinman planned a tile that would be easy to make into a seamlessly repeating pattern: None of the graphic elements would touch the tile edges, and the texture behind the graphics would be randomized and not too coarse. (For information on creating a more complicated pattern in which elements touch the edges and the "seams" have to be edited, see "Exploring Patterns," in Chapter 7 on pages 177–178.)

Choose a design element that you want to use in your pattern. To capture an element to use in her pattern design, Weinman scanned a hand graphic and opened the scan file in Painter. You may want to follow Weinman's process of scaling, rotating and duplicating to create your own design.

Select your design element with a selection marquee or the Lasso tool and copy it to the clipboard. Then open a new image to use for developing your pattern tile (Weinman's was 200 x 200-pixels),

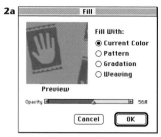

2a

Filling the tile with an overall tint

2b

Adding relief with Apply Surface Texture

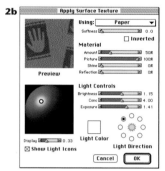

3

Moving the pattern in the Capture Pattern window to look for seams

4a

Detail of the background file with pattern

4b

Saving the file as a GIF with 64 colors

and paste the copied graphic into it. Before dropping the pasted graphic, Weinman used Effects, Orientation, Scale to reduce its size. She reduced its Opacity to about 50% using the Controls: Adjuster palette. Then she chose Effects, Orientation, Rotate and turned the graphic by dragging on a corner handle. She made a copy by Option-clicking on the graphic with the Floater Adjuster tool, dragged the copy to a new position, and rotated the copy to the right. She Option-clicked, scaled and rotated to produce more elements to balance the design within the pattern tile.

When you have all of the elements of your tile in position, choose Drop All from the Objects palette's Floater menu to drop the floaters (they must be merged with the canvas to use the Capture Pattern command in step 3).

2 Coloring and texturing the tile. Next, Weinman added a subtle brown color and texture to the tile. To color your tile, give it a transparent overall tint by filling it (Effects, Fill at about 50% Opacity.) Now make a mask so you'll be able to color the darker areas (the hand graphics, in this case) without affecting the background. From the Objects palette's Mask menu choose Auto Mask using Image Luminance, clicking the Invert checkbox. Shut the mask eye icon, target the RGB-Canvas and choose Select, Load Selection. Now give the graphic a darker tint with Color Overlay (Effects, Surface Control, Color Overlay, using Mask, clicking the Dye Concentration button).

Next, to add a colored texture to the entire tile, choose an interesting Paper texture; you may want to scale your texture down using the Scale slider on the front of the Art Materials, Paper drawer. Then apply Color Overlay, this time using Paper, clicking the Hiding Power button. Finally, add highlights and shadows that will enhance the texture using Effects, Surface Control, Apply Surface Texture using Paper. (Use the same Paper texture, at the same size you used to apply the Color Overlay.)

3 Capturing the pattern. When you have colored and textured your tile, it's ready to make into a pattern. To capture your pattern, choose Art Materials, Pattern, Capture Pattern. Click and drag in the Preview window to check your pattern for any seams. If you need to eliminate seams, refer to "Exploring Patterns," in Chapter 7. Weinman also captured her tile as a paper texture (Art Materials, Paper, Capture Paper) so she could apply it to her files as a repeating texture.

4 Setting up a page. This step sets up the Web page design itself. There are no absolute size restrictions on Web pages. They can be any length, because the viewer can scroll. But it's best to make the page no wider than 640 pixels (the width of the average monitor screen display). Weinman created her new page file at 500 x 600 pixels, to fit within the default page size of Netscape, a popular browser.

For your prototype Web page design, create a new file and fill it with your pattern (Effects, Fill, Pattern). When you've filled the file

5a

The logo mask (top) and hand graphic with type mask (bottom) shown by opening the mask eye icon and shutting the RGB-Canvas eye icon in the Mask List.

5b

The finished hand GIF with type; relief added with Apply Surface Texture

6a

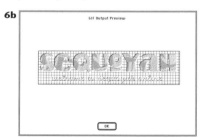

The GIF Options dialog box with settings for Transparency and colors

6b

The GIF Options preview window shows the logo background "dropped-out," so the user can test the mask and preview transparency.

with your pattern, choose File, Save As, GIF. Choose the number of colors and click the Quantize to Nearest Color radio button. (For advice on reducing Web page color palettes, see pages 241–242.)

5 Setting type and filling it with a pattern. It's often easier to build source graphics in separate files and paste them into the final screen image when all of the elements are done. Start a new file the same width as the page and as high as the graphic you want to add. Using the Text tool with black as the current color, set large bold letters for a logotype. Weinman made a 500 x 100-pixel file and typed "Sequoyah" using Hot Coffee, a font by Ethan Durham at Fonthead Design (http://www.mediabridge.com/fonthead/main.html).

Since you'll be treating all the letters as a unit, group the selected type shapes (Command-G) and collapse them to make one floater (Collapse button, in the Floater List). (A mask is saved when you convert a shape to a floater.) To fill the logotype floater with a gray version of her pattern, Weinman used Effects, Fill, Pattern and then stripped the color out by using Effects, Tonal Control, Adjust Colors, and dragging the Saturation slider to the left. She added texture to "Sequoyah" (Effects, Surface Control, Apply Surface Texture using Paper) using the Paper she had saved in step 3, so it lined up perfectly with the pattern fill. Then she added the subhead type to the logotype file with the Type tool, in a gray color she sampled from the logotype using the Dropper.

Next she created another new file (416 x 283 pixels) and copied and pasted her original hand scan into it and dropped it by clicking the Drop button on the Floater List. She masked the hand (from the Objects palette, Mask menu, Auto Mask using the Current Color, black). Then, as she had done for the logotype, she filled it with the pattern, grayed it out, and added text. (To create a masked floater that you can easily copy and paste into your layout in step 7, choose Select, Load Selection and choose the mask you made for the graphic. Now click inside the active selection to float it.)

6 Embossing. For the logotype and the graphic, Weinman built a crisp-edged embossed effect that would display well on the screen using limited bit depth. To do this you'll need to make two copies of your graphic. Select the Floater by clicking on it with the Floater Adjuster tool. Now, Option-click twice to make two more copies, one for the highlight (the middle one in the Floater List) and one for the shadow (the bottom one in the list). Select the shadow floater in the Floater List and use the arrow keys to offset it a few pixels to the left and up to create a hard-edged shadow (you'll be simulating lighting from below, right). Then darken it by choosing Effects, Tonal Control, Adjust Colors and dragging the Value slider to the left. Now select the highlight floater in the Floater List, move it a few pixels down and to the right, and lighten it (this time the Value slider goes right).

After collapsing the floaters (Shift-select all three floaters in the Floater List, press the Group button, and then press the Collapse

7a

Selected rectangular floaters that will define bounding boxes of the buttons

7b

- ★ 👁 ✏ chat
- ★ 👁 ✏ events
- ★ 👁 ✏ admission
- ★ 👁 ✏ teacher
- ★ 👁 ✏ student
- ★ 👁 ✏ phoenix
- ★ 👁 ✏ mission

The Floater List with the named floaters

7c

```
              Floater Attributes
Name:     mission
Position:  Top: 229    Left: 267
URL:      http://www.lynda.com/mission
          .html


Selection Interaction:
   ● None
   ○ Selection Reveals Floater
   ○ Selection Conceals Floater
Floater Visibility Mask:   ○ Disabled
                           ● Normal
                           ○ Inverted
☒ WWW Map Clickable Region
Region: ● Rectangle Bounding Box
        ○ Oval Inside Bounding Box
        ○ Polygon Region
                    Cancel      OK
```

Entering the URL into the information field

8a

```
        sequoyah main.GIF.NCSA.map
# WWW NCSA Image Map file for 'sequoyah main.GIF'
#
# Created by Fractal Design Painter 5.0
#
#
# mission
rect http://www.lynda.com/mission.html 267,229 483,260
# phoenix
rect http://www.lynda.com/phoenix.html 264,262 485,293
# student
rect http://www.lynda.com/student.html 263,295 487,321
# teacher
rect http://www.lynda.com/teacher.html 263,324 488,352
# admission
rect http://www.lynda.com/admissions.html 263,354 489,381
# events
rect http://www.lynda.com/events.html 262,383 490,410
# chat
rect http://www.lynda.com/chat.html 264,410 458,443

# 7 total floaters, 7 have URLs
```

The image map's HTML code as it appears in Simple Text

button), drop the floater to the canvas with its mask, by choosing Drop and Select from the Objects palette's Floater menu. Choose Select, Save Selection to save the selection as a user mask.

Now, save the image as a transparent GIF with a reduced color palette (Weinman saved the gray logotype and the graphic with 8 colors). Choose File, Save As, and select GIF format. In the Save As GIF Options dialog box, click the Preserve Transparency radio button, and choose the number of colors. Preview the transparency (by clicking the Preview button) to make sure it works, for example, the background needed to show through the counters of the "e," "q," "o" and "a" in "Sequoyah" and through the hand in the graphic.

7 Completing the layout and making the image map. Open the background file (from step 4; this was Weinman's 500 x 600-pixel pattern-filled file). Then copy and paste your logotype and graphics images into it (from steps 5 and 6; for example, the "Sequoyah" and hand graphic files). Position the elements and drop the floaters by clicking the Drop button in the Floater List.

Painter allows you to define an image file as an image map (a document that's divided into nonoverlapping regions, each of which lets you link to a different URL or location on the Web). Open the finished layout and drag with the Rectangular Selection tool to create a marquee around one of the button elements that will become a clickable region. Click to float the item. Repeat this process for as many clickable regions as you need.

Now tell Painter what to include in the map definition file: Double-click on each floater name in the Floater List to open the Floater Attributes dialog box. Enter a new name for the floater in the Name field, if you like. Use the checkbox to select WWW clickable map (the Region button will default to Rectangle), and type the URL into the URL field. Choose File, Save As, GIF, and when the Save As GIF Options dialog box appears, use the NCSA map or CERN map checkbox, depending on which type your Web server requires.

8 Finishing the HTML. Ask your service provider where the CGI script for image maps is stored and how to use it (CGI is an acronym for Common Gateway Interface). Or convert the image map information to a client-side image map for use within the HTML document. And check out these URLs on the World Wide Web to learn how to set up programming for client-side and server-side image maps: http://www.utexas.edu/learn/pub/maps/ and http://www.hway.com/ihip/.

Painter will make the map definition file for you—which lists each region, defines each region using x and y coordinates and lists the URL it links to. You'll also need additional HTML programming to make the links work. 🐾

8b

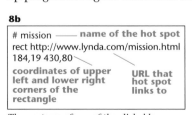

The anatomy of one of the clickable regions in the map definition file that Painter automatically generates.

Building an Online Suite

Overview *Scan pencil sketches into Photoshop; paint flat color onto layers; take the image into Painter to render details with brushes and textures; convert the color palette; compress the files.*

©1996 WARNER BROS.

© 1998 WARNER BROS.

The original pencil sketch

The in-progress layered file in Photoshop with flat color

Flat type shapes with a drop shadow applied

© 1998 WARNER BROS.

Angorn created an irregular edge for the rock by making a freehand selection, and floating it, in the final logo button before it was distorted to fit the right wall. He gave the type a three-dimensional look with Effects, Apply Surface Texture using Mask.

IF YOU'RE ONLINE LATE AT NIGHT, check out the work of the Warner Bros. Online creative team on America Online (use Keyword: Insomniacs). Some might say that Matthew Angorn's cartoon style is reminiscent of 1960's psychedelic art. Angorn coordinated with other members of the Warner Bros. Online team—including art director Suzanne Abramson and a site producer—to create the artwork for the "rooms" in the *Insomniacs Asylum*™ suite. He worked with many separate elements (layers in Adobe Photoshop and floaters in Painter) so it would be easy to make the changes required by the production team.

1 Making sketches and scanning. Angorn began each room in the suite by scanning a pencil-and-paper sketch using Adobe Photoshop's File, Acquire command. He saved the scan for the Lounge (the site hub, shown above), as a 1389 x 806-pixel file. Although the final art used online would be smaller, he preferred to work at a larger size so he could zoom in and paint details.

2 Adding flat color to the sketch. Using the sketch as an underlay (it was on the Background layer in Photoshop), Angorn blocked in large areas of color, creating new layers as he needed them. He saved the files in Photoshop 3 format so he could open them in Painter, automatically preserving the layers as floaters.

3 Creating elements using shapes. All of the furniture was drawn with Painter's Pen tool using Bézier curves. He converted the shapes to floaters (Shapes, Convert to Floater), then distorted them into the perspective of the room using Effects, Orientation, Distort. Type was set with the Text tool and converted to floaters in the same way.

4 Adding brushstrokes and texture. Enjoying the natural feel of Painter's brushes and its ability to apply textures, Angorn began rendering the characters who inhabit the room, each on its own floater. Using the Feather Tip Airbrush, he blocked in general values. To add detail to the people, he used both the Fat Stroke Airbrush and the Large Chalk variant (at about 70% opacity). On the furniture

4b

Angorn drew the Insomniacs Asylum™ *logo type with the Pen tool; then floated elements and applied color fills, brushstrokes and Apply Surface Texture*

5

Close-up detail showing a few of the regular Insomniacs

6

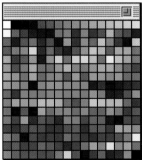

The producer used Debabelizer to convert the 24-bit file to an 8-bit BMP file (top) with these colors.

and type elements, he used Effects, Surface Control, Color Overlay and Effects, Surface Control, Apply Surface Texture using Mask, then touched up the highlights and shadows with the Feather Tip Airbrush.

5 Adding painted details. Using a small modified Feather Tip Airbrush, Angorn added highlights and shadows to the lounge regulars and the furniture, and added final touches to the logo buttons. When the details were complete, he saved the files in Photoshop 3.0 format, to make it easy for a site producer to prepare the files to be sent to America Online.

6 Converting and compressing. The site producer opened the files in Photoshop and saved a new version of each one, reducing the file size from 1389 x 806 pixels to 500 x 290 pixels at 72ppi, the resolution used for screen display. After reducing the number of layers by combining some of the smaller elements with the Merge Layers command, the producer saved each layer into its own file. Then the new files were opened in Equilibrium Debabelizer and each 24-bit working file with millions of colors was converted into an 8-bit nondithered BMP file with 256 colors. (America Online accepts both 4-bit [16 color] and 8-bit [256 color] files.)

To prepare the files to be sent to America Online, the producer moved the illustration file (now in BMP format) to a PC running Windows 95, then saved individual files in ART format with Johnson-Grace ARTpress, a compression format used by AOL. Originally created for working with photos, ARTpress works well with any continuous-tone images.

At AOL, producers programmed the art into their system and database and sent files back to the Warner Bros. Online team. The production team at Warner Bros. Online wrote code for links to screens and developed script content for the site, adding stories and photos with a language similar to HTML. ◆

Cafe.com, reached by clicking the Cafe.Com button on the Lounge back wall, was created using the same layering and brush techniques as the Lounge (Salon hub screen shown on page 247).

■ **Dewey Reid** is an accomplished creative director, film artist and virtuoso with special effects. *The Storyteller* is compositional layout for a scene in *Vanishing Point,* an interactive online drama published by Microsoft. Reid began the image by making pencil sketches and scanning these drawings and a photo. He painted the characters in Painter, using the Chalk variants and blended color using a custom Grainy Water variant that incorporated a chisel tip. To help the image load faster on screen, Reid used a reduced color palette and painted a solid black background, saving valuable colors for the characters' clothing and skin tones. He enhanced the focal point of the image by creating a custom "Renaissance" lighting effect (based on the Center Spot light in Effects, Surface Control, Apply Lighting). To complete the image, Reid subtly increased the saturation of the storyteller's hand and jacket using Effects, Tonal Control, Adjust Colors.

■ A versatile designer and fine artist, **Debi Lee Mandel** designed and illustrated *Campsite* (top) and *Hearth* (bottom), two screens for the DuraFlame Web site. She began the images by sketching in Painter with a custom "indigo-color crayon" (based on the Waxy Crayon variant) on a black background. Both screens incorporate animations. Mandel began by painting elements for the animations (the comet and fire in *Campsite,* and the fire in *Hearth*) using Painter's frame stacks. When she was happy with the progression, she exported the animations from Painter 4 as Quicktime movies, then she used GIF Builder to resave the movies as GIF animations. (With Painter 5, you can export frame stacks directly to GIF animations.)

After completing the crayon drawing for *Campsite,* Mandel painted crisp-edged brushstrokes using flat color. To build up deep color saturation, she used custom Oil Paint brushes with oval-shaped tips for a calligraphic feel.

To complete *Hearth,* Mandel smoothed the crayon drawing with the Just Add Water variant. She used a custom Water Color brush with an oval tip to lay in large, loose areas of color, then she switched to a smaller brush to add details. When she was satisfied with the watercolor, she dried the image (Canvas, Dry). Then she added deeper color and more detail using her own custom Oil Paint brushes.

■ **Hugo Hidalgo**, a gifted artist and innovative Web designer working with Boxtop Interactive, built the graphics for the *Lenny Kravitz* Web site for client Virgin Records. The site features many exciting screens that work together in a unified design. Hidalgo used tiled patterns built from images he had captured from video. He opened each video clip in Painter as a frame stack, and saved single frames by choosing File, Save As, Save Current Frame As Image. He also used the video grabs and photos supplied by the client to build button graphics in Painter.

To make it more inviting to enter the site, Hidalgo created an animated color button for the *Main Hub* (top). He put together a simple low-memory color animation for the button by making different color versions, saving the series as numbered files, and animating them in GIF Builder, a nifty freeware program that animates GIF 89a files, written by Yves Piquet (yvespiquet@ia.epfl.ch). First, Hidalgo applied a red color to the button with Effects, Color Overlay, using Image Luminance and Dye Concentration and saved the file as "01." He cloned the file and used Effects, Tonal Control, Adjust Color to change the Hue from red to purple. He saved the second file as a numbered file ("02"), and repeated the process to save the other files, moving around the color wheel.

For the *Videos* screen (bottom), Hidalgo drew a vertical, irregular shape with the Pen tool in a separate source file that included a pattern made from a montage he had built from video grabs. He converted the shape path to a selection and used the selection to capture a section of the montage that he could paste into the final *Videos* screen image. The vertical pattern also appears on several other screens within the site.

He designed the *Videos* screen to take advantage of Netscape 2.0's ability to play movies with sound in response to clicking a button on a Web page. Hidalgo programmed the buttons to link to small video clips stored in a folder. He used Adobe Premiere to compress the clips using Cinepak compression to about 1 MB in size. When the user clicks on a button linked to a video clip, Netscape boots Simple Player and saves a movie to the user's hard disk. To play the movie, the user clicks the Simple Player forward arrow button. You can visit the Kravitz site at http://www.underground.net/lennykravitz.

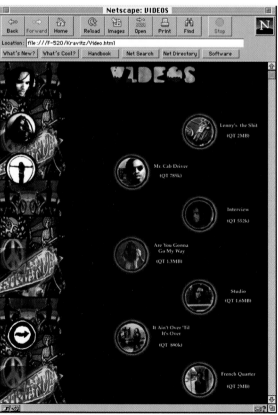

■ To build the images for the *UPN* Web site, **Hugo Hidalgo** used Painter's brushes, special effects and image map features.

He began the *opening screen* (top) by scanning a black-and-white photograph of an Art Deco building. He cut the top off the building to make room for the glowing logo that was to come. He cloned the photo (File, Clone) and after deleting the contents from the clone, he used Tracing Paper to make a drawing with the Pencil brushes. Then, he cloned portions of the photo into the drawing. He applied tints to his image using the Wet layer and the Simple Water Watercolor brushes. Then he used various Airbrushes to add atmosphere. Hidalgo built the logos for the screen in separate source files.

He set type shapes and drew Bézier shape paths to build the Telescape and Info logo outlines, and added realism to both logos with various Airbrushes; Effects, Apply Surface Texture; and Apply Lighting. When the logos were complete, he copied each one and pasted it into the final screen image.

Taking advantage of Painter's ability to make an image map definition file, Hidalgo created two links for the opening screen image, making the *Telescape* and *Site Info* logo floaters into hot spots (clickable regions). Using the Rectangular Shape tool, he dragged a shape around each logo to define the bounding box of the button, and entered the appropriate url information into the Floater Attributes dialog box for each region.

The *Telescape Lobby* (bottom), can be reached by clicking on the *Telescape* button on the opening screen. Hidalgo used the same techniques he used to build the opening screen to create the *Telescape Lobby* image and other rooms in the site. Check out the *UPN* site at http://www.upn.com.

PRINTING AND ARCHIVAL CONCERNS

Sybil's Fear, by Dorothy Simpson Krause, was created for a Media West Editions Pixel Pushers exhibition. Krause printed the image at 30 x 22 inches on an Iris 3047 printer. She plans an edition of 75 prints.

HOW WILL YOU PRESENT YOUR PAINTER ARTWORK to the world? Will it be as a limited-edition digital painting, printed on archival paper by a print studio or service bureau, then matted, framed, and hung on a gallery wall? Or as an illustration in a magazine, where it's part of a page layout that's output to negative film by an imagesetting service bureau, turned into a printing plate and printed on an off-set press? Or as a desktop color print? Or as part of a slide show? For each of these and other output options, there are things you can do to prepare your Painter file so the output process runs smoothly. We hope the tips that follow help you as you plan your own project.

COLOR FOR PRINTING

Most types of printing involve the use of four-color process, or CMYK (cyan, magenta, yellow, black) inks and dyes. Painter's native color mode is RGB (red, green, blue), which has a larger color *gamut* (range of colors) than the CMYK color model. (An illustration that compares RGB and CMYK color gamuts is on page 10 in Chapter 1.) Although Painter doesn't let you specify CMYK color mixes like Adobe Photoshop and some other programs do, it does allow you to work in Output Preview mode, using only those colors within the RGB gamut that are realizable in CMYK. You can also output CMYK EPS files for color separation directly from Painter.

Using Output Preview. When you'll be turning a file over to an imagesetting service bureau or printer for output in a form that will be used for CMYK printing, consider using Output Preview. Painter 5's new Output Preview incorporates the Kodak Color Management System. With this system you can set up a monitor-to-printer calibration loop that will allow you to see an on-screen approximation of how your printed image will look. (A word of caution: There are many variables besides the RGB-to-CMYK

Click the Output Preview icon to toggle between RGB and the Output Preview.

For an approximation of how a default Photoshop CMYK conversion of a Painter RGB image will look, choose the Photoshop RGB to CMYK Output Profile. Check the Gamut Warning box to show colors that are beyond the color range of the selected Output Profile. In our example, bright, saturated colors on the skiers' clothing are out of range for the Photoshop RGB-to-CMYK color conversion. The out-of-gamut colors are shown here covered by a bright green overlay.

conversion that will affect how a color print will look—for instance, the color cast of your particular monitor and the color of your paper.) Begin by choosing Canvas, Output Preview and selecting Kodak Color Correction. Now choose Canvas, Preview Options, and in the dialog box, choose a Monitor Profile and an Output Profile. When you perform a Painter Easy Installation the program automatically installs a selection of Output Profiles into your system folder. And you'll find more profiles in the ICC folder on the Painter 5 CD-ROM. (If you don't see your monitor or printer profile in the list, it can often be obtained from the manufacturer.) To add profiles to your system, run a Custom Installation, choosing the Additional ICC Profiles option; or copy them from the Painter 5 CD-ROM as follows: Macintosh users should drag the profiles into the System Folder, Preferences, Colorsync™ Profiles folder. And Windows 95 users should copy profiles into the Windows\Color folder.

To toggle between the broader-gamut RGB image and the Output Preview, click the Output Preview icon above the right scroll bar. Remember to change the Device Color Profile settings if you plan to print to another device. For more information about Painter's color management tools see "Color Management," in Chapter 17 of the *Painter 5 User Guide*.

Making CMYK conversions in another program. Some Painter artists prefer to work in the broader RGB color gamut and convert their finished images to CMYK in another imaging program such as Photoshop or Equilibrium Debabelizer, because these programs allow more control of how the conversion is made. There are several good resources that give detailed explanations of color conversion using Photoshop, including the *Adobe Photoshop User Guide* and *The Photoshop 4 Wow! Book* and *Photoshop in 4 Colors* (both from Peachpit Press). Some printing studios—for example, Cone Editions—prefer to receive RGB files from artists and make the conversion themselves using custom color tables they create in Photoshop especially for that image. (See "Making a Fine Art Master Print" on page 264 for an explanation of Cone Editions' process.) Check with your printer or service bureau to work out a conversion method.

PHOTO: DIGITAL STOCK

LINE SCREEN AND RESOLUTION

When you're preparing files to be printed on an offset press, ask what line screen will be used for printing so you can begin your file with a high enough resolution (ppi) to accommodate it. A factor of 1.5 to 2 times the line screen is typical. For example, to accommodate a 150-line screen, set up your file with the dimensions you need at a resolution of 225 to 300 ppi.

USING KCMS TRANSFORMS

Output Preview provides a preview only and makes no permanent changes to the file unless the file is saved as an EPS-DCS with KCMS Transforms. To include the transforms in an EPS file, choose Output Preview and select the Device Color Profiles in Preview Options before you save the EPS-DCS in Painter.

When saving a file as an EPS-DCS, remember to preserve your original Painter file by giving the EPS file a different name. Painter can save in EPS format, but the program cannot open EPS files.

Pulling a print on the Vutek system (top), and a close-up view of the nozzle heads on the Vutek machine (bottom)

Detail of Old World, by Bonny Lhotka. She hand-worked and treated Rives BFK paper, then printed the image on a Hewlett-Packard XL 300.

Writing EPS-DCS files from Painter. Many illustrators prefer to have control over the prepress process by ordering their own four-color film for illustrations. Rather than an electronic file, they send the film separations and a laminated proof (a Match-print, for example) to the client. Whether you or someone else will be ordering the film, check with the service bureau operator who will be doing the output. He or she should be able to tell you the correct setup for the equipment that will output your job.

FINE ART PRINTING

If you plan to present your image as fine art, choose a service bureau or master printer who specializes in output for fine art printmaking. The expertise needed differs greatly from that of a commercial service bureau accustomed to making film and proofs for offset printing. Choose a printer who has experience working with artists and who understands archival and editioning issues. (See Appendix C for a list of service bureaus that specialize in working with fine artists.)

Printing digital watercolors with the Iris. Iris printers (Iris is a division of Scitex, a well-known maker of image hardware and software) are special inkjet machines capable of producing images with luminous color and no visible dot, making the output desirable for fine art printmaking. The Iris sprays water-soluble, vegetable-based CMYK dyes (similar to watercolors) through four extremely narrow nozzles. The paper or other substrate is taped to a rotating drum in the machine and sprayed with millions of droplets per second. Many fine art printers modify the Iris 3047 (the largest of the Iris printer line) so it can handle thicker substrates. Cone Editions, The Digital Pond and Nash Editions were among the first printers to pioneer this technique; they moved back the printing heads, allowing 400-lb. watercolor paper, canvas and metal to be taped onto the drum.

Outputting to large canvas. Richard Noble is a traditionally trained artist and commercial illustrator who has worked with the computer for several years. He researched large output options and discovered Vutek, a large-format, low-resolution technology originally devised to print billboards. Noble established a partnership with Vutek and adapted the technology to print large-format fine art. The machine sprays acrylic-based pigments through four nozzles simultaneously, producing soft-edged images very much like an airbrush painting on canvas. Once they dry, the acrylic-based pigments are not water-soluble and offer permanency similar to that of acrylic paint. Images can be printed up to 4 feet wide and as long as you like, with enough canvas remaining around the perimeter of the image for stretching around a frame. Although the prints look good right off the Vutek, you can add even more dimension by working back into them with conventional brushes and acrylic paint. Since the Vutek prints at 18 ppi, files can be fairly

TRY COLORSYNC WITH RGB

You can get good results when printing from Painter using a desktop inkjet (such as the HP 550C or 560C) without first converting your image to CMYK. In the Print dialog box, choose Best Quality, and in the Options dialog box, choose Colorsync from the pop-up menu.

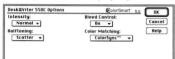

To check color and detail before printing on an Iris inkjet, Cher Threinen-Pendarvis proofed Sunrise *as an 8 x 10-inch Fujix Pictrography print. (Fujix Pictrography prints are described on page 258.) The print was sent along with the digital file to the service bureau (The Digital Pond), where the image was printed at 12.5 x 20 inches on bright white Somerset paper.*

DYE-SUBLIMATION PRINTERS

Dye-sublimation printers such as the Kodak XL7700 and 8600PS and the 3M Rainbow offer continuous tone (no obvious dot pattern) and bright color. Many designers use dye sub prints for comps. However, they are very susceptible to humidity and can smear if rubbed. If you make dye-sublimation prints for a portfolio presentation, do not permanently store them in acetate sleeves—the trapped humidity can ruin the color in the print.

small. For example, to produce a 4 x 6-foot painting, you'll need to set up a 864 x 1296-pixel file (only about 5 MB).

Printing digital watercolors with desktop printers. Desktop inkjet printers can deliver beautiful color prints if they are set up properly. The affordable HP Desk Writer (or Desk Jet) series and the Epson Stylus series are great little printers not only for pulling test prints before sending images to an Iris, but also for experimental fine art prints. Inkjet inks are water-soluble; try painting into a print with a wet brush. Although most desktop printers work best with slick paper, archival-quality cotton papers produce excellent results on some machines. For example, the HP 550C/560C/660C series prints on thicker acid-free papers if you feed the paper manually. (Two papers to try are 80–120 lb. Arches cold-pressed watercolor paper and Rives BFK printmaking paper.)

TURN OFF POSTSCRIPT

If possible when printing Painter artwork files with Postscript inkjet printers (such as the Hewlett-Packard XL300 and 1200c), turn off the Postscript option. If you leave it on, the Postscript software prevents the printer from producing the scatter spray that is desirable in a fine art print, giving you instead a halftone dot pattern. A scatter spray overlaps colors on the surface of the print where they mix, giving a result similar to fine dithering.

PHOTOGRAPHIC IMAGING OPTIONS

Many new technologies are available for Painter output at graphic arts service bureaus and photo labs that use digital equipment.

Imaging to transparencies using a film recorder. Small- and large-format film recorders are used to image digital files such as Painter artwork to transparencies ranging from 35mm to 16 x 20 inches. For output via a film recorder, images should be in landscape orientation (horizontal) to take full advantage of the width of the film.

To avoid *pixelation* (a jaggy, stair-step look caused by lack of sufficient resolution) on transparencies generated by a service bureau's film recorder, here are some guidelines from Chrome Digital (San Diego) and The Digital Pond (San Francisco) for creating or sizing your files. Most professional-quality 35mm film recorders (such as the Solitaire 16 series) use a minimum resolution of 4000 lines; for this resolution, your image should be 4096 x 2732 pixels. The minimum resolution for 4 x 5-inch transparencies is 8000 lines, requiring an 8192 x 5464-pixel file. For even more crispness, devices such as the Solitaire 16XPF will image at a

Dorothy Krause and Bonny Lhotka printed Krause's image, Procession, *on the Alpha Merics Spectrum printer. The large-format printer is outstanding for printing on thick material. The Spectrum's variable "Z" axis can be adjusted to the thickness of the substrate, allowing it to print on materials up to .75-inch thick (such as the wood shown in the photo above).*

resolution of 16,000 lines (a 16,384 x 10,928-pixel file). Two new, powerful film recorders used to create 4 x 5-inch, 8 x 10-inch and larger-format transparencies are the LVT (from Light Valve Technology, a subsidiary of Kodak) and the Lightjet (from Cymbolic Sciences, Inc.). Plan to create huge images (up to 800 MB) to take full advantage of the resolution capabilities of these machines.

Outputting to a digital positive. Prints made from the Fujix Pictrography 3000 offer better registration and permanency and more natural color than a dye-sublimation print such as the Kodak XL7700 or 3M Rainbow. The Fujix uses a laser to image the digital file onto a "donor" sheet, which is then printed onto photographic paper using a single-pass, silver-halide printing process. The appearance and permanency (about 20 years) of the Fujix are similar to those of a photographic Cibachrome (C-print). Prints can be laminated with a coating that includes an ultraviolet inhibitor, extending their life even further.

Printing your images as Fujichrome. For fine art images, Fujichrome prints made from transparencies offer excellent detail and saturated color, and can be ordered with a high gloss. Prints can be made from 35mm slides or 4 x 5-inch transparencies. To print to the maximum size of 20 x 24 inches, a 4 x 5 transparency is recommended. The permanency of the Fuji print is 40–50 years, and this can be extended by adding a lamination with an ultraviolet inhibitor. Diane Fenster, a noted fine artist and photographer, produces much of her digital work as large-format Fujichrome prints.

PRINTING AN IRIS PRINT USING SELECTIVELY ENHANCED COLOR DENSITY

Sometimes getting the kind of print you want involves doing research. (Some print studios will make special color tables with ink density settings customized for an artist's work. See "Making a Fine Art Master Print," on page 264.) S. Swaminathan is an innovative photographer, artist and printmaker who often makes a special color table for each print. "The Iris printer has powerful software with sophisticated color controls that take printmaking beyond the mechanical printing process to an art in itself," says Swaminathan. The Iris has a *double strike* function, which means the nozzles apply twice the default amount of ink. This is good for intensifying overall color, but doesn't help to emphasize a certain color family, such as cyan or yellow. To emphasize the yellow sunflower, Swaminathan began by making several test proofs of his

S. Swaminathan removed the Artichoke and Sunflower *print from the Iris drum after the second print pass was complete.*

Artichoke and Sunflower image to arrive at a print that balanced the emphasis between the artichoke and the sunflower. His maximum ink settings were Yellow, 65%; Cyan, 55%; Magenta, 55%; and Black 55%. (Iris prints are often made at less than 100% ink coverage, producing full-intensity colors, even at lower settings.) Then he applied a second "hit" of ink (without removing the print from the drum) using these settings: Yellow, 65%; Cyan, 0%; Magenta, 0%; and Black, 0%. The two print runs produced a combined yellow ink density of 130%. This produced richness and warmth, making the sunflower stand out in the image without being overpowering. "When you analyze your image, look for the predominant color that you want to emphasize," Swaminathan recommends. "Ask the print studio to make and save a color table using the ink settings for the best single-pass proof, then work with them to make a second color table that isolates the color you want to emphasize. Request that the print studio run a print beginning with the base color table, then print again using the enhanced color density table. It may cost more to do the second pass, but the results are well worth it."

Detail of The Game *by Carol Benioff, an Iris print overprinted with a copperplate etching*

EXPERIMENTAL PRINTMAKING

In today's world of experimental printmaking, anything goes if it works with your vision of the image you're printing. For instance, many different substrates can be used successfully with inkjet printers; among the favorites are archival-quality papers with a high cotton content. Browse your local art store for Saunders hand-made watercolor paper, Arches hot-press and cold-press watercolor paper, Rives BFK printmaking papers, and Canson drawing and charcoal papers. You can hand-feed these papers into a studio desk-top printer, or request that a fine art print studio create an Iris print with paper that you supply. Fine art print studios often keep special papers in stock—Cone Editions, for instance, has about 80 different fine art papers on hand. Some print studios also print on canvas, film or metal.

Mixing media. Prints from an Iris or another inkjet printer can be modified with traditional tools and fine art printing processes, such as embossing, intaglio and silkscreen. (Turn to page 262 to read about Carol Benioff's technique of overprinting a copperplate etching on top of an Iris print.) If you plan to hand-work an inkjet print with media such as pastels, pencils or oil paint—make the print on rag paper with enough body to hold together when you apply the traditional media to the print. Arches 140-pound watercolor paper and Rives heavy-weight printmaking paper are good choices.

Making Translite transfers. The Translite transfer technique was pioneered by Jon Cone. First, he printed a digital image onto Translite film using an Iris printer. He soaked archival quality paper (such as Rives BFK), and when it was partially dry, he transferred the image from the Translite "plate" onto the dampened printmaking paper using an embossing press—producing a monoprint with softly graduated color.

Overprinting a digital file onto a monotype. To create a surface that she would later use for printing *Day Job* (shown at left), Bonny Lhotka created a one-of-a-kind monotype "plate," by applying acrylic paint onto prepared acetate. She laid a piece of rag paper onto the "plate" and used a custom-made 40-lb. roller to transfer the painted image onto the paper. After transferring, she lifted the paper off the "plate," then allowed it to dry. Before printing, she applied two coats of Communicolor Proofplus Precoat Inkjet Receiver to the transferred image.

Bonny Lhotka created the digital file for Day Job *in Painter, by painting with brushes and using floaters to composite several source files. Before printing the digital image, Lhotka prepared a one-of-a-kind surface using gold- and ochre-colored acrylics. She painted an abstract design on a nonporous surface to create a monotype that she could transfer to a piece of rag paper using a large roller. After drying and coating the surface of the monoprint with inkjet receiver to help it absorb the ink, she printed the image on top of it using an Encad NovaJet 3. A photograph of the final print is shown above.*

Finally, she used a Novajet inkjet printer to overprint the digital file on top of the monoprint. She believes that the overprinting process produces a broader range of color than is possible with a standard inkjet print, resulting in a print with more depth.

DIFFERENTIAL AGING

If you plan to add another medium (such as acrylic or pastel) to a digital print, keep in mind that different pigments and dyes can age at different rates. So the strokes you carefully hand-work into the print may begin to stand out over time.

Bonny Lhotka creates one-of-a-kind "monotype" substrates to use as unique surfaces in the printing of her digital images.

White Buffalo, by Gary Clark, was printed by Cone Editions on Somerset paper at 12 x 28 inches. Clark plans an edition of 20.

Willow Pond, by Dennis Orlando, was printed with an Iris 3047 by Cone Editions on Somerset, a bright white paper. The print was approximately 30 x 20 inches; Orlando plans an edition of 150.

PRINTER BUNGEE-JUMPING

Fine artist and printmaker Bonny Lhotka shares some of her experiences while experimenting with various surfaces and printers:

"Artists can purchase primed or raw canvas and add their own surface. One-of-a kind substrates are much cheaper than commercially available canvases and can yield a more interesting print. I have printed on muslin, cheesecloth, silk, linen, buckram and drapery fabrics. First, stretch the material on a frame and coat it with white gesso. Let the gesso dry overnight before applying an inkjet receiver (from Communicolor in Seattle). Cut the fabric from the stretcher being careful not to make any creases. Store these sheets with a sheet of smooth butcher paper laid over the surface. Roll each sheet face out (covered with butcher paper) onto a 4-inch tube until you are ready to use it.

"Aluminum or copper, with a thickness of .003 to .005-inch and 36 inches wide, is a particularly interesting surface to print on. The metal must first be cleaned with a strong washing vinegar and roughed with steel wool or sandpaper. This is followed with a coating of artist's gesso. I generally run the metal through an etching press to flatten it out. Once the digital file is printed and sealed, the aluminum can be embossed using a cardboard plate by pressing the two in the etching press or using a hydraulic press. Both sides of the sheet can be printed on, allowing for the plate to be folded to create a dimensional image. The advantage is that the metal is more durable than paper and can be displayed without glazing.

"Par glass is a stiff fiberglas material less than .125-inch thick. It can be coated with rabbit-skin glue and an inkjet receiver. After printing and coating with UV protection, the sheets look like stained glass. It's possible to burn the edges of this material to give the art a fragmented look.

"Twinrocker Handmade Papers creates custom papers for art editions. The sheets can be made with a watermark to identify an authentic edition of digital prints (as an additional safeguard against unauthorized prints being made from a digital file). While the big deckles of these sheets are a desired aesthetic element and the mark of a handmade sheet, they can create problems when used with inkjet printers. The Alpha Merics is the only printer I've tried that prints on the sheets with the biggest deckle. When printing a handmade sheet with a large deckle on an Iris 3047, tape the deckle down."

PERMANENCY CONCERNS

Inks used by inkjet printers—including the Iris—are fugitive, which means they can fade when exposed to ultraviolet light. A few fine art printers (notably, Cone Editions and Nash Editions) have developed their own silkscreen coatings to protect Iris prints from fading. The coating merges with the ink on the substrate and doesn't change the appearance of the print. (Both Iris and desktop inkjet printers use water-soluble inks. Keep the print dry unless you purposely want to spot or mix the color with water.) For up-to-date information on new inks developed by Iris contact the company's web site at http://www.irisgraphics.com.

Treating inkjet prints in a studio setting. If you are printing your images to a desktop inkjet printer such as the HP 560C or 660C or the Epson Stylus, you can treat prints yourself so they'll last much longer. Artist Bonny Lhotka suggests buying a

Point Lobos Calm Light, by Cher Threinen-Pendarvis, was printed on Rives BFK printmaking paper on an Iris 3047 by Harvest Productions. The 22 x 17-inch fine art print was hand-worked with pastel pencils; Pendarvis plans an edition of 50.

CERTIFICATE OF AUTHEN

Title **Swimmers 2**

Image Size **12 x 18"**   Edition # **2/50**

Edition Size **50**   Artist Proofs **5**

Date Created **July 1, 1995**   Date Purchased **July 14,**

Art Media **Iris print on Rives BFK**

Uniqueness of this Print **This print is hand-worked with pa**

Artist *Cher Threinen-Pendarvis*

The above information contains all the information pertaining to this Edition. As or watercolor, do not display this artwork in direct sunlight. Frame it under UF3 p

Detail of a sample certificate of authenticity. You'll find a Pagemaker 6 file of this sample certificate on the Painter 5 Wow! CD-ROM.

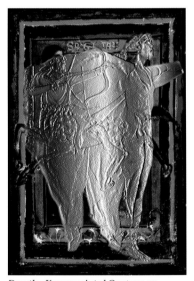

Dorothy Krause printed Centaur on canvas using an Iris 3047 at 46 x 31 inches in an edition of 20. The print was hand-worked after printing: Krause rubbed metallic pigment into the female figure and wrapped gold leaf around the outer edges and sides of the stretched canvas.

can of Golden MSA Varnish with UVLS (soluble with mineral spirits) from your local art supply store. Use a protective respirator and gloves for the process because the fumes from this coating are *very* toxic. To further minimize contact with dangerous airborne particles, dilute the varnish and apply it to your artwork with a brush.

Caring for prints. After a UV-protective coating has been applied to your print, treat it as you would a watercolor and avoid displaying it in direct sunlight. Frame it using UV-resistant glazing (glass or Plexiglas) and preserve air space between the surface of the print and the glazing.

FINE ART EDITIONS FROM DIGITAL FILES

Some artists scan finished, traditionally created artwork and then print it on an Iris. This process is actually *replicating* an original piece of work and is not original digital art. When artwork *originates* as a digital file—using a program such as Painter—and is then printed to an Iris, that print becomes an original. (Think of your Painter image as a kind of "digital printing plate" stored in your computer.)

Advantages of digital editions. Printing a digital edition has advantages over traditional, limited-run printing methods. Any number of multiple originals can be made from a digital file without loss of quality: The "digital plate" won't deteriorate. Also, the setup charge for the digital process is usually much less than when an edition is printed conventionally. And while an edition printed with traditional methods needs to be printed all at once, with digital editions, an artist may request prints from the fine art service bureau as needed.

Planning an edition. An edition should be carefully tracked and controlled, just as it would be if printed with traditional methods. It's wise to make a contract between the master printer and artist, stating the type of edition, the number of prints in the edition and that no more prints will be made. When an original is sold, the artist should give the buyer a certificate of authenticity that contains the name of the artist and the print, the date sold, the edition size, the print number, the number of artist proofs, the substrate, and any details of hand-working done on the print. Once the edition is complete, the artist should destroy the digital file, just as the screen would be destroyed after a silkscreen edition. (See "Making A Fine Art Master Print" on page 264.)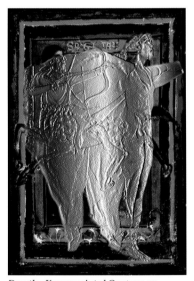

Building an Experimental Desktop Print

Overview *Create colorful, textured elements for a collage; roughen and coat the paper prior to printing; print the final image on a desktop inkjet printer.*

BONNY LHOTKA

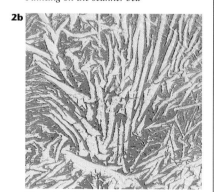

Lhotka's color sketch, created in Painter

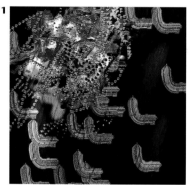

Painting on the scanner bed

The original scanned "paint skin"

"MOST OF MY ORIGINAL WORK has a strong tactile quality," says Bonny Lhotka of her printmaking experimentation. She often uses traditional printmaking equipment to prepare rich, complex surfaces for her digital collage work. To create *Old World*, Lhotka used three digital source files and composited them into a collage, then wrinkled and coated the paper before feeding it through her desktop inkjet printer. You may want to loosely follow Lhotka's image-making process and also experiment with your own effects.

1 Sketching with color. Open a new file and make a colorful, abstract sketch. Lhotka opened an 8-inch-wide, 100-ppi file with a black background. She created an abstract, color sketch using a variety of brushes in Painter, in much the same way she would paint an image with traditional tools. She saved the image for use later in the process.

2 Making a "paint skin." To create source images that she calls "paint skins," Lhotka applies paint directly on the glass surface of her scanner (or to a sheet of acetate) and scans it. To create your own paint skin in a process similar to Lhotka's, paint a textured design on a piece of clear acetate with acrylic paint. If you like, make marks in the paint with a palette knife or flat brush. When the paint dries, place the acetate on the scanner bed and scan it.

3 Compositing in Photoshop. Lhotka began the composite in Photoshop though she could have done the work in Painter. Without a preconceived idea, she opened the Painter file (from step 1) in Photoshop where she flipped, inverted and distorted the image. She copied and pasted the paint skin image (from step 2) into the developing, 11 x 11-inch, 300-ppi Photoshop composite as a layer (in Painter, it would have been a floater). She turned the skin nega-

3

4a

The image showing the emerging map-like design

The boat scan, ready to paste into the composite

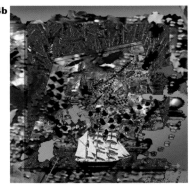
4b

The image as sent to the desktop printer

5a

Ironing the dampened, crumpled paper

5b

Painting a dark acrylic wash onto the paper to enhance the wrinkled effect

5c

Positioning the paper on the etching press to flatten it before printing

tive (Image, Map, Invert) to change the color spectrum to blue tones. As the image evolved, a map-like configuration emerged. She selected some of the dark areas in the skin layer with the Magic Wand and deleted them to make those areas transparent.

To give her image more depth, Lhotka created a new background image for the composite by copying a portion of her original sketch and resizing and softening it. She pasted the working composite into the new background image, combined the two layers using the blending modes, then flattened the image.

4 Refining the image in Painter. To make the evolving image appear more like a map, Lhotka opened the image in Painter and used the program's brushes and effects. She used the Magic Wand to select areas based on color in the top and right side of her image and filled the selections with blue (Command-F, Current Color) to create a sky and bodies of water. Then she painted an island chain in the lower right using a variety of brushes. She gave the sky and water more depth by reselecting all of the solid blue areas with the Magic Wand and filling the selections with a blue-to-white Two-Point gradation (Effects, Fill, Gradation). Lhotka created drop shadows beneath the "land masses" in her map and added linear elements and arrows to suggest an abstract compass. She chose a scan of a model boat from her archives and pasted it into the composite image. As a final step to finish the image, she used Effects, Tonal Control, Adjust Colors and experimented with the Hue Shift, Saturation and Value sliders.

5 Preparing the paper and printing. Many desktop inkjet printers will accept thicker papers that have been pretreated for more uniform printing. If your printer can do this, try using an archival-quality paper with a high rag content such as Rives printmaking or Arches watercolor paper. Lhotka used a cream-colored, heavyweight Rives paper. To give the paper an antique look that enhanced the Old World feel, she dampened and crumpled the paper, then flattened it with a steam iron. To add to the wrinkled look, she applied a wash of acrylic that soaked into the creases. She dried the paper and ran it through an etching press to flatten it.

As a final step before printing, she precoated the paper with an inkjet precoat (from Communicolor in Seattle) to enhance the uniform application of the inks and maintain color fidelity. She printed the 11 x 11-inch image on a Hewlett-Packard XL300 inkjet printer. She set the XL300 to print without Postscript software, which allowed the device to print the inks in a scatter pattern similar to that of an Iris, but coarser. The inkjet inks soaked into the paper and helped integrate the image with the character of the prepared paper itself. To protect the print from fading, Lhotka brushed a solvent-based UV varnish (from Golden Varnishes) onto the finished print. 🖊

Combining Digital and Intaglio Printmaking

Overview *Make a print using a traditional printmaking method; scan the print; use the scan as a guide to create a colored image in Painter; output the digital file to an Iris printer; overprint the traditional print on top the Iris print in register.*

CAROL BENIOFF

1a

Photograph of the copperplate etching. The composition is created in reverse.

1b

Grayscale scan of the black-and-white intaglio print

CAROL BENIOFF'S INNOVATIVE PRINTMAKING method combines classic intaglio techniques with digital printing. An award-winning fine artist and illustrator, she has illustrated for magazines such as *Atlantic Monthly* and *Parenting*—and her work appears in the *CA Illustration Annual*. Currently she works with The Graphics Arts Workshop in San Francisco: one of the oldest artists' cooperatives in the United States, it has been in existence since the 1930's. To create *The Game*, a self-promotional piece, Benioff overprinted a copperplate etching on top of an Iris print made on Daniel Smith archival printmaking paper.

1 Making an intaglio print. Benioff planned the 6 x 7-inch copperplate knowing that she would be adding a dimension of colored imagery created in Painter. Using primarily a hard ground etching technique, she etched fine lines into the acid-resistant coating on the copperplate with a fine-point diamond stylus. When making a classic hard ground etching, an artist scribes lines into an acid-resistant coating, exposing the metal underneath. Then the plate is soaked in a acid bath to etch the drawing deeper into the plate. The acid-etched lines hold the ink, yielding warm, velvety black lines when printed.

Benioff rolled black ink onto the plate, working it into the lines with a cardboard dauber, then rubbed off excess ink with tarlatan

2

The two images: A painted landscape (left), and a watercolor tint image to match the etching (right)

3

Photograph of the Iris print composite

4a

Inking the plate (left) and making registration marks on a clear acetate sheet to help align the copperplate to the Iris print (right)

4b

After lifting the press felts on the intaglio press, Benioff carefully pulled the finished print off the copperplate.

(starched open-weave muslin). Next, she chose a piece of archival printmaking paper and soaked it, so it would absorb the ink better. After letting the paper partially dry, she made a print using an etching press.

When the print was dry, she scanned it and saved the scan to use as a guide to help develop two color images (described in step 2). Benioff's grayscale scan was 2400 x 2800 pixels.

2 Creating color images and compositing. Open your scan, make a clone (File, Clone), and delete the contents of the clone (Select, All, and press the Delete key). Now, turn on Tracing Paper (Command-T). Using the scan as a guide, paint a colorful image that will complement your traditional print.

Benioff created two images: a painted landscape and a loose watercolor version of the etched composition. The landscape was designed to add dynamic tension to the composition. To begin the landscape, she sketched larger shapes with the Large Simple Water Watercolor brush, then added details with the Artists Pastel Chalk and the Brushy Brush. When the image was complete, she saved it for use later in the process.

To paint a second image, which would add colored tints to elements in the etching, she made a second clone of the scan, again deleting the contents. Using the scan as a guide, she painted a loose color composition with the Simple Water brush variants.

Benioff composited the images in Photoshop by merging the second image with the first using the Image, Apply Image and the Multiply blending mode. To merge two color images in Painter, open both images and make the second image active. Select, All, Copy, and Paste it into the first image. Choose a Compositing Method in the Controls:Adjuster palette that complements your image.

3 Choosing paper for the print. To achieve a good ink impression of the copperplate, paper should be softened by dampening so that it will mold to the detail etched into the plate. This poses a problem when printing over an Iris print, because Iris prints bleed when wet. To resolve this problem, Benioff extensively experimented with different papers. She found that some very soft papers will soak through—even when you spritz the back of the paper to dampen it slightly—destroying the water-based Iris image. The paper she chose is fibrous enough to soften and swell when slightly moistened but thick enough that the dampness did not soak through to the inks on the front. To print *The Game*, Benioff settled on Daniel Smith archival printmaking paper.

4 Overprinting the etching. After preparing the copperplate with ink, Benioff made an acetate template to register the image on the paper and plate. The elements in the Iris print needed to align perfectly with the copperplate, so she carefully traced the position of the figures and table onto the acetate. She aligned the template, the plate and the paper (Iris print) on the press bed and pulled the print.

Making a Fine Art Master Print

Overview *Make a custom color conversion of a Painter image; choose a textured, handmade paper that will enhance the image; after a first, light printing, paint an iridescent polymer onto some areas of the print; print the image a second time; apply a UV-protective coating to the print; document the edition.*

Cone at the Power Mac 9150 that's connected to the Iris system

One of Cone's custom ink settings

JON CONE OF CONE EDITIONS PRESS has been making prints and editions for artists since 1980. In 1985, Cone Editions began using computers in printmaking, pioneering techniques such as digital gravure, digital silkscreen and various digital monotype techniques. The firm has made Iris prints since 1992 and has become a leader in Iris printing technology, sharing methods, materials and techniques with other fine art service bureaus.

When he makes a fine art Iris master print, Cone interprets the artist's image in a collaborative manner. Often the selection of a paper, a special color transformation or perhaps even an experimental printing method can enhance an image. Cone used all three of these to realize the Painter image above.

1 Resizing and converting the color mode. An image may need to be resized to take advantage of the Iris printer's resolution (300 dpi) and replication capabilities. The Iris achieves the look of a much higher resolution because of the way the ink sprays onto the paper. Although the optimal resolution for files that will be printed on the Iris is 300 ppi, the printer can interpolate resolutions of 150 ppi or 100 ppi to produce high-quality prints.

Cone prefers to use Adobe Photoshop for a monitor-to-output calibration loop. He has written a proprietary color transformation engine for Photoshop that he uses to convert images from RGB to CMYK. This interface also helps him calibrate the Iris, allowing the monitor to show a close approximation of the printed image. After converting this image, Cone used Photoshop's Image, Adjust,

IRIS FACTS

The Iris printer's drum spins at 110 inches per second; up to 1 million droplets of ink per second are sprayed at 90 mph through each of its four nozzles. Using only cyan, magenta, yellow and black inks, it can simulate millions of colors.

Positioning the paper on the Iris drum

Carefully painting the iridescent polymer coating on the print

Drying the iridescent solution

Stopping the printer to show how the cyan, magenta, yellow and black inks are printed in sequence on the substrate

Using a silkscreen process to add a protective archival coating

Curves dialog box to compensate for out-of-gamut blues that had been lost. (Since RGB has a broader color gamut than CMYK, out-of-gamut colors are dulled when an image is converted to CMYK.) The black plate was adjusted separately to bring out detail in the darkest areas of the image. Finally, a proprietary plug-in Iris format RIP (raster image processor) was used to save the image in a form that the Iris can use for printing.

2 Choosing a paper and setting up the Iris. Cone selected a sheet of heavy, handmade paper with a very soft, large surface grain and an exaggerated deckled edge that would complement the vivid color and lively brushstrokes in the image. He taped the paper to the drum of the Iris.

3 Printing, painting and drying. Cone used the Iris to print this particular image twice. For the first pass, he adjusted the ink tables in the Iris's RIP to print a faint version of the image. With the print still taped to the drum, Cone brushed an experimental iridescent solution (composed of titanium dioxide-coated mica and hydroscopic polymer) onto the lily only. Then he dried the hand-painted coating with a hair dryer.

4 Printing the image a second time. Cone loaded a new set of rich-printing color ink tables into the Iris's RIP and made a second printing pass. The transparent Iris inks adhered to the polymer coating on the lily as easily as they did to the uncoated paper; the iridescent polymer provided a subtle reflection, adding luminance to the lily.

5 Applying a protective coating to the print. Michael Pelletier, Systems and Production Manager for Cone Editions, applied a silkscreen coating of hindered amine light stabilizers (HALS) and UV absorbers (UVA) to the finished print. This solvent-based coating developed by Cone carries the protective additives deep into the printed image where they fully encapsulate the dyes, helping to produce what Cone Editions says is "the longest-lasting archival Iris print available today."

Documenting the edition. The artist now signs the finished print to make it the "right-to-print proof" against which future prints in the edition will be compared. After the artist has signed approval, an edition can be printed on demand while the image file is stored safely on CD-ROM at Cone Editions. A documentation sheet signed by both master printer and artist details the size of the edition, number of proofs printed, methods used and dimensions. Most importantly, it specifies that no other proofs or prints can or will be made. (After completing an edition, Cone destroys all copies of the image file.) Each print will bear a unique print identification number and will be signed and numbered in pencil by the artist.

■ **Helen Golden** created *Reflections And Breezes* by beginning with two source images, a photo she took of a window at an Italian country inn and a scan of a pen-and-ink drawing. After painting on the source images with Painter's brushes, she used both Painter and Photoshop to composite the pieces into one picture. Then she painted on the composite image using the Wet layer and Watercolor brushes in Painter.

Golden plans to print three different versions of the digital file, on different surfaces and using different printers. She printed the first version on prepared canvas at 48 x 30 inches, coating the print with Golden UV Filtering Varnish to protect it and to add a sheen that would enhance the feeling of transparency in the windows. She plans to print the second version on Tuxedo Parchment paper at a slightly smaller size. Tuxedo Parchment has a translucent look reminiscent of the soft light emanating from the window. The third version will be 48 x 30 inches, and will be built using two layers: a heavy coated paper topped with Hewlett-Packard Clear Acetate Film. The printed film is placed over the print on the paper, producing an image with both transparency and greater color depth. All three of these prints will be printed on the Hewlett-Packard DesignJet 755CM. Golden plans an edition of 30 works.

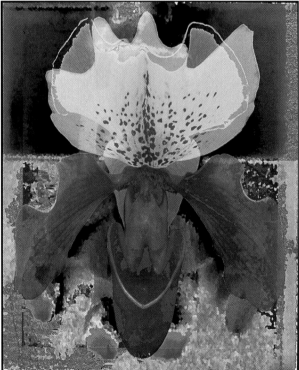

■ To begin *Metaphor* (left), one work in her series *Variations on a Theme*, **Judi Moncrieff** shot many photos of flowers at an orchid ranch in Livermore, California. Inspired by the beauty of the rare flowers, she chose one photograph from the shoot as a basis for the digital image and worked with it in Painter and Photoshop—adding textures, color and brushstrokes in Painter. Moncrieff prepared canvas by painting it with gold and bronze acrylics and interference colors. Then she treated the canvas with an inkjet precoat and printed it on a large-format Encad NovaJet 3 Printer with an Onyx RIP. After drying the print, she worked back into it with gold leaf, pencils, inks and pastel. The size of the final print is 34 x 46 inches.

■ In creating the series *Women of the World*, fine artist **Dorothy Krause** spent as much time preparing surfaces and working the printed image as she did making the original images on the computer. She created the digital work for *Lady of the Flowers* (the digital file above and the printed work, right) and *Marketplace* (the digital image shown below, right) in Painter and Photoshop. Both images were printed on the Alpha Merics Spectrum printer, which prints on 4 x 8-foot materials up to ¾-inch thick.

For *Lady of the Flowers*, Krause coated loosely woven linen with spackling compound and modeling paste, then rolled it to make it crack and chip. *Marketplace* was printed directly onto a plywood surface, then textured heavily with modeling paste. She glazed the border with washes of oil color.

To help unify the series, Krause rubbed metallic pigment onto the printed surfaces of the works until they looked like a blend of old stucco and burnished metal. Next, she added a 2-inch deep structure with cross supports to the back of each piece and textured and colored the surfaces. Then she brought some of the same texture and color into the images. As a last step, she drew onto the works with graphite, scratched their surfaces with a scribe and added bits of gold leaf.

Krause plans an edition of 20 works based on each of these digital images. She may decide to print each of the works on a different printer, on a different surface and at a different size.

Appendix A
Images on the *Wow!* CD-ROM

These vendors provided photos or video clips from their collections for the Wow! CD-ROM *in the back of this book.*

Artbeats
Three volumes of backgrounds and textures, including Wood and Paper and Leather and Fabric; sizes to 16.5 MB; Reel Textures, a collection of 40 animated backgrounds

Cascom International
Select Effects: A three-volume set of digitized clip video, including high-tech animation, titling effects and moving backgrounds; sizes to 320 x 240 pixels

Color Bytes
3 Sampler volumes (nature and urban photos); 2 Designer volumes (background and texture photos); sizes to 25 MB

Digital Stock
85 photo volumes (e.g., Active Lifestyles, AntiStock™, Skylines of North America, Medicine & Health Care, Urban Textures, Transportation, Undersea Life); sizes to 24 MB

Digital Wisdom
Body Shots: One volume of photographs shot with twelve models in various business situations against a white background; sizes to 4 MB

Form and Function
Wrapture Reels: One volume of animated textures including time-lapse clouds, rushing water, and hand-drawn animations; sizes to 640 x 480 pixels

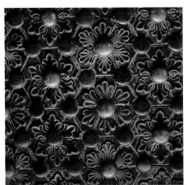

Image Farm
10 volumes including Arizona Desert, Berlin Walls, Cottage and Country, Real Rock, Streets of London, and Industrial Backgrounds and Objects; high quality photographic textures and backgrounds; sizes to 18 MB.

Mediacom
Adclips: One volume (2 CDs) of video clips including Recreation, Corporate, Historical, Lifestyles, Wildlife; sizes to 320 x 240 pixels

MetaCreations
KPT Power Photos: 4 volumes of object and background photos, many with masks; sizes to 24 MB

PhotoDisc
46 standard photo volumes; 24 Signature Series (from a single photographer) discs; 20 Object Series (with clipping paths) discs; 8 Fine Art disks; 18 Background Series; sizes to 28.5 MB

Visual Concept Entertainment
Pyromania 1, 2 and Pyromania! Pro: 3 volumes of digitized video of explosions, fireworks, smoke, and other incendiary displays; sizes to 640 x 480 pixels

Xaos Tools
Fresco: One volume of painterly computer-generated textures; sizes to 30 MB

Appendix B Vendor Information

IMAGE COLLECTIONS

Artbeats, Inc.
2611 S. Myrtle Road
Myrtle Creek, OR 97457
541-863-4429 541-863-4547 fax

Cascom International
806 4th Avenue South
Nashville, TN 37210
615-242-8900 615-256-7890 fax

Color Bytes, Inc.
2525 S. Wadsworth, Suite 308
Lakewood, CO 80227
800-825-2656 303-202-9200
303-202-5946 fax

Digital Stock Corporation
750 2nd Street
Encinitas, CA 92024
760-634-6500 760-634-6510 fax

Digital Wisdom, Inc.
300 Jeanette Drive, Box 2070
Tappahannock, VA 22560
800-800-8560 804-443-9000
804-443-3632 fax

Form and Function
3394 SE Woodward Street
Portland, OR 97202
503-731-0985 503-731-0986 fax

Image Farm
110 Spadina Avenue, Suite 309
Toronto, Ontario
Canada M5V 2K4
416-504-4161 416-504-4163 fax

Mediacom
12701 Cottage Mill Terrace
Midlothian, VA 23113
804-794-0700 804-794-0799 fax

MetaCreations
6303 Carpinteria Avenue
Carpinteria, CA 93013
805-566-6200 805-566-6385 fax

PhotoDisc, Inc.
2013 4th Avenue, 4th Floor
Seattle, WA 98121
800-528-3472 206-441-9355
206-441-9379 fax

Visual Concept Entertainment
P.O. Box 921226
Sylmar, CA 91392
818-367-9187 818-362-3490 fax
http://www.vce.com

Xaos Tools, Inc.
300 Montgomery Street, Floor 3
San Francisco, CA 94104
415-477-9300

HARDWARE

Apple Computer, Inc.
800-767-2775

Hewlett-Packard / *Desktop color printers*
16399 West Bernardo Drive
San Diego, CA 92127
619-592-8308

Epson America / *Desktop color printers*
P.O. Box 2854
Torrance, CA 90509
800-289-3776 800-873-7766

Iomega / *Removable drives*
1821 West Iomega Way
Roy, Utah 84067-9977
800-456-5522 801-778-3000

IRIS Graphics / *Specialized inkjet printers*
Six Crosby Drive
Bedford, MA 01730
617-275-8777

Mitsubishi Electronics Inc. / *Monitors*
5665 Plaza Drive, P.O. Box, 6007
Cypress, CA 90630
1-800-843-2515

Number Nine Visual Technology
Graphics accelerators
18 Hartwell Avenue
Lexington, MA. 02173-3103
781-674-0009 Fax: 781-674-2919

Wacom / *Drawing tablets*
115 Century Road
Paramus, NJ 07652
800-922-6613

SOFTWARE

Adobe Systems / *After Effects, Dimensions, Gallery Effects, Illustrator, Pagemaker, Photoshop, Premiere*
345 Park Avenue
San Jose, CA 95110
800-833-6687

Auto F/X / *Photographic Edges*
Black Point
HCR-73, Box 689
Alton Bay, NH 03810
603-589-8800

Baseline Publishing, Inc. / *Screenshot*
1770 Moriah Woods Boulevard, Suite 14
Memphis, TN 38117-7118
901-682-9676

Macromedia / *Director, Freehand*
600 Townsend Street, Suite 310-W
San Francisco, CA 94103
800-989-3762
415-252-2000

MetaCreations / *Bryce, Color Studio, Dabbler, Expression, Infini-D, KPT Convolver, Kai's Power Tools, Painter, Poser, Ray Dream Studio, Sketcher, and add-ons such as Really Cool Textures*

In Scott's Valley:
5550 Scotts Valley Drive
Scotts Valley, CA 95066
408-430-4000

In Carpenteria:
6303 Carpinteria Avenue
Carpinteria, CA 93013
805-566-6200

Customer Service:
800-846-0111 888-501-META fax

Netscape Communications Corp.
Netscape, Netscape Navigator
501 East Middlefield Road
Mountain View, CA 94043
415-528-2555

Strata, Inc. / *Studio Pro*
2 West St. George Boulevard, Suite 2100
St. George, UT 84770
800-787-2823
801-628-9756

Xaos Tools, Inc. / *Paint Alchemy, Terrazzo, TypeCaster*
300 Montgomery Street, Floor 3
San Francisco, CA 94104
415-477-9300
www.xaostools.com

Appendix C
Fine Art Service Bureaus

These print studios specialize in fine art printmaking with Iris equipment. More studios are listed on the Wow! CD-ROM.

David Adamson Editions
Glen Echo, MD
301-320-9386

Altron Color Imaging
Moncton, NB, Canada
506-852-3510

The Color Space
Peter X (+C) Design
New York, NY
212-366-6600

Colibri Digital Imaging
Old San Juan, PR
809-721-4069

Cone Editions
East Topsham, VT
802-439-5751

Digicolor
Seattle, WA
206-284-2198

Digicolorado
610 South Lipan Street
Denver, CO 80223
303-777-6720

The Digital Pond
San Francisco, CA
415-495-7663

Electric Paintbrush
Hopkinton, MA
508-435-7726

Hunter Fine Art
Kennebunkport, ME
207-967-2802

Imagestation
Kihei, HI
808-536-1718

Nash Editions
Manhattan Beach, CA
310-545-4352

Paris Photo Lab
Los Angeles, CA
310-204-0500

Urban Digital Color
San Francisco, CA
415-626-8403

Appendix D
Contributing Artists

Matthew Angorn
4100 W Alameda Avenue, # 207
Burbank, CA 91505
818-977-0868

Richard Biever
117 N. Fredrick Street
Evansville, IN 47711
812-476-1778

Ben Barbante
1176 Key Avenue
San Francisco, CA 94124
415-657-9844

Caty Bartholomew
198 Seventh Avenue #4R
Brooklyn, NY 11215
718-965-0790

Carol Benioff
2226 11th Avenue #4
Oakland, CA 94606
510-533-9987

Jeff Brice
2416 NW 60th Street
Seattle, WA 98107
206-706-0406

Marc Brown
3042 S. Flamingo Way
Denver, CO 80222
303-782-5484

Jeff Burke
8755 Washington Blvd.
Culver City, CA 90232
310-837-9900

Steve Campbell
1880 Fulton #5
San Francisco, CA 94117
415-668-5826

Gary Clark
823 Lightstreet Road
Bloomsburg, PA 17815
717-387-1689

James D'Avanzo
1446 Jennings Road
Fairfield, CT 06430
203-255-6822

Ellie Dickson
185 West End Avenue #3L
New York, NY 10023
212-724-3598

Linda Davick
4805 Hilldale Drive
Knoxville, TN 37914
615-546-1020

Jack Davis
1315 Belleview Avenue
Cardiff, CA 92007
619-944-7232

John Derry
c/o MetaCreations
5550 Scotts Valley Drive
Scotts Valley, CA 95066
408-430-4000

John Dismukes
2820 Westshire Drive
Los Angeles, CA 90068
213-464-2787

Pamela Drury Wattenmaker
17 South Palomar Drive
Redwood City, CA 94061
415-368-7878

Mary Envall
1536 Promontory Ridge Way
Vista, CA 92083
619-727-8995

Grace Ferguson
2226–11th Avenue
Oakland, CA 94606

John Fretz
707 S. Snoqualmie Street, #5D
Seattle, WA 98108
206-623-1931

Lawrence Gartel
P.O. Box 971251
Boca Raton, FL 33487
561-477-1100

Kerry Gavin
154 East Canaan Road
East Canaan, CT 06024
203-824-4839

Fred Gillaspy
465 Sugarloaf Road
Scotts Valley, CA 95066
408-354-2809

Jack Gold
12939 Indian River Dr. #6
Sebastian, Fla. 32958
561-388-2620

Helen Golden
460 El Capitan Place
Palo Alto, CA 94306
415-494-3461

Steven Gordon
P.O. Box 752
Madison, AL 35758 USA
205-772-0022

Rhoda Grossman
216 Fourth Street
Sausalito, CA 94965
415-331-0328

Francois Guerin
33 Rue Alexandre Dumas
75011 Paris, France
0-11-331-43-73-36-62

Andrew Hathaway
805 Page Street
San Francisco, CA 94117
415-621-0671

Hugo Hidalgo
9014 Reichling Lane
Pico Rivera, CA 90660
310-942-7526

Philip Howe
540 First Avenue South
Seattle, WA 98104
206-682-3453

Geoff Hull
4054 Cartwright Avenue
Studio City, CA 91604
818-761-6019

Donal Jolley
1506 Black Spruce Court
Lilburn, GA 30047
770-279-7753

Rick Kirkman
2432 W. Peoria, Suite 1191
Phoenix, AZ 85029
602-997-6004

Dorothy Simpson Krause
P.O. Box 421
Marshfield Hills, MA
617-837-1682

John Lee
2293 El Contento Drive
Los Angeles, CA 90068
213-467-9317

Susan LeVan
30 Ipswich Street, Studio 211
Boston, MA 02215
617-536-6828

Bonny Lhotka
5658 Cascade Place
Boulder, CO 80303
303-494-3472

Michele Lill
4503 Kleffer Court
Valparaiso, IN 46383
lill@netnitco.net

Patrick Litchy
8211 E. Wadora NW
North Canton, OH 55720
330-494-5593

Debi Lee Mandel
Box#2, Dutch Flat, CA 95714
916-389-8312

Janet Martini
4857 Biona Drive
San Diego, CA 9211
619-238-7895

Craig McClain
9587 Tropico Drive
La Mesa, CA 91941
619-469-9599

Pedro Meyer
1333 Beverly Glen #1004
Los Angeles, CA 90024
Pedromeyer@aol.com

Judi Moncrieff
4543 SW Water Avenue
Portland, OR 97201
503-294-9947

Bill Niffenegger
1007 Grand Boulevard
Cloudcroft, NM 88317
505-682-2776

Richard Noble
899 Forest Lane
Alamo, CA 94507
510-838-5524

John Odam
2163 Cordero Road
Del Mar, CA 92014
619-259-8230

Corinne Okada
657 Evert Avenue, Apt. 1
Palo Alto, CA 94301
415-325-3549

Dennis Orlando
79 Brookline Road
Ivyland, PA 18974
215-355-5524
dorlando@voicenet.com

Dott. Lorenzo Paolini
Rome, Italy
conor@mware.it

Chet Phillips
6527 Del Norte
Dallas, TX 75225
214-987-4344

Jean Francois Podevin
5812 Newlin Avenue
Whittier, CA 90601
310-945-9613

Abbie Rabinowitz
7 Yellow Ferry Harbor
Sausalito, CA 94965
415-331-0878

Cindy Reid
11018 122nd Lane NE/91
Kirkland, WA 98033

Dewey Reid
c/o Microsoft Corporation
1 Microsoft Way, 13/1052
Redmond, WA 98052-6399

Peter Mitchell Rubin
c/o Production Arts Limited
310-915-5610

Cecil Rice
5784 Salem Terrace
Acworth, Georgia 30102
770-974-0684

Chelsea Sammel
482 South Street
Holister, CA 95023
408-636-7443

Larry Scher
11821 North Circle Drive
Whittier, CA 90601
310-699-8797

Karin Schminke
5803 NE 181st Street
Seattle WA 98155
206-483-3011

Beth Shipper
2151 Cumberland Parkway
Apartment #515
Atlanta, GA 30339
770-803-3351

Nancy Stahl
470 West End Avenue
New York, NY 10024
212-362-8779

Sharon Steuer
205 Valley Road
Bethany, CT 06524
203-393-3981

Jeremy Sutton
245 Everett Avenue
Palo Alto, CA 94301
415-325-3493

S. Swaminathan
P.O. Box 1547
Capitola, CA
408-722-3301

Margaret Sweeney
12939 Indian River Dr. #6
Sebastian, FL 32958
561-388-2620

Will Tait
1357 93rd Avenue
Oakland, CA 94603
415-329-3684

Lorraine Triolo
8755 Washington Blvd.
Culver City, CA 90232
310-837-9900

Ayse Ulay
146 South Michigan Avenue, #101
Pasadena, CA 91106
818-796-4615

Trici Venola
911 Marco Place
Venice, CA 90291
310-823-7308

Lynda Weinman
908 West Cyama Road
Ojai, CA 93023
http://www.lynda.com

Appendix E
Reference Materials

Here's a sampling of recommended references for both traditional and digital art forms.

ART BOOKS

Art Through the Ages
Fifth Edition
Revised by Horst de la Croix and Richard G. Tansey
Harcourt, Brace and World, Inc.
New York, Chicago, San Francisco, and Atlanta

The Art of Color
Johannes Itten
Van Nostrand Reinhold
New York

Drawing Lessons
from the Great Masters
Robert Beverly Hale
Watson-Guptill Publications
New York

Mainstreams of Modern Art
John Canaday
Holt, Reinhart and Winston
New York

Printmaking
Gabor Peterdi
The Macmillan Company
New York
Collier-Macmillan Ltd.
London

The Natural Way to Draw
Kimon Nicolaïdes
Houghton Mifflin Company
Boston

The Photographer's Handbook
John Hedgecoe
Alfred A. Knopf
New York

TypeWise
*Kit Hinrichs
with Delphine Hirasura*
North Light Books
Cincinnati, Ohio

COMPUTER IMAGERY BOOKS

Creating Killer Web Sites
David Siegel
Hayden Books
201 West 103 Street
Indianapolis, IN 46290

Designing Web Graphics
How to Prepare Images and Media for the Web
Lynda Weinman
New Riders Publishing
Indianapolis, IN

The Illustrator Wow! Book
Sharon Steuer
Peachpit Press
Berkeley, CA

The Photoshop 4 Wow! Book
Linnea Dayton and Jack Davis
Peachpit Press
Berkeley, CA

Photoshop in 4 Colors
Mattias Nyman
Peachpit Press
Berkeley, CA

PUBLICATIONS

Communication Arts
Coyne & Blanchard, Inc.
410 Sherman Avenue
Palo Alto, CA 94306

Design Graphics
Design Editorial Pty. Ltd.
11 School Road
Ferny Creek
Victoria 3786 Australia

Electronic Publishing
Ten Tara Boulevard, Fifth Floor
Nashua, NH 03062

Graphis
Graphis US, Inc.
141 Lexington Avenue
New York, NY 10016

How
Ideas and Techniques for Graphic Design
104 Fifth Avenue
New York, NY 10011

Print
RC Publications
104 Fifth Avenue
New York, NY 10011

Step-by-Step Graphics and
Step-by-Step Electronic Design
Step-by-Step Publishing
6000 Forest Park Drive
Peoria, IL 61614

Index